Faces of Islam in African Literature

STUDIES IN AFRICAN LITERATURE: NEW SERIES

▼▼▼▼▼▼▼▼▼▼▼▼▼▼▼▼▼▼▼▼▼▼▼▼▼▼▼▼▼▼▼▼▼▼

SIMON GIKANDI
Reading the African Novel

SIMON GIKANDI
Reading Chinua Achebe (forthcoming)

KENNETH W. HARROW (ed.)
Faces of Islam in African Literature

ADEOLA JAMES (ed.)
In Their Own Voices: African Women Writers Talk

ELDRED DUROSIMI JONES
The Writing of Wole Soyinka

MILDRED MORTIMER
Journeys Through the French African Novel

EMMANUEL NGARA
Ideology and Form in African Poetry

NGUGI WA THIONG'O
Decolonising the Mind

▼▼▼▼▼▼▼▼▼▼▼▼▼▼▼▼▼▼▼▼▼

Faces of Islam in African Literature

Edited by
KENNETH W. HARROW
Michigan State University

HEINEMANN
Portsmouth, NH

JAMES CURREY
London

Heinemann Educational Books, Inc.
361 Hanover Street   Portsmouth, NH 03801
Offices and agents throughout the world

James Currey Ltd
54b Thornhill Square, Islington
London N1 1BE

Chapter 11 first appeared in *Africa* 55(4), 1985, 447–464. Reprinted by permission. Chapter 16 first appeared in *Research in African Literatures* 11.1, 1980: 26–49. Reprinted by permission.

Library of Congress Cataloging-in-Publication Data
Faces of Islam in African literature/edited by Kenneth W. Harrow.
    p.   cm. — (Studies in African literature)
  Includes bibliographical references.
  ISBN 0–435–08025–3
    1. African literature — History and criticism. 2. Islam — Africa,
Sub-Saharan — Influence. 3. Islam in literature. I. Harrow,
Kenneth W. II. Series.
PL8010.F3   1991
809'.93382 — dc20   90–39807
                                         CIP

British Library Cataloguing in Publication Data
Faces of Islam in African literature.
  1. African literature-Critical studies
  I. Harrow, Kenneth W.
  896

  ISBN 0–85255–528–8

Designed by Jenny Greenleaf.
Printed in the United States of America.
91 92 93 94 95 9 8 7 6 5 4 3 2 1

Contents

▼▼▼▼▼▼▼▼

Notes on Contributors   vii

Preface   xi

I THE APPROACH TO ISLAM
▼
   1. Introduction: Islam(s) in African   3
      Literature   KENNETH W. HARROW

II EAST AFRICA
▼
   2. An Historical Context for the Study of Islam in
      Eastern Africa   JAY SPAULDING   23
   3. Islam and Secularity in Swahili Literature: An
      Overview   IBRAHIM NOOR SHARIFF   37
   4. Language, Poetry, and Power: A Reconsideration of
      "*Utendi wa Mwana Kupona*"   ANN BIERSTEKER   59
   5. Of Poets and Sheikhs: Somali Literature
      ALI JIMALE AHMED   79
   6. The Two-Sided Image of Women in *Season of*
      Migration to the North   SONIA GHATTAS-SOLIMAN   91

III WEST AFRICA
▼
   7. An Approach to Islam in West African
      History   DAVID ROBINSON   107
   8. Can a Single Foot Follow Two Paths? Islamic and
      Songhay Belief Systems in the Timbuktu Chronicles
      and the Epic of Askia Mohammed
      THOMAS A. HALE   131
   9. Amadou Hampâté Bâ and the Islamic Dimension of
      West African Oral Literature   GABRIEL ASFAR   141
   10. *Kaïdara*: Islam and Traditional Religion in a West
      African Narrative of Initiation   DENISE ASFAR   151
   11. Islam in Senegalese Literature and Film
      MBYE B. CHAM   163
   12. Women, Tradition, and Religion in Sembène
      Ousmane's Work   EDRIS MAKWARD   187

13. Mouridism in Senegalese Fiction
DEBRA BOYD-BUGGS   201

14. The Image of Islam in Selected Tales of Birago
Diop   I. C. TCHEHO   215

15. Islamic Elements in Camara Laye's *L'Enfant
noir*   ERIC SELLIN   227

IV COMPARATIVE APPROACHES

16. Crescent and Consciousness: Islamic Orthodoxies
and the West African Novel   LEMUEL A. JOHNSON   239

17. Camara Laye, Cheikh Hamidou Kane, and Tayeb
Salib: Three Sufi Authors   KENNETH W. HARROW   261

18. Through a Prism Darkly: "Orientalism" in
European-Language African Writing
GEORGE LANG   299

Select Bibliography   313

Index   319

Notes on Contributors

▼▼▼▼▼▼▼▼▼▼▼▼▼▼▼▼▼▼▼▼

ALI JIMALE AHMED: Assistant Professor of comparative literature at Queens College, CUNY. A former editor-in-chief of *Ufahamu*, his research interests include Islam in African literature; the novel genre in the Third World; and literature and politics in the Horn of Africa.

DENISE ASFAR: Associate examiner in foreign languages at the Educational Testing Service. As consultant to the Peace Corps Language-Training Programs, she has conducted seminars in North Africa and West Africa on oral-language testing for French and African languages.

GABRIEL ASFAR: Director of the Foreign Language Institute at Simon's Rock of Bard College, where he teaches French and Francophone literature. He is currently at work on an annotated translation of West African folktales based on the oral narratives of Amadou Hampâté Bâ.

ANN BIERSTEKER: Assistant professor, linguistics and African and African American studies; director, Program in African Languages, Yale University.

DEBRA BOYD-BUGGS: Assistant professor of French and African studies, Wake Forest University in Winston-Salem. Fulbright researcher in Senegal, 1983–4, with Ph.D. thesis, "Baraka: Maraboutism and Maraboutage in the Francophone Senegalese Novel." Has published articles on African, Caribbean, and Afro-American literatures.

MBYE CHAM: Director, African Studies Program, Howard University. Author of numerous studies on African literature and film.

SONIA GHATTAS-SOLIMAN: Received her B.A. from the University of Alexandria, Egypt, and her Ph.D. in French from the University of California at Irvine. She has done field research on Egyptian women. She teaches at Southern Methodist University. She writes and lectures on the Arab woman, Middle Eastern society, and Arabic literature in translation.

THOMAS A. HALE: Professor of African, French, and Comparative Literature at The Pennsylvania State University. A founder and former president of the African Literature Association, he has published

vii
▼

widely on African and Caribbean literature. His most recent book is *Scribe, Griot, and Novelist: Narrative Interpreters of the Songhay Empire. Followed by the Epic of Askia Mohammed Recounted by Nouhou Malio* (University of Florida Press, 1990). Currently he is working on a study of griots from the 14th century to the present.

KENNETH W. HARROW: Professor of English at Michigan State University. Co-editor (with Jonathan Ngaté and Clarisse Zimra) of *Crisscrossing the Boundaries in African Literature*; past president of the African Literature Association; Fulbright teaching and research grants in Cameroon and Senegal.

LEMUEL JOHNSON: Professor of English, the University of Michigan. Past president of the African Literature Association. Author of *Highlife for Caliban, Hand on the Navel*, and *The Devil, the Gargoyle, and the Buffoon: the Negro as Metaphor in Western Literature*, as well as numerous articles on African and Caribbean literature.

GEORGE LANG: Canada Research Fellow in Comparative Literature at the University of Alberta and the author of various studies of African and Caribbean literatures, as well as the forthcoming *Three Literary Pidgins: Lingua Franca, Chinese Pidgin English, and Chinook Jargon*.

EDRIS MAKWARD: Professor of French and African literature, University of Wisconsin-Madison. Former president, African Studies Association. Currently, director of African Studies Program. Co-author of *Contemporary African Literature*; author of articles on contemporary African and Caribbean literature and oral African traditions. Contributor to forthcoming *History of Twentieth Century African Literature* and *Afrique 2000*.

DAVID ROBINSON: Professor of History, Michigan State University. Author of *The Holy War of Umar Tal, The Western Sudan in the Mid-Nineteenth Century*, and *Sources of the African Past* (with Douglas Smith). Currently editor of the *Journal of African History* and administrator of an NEH grant, "Translations of African Historical Sources."

ERIC SELLIN: Professor of French and comparative literature at Temple University. He is director of the Centre d'Etude sur la Littérature Francophone de l'Afrique. Sellin has published numerous articles on African francophone literature both north and south of the Sahara.

IBRAHIM NOOR SHARIFF: Professor at Rutgers, the State University of New Jersey. He teaches Kiswahili and Fine Arts. He has exhibited his artwork in East Africa, Arabia, and the United States. His numerous publications include *Umbuji Wa Kiwando* (East African Publishing House, 1985) and *Tungo Zetu* (The Red Sea Press, 1988).

JAY SPAULDING: Author of *The Heroic Age in Sinnar* and *Arcangelo Carradori's Dictionary of Seventeenth-Century Kenzi Nubian*; he is co-author (with R.S. O'Fahey) of *Kingdoms of the Sudan*, (with M.I. Abu Salim) of *Public Documents from Sinnar*, (with Lidwien Kapteijns) of *After the Millenium: Diplomatic Correspondence from Wadai and Dar Fur on the Eve of Colonial Conquest* and *Een Kennismaking met de Afrikaanse Geschiedenis*.

I. C. TCHEHO: Senior lecturer in African literature at the University of Yaoundé, Cameroon. His area of interest is the cross-cultural dialogue between the Arab and Black worlds. He has published in several journals and is co-editor of *Oral Literature in Africa Today: Theoretical and Practical Approaches*.

Preface

▼▼▼▼▼▼▼

The need for a volume of critical essays on Islam in sub-Saharan African literature could not be greater. There is a vast body of literature in Africa that is of Islamic inspiration or that deals in a substantial way with Islamic beliefs, cultural practices, or social patterns. And, amazingly enough, there is no serious study available to the scholar dealing with this topic. The closest one could come to such a study would be Albert Gérard's *African Language Literatures*, an admirable, thorough literary history of all the African literatures written in African languages. The limitations of this study, however, are imposing. Swahili literature, for example, is comprised in large measure of oral elements which are outside the scope of Gérard's text. Indeed, all African literatures, other than those written in European languages, have important oral components — components that often include Islamic elements, or that have helped to shape the forms of culture in Islamic societies.

Furthermore, the bulk of scholarship on African literature deals with contemporary fiction, poetry, and drama, most of which is Europhone. This, too, lies outside the scope of Gérard's study. And a very large portion of that recent literature is Islamic, in the sense employed above. Thus the frustration of the scholar who wishes to learn about Islam with respect to the novels or stories of Cheikh Hamidou Kane, Ousmane Socé, Camara Laye, Sembène Ousmane, Nurrudin Farah, Tayeb Salih, Yambo Ouologuem, Ayi Kwei Armah, Mariama Bâ, Hampâté Bâ, Ahmadou Kourouma, Birago Diop, Seydou Badian, Shaaban Robert, Abdoulaye Sadji, Aminata Sow Fall, or with respect to the films now emerging especially from Senegal, Burkina Faso, and Mali, not to mention dozens of other poets, novelists, and dramatists.

My own experience in attempting to learn about the Sufi elements in Camara Laye's work was of this sort. Many well-known critics, like Janheinz Jahn and Eustace Palmer, had written about *Le Regard du roi*. But wrong-headed notions about Clarence as a Christ figure, or in Jahn's case, as a universal quester, ignored the essential background of the author, who was raised in a region of Guinea where Islam has been present for hundreds of years, and where the Tijani influence was paramount. The Western, New Critical approach to

African literature, as well as the general ignorance in the West concerning Islamic beliefs and traditions, may have been responsible for this unforgiveable lacuna.

This volume represents a beginning, an attempt to redress the imbalance in the scholarship, and is not by any means an exhaustive survey. Critical problems involving context, historical formulations, ideological frameworks, the treatment of women, the importance of language — the special place occupied by the Word in Islam — and especially the impact of the meeting of Islam and African traditions, are featured in the essays in this volume. The regions under consideration span both East and West Africa, and although the focus is on contemporary literature, also included are studies on the older works, such as the *Tarikh-el-Fettach* or the *Utenzi wa Mwana Kupona*. Overall, the appreciation of Islam and its literature in sub-Saharan Africa as a long-standing tradition is recognized and celebrated in this volume.

Our collective work was greatly facilitated by the generous support of David Wiley and the African Studies Center, and John Cantlon and the Office of the Vice-President for Research at Michigan State University, who made it possible for a conference on the topic of Islam in sub-Saharan African literature to be held at Michigan State University in 1989. There the contributors to this volume met, along with Nurrudin Farah, Stephen Arnold, Mohamed Mbodji, and many others whose commentaries were greatly appreciated.

I am extremely grateful to David Robinson for his support for this project, and for his critical suggestions. Mohamed Mbodji gave unstintingly of his ideas and time in helping me shape the broad lines of the introduction, and Elizabeth Wettroth Harrow helped not only to give the ideas a critical focus but also whatever modicum of style they enjoy. Her help in the preparation, and especially in the editing, of this volume was invaluable — I could not imagine having finished without it.

Finally my thanks to John Watson of Heinemann Educational Books for his patience, suggestions, and encouragement.

Part I

THE
APPROACH
TO ISLAM

Chapter 1

▼▼▼▼▼▼▼▼

Introduction:
Islam(s) in African Literature

KENNETH W. HARROW

For the New Historians, patterns of rhetoric that inform historical discourse are responsible for the reification of culture. Nowhere is this more evident than in the Orientalist view of Islam in Africa. When viewed as an object, and specifically as a foreign object introjected into a land distant in space and culture from its point of origin, Islam has conventionally been reduced to the notion of a predetermined monolith. Sweeping characterizations of Islam have more or less succeeded in transforming various groups of people into one undifferentiated body, "Muslims." This totalizing tendency reduces Islam to an unchanging doctrine, and its multitudes of adherents to a single entity.

In contrast, what this collection demonstrates quite simply is the multivalent nature of what is meant when "Islam" is employed by writers from across the continent of Africa. Despite the common understanding of the term, "Islam" varies considerably with time, place, and text — reflecting all the diversities of African culture, as well as particular idiosyncrasies of individual authors. Nonetheless, common features of history, and similar institutional patterns, allow us to postulate the existence of an African Islamic culture and literature.

The first element of that identity consists in the self-conscious adherence to the community of believers and their doctrinal elaborations, as in the elucubrations of Samba Diallo's father in *L'Aventure ambiguë*; equally, it can be located in the attack on doctrine or practice, as in the case of *Ceddo*. The discourse may lack what

3
▼

Foucault would call an author, but those who elaborate it share common religious assumptions. The "brotherhood of believers," and more specifically, the characteristic beliefs and practices of groups like the brotherhoods, or *tariqa* (Sufi orders), can be reflected in a body of novels, like those of the Senegalese Mourids or Tijanis. **Debra Boyd-Buggs**[1] has shown that much contemporary Senegalese fiction bears direct relation to the dominant position of Mouridism in Senegalese society.

Just as participation in the group implies participation in a power structure, so, too, does the discourse or the text represent as well as share in power. The griots of the past have been termed "masters of the word"; the sheikhs and marabouts have always understood their dominion to be grounded in the word, and, indeed, **Ali Jimale Ahmed** represents the basic conflict that has animated Somali poetry as the struggle between sheikh and poet for authoritative dominion over the spoken word. Similarly, I have attempted to demonstrate that Cheikh Hamidou Kane's "ambiguous adventure" can best be viewed in terms of the struggle between secular and sacred authorities for control over representations of the word. Birago Diop has given memorable features to these Islamic mysteries in his story "La Biche et les deux chasseurs": as a marabout's spittle is ingested by a deer when it chews some grass, the deer puts on the knowledge and the power of the marabout's word. In this story, Birago succeeds in appropriating and synthesizing Islamic and Wolof elements. In a thousand ways of representing the paradoxes, the illusions, the mysteries, and the ambivalences of life, African writers have constructed a distinctively African Islamic edifice with their words — by stringing the pearls of their verses, as the Swahili conceit would have it.

The central issue being raised here is not the perplexing one of what Islam is (to author, to reader, to discourse), but the straightforward notion of a religious/cultural tradition that represents itself in orature and in literary texts. What Foucault has made clear is that the act of representation itself is part of an evolving process into which power always enters. Nowhere in traditional Islamic society is that relationship of power to discourse more apparent than in the male-female relationships, which is why Fatima Mernessi's analysis of the act of representation turns on the issues of feminism in the Islamic world (Mernessi, 1987). For Mernessi the gap between fact and word — between event and its representation — is considerable. The first she terms reality and associates with acting, or what people actually do; the latter are discourses people develop about themselves which respond to the need for self-presentation and identity-building, needs we would expect to be all the greater in colonial or post-colonial societies. Reality obeys "harsh time-bound laws" — thus the need for identity-building as corresponding to the demands generated in a "confusing and shifting reality" (Mernissi 1987, viii). The drive to make sense out of our lives springs from our impulse to have control over our lives, to exercise power, so that "as fragile as one may be, one can still have an impact on one's surroundings" (viii-ix). This need to exercise control is all the more acute in times of radical change, all the more evident when Islam measures its strength against non-Muslim elements within societies it purports to make into its own — or when its purists launch their campaigns against *al-mukhlit*, or those who mix Islam with non-Islamic elements. Thus, Mernissi concludes, "Everyone is afraid of change, but Muslims are more so, because what is at stake are their fantasies about power. And women all over the world know very well how important power fantasies are to one's self-empowerment" (x).

For Kourouma, fantasies of power are all that is left for Fama and Salimata in *Les Soleils des indépendances*; while the forces of traditional religious authority were responsible for scarring Salimata's past, the marabouts seem no more capable of restoring her wholeness in the present. Kourouma's vision of the abuses of religious power finds echoes in much contemporary Islamic African literature — from Sembène to Farah — revealing the aptness of Mernissi's remarks. In a careful analysis of Koranic law versus Sudanic practice, **Sonia Ghattas-Soliman** shows how Tayeb Salih portrays the destruction of an independent woman in *Season of Migration to the North*. There it is a concerted effort by the entire village male hierarchy, whose actions are rationalized along forced readings of the Koran, that combine to impose a marriage on the unwilling widow, Hosna.

However, merely to associate discourse with power or its fantasies is to ignore cultural specificity. In his discussion of Moroccan institutions, Clifford Geertz elaborates three forms of Islam which we might consider as models for our texts themselves. The first he labels the *siyyid* complex, "after the name given both to dead saints and to the tombs in which they are thought to be buried" (1968, 49). By metonymic extension, the patrilinear descendants of the saint, and the cult through which his baraka is extended, are included. The second form is termed the *zawiya* complex, referring to the brother-hoods with their lodges or *tariqa*, their founding sheikhs, and especially with the practice, or *dhikr*, which is taught to successive generations of adherents. These, of course, became particularly active in much of sub-Saharan Africa. The common element in *siyyid or zawiya* complex patterns is the focus on the holy man—saint or marabout—who provides the center for each movement. The individual mystic appears most prominently in Salih's *Wedding of Zein*, while the marabout or master features in Kane's *L'Aventure ambiguë*. In Laye's *Le Regard du roi*, the classic text of the Sufi way, it is the guide, or *murshid*, who figures prominently, while the notions of *tariqa* and *dhikr* inform the novel. In general the positive religious depictions give us representations of holy figures around whom *siyyid* and *zawiya* complexes are focused.

Geertz's last term for institutional Islam is the *maxzen* complex; that is, royal assumption of sacred power assured through descent in the Prophet's line. As sacred kingship was commonly held in much of what is now Muslim sub-Saharan Africa, the association of Islam with central government was naturally linked to still broader distinctions that clearly emerged within the patterns of the *maxzen* complex. When we understand that the power of the monarch was linked with public displays, such as holidays connected with the sultan or king's reign, the appointment of Islamic judges, the pronouncement of the Friday sermon in his name, and generally dominion over the elements of worship within the city (Geertz 1968, 53), it becomes clear that the traditional opposition between the mystic holy man or saint, and the formal, legal exponents of religious authority (what Lings refers to as the esoteric versus the exoteric approach), can apply here as well (see Lings 1987). Although Geertz presents the *maxzen* complex as yet another example of the mystification of individual power, it is clear that the power of the state is institutionally bound to the formal, scriptural reading of Islamic text, what can be termed the legalistic discourse. This provides the focus upon ethical behavior, which is naturally employed by a wide range of critics: **Edris Makward** has argued that much of Sembène's apparent criticism of Islam is more obviously a criticism of the unethical deployment of religious authority; **Sonia Ghattas-Soliman** makes similar arguments in her analysis of Salih's *Season of Migration to the North*; while **I. C. Tcheho** sees Birago Diop's attitude toward Islam as driven into ambivalences over contradictory formal positions. The larger criticisms of Ouologuem and Armah are also best understood within the framework of the cult of the State. Other depictions of Islam in terms of Muslim models of righteousness are numerous. The majority of Muslim characters in much recent African fiction—as in Soyinka's *The Swamp Dwellers*, *The Interpreters*, and *Season of Anomy*, the more recent works of Nigerian writers, such as Ibrahim Tahir's *The Last Imam* and Zaynab Alkali's *The Virtuous Woman*, as well as popular Hausa fiction—testify to a growing desire of writers to focus entirely upon comportment as defined according to a Muslim ethos.

Geertz's formulations often suggest models for binary oppositions that operate along parallel lines. Mysticism and legalism, *baraka* and scripture, marabout and *faqih* (legal scholar) are often at odds with each other. When the division fails to break into such neat patterns, different parties vying for power, like sheikhs and poets (or princes and marabouts, as Coulon [1981] would have it), still retain their institutional associations, and thus suggest broad cultural divisions which give coherence to a Muslim identity and discourse.

While not terminating these struggles and divisions, colonialism brought an additional element into this pattern. In some cases it merely substituted its word, its authority for that of the sultan, appropriating the *maxzen* complex for itself. In others, it either suppressed the "maraboutism" or co-opted it, generating considerable alienation as the inevitable consequence of its efforts at supplanting African institutions. Kane's famous formulation in *L'Aventure ambiguë* best sums up the foreboding mood of the times: As the *maître*, the *chef*, and Samba Diallo's father are talking early in the novel, the latter opines, "Nous sommes parmi les derniers hommes au monde à posséder Dieu tel qu'Il est véritablement dans son Unicité ..." (1961, 20) [We are among the last people on earth to possess God such as He truly is in his Oneness].

Great though the impact of the West may have been, the central issue posed by the study of Islam in African literature is the way in which Africans appropriated the new religion and made it their own. For Arabists, purists, and fundamentalists, as Mernessi put it, change poses a threat, and deviation from orthodox forms is to be opposed. But the realities of social change, and of cultural practice, are more complex: processes of appropriation, grounded in power, have always accompanied the elaboration of any belief system—while the ideological explanations for those beliefs have tagged along afterward. As concerns Islam in Africa, and its subsequent literary expression, what occurred was a series of adaptations in which Islam came to occupy increasingly important spaces in the lives of various people—psychological spaces, governing first the territory of the mind, at times motivated by economic or other self-interested concerns, and then larger, external spaces of an increasingly political and social nature.

This process could be termed Africa's appropriation of Islam, and, to be sure, could be compared with the similar process of appropriation that Islam underwent everywhere, cutting across both geographical and temporal boundaries. With each different culture it took on its own specific form, despite sharing much of a common theology. As **George Lang** has pointed out, "Africa is but one of the five cultural spheres in which Islam has found a home, and the Arab heartland is but another." And in rebuttal to the slander that African Islam is particularly given to schism and heresy, Lang remarks upon the "proliferation of sects within each of [the five cultural spheres]." Works of literature, like *Les Soleils des indépendances*, exemplify perfectly the way in which Islamic realities dovetail with the immediate cultural context, in this case a Malinke one. In addition to plot, the implied views of the semi-ironic narrative voice, the articulation of sensitivities and values, all attest to the tensions faced by Fama and Salimata in contemporary Muslim West Africa, and specifically the Côte d'Ivoire. (Here we are in disagreement with Mohamadou Kane for whom Fama's ultimate choice of accepting the direction of the *féticheur royal* places Fama in the camp of the *animistes* [1982, 435].)

Ultimately, to appreciate how literature fits within the context of cultural Islamization, we must have access to the historical approach, which will help us account for the meeting of Islam and traditional African culture, as well as for the impact brought to that conjunction by the harsh realities of colonialism. At the outset of the historical investigation one immediately encounters the Orientalist bias as opposed to the native perspective. The opposing approaches turn on the difference between an Islam *reaching* Africa, influencing Africa (as though it were some outside or foreign element grafted onto African soil),[2] and Islam itself developing in Africa, being a tradition in Africa upon which Muslims of today can look back. The difference in approaches is clearly seen in the observations of the fourteenth-century Maghrebian traveller, Ibn Battuta, and the viewpoint of the contemporary writer, Cheikh Hamidou Kane, especially with regard to the latter's characterization of the *maître*. The former offers a reconstructed view that begins in the past and from the outside, and moves into Africa and into the present. The standard of *istihan* (beauty/good) and *istiqbah* (ugly/bad) is provided by norms to which he is accustomed in Arabic society, and he rejects Malinke values as *istiqbah* on the ground that they are "pagan," pre-Islamic intrusions.

We can define the contrasting view as starting from the perspective of the text into which one enters always here and now, beginning at the moment one encounters the sphere of the text. Here tradition and religion are not the product of some past foreign, missionary activity which provided the point of origination, but are contemporary realities, grounded, to be sure, in the ancestors' words and wisdom, but occupying the present territory. The *maître* in *L'Aventure ambiguë* has no predecessor identified other than by the term *maître* — in a sense he has only successors.

For the historian, **David Robinson**, the Orientalist approaches have occluded our understanding of the different Islamic realities that developed in West Africa. In its most extreme form, the Orientalist view of African Islam denies its authenticity, insisting that all genuine forms of the religion be tied to Arabic culture and language. Thus all syncretism is denied, while the language, faith, and practice of Islam are all frozen in 622 A.D. This "hegira" view of religion revealed its ethnocentric bias when it came to Islam on the Margins where historical change or mixing is not only conceded, but blamed for the impure nature of the indigenous form. We see this tendency in Trimingham's well-known description of the stages of Islamization in Africa (1949; 1959; 1962; 1964). We also see it in the radical divisions of space into the Muslim world (*dar al-Islam*) and the non-Muslim (*dar al-Harb*); and radical divisions of time into the *Jahaliya* (the time before the coming of Islam, called a state of ignorance) and the era of Islam beginning with the Hegira.

Robinson's reformulation of the issue focuses on the practice of Islam in new spaces, as well as the re-formation of old spaces with the coming of historical change. Although the order of conversion might vary, especially in West Africa it was seen to be associated first with merchants and traders, next with the ruling classes, and finally with the rural masses. At the heart of these changes lies the consciousness of Islamic identity which governed the sense of participation in the *dar al-Islam*. The instruments for the emergence of this consciousness were multiple, and again varied from region to region. **Robinson** has shown how in the savannah of West Africa these instruments involved "quietistic and militaristic modes" — networking through trade and scholarship, jihad and reformism, culminating in the conquest of the region. Conquest occurred in the full sense of the term under the impetus of al-Hajj Umar, leaving the majority of the inhabitants of the region conscious of a Muslim identity for themselves and their land. Historians thus demonstrate that reterritorialism, whether peaceful or militant, entails conquest of space.

In Eastern Africa, **Jay Spaulding** demonstrates similar patterns with the careful initial quarantining of the foreign merchants, followed by the conversions at the courts, and eventually, as in the Western savannah, a series of reforming, expansionist jihads. **Spaulding** emphasizes the theme of continuity whereby the Islamic cultural tradition perceives itself as participating in common currents, while he places this sense of continuity within the historical theme of change to which all temporal institutions are subject. The constant interplay of external forces and local plenipotentiaries marks the centuries of Islamization of the region. Again, in terms of the crucial question of how the foreign entity was integrated into the native culture, **Spaulding** notes that while the eye of faith would prefer to have it that realities drawn out of the mainstream of Islamic tradition were appropriated into the cultures of Eastern Africa, the historian sees always "a sequence of changing epochs, a wider context, a diversity of cultural preferences," with "alternative possible outcomes to every historical process."

Thus, in place of the comforting *divisions* of people, space, time, or belief, we see as more realistic the concept of a *continuum*, such as that observed by Ibn Battuta as he journeyed south across the Sahara. Moreau's description of the famous traveler's geographical encounters could well serve to characterize temporal, and indeed cultural change: "En s'approchant du pays des Noirs, il rencontrait des marchands blancs de toute obédience, kharijites comme sunnites, et des *Wangârata* [black merchants]. Sur ces marchés, l'éclecticisme des croyances devait être très grand; là pourtant s'élaborait ce qui se raconterait d'escale en escale à l'intérieur, et qui deviendrait traditions . . ." (Moreau 1982, 99). [As he approached the land of the Blacks, he encountered white merchants of all persuasions—Kharijites as well as Sunnis, and the *wangarata* [black merchants]. On these routes, the eclecticism of beliefs had to have been quite considerable; there, on the other hand, are found elaborations of what was recounted from stopping point to stopping point to the interior, and which became traditions . . .].

This mixing is perhaps better understood as a normal process of culture practice, a characteristic of all vital processes, just as the reformist tendency would seem to be an inevitable feature of religious/ culture formation, no less inevitably joined, as Mernessi has said, to the fundamentalist reaction.[3] **Thomas Hale**, **Gabriel Asfar**, **Denise Asfar**, and **Lemuel Johnson** offer interesting variants of this view. **Hale** dissects the famous *Tarikh el-Fettach* and *Tarikh es-Sudan*, which celebrate the rise to power of the Songhay monarch Askia Mohamed. The documents are described as exhibiting the properties of dynamic growth: "They are hardly static documents fixed in the past, but constitute instead many layers of interpretation which continue to evolve in the present." Those layers of interpretation reflected pre-Islamic Songhay belief as well as orthodox doctrine. For example, in the battle for Gao, Askia Mohamed's descendants relied on three protective spirits, incarnated in a snake, a hen, and an ox, "thanks to whom the city maintains its invulnerability." All the same, when Askia Mohamed was endangered in battle with the Bargantche, he sought salvation by addressing a prayer to Allah: "Oh my God, I implore you in memory of that day when I stood next to the head of your messenger in his mausoleum . . . ." The examples are multiplied by **Hale**, who concludes that "the epic appears to be a syncretic portrait of two systems of belief . . . ."

In a close study of Fulani oral literature and of the Sufi orders (especially the Tijaniyya) of the region of Mali, **Gabriel Asfar** describes Hampâté Bâ's project to remain faithful to both the Islamic and the Fulani traditions. For Bâ the meeting of the two was not confrontational but harmonious, mutually stimulating because of the capacity of the Fulani base to grow and incorporate the Muslim values. Affirming that strong compatibilities may be shown to exist between Islam and the tenets of traditional African religions, Bâ concludes that "Islam took hold and grew in sub-Saharan Africa upon the foundations of traditional religion." **Denise Asfar** then proceeds to demonstrate the truth of this assertion by examining one of Bâ's masterpieces, *Kaïdara*. Indeed, it is her view that the "underlying compatibility of these traditions ensured their continuing intermingling beyond the rise and fall of the savannah states . . . ." The quest tales of Fulani initiation, like the trilogy to which *Kaïdara* belongs, offer striking examples of this compatibility, but we might also find comparable examples in Birago Diop's "L'Héritage," as well as in Camara Laye's *Le Regard du roi*.

If the traditional oral literature testified to a basic harmony, the same could not always be said of contemporary literature. Mohamadou Kane posits the movement towards syncretism as a result of the ruptures, aporias, introduced into traditional belief by Western values, values ultimately purveyed under the mantle of modernity: "L'attention accordée à l'éloignement des personnages de la religion conduit les romanciers au thème des contradictions que suscite le contexte de modernisation. Ils ne s'y attardent pas particulièrement, préférant le plus souvent insister sur le progrès du syncrétisme" (M. Kane 1982, 427). [The attention devoted to the alienation of characters from religion leads the novelists to the theme of contradictions to which the context of modernization gives rise. They don't remain focused on this point, however, preferring more often to stress the progress arising from syncretism.]

In an original approach, **Lemuel Johnson** argues that this kind of syncretism is also characteristic of contemporary African fiction that he labels *al-mukhlit* writing, that is, writing of "the mixers." The term, he explains, is not disinterested. Although he employs it in reference to aesthetic practice, it is in essence "religious and inquisitional," implying a "purist concern with apostasy, heresy, and syncretism." At the limit, **Johnson** concedes an approximation to this purism in the "near-pathological excesses of mortification and ecstasy" in the *maître* in *L'Aventure ambiguë*.[4] For **Johnson**, the type of "dual consciousness" that characterizes *al-mukhlit* writing is best found in *L'Enfant noir*, in which the culture's "magico-religious syncretism" recurs repeatedly in ritual and practice. The elixir from Kankan, prepared by the marabout from water used to wash a slate on which appropriate Koranic verses have been written, is a familiar example of "popular" Islam, although careful attention to the speech acts, as well as to the calendar, as **Eric Sellin** points out, offer more striking examples. This is particularly evident in the characterization of illness and death as the road to God. A more recent example of the most creative sort of cultural cross-fertilizing might be seen in Nurrudin Farah's *Maps*. There Farah informs dreams and memories, mixed fantasies and collected world visions, with Islamic figures like the winged white horse, al-Buraq, that bore Mohammed aloft, and with pre-Islamic Somali images of the deity, like the crow. In his works the personal, the fantastic, and the transcendental all intersect.

In his analysis of the broad range of positive and negative writings about Islam, i.e., from Kane and Laye to Sembène and Ouologuem, Johnson points out that in all cases there is a tension, albeit a muted one, which results from the pressures of the varied religious forces at play. It might be argued that tension is a permanent feature of all religious as well as cultural formation, as a result of the resistance of past patterns, or of well-defined bodies of belief—that is, a resistance to admit the integration of foreign elements or to accede to the pressure to change. The concept of purity is the form taken by that resistance, and the tension exhibited across the literature might be better understood not as a result of an authentic Islam resisting the infiltration of "pagan" practice, but as the natural and inevitable dynamic of an on-going religious/cultural process — just as the absence of that tension might be viewed not as the triumph of purity, but as the manifestation of that process in a moribund stage.

By that interpretation, Ouologuem's vituperation no less than Laye's or Salih's exultation testifies to the metabolic vitality of Islam in their culture. More generally, from Ousmane Socé's *Karim* to the more recent present with Mariama Bâ's *Une si longue lettre*, dozens of novels, plays, and films from Senegal and other parts of West Africa continue to evoke Muslim personnages and practices of the *al-mukhlit* variety. **Mbye Cham**'s study of Senegalese literature and film demonstrates the range of attitudes developed towards Islam: the extremes he labels as promoters or as apostates. The former demonstrate the zealous embrace and vigorous advocacy of Islam, while the latter posit "a fundamentally materialist ideology" in which Islam is portrayed as "colonial in nature." In between these two poles lies "a range of artistic responses which share an acceptance of the basic ideals of Islam yet are separated here by less zeal and didacticism, there by a constant alternation between reverence and mockery of Islamic holy men, and there again by a strident iconoclasm which indicts religious charlatans and distorters of Islam." In his conclusion Cham makes the claim that whether it is the apologists or agnostics who speak, Islam occupies a central position in their thoughts, attesting to "the almost absolute hegemony of Islam in Senegal."

Cham's Senegalese model resembles that of Mohamadou Kane, for whom the contemporary African novelist has had three responses to the encounter between Islam and modernity, and the accompanying loss of tradition. One response is of praise: Traditional religion — and, by extension, Islam — is glorified, as in the case of Seydou Badian. The second is of regret: There is an apparent resignation to the fact that traditional ways have passed, as may perhaps be seen in the nostalgic backward glance of Laye or Kane. The third response is of rejection: The pessimistic theme of the loss of God ("la mort des dieux") is developed — this extreme position being the most common response, according to Kane (1982, 437). Though Kane draws his examples from those attesting to the loss of traditional beliefs, we can apply this theme equally to Islam in the work of Sembène, and even more especially to *Le Devoir de violence*. At the limit we pass from rejection to vituperation with Armah's *Two Thousand Seasons*.

When Islam is presented in a positive light, it is often in the form of a jihad whose twin meanings include struggle against external evil, and against evil impulses and weaknesses within. The latter conflict is commonly represented in novel or short story where the struggle within takes the form of a self-overcoming. The quest versions, mythic projections of this theme, are seen in the tales, epics, or Sufi-inspired novels that depict man or woman in a state of weakness or ignorance, overcoming obstacles to greater self-fulfillment. Islamic virtue is then a matter of inner strength, the key to self-transformation and to self-realization. On a quieter note, it is associated with those models of deportment or self-control whose character had been formed by this struggle. One thinks of Samba Diallo's education at the hands of the *maître* as an example of this struggle for self-control, and of his father, or of Laye's Uncle Mamadou as the role models. Cham points out that poetry is the favored medium among the "traditional promoters" of Islam — a generalization one could apply broadly across the continent to Islamic writings in African languages.

On the other hand, when Islam is depicted in a negative light, the inner struggle is absent, and corruption takes external form: hypocritical behavior, contradictions between word and deed, and typically base motivations of power and greed betray the absence of any inner strength or outward opposition to evil. Jihad is absent. In this emphasis on morality, and implicitly on obedience to higher moral principle, if not to higher authority, we are not only in the realm of legalistic Islam, but of *maxzen* Islam. Thus, Islam (especially corrupt or hypocritical Muslim authority) is reduced to the arch-villain in the tragedy. Sembène writes the history of its villainous usages, beginning with the false marabout or charlatan, gradually hardening the attack over the years. In "Tauw" the marabout was just another feature of a corrupt society; in *Ceddo* the marabout imposed an oppressive system in the form of Islam. Nonetheless, **Edris Makward** notes that Sembène's denunciation of social abuses "does not generally amount to a sweeping condemnation of tradition or religion," but of unethical behavior or corrupt practices. Sembène's intent in the film was "to remove the untouchable aura of Islam in his country by portraying its implantation and insertion in his society as a result of a merciless struggle for political control." For the materialist, tradition may have its saving graces, but religion never offers a genuine ontological or metaphysical conception. Thus, while Sembène does not call into question the specific theological truths of Islam, Makward affirms that he "seems to be accusing it for its spirit of fatalism and its inherent message of inertia and passivity." This evaluation might well apply equally to a large body of films and novels from West Africa, such as Johnson Traore's *Njangaan*. Cham points out that film and novels in French are the favored genre employed by the "iconoclasts," those most critical of Islam.

The closed door on history as well as on metaphysics — on dialogism of any form — explains further the vituperative nature of the attacks launched on Islam by Ouologuem and Armah. The object of the former's parody, and of the latter's scorn, is an Islam portrayed solely as an institution — that is, as the source of power of the sort derived from the *maxzen* complex.

The opposite of these portraits of radical evil is to be found in African Islam's most inspirational effusions. In the long-standing traditions tied to maraboutic institutions, *siyyid* or *zawiya*, otherworldly power is married to religious thought, as in the voluminous writings of the "anti-sultan," al-Hajj Umar. Mamadou Dia has traced this tradition from the Middle Ages down to the present: "Des études récentes . . . révèlent la continuité d'une tradition qui, inaugurée par d'illustres noms du Moyen Age comme *Al Maghili, Al Bilbâli, Ahmed Baba*, se prolonge au XVIIe siècle avec les érudits haoussas: *Dan Marina* et *Dan Massanih* et au XVIIIe siècle avec l'imam *Al Barnawi*, théologien, critique, précursor de Osman Dan Fodio et de Djibril d'Agadès . . ." (Dia 1980, 35). [Recent studies . . . reveal the continuity of a tradition, inaugurated by illustrious names of the Middle Ages like al-Maghili, al-Bilbali, Ahmed Baba, that continues into the seventeenth century with erudite Hausas, Dan Marina and Dan Massanih, and, in the eighteenth century, with the imam al-Barnawi, theologian, critic, precursor of Usman Dan Fodio and of Djibril d'Agadès.] Dia concludes that this ancient tradition is most richly fulfilled in the spiritual writings to which it gave rise: "Cette littérature d'exégèse savante n'épuise pas, au demeurant, l'apport culturel de l'Islam: la littérature mystique, à peine explorée, nous paraît plus originale, plus riche de spiritualité." [This literature of scholarly exegesis does not exhaust, however, the cultural contribution of Islam: the mystical literature, hardly explored, appears to us as more original, richer in spirituality.][5]

In his magisterial study of African language literature, Albert Gérard has shown how the lines of Islamic writing have extended far back into the past of several major societies. In the Western Sudan, Gérard begins with Arabic language texts, centering on the regions of the Songhai kingdom and the Hausa states. Not surprisingly, this literature is close to the homiletic or doctrinal sources of the Arab world, and can be characterized as anti-*Mukhlit*, as we see in the title of one of Usman Dan Fodio's treatises, *Ihya al-sunna wa ikhmad al-bid'a* ("Revivification of Orthodoxy and Extinguishing of Innovation"), an appropriate marker of the link between jihad and literature in much of the Arabic, Hausa, and Fulani writings. In Senegal it was Wolof poetry and treatises which appeared prominently in the nineteenth century, again carrying a strong moralistic message. The Sufi influences over epics and poems by authors like Amadou Bamba and Moussa Ka were dominant, but traditional oral influences remained strong, attesting to what Cheikh Anta Diop called the "Africanization of Islam" when referring to Mourid poetry. Moussa Ka's assertion that religious values ought to hold pride of place in literature of any language is expressed in the following verse: "Wolof, Arabic, and all other languages are equally valuable/All poetry is fine, that aims at praising the Prophet ..." (Gérard, 73). In East Africa, Gérard notes the presence of the Muslim influence in Madagascar, but focuses his efforts on Swahili and Somali writings. Again it is the Islamic character of the society that leads Gérard to focus upon the religious element in the literature. Wilfred Whitely is cited to substantiate this claim. "The inspiration [of the early poets] was Islam, and Islamic culture and thought impregnate all the early verse" (Gérard, 95).

In contrast to this position, **Ibrahim Noor Shariff** holds that the emphasis placed on *written* sources by Western scholars — including many of Gérard's primary authorities, like Whitely, Knappert, Harries, and Allen — has led to the erroneous conception that the vast preponderance of Swahili literature is devotional in nature. This error sprang, in part, from the belief among the Swahili Muslims that the preservation and propagation of Islamic doctrine, as in the form of homiletic verse, "are acts which are believed to give the mortals *thawab* — or Heavenly credit — that is expected to help them enter Paradise." It was these manuscripts that received the attention of the colonialists and later scholars. However, **Shariff** asserts that a continuous secular oral tradition has always been a strong feature of Swahili literature, resulting in great prestige attached to verbal skills in the culture. This leads Ali Mazrui to comment on the extraordinary blending of cultures which arises when one discovers Swahili poetry on a wide variety of topics in one's morning newspaper. The most striking Swahili poetical form to have developed, the *utenzi*, exhibits traits of both religious and secular traditions. For **Shariff**, the poetic tradition joined the resources of the Swahili language with the religious persuasion of the culture, resulting in the fulfillment of "a noble task," one most deserving of *thawab*, because it manages "to exploit [one's] innate possibilities to the full in the service of Allah."

Not surprisingly, **Ali Jimale Ahmed** has attested to vibrant poetic traditions of Somali literature which bear resemblances to the Swahili. **Ahmed** asserts that Islam and poetry meet in several ways in Somalia. The poet shares in the power of the judge for whom Islamic law forms the basis for passing judgments, thus competing with the sheikhs. The oral tradition creates a reverence for the word, for recitation, and for the one who memorizes text, just as the passage through the gateway of faith is begun with the learning and recitation of the *chahada* — the credo — and culminates with the night of the recitation, in which the youthful initiate recites the entire Koran by heart.[6] Reverence for the spoken word is at the heart of Somali and Swahili beliefs: According to **Shariff**, *thawab* is obtained by repetition of the holy verse. Conversely, the power invested in the oral curse springs equally from the ability of the sheikh to evoke Allah's punishment for transgressors. Here poetry itself becomes, in the words of the Prophet addressed to the poet Hassan Ibn Tabit, "more potent than falling arrows in the darkness of dawn." **Ahmed** has indicated a beautiful Somali version of this concept in the words of the poet Qamaan Bulxan: "O Cali, the Everlasting One has driven on the words of your poem/the rustling wind of the warm breeze has carried them." It is no surprise that the poet's vaunting is hedged by the sheikh's accusations of irreverence, summed up in the Koranic warning, "Poets are followed by none save erring men" (26:227).

This ambiguity is also drawn in the famous Swahili classic, the *Utenzi wa Mwana Kupona*. **Ann Biersteker** has shown how the subtleties of Swahili verbal art inform this *utenzi*: the messages that radiate out from the poem could be seen to indicate ironic contradictions to its surface meanings. Ostensibly the *utenzi*, the only canonical Swahili text to be authored by a woman, deals with the theme of wifely virtue as defined within the contours of patriarchal Islamic ideology. Yet closer readings deconstruct the surface moralizing: Virtue turns out to be "seductive verbal eloquence," a form of manipulation which justifies the Koranic warnings against the poets. Submission — as wifely virtue, or as *the* proper religious attitude — is turned/troped into empowerment, at the expense of those (males) who overtly control the reins of power.

Thus the Swahili and Somali traditions, like their Songhai, Hausa, and Wolof counterparts in the West, converge at the one central point of the Islamic discourse — the special powers of the poetic, spoken, recited, chanted, evocatory word. Its esoteric properties rest upon exoteric form, allowing for the interplay between outward 'and inner meanings. Unlike the printed sign whose primary quality is its interchangeability, its capacity to be translated and telegraphed, the *baraka* or power/blessing of the word is inseparable from the status of the agents who articulate it: poets, sheikhs, marabouts, *murshids* (guides), *faqih* (legal scholars) — as Mamadou Dia has said, these voices which can be traced from the distant past to the present — have elaborated an anthology, a discursive tapestry, "autant de manifestations éblouissantes d'un esprit de création et d'une finesse philosophique qui doivent à l'Islam d'avoir pu s'épanouir" (Dia 1980, 36) [so many dazzling manifestations of a spirit of creation and of a philosophical finesse whose fulfillment was made possible by Islam]. And if the europhone literary production has inclined toward critical positions, it has had to couch its formulations no less in the terms of this long-standing tradition. The objective of this volume is to lift the veil of silence that has been imposed by a europhone critical pattern, so that future volumes on African literature can have no excuse for omitting all references to Islam.[7]

Notes

1. The names of contributors to this volume will be indicated in boldface.
2. The language with which Islam is described as reaching Africa has been naturalized, as if it were the only way to discuss the topic. Thus Moreau, in describing the situation in East Africa states, "cette côte fut très tôt visitée par les Arabes et arabisés musulmans, avec des avancées toujours plus accentuées vers le sud; Kilwa fut *atteinte* en 957 ..." (Moreau 1982, 50). [this coast was visited quite early by the Arabs and Arabized Muslims, with ever-increasing sorties being made towards the south; Kilwa was *reached* in 957 ....]; and for the West, "Tout au long de l'histoire, ce sont les Maures eux-mêmes qui *pénetrait* lentement .... Ce n'est qu'au XVIIe que l'islam *s'implanta* plus profondément dans le pays ...." [Throughout history it was the Moors who slowly *penetrated* .... It wasn't until the seventeenth century that Islam was more profoundly *implanted* in the country]; and finally, "Les témoignages de ce genre, émanant des traditions locales, apportent de nouvelles lumières sur les étapes de *l'impregnation* islamique des sociétés ..." (66–67, my stress in all quotations) [The testimonials of this sort, emanating from local traditions, brought new light on the stages of Islamic *impregnation* of the societies].
3. See her introduction to the revised edition of *Beyond the Veil*, "Muslim Women and Fundamentalism."
4. Kane himself would seem to favor the softer path of reconciliation. In an interview with Debra Boyd-Buggs, he puts a negative construction on

the *fou*'s final refusal to accept Samba Diallo's decision not to pray, indicting the *fou* for his failure to accept the kind of reformist change anticipated in the "new" Samba Diallo who has returned from France. See Boyd-Buggs 1986, 299−308.

5. Dia then elaborates: "Nous pensons à la poésie mystique en langue arabe telle que les 'Javair mâni' [Jawahir al-ma'ani] de El hadj Omar, 'l'Al-Ibris' d'Ad-Dabbagh, les poèmes du mouride Ahmadou Bamba, du Sage érudit de Tivaouane Malick Sy, mais à toute une florissante littérature en langues africaines, notamment les poèmes peuls à thèmes religieux. Ainsi la méditation sur la mort que développe le poème intitulé *les Créatures* ou cette évocation des traditions musulmanes sur les *Signes de l'Heure* que représente cet autre chef-d'oeuvre: *La fin des Temps* . . . . Chose étonnante, la vie paysanne elle-même trouve des chantres à la faveur de la mystique musulmane qui sous le ciel africain fait éclore une poésie bucolique porteuse des premices d'une géorgique, peut-être la première, en Islam" (35−36).
[We are thinking of the mystical poetry in Arabic such as the "Jawahir al-ma'ani" of al-Hajj Umar, the "'Al-Ibris" of ad-Dabbagh, the poems of the mourid Ahmadou Bamba, the erudite sage of Tivaouane, Malick Sy, and of a flourishing literature in African languages, notably the Pular poems with religious themes. Additionally, there is the meditation on death which is developed in the poem entitled *The Creatures* or that evocation of Muslim traditions on the *Signs of the Hour* which represents that other masterpiece, *The End of Time* . . . . It is amazing that peasant life itself finds singers who favor Islamic mysticism and who, under the African sky, have created a burgeoning bucolic poetry, adumbrating the springtime of a georgic, perhaps the first, in Islam.

6. Beautifully evoked in Kane's *L'Aventure ambiguë*.

7. One of the more glaring examples, because it purports to survey East African writing, is G. D. Killam, ed., *The Writing of East and Central Africa* (1984). Other than Gérard's lengthy study on African language literature, one could cite virtually any well-known critical text dealing with African literature and find the topic of Islam scanted.

References

ALKALI, ZAYNAB. 1987. *The Virtuous Woman*. Ikeja, Nigeria: Longman Nigeria.

ARMAH, AYI KWEI. 1968. *The Beautyful Ones Are Not Yet Born*. Boston: Houghton Mifflin.

———. 1970. *Fragments*. Boston: Houghton Mifflin.

———. 1972. *Why Are We So Blest?* New York: Doubleday.

———. 1973. *Two Thousand Seasons*. Nairobi: East African Publishing House.

BÂ, AMADOU HAMPÂTÉ. 1969. *Kaïdara*. Paris: Julliard (Collection classiques africains).

BÂ, MARIAMA. 1980. *Une Si Longue Lettre*. Dakar: Nouvelles éditions africaines.

BOYD-BUGGS, DEBRA. 1986. "Baraka: Maraboutism and Marabutage in the Francophone Senegalese Novel." Ph.D. thesis, Ohio State University.

Dissertation Abstracts 47:899A.

COULON, CHRISTIAN. 1981. *Le Marabout et le Prince: Islam et pouvoir au Senegal.* Paris: A. Pedone.

DIA, MAMADOU. 1980. *Islam et civilisations négroafricaines.* Dakar: Nouvelles éditions africaines.

DIOP, BIRAGO. 1947. *Les Contes d'Ahmadou Koumba.* Paris: Présence africaine.

FARAH, NURUDDIN. 1986. *Maps.* London: Pan Books.

GEERTZ, CLIFFORD. 1968. *Islam Observed.* Chicago: University of Chicago Press.

GÉRARD, ALBERT. 1981. *African Language Literatures.* Harlow, Essex: Longman.

KANE, CHEIKH HAMIDOU. 1961. *L'Aventure ambiguë.* Paris: Juilliard.

KANE, MOHAMADOU. 1982. *Roman africain et tradition.* Dakar: Nouvelles éditions africaines.

KILLAM, G. D. 1984. *The Writing of East and Central Africa.* London: Heinemann.

KOUROUMA, AHMADOU. 1968. *Les Soleils des indépendances.* Paris: Le Seuil.

LAYE, CAMARA. 1953. *L'Enfant noir.* Paris: Plon.

———. 1954. *Le Regard du roi.* Paris: Plon.

———. 1966. *Dramouss.* Paris: Plon.

LINGS, MARTIN. 1977. *What Is Sufism?* Berkeley: University of California Press.

MERNISSI, FATIMA. 1987. *Beyond the Veil.* Bloomington: Indiana University Press.

MOREAU, RENÉ LUC. 1982. *Africains musulmans.* Paris: Présence africaine.

OUOLOGUEM, YAMBO. 1968. *Le Devoir de violence.* Paris: Le Seuil.

SALIH, TAYEB. 1969. *Season of Migration to the North.* Trans. Denys Johnson-Davies. London: Heinemann.

———. 1968. *The Wedding of Zein, and Other Stories.* Trans. Denys Johnson-Davies. London: Heinemann.

SEMBÈNE, OUSMANE. 1981. *Le Dernier de l'empire: roman Sénégalais.* Paris: L'Harmattan.

SOCÉ OUSMANE. 1937. *Karim.* Paris: Nouvelles éditions latines.

SOYINKA, WOLE. 1965. *The Interpreters.* London: A. Deutsch.

———. 1964. *The Swamp Dwellers.* Oxford: Oxford University Press.

———. 1973. *A Season of Anomy.* London: Rex Collins Ltd.

TAHIR, IBRAHIM. 1984. *The Last Imam.* London: Routledge and Kegan Paul.

TRIMINGHAM, J. SPENCER. 1949. *Islam in the Sudan.* London: Oxford University Press.

———. 1959. *Islam in West Africa.* London: Oxford University Press.

———. 1962. *History of Islam in West Africa.* London: Oxford University Press.

———. 1964. *Islam in East Africa.* London: Oxford University Press.

———. 1971. *The Sufi Orders in Islam.* London: Oxford University Press.

Part II

EAST AFRICA

Chapter 2

▼▼▼▼▼▼▼▼

An Historical Context for the Study of Islam in Eastern Africa

JAY SPAULDING

An important theme within the Islamic cultural tradition is a sense of continuity, a perception that important values, correct ways of behavior, and the criteria for the evaluation of the human experience are constant throughout time; one important vehicle for the transmission of this sense of continuity down the centuries has been the written literature of the Islamic heartlands. The Islamic cultural tradition also embodies a wide variety of intellectual countercurrents and alternative visions of reality; these too have found their places within the body of Islamic literature.

An important theme in historical studies is change, a perception that human institutions and values are contingent and subject to transformation. The historical investigation of eastern Africa is not yet mature, and much remains conjectural or unknown.

A creative writer whose work touches the lives of Muslims in eastern Africa past or present may occasionally wish to expand his or her personal world of perception through reference to a relevant wider body of experience. For him or for her the Islamic literary tradition is a mighty instrument, which, when manipulated with artistry, can produce rich and deep resonances. The historical literature about eastern Africa is a conspicuously lesser instrument, which, no matter how skillful its player, is apt to emit occasional discords. Yet it possesses one merit that its noble rival does not — a specific commitment to the concrete experiences of the people of eastern Africa.

The appropriation of realities out of the mainstream of Islamic tradition into the cultures of eastern Africa is in itself one of the themes treated by historical scholarship, and through the eye of faith this may seem the most meaningful or even the only meaningful one. But for the historian there is always more — always a sequence of changing epochs, a wider context, a diversity of cultural preferences, other social forces at work, alternative possible outcomes to every historical process. The purpose of the present essay is to offer one possible reading of the wider historical context to which the story of Islam in eastern Africa belongs.

"To be colonized," said Walter Rodney, "is to be removed from history." The colonial masters undertook to render null the power and validity of the historically formed cultures of eastern Africa, and then to fill the void with an artful structure of other elements, some intrusively European, but others carefully selected on the basis of expediency from the older cultural archive itself. In the hands of foreign masters, all became foreign. Important aspects of the mission undertaken by many of the authors and critics considered in this volume are the reestablishment of meaningful dialogue between the living community and the preserved memory of its historical experience, and the recovery of both a sense of continuity and of cultural balance and proportion across the span of generations toward which the living community feels itself accountable. Given the magnitude of scope and radical quality of this imaginative and scholarly mission, however, it is not surprising that at some points the perspectives of both authors and critics reflect some measure of the recently dominant colonial aura of alienation and discontinuity, if only through portentous silences.

Eastern Africa at the Rise of Islam: During the millennium before the prophetic vocation of Muhammad large parts of eastern Africa were incorporated into the Hellenistic world, and the terms of this relationship were to have a significant bearing upon the fortunes of Islam there during its early centuries.

Alexander himself conquered Egypt, establishing a long legacy of rule over this community of Africans by an alien Greek elite. He also founded the city of Alexandria, home to the first community of middle-class private merchants the ancient kingdom had ever known, men who used Greek as a *lingua franca* to bridge their extremely cosmopolitan ethnic origins. With the passage of time the Hellenistic world fell under the political authority of Rome, which adopted Christianity as its state cult and bequeathed its laws and name to the later empire.

Throughout the Hellenistic age, Graeco-Roman rulers, mission-aries, and merchants cast curious and acquisitive eyes toward the wider African continent adjoining the imperial heartlands, and a wave of Mediterranean political, economic, and cultural influences gradually pervaded large parts of eastern Africa. Two contrasting patterns of relations developed, the choice of destinies being deter-mined by the size and degree of political centralization of each respective African community as it established contact with the Hellenistic world.

The larger states of northeastern Africa — initially Meroe and Axum, and subsequently also the Nubian kingdoms of Nobatia, Makuria, and Alodia — established formal and correct diplomatic re-lations with the empire, relations nourished by the periodic dispatch of embassies from either side, though occasionally ruffled by outbreaks of the ageless disputes to which international *Realpolitik* is prey. The Nubian kingdoms and Axum followed Rome in the adoption of Christianity as the religion of state. The conversions were formalized by missionary agents of the empire, and should probably be seen as part of the wider nexus of diplomatic relations. Within each realm the conversion of a king meant the formal conversion of his subjects also. However, the official collective Christianity of these communities did not necessarily imply immediate or radical changes in the older cultures, nor did it mean that the cultures of these kingdoms necessarily bore a close resemblance to the usages of any other Christian land. Hellenistic merchants were welcomed by the kings, but closely super-vised. Though individuals were occasionally summoned to court and honored as diplomats, both traders' settlements and the bulk of their exchange activities were confined to royally designated enclaves, often at the periphery of the kingdom. The traders' profits depended upon their ability to obtain raw materials of small bulk and high unit value, such as gold, ivory, and aromatics, in exchange for cheap and shoddy Mediterranean manufactured goods made specifically for export to remote places. The merchants had nothing to gain from excessive intimacy with their client hosts.

From an imperial perspective the small-scale societies of eastern Africa offered no kingly counterparts with whom to conduct conven-tional politics; at some sensitive points along the immediate periphery of the empire garrisons of military raiders were stationed to keep their African neighbors eternally on the defensive. There were few or no conversions to Christianity among African peoples outside the large kingdoms. Contacts with more remote African communities were established and maintained almost exclusively by seaborne

Hellenistic merchants, who regularly made many ports of call along the east coast as far south as a place called Rhapta, possibly in Tanzania. The basic economic logic governing their enterprises did not differ materially from that prevailing at the merchant enclaves within the kingdoms of Ethiopia and the Nile valley, but among small-scale societies the political conditions governing their presence and the conduct of exchange varied considerably from region to region. Trade was brisk at numerous seaside entrepots down the long "Aromatics Coast" of modern Somalia, for example, but the foreigners did not settle there. They did establish permanent homes, however, at Rhapta, along the African coast of the Red Sea, and in Cyrenaica.

The Hellenistic commercial settlements were to constitute the living models of society and economy upon which the later analogous communities of the Islamic age would be patterned. They took the form of towns, usually located at the coast, or even better, on islands immediately offshore. While their internal affairs are now usually dark, two meaningful details may be extracted from the surviving record. One is told that even remote Rhapta publicly acknowledged the overlordship of the contemporary ruler of South Arabia, in turn a tributary of Rome. Both in Rhapta and in the five little towns of pre-imperial Cyrenaica, the Hellenistic settlers intermarried with their African neighbors. In Cyrenaica, a bitter conflict ensued as later generations, men of partly African descent, struggled to win full rights of citizenship against a very resilient settler exclusiveness. Both the stubborn defense of a culturally circumscribed urban citizenry against a surrounding rural *WaShenzi* and the conspicuous appeal for legitimation to a prestigious but distant universal authority were to constitute important themes in the subsequent Islamic history of eastern Africa.

The Early Islamic Centuries, 600–1500: Egypt and the other African provinces of Rome fell to the initial wave of Arab conquest during the seventh and eighth centuries, and became important components within a new and wider Mediterranean Islamic *imperium*. Arabic replaced Greek as the *lingua franca* of the trading community, and the majority of merchants became Muslims. The ensuing relations between the Islamic heartlands and eastern Africa tended to follow the structure and obey the logic of Hellenistic precedent; one pattern governed relations with the northeast African kingdoms, while a second prevailed where societies were small in scale.

The Christian kingdoms of northeastern Africa enjoyed no prin-
cipled exemption from the tide of Arab conquest; early Muslim
commanders expeditiously annexed the South Arabian dependencies
of Axum and, having consolidated their hold upon Egypt, launched
a series of invasions up the Nile into Nubia. There, however, they
suffered both lesser and greater defeats at the hands of Makuria, and
it became clear that prospects for expansion were brighter elsewhere.
In retrospect, a prophetic tradition was adduced to the effect that the
Abyssinians should be left alone, while relations with northern Nubia
were normalized through an agreement called the *baqt*. Islamic legal
theorists were able to rationalize the *baqt* by construing it as a treaty
conferring tributary status upon Makuria, but in substance the pact
established and formalized a reciprocal, governmentally administered
commerce between the Nubian monarch and his Egyptian counterpart.
Since this pattern of royal exchange via accredited diplomatic agents
was normal practice among northeast African kings, but characteristic
neither of Hellenistic commerce nor of the usages peculiar to Islam,
it is probable that the terms of the *baqt* were proposed by the
victorious Makurians. The agreement was renegotiated and renewed
at intervals from the late seventh century into the thirteenth.

In addition to royal trade, Muslim private traders like their
Hellenistic predecessors were admitted to commercial enclaves at the
periphery of the several Christian kingdoms, and there the basic
patterns of exchange laid down for the African trade in Greek days
were preserved. Records originating in the experience of these enclaves, however, reveal a significant clash between the merchant
capitalist assumptions of the Muslims and the terms of trade dictated
by the African kings. For example, when Muslim traders ventured to
buy land within the designated entrepot at Makuria's northern border,
the Nubian monarch simply expropriated their purchased property
on the grounds that since both kingdom and subjects belonged
inalienably to him, the latter had neither right nor capacity to dispose
of the former. The aggrieved Muslims appealed their case to the
incumbent 'Abbasid caliph, but the Makurian lord could not be
swayed. Or again, the Islamic trading community at Ethiopia's
designated commercial entrepot at the dawn of the sixteenth century
was obliged to accept on permanent consignment 1,000 ounces of the
emperor's gold, and to repay him 1,000 ounces every year. The
emperor motivated the Muslims to police themselves and to exercise
both probity and acumen in their transactions through the expedient
of holding them collectively responsible for their obligations. In

sum, the Christian kingdoms of northeastern Africa maintained relations with the Islamic world that were correct and mutually advantageous, but decidedly limited.

During the early Islamic centuries the rise and decline of northeast African kingdoms continued to obey its own internal dynamic. In Ethiopia the kings of Axum gave way to rulers of the Zagwe line, and they in turn to the Solomonic dynasty, but relations with the Islamic world followed time-honored precedent. In the Nile valley, however, when the Christian Nubian kingdoms entered a period of decline from about 1200 to 1500, would-be renewers made the adoption of the currently prevailing Mediterranean religion as their own state rite a component of their political program. The lords of Makuria converted during the fourteenth century, and in about 1500 the founders of the Funj dynasty reunified most of the Nile valley Sudan as an Islamic kingdom later called Sinnar. A similar logic prevailed in areas where new kingdoms were coming into being at this period; Islam was to be the religion of the sultanates of Dar Fur in the western Sudan and Wadai in eastern Chad, and of the sultanate of 'Adal located south and east of Christian Ethiopia. Yet the cultures of these realms did not necessarily resemble those of any other Islamic country. Their most conspicuous feature was conformity to the long-standing canons of northeast African kingship, according to which formal allegiance to the cult of a Mediterranean metropole was not allowed to interfere with the orderly conduct of government and daily life of a conservative, primarily agrarian, inward-looking society. The kingdoms were open to outsiders, Muslims or otherwise, only under the same type of rigorous restrictions enforced by their non-Islamic predecessors.

The early Islamic centuries brought prosperity to the commercial settlements of the eastern coast. In the far south, pioneering seaborne Muslim merchants made contact with agents of the kings of Zimbabwe, another major African monarchy, and a new royally administered gold-trading entrepot developed near the mouth of the Zambezi. By 1500 the long chain of settlements extended from Sawakin on the Red Sea coast to Sofala at the head of the Mozambique Channel; Arabic speech prevailed at the northern settlements, Somali along the Somali coast, and Swahili farther south, but all the communities shared an allegiance to Islam, typically Sunni and Shafi'i, and they also observed in common many similar principles in the conduct of politics, economy, and cultural life. The communities may be viewed as middlemen in two senses: they mediated between the wider Indian Ocean maritime world and the inland African peoples who adjoined them on the mainland; and each major settlement vied with its rivals to halt on its beaches foreign shipping along the sea lanes both north and south, thus to monopolize all trade to ports more remote in either direction. In the latter regard Mogadishu in Somalia, Kilwa in Tanzania, and Mombasa in Kenya seem each in turn to have enjoyed an age of preeminence (by no means uncontested) south of Ras Hafun in the centuries before 1500.

The impressions of European visitors at the close of the early Islamic centuries are useful to modern western readers in placing the settlements in a broader comparative historical context. To Europeans who arrived at the dawn of the sixteenth century, the settlements constituted a first glimpse of the fabulous prosperity of the Indies; even a patriotic Portuguese seaman concluded that Sawakin could be compared only to Lisbon. Modern archaeological studies of settlements such as Kilwa and Shanga tend to justify the contemporary observers' enthusiasm, for they have exposed the remains of a rich material culture indicative of a vibrant tradition of creativity. Or again, to one familiar with the city-states of Renaissance Italy, it seemed obvious that a settlement such as Barawa was governed according to principles analogous to those of a contemporary Mediterranean commercial republic. From the perspective of a modern historian, the social structure and political style of the Islamic city-states of eastern Africa bear significant resemblances to their Mediterranean counterparts.

The human community of each east African city-state was comprised of lineage groups, each defined in terms of kinship through the male line and governed by senior men, each dedicated primarily to one economic activity and resident in one urban quarter. These lineages were not equal, for those engaged in agricultural pursuits or crafts enjoyed less wealth and prestige than the limited clique of wealthy merchant lineages who organized and deployed the bulk of the community's venture capital and who dominated city politics. However, all able men were expected to help defend their community militarily, and there prevailed a sense of common citizenship — a belief that no native son, however humble, should be excluded from participation in civic life.

Most communities supported a textile industry of modest scale that produced high-quality cloths suitable for international markets, but the most conspicuous economic activity was the exercise of dominance over the long-standing maritime transit trade. Foreign boats were constrained to halt by the need for water and provisions (these could be obtained from the subordinate lineages of the city) or by force, and they were then discouraged from continuing on to trade by elaborate and confiscatory customs codes. Having persuaded the foreigners to sell, the merchant elite organized the further conduct of trade goods by sponsoring the dispatch of ships. These were financed according to a system of shares in which any citizen with capital to risk might choose to invest. The search for safe passage for the ships of one's own city was a perennial theme in coastal politics, and the right to send a ship untaxed through another city's territory was a frequent bargaining chip in diplomatic interactions among the city-states.

In many city-states political authority was exercised by a council of lineage leaders. Given the social inequalities within each city and the uncertainties of economic and political fortune to which even the elites were subject, political life tended to be turbulent. It was not unknown for a troubled community to name one strong man as its prince, or to create a second or third influential if vaguely defined office for the representatives of rival powerful lineages, or for a subsequent round of new upheavals to restore republican institutions. Unseated and exiled leaders often sought allies abroad, which introduced a wider and threatening dimension into local disputes. There were no serene republics in east Africa.

Concerning the quality of religious life in the city-states of this age, the account of the fourteenth-century traveler Ibn Battuta attests to the general piety of the communities, and to the practice of conventional orthodox jurisprudence. The subtleties of local usage remain unknown; however, to the extent that anachronistic evidence from the age to follow may be accepted, it would seem that the Islamic communities of the coast probably responded defensively to a surrounding African continent that they perceived to be militarily threatening and spiritually polluting. Their role as commercial middlemen between the maritime world and the interior was largely passive; it was the interior peoples who initiated contacts at the coast and extended them from one small-scale community to another up a long chain of link commerce into the interior. Some non-material aspects of coastal culture may also have ascended these routes, but Islam, as far as is known, was not among them.

The Later Islamic Centuries, 1500–1900: The long sixteenth century witnessed an early scramble for Africa by alien maritime powers. The Ottoman Turks occupied Egypt and much of the Mediterranean littoral, and contended at length with seaborne Portuguese empire-builders for control of the east African coast. The major protagonists tended to interpret this clash in terms of a primal rivalry between Islam and Christianity, and the African communities who constituted the object of the newcomers' acquisitive attentions often found themselves impelled to agree. As the maritime powers gradually reached a military stalemate that had the effect of partitioning the coast near the modern Kenya-Somalia border, the course of events in the northern and southern spheres of influence obeyed a measure of logical symmetry.

Both powers annexed coastal settlements and established garrisoned bases; the Turks at Sawakin and Massawa, the Portuguese at Mozambique and Mombasa. At best, foreign control of the sea and hegemony over the coast had a deleterious effect upon the commercial life and prosperity of the old city-states — after 1550 no one would ever compare Sawakin to Lisbon again, and it may plausibly be assumed that Ethiopian coastal interests suffered — but the cities of the Ottoman sphere were not asked to endure the degree of punitive military devastation and confiscatory taxation experienced by townsmen of the Portuguese zone. Both foreign powers organized major invasions of the African interior, in each case a major objective being direct access to sources of gold, the export of which had hitherto been monopolized and regulated by commercially conservative African kings. The respective roles played by the coastal peoples of the north and south in these invasions differed sharply, however, and in this religion was probably a significant determining factor.

As initial Ottoman incursions into northern Ethiopia gained momentum, they found increasing local support among Muslim peoples of the lowlands and coast, not least from among the folk of a sultanate of 'Adal subjected to severe blows in recent times by the Ethiopians. While Ottoman imperial ambitions and material support remained a significant motivating factor, the invasions acquired African leadership in the person of Ahmad b. Ibrahim and took on the character of a holy war. A modest but conspicuous Portuguese military intervention in support of the Ethiopians was primarily expected to yield a harvest of souls for Roman missionaries rather than profits for Lusitanian merchants — for such were the issues to exercise these parties in the postwar period. The war was costly to all; the jihad failed. Yet in the end the preeminence of Muslim merchants in mediating the foreign trade of Ethiopia remained unchallenged. The city-state of Harrar at the eastern brink of the highlands emerged to new prominence, and networks of Muslim traders quietly permeated the fragments of the old kingdom as it sank into an age of internal discord. A new unregulated private traffic in firearms and slaves, both cause and effect of the troubled times, came to rival or exceed older sources of commercial profit.

Portuguese advances against Zimbabwe paralleled Turkish involvement in Ethiopia. In the end, despite victories on the battlefield, the effort failed, but the incursions left the inland kingdom in vulnerable disarray. The Portuguese were in no position to harness the aspirations of the Muslims of the coast; the latter preferred to side with the Zimbabwean resistance, and encouraged the conversion to Islam of some of its most prominent leaders. (The Christians also found allies and converts as years of crisis fragmented the Zimbabwean elite.) Private merchants both Christian and Islamic stood to profit as the hand of the old monarchy loosened its grasp upon foreign trade, and an unregulated private traffic in slaves came to rival or surpass the importance of gold.

A major historical development of the seventeenth and eighteenth centuries in eastern Africa was the rise to prominence of a new Islamic leadership. It was usually said of these holy men that they or their forefathers had immigrated from the Islamic heartlands and were biological descendants of Muhammad or other prominent individuals of Islamic antiquity. However, since one of the most obvious things about them was their highly successful adaptation to the social environment of eastern Africa, the significance of real or alleged foreign qualities should not be exaggerated. The holy men brought to eastern Africa a missionary vocation hitherto uncommon in the region, and they held a world view less parochial and more confident than that characteristic of the older societies. Typically, the holy men were educated not only in the conventional Islamic sciences but also in the traditions of Islamic mysticism. A Sufi training inculcated subtle and powerful leadership skills and provided an array of arcane paradigms of knowledge by which all but the most complex or recalcitrant of social situations could be manipulated and reordered.

The holy men introduced new forms of social organization, usually referred to as Islamic brotherhoods. While these new communities differed considerably one from another in detail, they had in common the fact that they exemplified a viable alternative to the established institutional arrangements of older communities, whether kingdoms, city-states, or small-scale societies. The brotherhoods were usually open to newcomers if not actively engaged in recruitment, and they tended to redefine the criteria for the achievement of status in ways that made them attractive to individuals who would not easily have advanced elsewhere. Would-be private merchants from among the peasant subjects of the kingdom of Sinnar, freedmen and foreigners squatting at the outskirts of the city-state of Lamu, networks of Muslim traders twined through the interstices of Ethiopia's agrarian fiefdoms, hapless and herdless refugee cultivators among the Somali, Oromo victims of renewed Ethiopian expansion — such were typical constituencies who responded to the call of holy men. The role of the brotherhoods in gathering and reintegrating socially lost souls could only assume ever-greater significance in an age of burgeoning slave trade and accelerating violence.

The governance of a holy man was characteristically benign but authoritarian, and while the community might well afford avenues for advancement to the humble, nothing was allowed to challenge the preeminence of the leader and his family. The holy man demanded regular and generous payments from his followers, a substantial portion of which he would return to them as charity or largesse. Here as elsewhere, the adoption of a system of significant material redistribution by a charismatic and ambitious leader had the effect of stimulating an intensification in the economic efforts of his followers. The latter pursued diverse vocations as circumstances permitted, but many became private merchants, conspicuously in slaves. The rising economic power of the holy men often rendered them tangible as well as cultural rivals to the leaders of the older societies on every hand. In the main, however, the relatively modest processes of change initiated during the seventeenth and eighteenth centuries were overtaken and absorbed by the mightier currents of the nineteenth.

Far-sighted imperialists among the Portuguese, even during the heyday of the Atlantic slave trade, perceived that given an adequate coercive apparatus, they could have exploited African labor more efficiently in Africa; by the dawn of the nineteenth century the modernizing Islamic monarchies of Egypt and Oman were poised to act upon this principle. Both states gathered foreign capital, technical advice, and weaponry, and dispatched soldiers bearing their respective flags out of Cairo and Zanzibar. By century's end these expeditions had swept over much of the eastern half of the continent north of the Zambezi, clashing briefly in Uganda and on the southern Somali coast. Specific events of the period lie beyond the scope of this essay, but the quality of dominance admits of simple summary. Force was used to break each society in turn, while the incentive of the slave trade served to hurl each stricken community in sequence against its neighbors in the service of the foreign masters of the market. As the geographical grasp of the new elites widened, they asserted new patterns of dominance over the societies they had broken, patterns often couched in the idiom of slavery. In some favored situations plantations were introduced to produce cash crops for export — the cloves of Zanzibar and the indigo, sugar, and cotton of the northern Sudan provide examples. In all cases, slave labor was expected to support both the foreign conquerors and their numerous native servitors high and low. The empire-builders of the day were Muslims, and Islam provided them with an ideological rationale for capitalist conquest. Islam also provided an integrative framework for the incorporation into the new Arabic or Swahili-speaking society of individuals whose previous lives had been irrevocably interrupted by the troubled times, and who found themselves at the mercy of the vicissitudes of the new order — plantation slaves and concubines, soldiers and servants, traders and townsmen, chiefs and bandits, butchers and gunsmiths, boatmen and hired laborers, and many others. A substantial portion of the modern contours of society in eastern Africa took shape during the nineteenth century, and unless a deliberate effort is made to see beyond the realities of this age into more remote epochs, this period is likely to loom large in the historical memory of living men and women.

Some communities of eastern Africa avoided conquest during the nineteenth century through determined resistance, and occasionally, resolute xenophobia; none, however, emerged unscathed. Prominent among the resisters was Ethiopia, which emerged from its time of troubles after mid-century, acquired foreign patronage, and pursued its own manifest destiny toward the east, west, and south across rugged terrain toward the modern national boundaries. An influx of European traders, including many individuals of modest means, directly challenged the livelihoods of hitherto-dominant Muslim merchants in many parts of the new Ethiopian empire. A final set of eminent opponents to the nineteenth-century empire-builders were a new generation of Islamic holy men, heirs to the cultural traditions of their predecessors. After mid-century Muhammad al-Sanusi and his followers formed a brotherhood that brought a substantial measure of political unity to the peoples of eastern and southern Libya and the east-central Sahara. The Sanusi movement helped deter Egyptian ambitions along their western flank, and the brotherhood fought a long and bitter resistance against the subsequent imperial ambitions of the French and Italians. Within Egyptian territory, Muhammad Ahmad the Sudanese Mahdi launched a movement that broke foreign domination and liberated the greater part of the Sudan; his successor, the Khalifa 'Abdallahi, organized a new national administration that sought a synthesis between the useful technological innovations of the Egyptians and the inherited traditions of Sudanese royal statecraft. In Somalia, Muhammad 'Abd Allah Hasan built a powerful movement to resist Ethiopian encroachment upon Somali lands, and simultaneously fought off the acquisitive ambitions of the British and Italians. These movements earned a significant and respected position in the national histories of Somalia, the Sudan, Libya, and Chad; each had its failures and opponents, however, and the legacy to modern times has not been free from controversy.

The Twentieth Century: Living memory embraces the twentieth century, which thus lies open to perception unmediated by the testimony of aged texts. Insofar as Islam is concerned, two broad themes merit special consideration, for they articulate a wide range of current tensions within the societies of eastern Africa, and evoke relevant questions about the future.

The age of Western colonial and neocolonial hegemony harnessed much of the machinery of dominance imposed in the nineteenth century, while vastly refining and extending its mechanisms of exploitation and control. Foreigners delineated the political boundaries that set the series of colonial (and subsequently, national) contexts within which the modern experience of Islam has worked itself out. Their policies encouraged the growth of towns, a social setting within which many immigrants, in committing themselves to modest urban occupations, also chose to define themselves as Muslims for the first time. The non-Muslims who exercised power regarded Islam with a patronizing snobbery, but usually conceded to the Muslims a status somewhat superior to that of other subject peoples — the classification of Somalis as statutory Asians under the race laws of colonial Nairobi may serve as an illustrative example of this sentiment.

During the era surrounding World War I, Muslims in eastern Africa were often perceived as potentially subversive supporters of a wider pan-Islamic mission; the European colonial powers of the region devoted considerable effort and expertise to the containment and control of such tendencies, and took pride in their success, but the government of Ethiopia was unable to avoid a dramatic confrontation with its would-be-Muslim emperor, Lij Iyasu. Where the Islamic community was perceived to have geopolitical limits, the responsible British and Ethiopian authorities often undertook to contain it by admitting Christian missionaries around the periphery — a policy conspicuous in the Sudan, for example. Higher education, which in the end bestowed access to the threshold of power, was inherently secular in content and rarely if ever conveyed in a culturally Islamic ambience; thus the colonial regime and its successors elevated new elites, not necessarily Islamic, at the expense of the old.

A second prominent theme of the twentieth century, particularly since the growth of oil wealth in the Middle East following the Second World War, has been a renewed sense of unity and confidence on the part of the wider community of Muslims, a vision that embraces wide portions of eastern Africa. Some important channels of renewal have included increased levels of participation in the pilgrimage, recourse to Islamically oriented institutions of higher education in Egypt and the Middle East, and missionary outreach programs communicated via radio, publications, and Islamic charitable and educational institutions in eastern Africa. The role of labor migration to the oil states, and of oil state investments in eastern Africa, has also been significant.

The new Islamic vision challenges the existing social order in many quarters, sometimes by calling into question the legitimacy of existing political boundaries or regimes, but more generally through its attack upon both the specific failures and general underlying principles of secular society. The quality of this critique, however, is limited by the terms in which it is conceptualized. The intellectual content of the new age of piety has been narrowly legalistic, and has usually interpreted the eternal verities of religion in terms of middle-class urban respectability to the exclusion of other conceivable readings of the content of the faith. The execution for apostasy of the Sudanese religious leader Mahmud Muhammad Taha (18 January 1985) exemplifies the rigor with which the new bourgeois innovators have been willing to renounce the accumulated wisdom of their own cultural heritage, while the circumstances surrounding the execution — national starvation by the many amidst rampant grain-profiteering by the local agents of Arabian Islamic banks — expose the innovators' vision of the preferred society of the future.

Chapter 3

▼▼▼▼▼▼▼▼

Islam and Secularity in Swahili Literature: An Overview

IBRAHIM NOOR SHARIFF

Introduction

The Swahili language has a rich literature in both the oral and written modes, and while most of the traditional literature has historically taken the oral form, there is in both the oral and written traditions, in prose as well as poetry, a great variety of both secular and religious themes and texts. This article seeks to put forward a panoramic view of the Islamic themes in Swahili literature, and of the literary forms in which these are presented. It is also imperative to survey, however briefly, the secular literature and its place in society. We will then touch upon the place poetry generally occupies in Swahili culture. We shall also discuss the religious tradition in Swahili poetry and the place of that tradition in society at large. But, first, it is essential that we mention the earliest known evidence of the verbal arts so that we give a sense of the longevity of the tradition.

The Earliest Known Swahili Poet

The earliest of the known Swahili poets is the legendary poet-warrior-hero Fumo Liyongo wa Baury (or al-Baury) who grew up in the city-state of Shanga in Pate Island during the reign of Daudi Mringwari. Reliable Swahili historians tell us that Shanga city-state was attacked in 1292 A.D. by the city-state of Pate, "plundering it and killing the males. The youths and the old women and maidens they made prisoners" (Freeman-Grenville 1966, 242). Recent archaeological excavation of Shanga using modern scientific dating methods places the bottom layer of the city in the eighth century and "a complete set of 14th century ruins on the surface" (Horton 1987, 87–88). I argue elsewhere (1988) that given all the evidence available to date, Fumo Liyongo must have lived during the heyday of Shanga's glory, perhaps in the tenth century or even before that time. Indeed, a letter, published in 1943, from the Arabs and Swahilis of Kau and Kipini addressed to the district commissioner of Kipini places the hero in the eighth century (Darroch 1943, 252).

Fumo Liyongo composed many poems, fragments of which are now recited in collective rituals such as the harvest celebrations known as *wawe*. But two poems stand out, partly because of their integrity and partly because of their contents. The first is his poetic message through his servant Sada to his mother when he was in prison condemned to death. The other is his famous epic describing the beauty of a woman, possibly his wife, from hair to toe, leaving no part of her body unpainted by his verbal genius. Both these poems[1] are in perfect meter and rhyme, popular even today.

Secular Swahili Prose

Compared to the volume of poetry that has come to us in the written form from the previous centuries, very little Swahili prose was ever written down in manuscript form using Arabic letters. Until a few decades ago, prose in Swahili remained essentially in the oral tradition. Some of it is clearly derived from Arabic texts, which not a few Swahili read in the original language. The Swahili literati extracted the parts that took their fancy and made modifications in their translations and renderings to suit local needs. Those texts have now become part of the corpus of Swahili oral literature. However, a very significant part of the literature originated from local Swahili sources and, no doubt, some also from neighboring non-Swahili societies such as the Somali, Boni, Pokomo, Digo, and Zaramo. Until recently, the oral prose tradition in Swahili society served as one of the primary means of teaching societal values and ethics and were an indispensable part of growing up.

Traditional riddles, animal fables, and allegorized historical tales are the first form of folkloric wisdom that children customarily encounter. The characters in the children's stories usually take the form of animals. In addition, each Swahili littoral has its own local human characters, based on true personalities of the area's past. There is also a body of oral prose that deals with past Swahili heroes. Some are heroes for individual city-states while others are revered by all Swahili. Literature about such historical personages, until recently, was abundant. These historical personages often serve as central characters in exemplary tales and moral fables, whose function is to elucidate certain virtues or vices. History is thus used as a form of allegory.

As mentioned earlier, there is also a very large body of prose that originates from the other Indian Ocean basin countries, especially the Arabian Peninsula and Persia (Iran) which has been incorporated into the main body of Swahili literature. Many of these stories play the same role as do the animal fables. As the hare represents wisdom and cunning in the fables surrounding him, Abunuwas (Ar. Abu-Nawas) represents these same qualities in the stories that have grown around his name. In Swahili folklore, Antar ibn Shaddad of Arabia and Rastam of Persia represent bravery; Harun al-Rashid represents power and wealth, the Banu 'Udheira are emblematic of a family of great lover-poets; and there are also characters who serve as the Swahili counterparts of Romeo and Juliet. Similarly, there are countless characters and episodes originating from Arabic sources that deal with various aspects of Islam.

Early training in the riddling tradition plays a major role later in life in both the composition of poetry on the part of the poets and the understanding of the verses on the part of the audience. No matter how taboo the public discussion of a subject may be for reasons of ethics and custom, or for fear of political reprisal, the poets and prose masters somehow find ways of expressing their concerns through the use of metaphors, similes, and riddles, and to represent and refer to living personalities by using animal characters. Until a few decades ago, a man of letters among the Swahili was recognized by his Islamic knowledge and his awareness and use of all the categories we have mentioned above.

Since the Swahili are Muslims, Islamic themes feature very significantly in both their prose and poetry. Swahili Islamic prose is also used in the education of the young and the old. One pronounced feature of this literature, whose primary means of delivery to the audiences still remains oral, are the stories of the prophets of Islam — including Muhammad, Isa (Christ), Musa (Moses), Suleiman (Solomon), Daud (David), Adam, Ibrahim (Abraham), Ismail (Ishmael), Is'haq (Isaac), Yusuf (Joseph), and Nuh (Noah). In the course of educating the children, these traditional narratives are constantly amplified in relation to everyday experiences.

The Western Impact

The earlier system of learning began to change after the imposition of Western education, which included its own curriculum and literature. Before the introduction of Western schooling the Islamic *madrasa*, whose curriculum was made up largely of theological studies and Arabic language learning, was the only means of formal education, while trade was learned by living and doing and by apprenticeship in vocations such as farming, fishing, carpentry, and masonry. Mastery of the language and literature was also obtained by observing and listening to elders' eloquence as they expressed themselves. Western schooling began to take over most rapidly from the end of the first quarter of this century. In the area of language and literary study, it would be accurate to say that the European colonial administrators and educators *invented* a new language and a literature, for what came to be taught in the colonial classroom was neither the traditional literature of the Swahili people nor a literature *written* by the Swahili themselves outside the narrow social perimeters of the missionary educator. This is shown by the fact that "[b]etween the years 1900– 1950, there were approximately 359 works of prose published in Swahili; 346 of these were written by Europeans and published mainly in England and Germany" (Rollins 1985, 51).

It is ironic that the first published Swahili translation of the Qur'an was done by the Society for Promoting Christian Knowledge. In spite of the many centuries of Swahili adherence to Islam, Muslim theologians saw no need to publish a Swahili translation of their Holy Book. Although oral translations of the Qur'an continue to be made by the Swahili sheikhs, and hand-written translations of many chapters do exist and have been used in the teaching of the Scriptures, for the most part the sheikhs preferred the texts to be studied in the original language.[2] As a result, both Swahili and Arabic became the languages of learning in the Islamic institutions in East Africa. The need to publish a Swahili translation of the Qur'an became more pressing to the Christian clergy in their desire to debate with the sheikhs in order to show the weaknesses of Islam and to undermine Muslim initiatives, than to the Muslim sheikhs themselves in their attempt to spread Islamic doctrine. Such reasons are very candidly and often condescendingly spelled out by Reverend Godfrey Dale, the translator, in his Swahili preface of the translation first published in 1923 and also in his essay on the translation published in *The Moslem World* in 1924 (5–9). It was not until the 1960s that we began to see a noticeable participation of the Swahili themselves in published prose. Since the tradition of prose writing in Swahili is a rather new phenomenon, when compared to poetry manuscripts, we shall let future crities pass judgment on the impact of such works.

The Place of Poetry in Swahili Society

At every stage of history, the Swahili have produced a far greater volume of secular poetry than of homiletic verse. Even a quick survey of the poetry aired from the broadcasting stations in East Africa, or a glance at the Swahili newspapers — and most papers print whole pages of poetry where the speakers of the language unravel their most profound thoughts — will at once reveal this fact. Similarly, a substantial number of books written in Swahili on its poetry happen to be on secular verse. Among these are: *Diwani ya Muyaka bin Haji al-Ghassaniy* (Hichens 1940), *Masomo Yenye Adili* (Robert 1959), *Sheria za Kutunga Mashairi na Diwani ya Amri* (Abedi 1954), *Malenga wa Mvita* (Bhalo 1971), *Sauti ya Dhiki* (Abdala 1975), *Malenga wa Mrima* (Mwinyihatibu 1977). On the other hand, most of the volumes on the subject of Swahili poetry written in English have concentrated on religious verse. Noteworthy among these are: *Swahili Poetry* (Harries 1962), *Traditional Swahili Poetry* (Knappert 1967), the three volumes entitled *Swahili Islamic Poetry* (Knappert 1971), and *Tendi* (Allen 1971).

If it is indeed true that most Swahili poetry has focused on secular themes, how can we account for the fact that books written in English tend to concentrate on religious themes? This can be explained easily if we examine on the one hand, the motives — on the part of the poet, the scribe, and the society in general — that underlie the process of collection and preservation of poems, and on the other hand, the interests of and limitations confronting the European researcher.

As a society that is overwhelmingly Muslim in its social composition, many of whose members are devout, Swahili society has traditionally attached great importance to the *preservation* of religious verse for posterity. More often than not, such verses are carefully written down, either by the poet himself or by a scribe, and they quickly become a part of the collective heritage of *written* poetry. Literacy among the Swahili has been a phenomenon of the mosque and the Quranic *madrasa*. Until the more recent days of German and British colonization of East Africa, when Western formal schooling became the order of the day (and the script changed from Arabic to Roman), the most literate among the Swahili were themselves students, former students or Islamic scholars who acquired their writing craft from the religious institutions. Hence, most of the scribes attached greater importance to the preservation of homiletic verse than of secular poetry. In addition, the preservation and propagation of Islamic doctrine are acts which are believed to give the mortals *thawab* — or heavenly credit — that is expected to help them to enter Paradise, and the wider the circulation of the doctrine, the more the *thawab*.

In comparison, the poetry on secular subjects, that reflects and reveals both private and communal experiences, has found fewer scribes than the homiletic genre. A significant number of the verses in this category has been composed and delivered orally in real-life situations and in everyday business; consequently, much of the poetry in this genre has passed into oblivion along with the events that had given rise to the poetry, since neither the protagonists nor the audience could later recollect the verses. And when they could recollect them, they cared little to preserve them in writing for posterity once the moment of its secular need had passed, as there was no incentive like *thawab* to do so. Likewise, in those cases when they did write down the poems, they usually did not record the context within which the poem arose.

The concentration on religious poetic manuscripts has led many scholars to make categoric and narrow conclusions on both the longevity of the Swahili poetic tradition and its diversity. For example, Jan Knappert writes:

> Swahili literature is entirely Islamic from its inception in 1728 until the advent of German administration in 1884. And even after that, up till the present day. ... (1971, 5)

Some scholars such as Lyndon Harries acknowledge the existence of secular poetry manuscripts. Harries writes that "[t]here are hundreds of short Swahili poems in the Library of the School of Oriental and African Studies in London which still defy interpretation partly because no one is able to provide the context in which the poem was written" (1962, 2). But Harries too had to justify his conclusions, which were based on the manuscripts he could understand. He writes:

> It is true that versification in Swahili is practiced today in roman script by many who cannot claim Swahili blood but usually they are Muslims ....
> It is not religious verse that they write for the popular press,

but the medium employed indicates familiarity with Swahili way of life, which is fundamentally Islamic.

This wider modern practice of Swahili versification has led to a departure from its earlier intention — to express the spirit and practice of Islam. Today the medium is employed for more secular ends. Any news item may be the subject of a few verses, but this is the tradition established during the nineteenth century by writers like Muyaka bin Haji of Mombasa, who brought poetry out of the mosque and into the market-place (1962, 2).

As we have noted earlier, the composition of Swahili secular verse has its roots many centuries prior to Muyaka's era. The art was so advanced by Muyaka's times and used by so many poets such as Bwana Zahidi Mgumi of Lamu, and Bakari Mwengo and Ali wa Athumani of Pate that it could not have been invented by Muyaka or his contemporaries. Similarly, the genius of Swahili literature (like that of other heterogeneous Islamic societies that have enjoyed economic prosperity over the ages, resulting in the attraction of continuous waves of emigrants from many different societies) cannot be analyzed in terms of "blood" lineage. Contrary to one rampant Germanic myth that has pervaded the intellectual discourse since the last quarter of the nineteenth century, the definition of Swahili ethnicity has little to do with blood descendancy and everything to do with language and culture, including the latter's religious practices and peculiarities.

The Swahilis' intimate involvement with their poetry prompted Ali Mazrui to pay homage to the Swahili verbal arts:

> There are occasions when the mixture of cultures can be particularly striking. For example, a daily newspaper is not an indigenous tradition in east Africa but was borrowed from the West. On the other hand, when one is sitting at the breakfast table in the Western world, one does not normally expect to be reading poetry in the morning newspaper. But in the world of Swahili culture, one does. There is a section in Tanzania's newspapers not only for letters to the editor but for poems to the editor. These poems are on a wide range of subjects: on inflation, or traditional medicine, or some recent government policy.
>
> There is a school of thought in English poetry, represented by such people as Wordsworth and Coleridge, to the effect that poetry should approximate to the ordinary language of conversation. But in Swahili culture there is a school of thought which would argue that ordinary conversation should try to approximate the elegant language of poetry. Those poems to the editor in Tanzanian newspapers, poems of dialogue, are part of this tradition (Mazrui 1986, 244–45).

In short, then, over the centuries the Swahili have created at least as many secular poems as religious ones, though, as we have stated above, the manuscripts in various libraries and in private collections do not represent the true balance between the two aspects of Swahili literature. We argue, moreover, that the literature on Swahili poetry in English, which depends heavily on religious manuscripts, does not represent a balanced picture of the verbal arts.

Utenzi Epics and Other Poetic Compositions

There are four major areas within which Swahili poetry plays a role: (1) admonition, (2) prayers, (3) epics, usually with Islamic messages and often based on the lives of Prophets of Islam and also verses dealing with Islamic law, and (4) matters that have much to do with everyday living.

In Swahili poetry, there are certain prosodic forms which are used strictly for religious compositions, while others include both the religious and secular themes. Except for a few forms such as the *utumbuizo*, which have rhymes but no syllable count, the other categories all have specific numbers of syllables to a line as well as rhyme patterns.[3] We shall briefly specify the characteristics of each of the major forms.

One of the ancient prosodic patterns is the *utenzi* or *utendi* (pl. *tenzi* or *tendi*). An *utenzi* verse is made up of two lines with a middle caesura often splitting the lines into equal halves. Therefore, the most common *utendi* verse has sixteen syllables to a line and an aaab rhyming pattern. One of the first known *tendi* composed by Fumo Liyongo, possibly sometime in the tenth century, had twelve syllables to a line and rhymed thus:

Pigiyani basi   pembe ya jamusi[4]
Kwa cha mtutusi   au mwana-ninga

Would you beat for me   the horn of a buffalo
With drumsticks made of *mtutusi*   or *mwana-ninga*

The *utenzi* verse has the fewest number of lines of any of the verse categories. Thanks to this feature, coupled with the fact that Swahili language has an abundant supply of rhyming words, the Swahili poets came to the realization, many centuries ago, that they could easily compose an unlimited number of verses using the *utenzi* form. Indeed, linked verses in some of the *tenzi* run in the thousands. Thus, *Utenzi wa Vita vya Uhuru*, an account on the Second World

War by Shaaban Robert (1967), the famous Swahili novelist and poet, is comprised of three thousand verses. No one knows how many *tenzi* have been composed by the Swahili over the centuries. The tradition is also alive and new *tenzi* are composed here and now as Swahili poets feel the need to compose.

The *utenzi* is essentially a narrative form, and although used most widely for the composition of epics, it is also a major medium for telling stories, recording historic events, admonishing the Swahili on matters of their faith, and so on. There is very little use of either ornate language, extended metaphors, or the riddle tradition. Normally, the language is simple and straightforward. When the verses are difficult to understand, it is usually because the dialect is different from that of the listener or reader, or because of an archaic vocabulary. Where men of letters in many other cultures express themselves in prose, the Swahili often compose using the *utenzi* meter. In addition to the technical meaning of the term *utenzi* described above, as a specific measure of versification, the term also means "long narrative." Hence one could say that the *utenzi*, according to the Swahilis' own definition, is a metered and rhymed narrative.

Any subject requiring long narration can be articulated in the *utenzi* form. The preponderance of *tenzi* composed at any given time and the diversity of their subject matter is breathtaking, from the celebration of heroic leaders to the building of ships, from the stories of the Prophets to ribald sexuality. The *utenzi*, bordering as it does on both verse and prose, plays a significant role in the education and entertainment of adults. There are *tenzi* compositions on the lives of all the major prophets of Islam composed by different poets over the years. One anonymous manuscript I read some years ago of an exquisitely composed *tenzi* on Joseph, for example, is comprised of 723 verses. Given a good reciter, many of these *tenzi* would hold any Swahili audience spell-bound throughout its recitation. I personally recall seeing several members of the audience sobbing when one talented reciter enchanted the verses of the famous *utenzi* on The Day of Judgment. Some were in tears, especially when the poet was revealing how the evil ones were being punished for their misdeeds.

The *utenzi* of Mwana Kupona binti Msham al-Batawy (ca. 1810–1860) is perhaps the most famous among all the *tenzi* composed over the centuries and a standard by which other epics are often judged. (See Biersteker's analysis in this volume for a discussion of levels of meanings in the poem.) The religious opinions Mwana Kupona expresses regarding the "divine" power a husband supposedly holds over his wife's fate in the hereafter is not a widely accepted dogma in much of Swahili culture; the poem nonetheless remains one of the finest *utenzi* ever composed in Swahili. The reasons why the work stands out is that it is at once religious and social; its accomplishment can also be attributed as much to tone and humor as to the flow of language and the form intrinsic to the work. The poem is a masterpiece of allusions that play up the male ego in a society where men see themselves as masters over their womenfolk, while at the same time instructing the intelligent woman to treat the opposite sex as she would an infant. In addition, the poem is in two major parts. The second part, almost half the poem of about one hundred verses,[5] is a prayer, composed in exquisite language, which could be used by any Swahili Muslim in seeking salvation. Mwana Kupona's *tenzi* and many others have played a major role in admonishing the faithful to avoid bad conduct and to seek good behavior as seen through the traditional Swahili-Islamic perspective.

Another popular verse form in which religious matters are discussed is the *shairi*, with double the number of lines of the *utenzi* and sixteen syllables to a line, with a middle caesura and rhymes in the first three lines, The *shairi* is also the most formal composition. It is in this verse form that the most serious subjects are discussed, from warnings of inevitable arms conflict to humorous verses, and from inculcation of good conduct to venomous poetic curses.

Religious scholar-poets have often used the *shairi* in discussing religious matters. Poets such as Muyaka b. Haji al-Ghassany (ca. 1776–1856) have also used the medium for both secular and religious didactic purposes. When, for example, Muyaka found out that an acquaintance had slept with a woman whose husband had just died, he unleashed his anger in *shairi* verse:

V.4 On the day of flaming Hell-fire
　　　The Muslim scurries from torment,
　　　　Yet you have approached her with her turban of mourning?
　　　She would have wanted to shout for help
　　　But you held her hips!
　　　That day of raising and lowering sail,
　　　　　Sir, have you forgotten it?

V.5 She was aching so to cry,
　　　Remembering her husband.
　　　The devil has entered you both
　　　The animal eats its own kind.

> You just kept telling her: "Strip off the turban!"
> That day of trumpets and screams,[6]
> Sir, have you forgotten it?

There have been many poems by religious scholars that discuss points of theological law and that derive their significance essentially as logical constructions and legal documents. The enthusiasm over some of these poems is thus not simply derived from their aesthetic value but also from the intellectual content of the debates themselves. A very fine example of this is the exchange of six poems between Sheikh Ali bin Saad (dubbed: Taji 'l Arifina, i.e., the crown among the informed) of Lamu and Bakari Mwengo of Pate, which took place sometime in the nineteenth century. The two debated the finer points of Islamic law pertaining to the dissolution of marriage initiated by the husband who had, perhaps inadvertently, uttered the Islamic divorce formula three times at a go. The couple, we are told, had a number of children and one more was on the way.

Such divorces are contentious among Muslim jurists; some consider them *divorce a vinculo*, while others argue that the three consecutive utterances should count no more than a single mention of the divorce formula. One point has to be borne in mind if the complexity of the issue is to be fully appreciated by the non-Muslim reader. That is, if the divorce formula is uttered *once* by the husband, he can — on realizing the error committed — offer his sincere apologies within the allowed period of separation, and the marriage will be re-instituted. There can be a second recurrence of a similar disruption (divorce), and if the renewal of marriage vows is mutually desirable, the two can re-unite in marriage. However, the third divorce will sever the bonds of matrimony for good. The only way that the two can live again as husband and wife is if the woman marries another man and if this other marriage breaks up, a condition that is rarely satisfied.

Keeping the above in mind, let us first examine the arguments used in the following *shairi* by Sheikh Ali bin Saad, who speaks on behalf of the woman:[7]

Paper from Hijaz, go and give my greetings
To my dearest friend; my friend from long ago.
He should open his ears, tell him politely;
What he must hear, is what has transpired.

I was married to a husband, arranged during our childhood,
With the consent of our mothers and our fathers and our people too.
I have been a fortress, not entered by another man.
But when a few days had passed, I saw him leave in distress.

I do not tire and do not rest my massage and my caress.
To my husband I do not speak any negative wrong word.
And I don't do anything of annoyance at all.
I have been obedient; he has married me obeying.

And now he has escaped; he does not come, he won't pass by
And he's taken back the dowry, even his engagement gifts.
What do you say about this that makes my heart cry out?
It's not one thing to keep inside; its not two things to tolerate.

What do you say, Abu-Bakr, my dear friend.
Give me some advice here and now, what shall I do?
One who bends his knee in homage doesn't find his legs in chains.
This was said so long ago and I've felt so bad about this.

Upon receiving this poem from Sheikh Ali bin Saad of Lamu,
Bakari Mwengo of Pate replied as follows:

Paper from Mecca, return to Lamu;
Give compliments to my friend, my friend from long ago.
I've understood the charges of the Lamuan.
The son of Adam can't erase what has been written for him.

You are the woman who wanted, it's you whom love has clutched.
Someone as clever as you, he still came and overwhelmed you;
And you don't see through him until years had passed;
Now it has dawned upon you, so now you want to be told.

That husband is not a friend; had he stayed he'd still have faults.
Massaging him in every way, not stopping even for a day.
What good would it be when we agree with you; hands don't need to
    scoop water.
It is the nature of a lady not to agree to defeat.

If he leaves, let him leave; he who gives to us is God.
Don't bother to think about him with bitter feelings in your heart.
Regret comes all alone; he will in the end regret it.
The best load is the lightest one; a heavy one just tortures you.

Those are my words, Dear friend from long ago.
Hold on to what I tell you; don't let it weigh heavy on you

One who is used to running away does not return anywhere.
Let him not be harassed should this deserter return.

Bakari Mwengo's verses contain three basic thoughts: (1) he blames the woman for not understanding the character of the husband earlier, before the marriage; (2) the husband is wicked, and, therefore, (3) the wife has no choice but to live with him as he is, without illusion or complaint; in fact to accept him at any time he decides to return regardless of the number of times he abandons her. But Sheikh Ali b. Saad is not content with an answer that only blames the woman. Moreover, Bakari Mwengo's argument does not even address the more basic question as to whether or not the woman is still married to the man who has not only divorced her but has also taken the dowry with him, thus making the divorce concrete. These issues and others are discussed and debated in other sets of poems that followed. The question as to whether or not the woman is married deals with a much more serious subject, in that any false statement uttered or action taken could result in one's punishment on the day of Resurrection, according to Islamic belief. Should the divorce be in place from the theological point of view, and should the couple nevertheless continue to live together as a result of wrong advice given them, they would, in the eyes of Islam, be committing adultery, and the punishment for such an indulgence is severe, both here and in the hereafter.

As can be noticed from the examples above, the *shairi* is one of the most formal among the Swahili verse compositions; while it is also one of the most popular for the audience, it is one of the most taxing to compose. As a rule, poets do not venture to create more than two dozen *shairi* verses on any subject. Suffice it to say, however, that *tenzi* and *shairi*, which move freely from the religious to the secular themes, are precisely the ones in which most Swahili poetry is composed.

There are five other categories of Swahili verse whose themes are entirely Islamic. Four of these—the *wajiwaji*, the *inkishafi*, the *ukawafi*, and the *hamziya*—were, in all probability, the creation of eighteenth- and nineteenth-century religious scholars, while the *tiyani Fatiha* is a more recent compositional form.

The syllabic form of lines of the *wajiwaji* and the *ukawafi* are identical. The difference is that the former is made up of five lines, while the latter has four lines to a verse. All the lines have fifteen syllables, with caesuras between the sixth and seventh, and also between the tenth and eleventh syllables. While the *wajiwaji* may be used for any religious theme, the *ukawafi*, on the other hand, deals exclusively with stories about prophets. One of the most famous of the *wajiwaji* is by Sayyid Muhyiddin bin Sheikh Qahtan (ca. 1798–1869). It is a prayer for rain during drought. As an example we present here the fourth and fifth verses of the poem, with our translation:

```
Ai Subhana      Mola wetu      uso shirika
Ndiwe Rahamana      Muwawazi      uso shaka
Warehemu wana      na wazee      wenye mashaka
Waijua sana      hali yetu      kati ya chaka
Jua la mtana      kula siku      lisilokoma

Tu waja dhaifu      mlangoni      pako twemele
Kwa niya ya kafu      shida yetu      Rabbi yondole
Hatuna wokofu      Mtatuzi      Uyatatule
Kwako ni khafifu      ni mafupi      yangawa male
Mwingi wa lutufu      Muwawazi      wawi na wema⁸
```

Our Glorious God, Our Lord who has no associate,
Thou art the Merciful One, Mighty Glorious Lord,
Be merciful to the children and the aged in difficulties.
You are well aware of our condition in the drought;
The heat of the day's sun, every day without pause.

We are weak beings, at your door we come to beg.
With urgent intent, our predicament Lord, remove.
We have no salvation our Savior, rescue us.
To You it is a light matter, it is easy; to us a heavy burden.
Lord full of kindness, Mighty to the good and evil.

Most Muslims believe that a prayer in verse is more potent than in ordinary language; hence poets are often summoned to compose prayer verses in times of difficulties.

One of the most famous of the *ukawafi* compositions, whose author is yet unknown, is a story about how the angels Jibril (Gabriel) and Mikail were sent by God to Moses in the form of a pigeon and a hawk respectively, to test Moses' sense of justice. The pigeon asked Moses for protection, while the hawk claimed it as food. Moses took a knife with the intention of cutting a piece of flesh from his own thigh to give to the hawk in place of the pigeon. It was at this point that the angels revealed themselves in order to stop Moses from cutting himself and to tell him that he had passed God's test, with flying colors.

The *inkishafi* verse is made up of four lines, each having ten, syllables, with a caesura on the sixth between the sixth and seventh. Unlike a *shairi*, there is no rhyme before the middle caesura. Though not as popular as the *utenzi*, some of the compositions in this genre are made up of a few dozen verses. The most popular of these is the original *al-Inkishafi* by Sayyid Abdallah bin Ali bin Nasir (ca. 1720–1820) from which the genre gets its name. It is a poem about the downfall of the once very powerful city-state of Pate, which the Sayyid witnessed. But the real purpose of the poem is to tell about the meaning and purpose of life as the poet-theologian sees it. The work is one of the finest examples of an Islamic verse composition in Swahili. Lyndon Harries observes:

> This poem is a homiletic on the inevitability of death, the transitoriness of even the richest forms of life, and a warning to the human soul against the danger of eternal damnation ....
> *Al-Inkishafi* was written after Pate had fallen to ruin and at a time when the once-lively houses still stood, desolate and void. The ruins of Pate were evidence of the truth of the poet's theme, the vanity of this transitory life. When the poem was written, probably between A.D. 1810–20, the Swahili of Pate and Lamu could remember well some of the prosperity of Pate, the downfall of which served the poet as a moral to his homily (1962, 88).

Harries has the following to add:

> The poem opens in the manner proper to all of the longer traditional Swahili verse, by setting forth the Attributes of Allah, with a prayer for the Holy Prophet, his Companions, and kindred. Then (in vv. 6–10) he explains the design of his work, to write a poem, likened to a string of pearls, whereby, from its regard, both he himself and all who heed his counsel may turn from sin to the good life. He then exhorts his heart to abandon the follies of mortal life, and mingling parable with exhortation reaches the climax of his theme in verses 33–54 where he depicts the glories of Pate, contrasting them with the pathos of its fall. In verses 65–77 he expounds on the penalties awaiting those who do not accept the counsel of righteousness, and he describes the punishment which awaits the sinful in the Seven Hells of Islam. (89)

Another famous poem in the same compositional form is known as *Dura mandhuma* by Sayyid 'Umar bin Amin al-Ahdal (ca. 1790–1870). The lines of this poem begin with the letters of the Arabic alphabet and continue to the end of the poem in their correct sequence. The theme of this poem, like that of the Inkishafi, is also a warning to the Muslims about the transient nature of life in this world and the importance of striving for the hereafter. In the opening two verses, for example, we clearly see how lines in each stanza begin with the same letter of the Arabic alphabet, while each of the lines in a given stanza combines the letter with a different vowel sound. The following examples are from the first two verses of the poem whose first three lines begin with A, I, U and Ba, Bi, Bu respectively:

> Andika mwandishi   khati utuze
> Isimu ya mola   utangulize
> Utiye nukuta   na irabuze
> Isiwalahini   wenye kusoma

> Baada ya ina kulibutadi
> Bijahi Rasuli   tutahimidi
> Bushura ya pepo   nasi tufidi[9]
> Mola atujazi   majaza mema

> Write, scribe, let your hand be steady
> Begin with The name of the Lord
> Dot the i's and cross the t's
> So that it may not give the readers any difficulty

> After inscribing first The Name
> In the honor of our Prophet we should pray
> So that we may be among those in paradise
> May The Lord bestow upon us His blessings

Another compositional form is known as *Tiyani Fatiha*. The original *Tiyani Fatiha* by Rukiya binti Fadhil al-Bakry (ca. 1892–1968) is a relatively recent prayer poem made up of nine lines, each two lines having the same number of syllables while each pair has a different syllable count. There are very few poems composed in this category.

There are several poems in Swahili on Islamic themes which were inspired by some poems in Arabic. Among these are the translations of the *mawlid*, praises on the life and deeds of Prophet Muhammad. Most of these poetic Swahili translations are based on what the Swahili refer to as *Mawlid Barzanji* by Ja'afar b. Hasan al-Barzanji (ca. 1690–1766). The most famous of the Swahili poetic translations is by Sayyid Abu-Bakr b. Abd al-Rahman, popularly known as Mwinyi Mansabu (ca. 1829–1922). All the versions that came to my attention have been composed in the 6+4+5 *ukawafi* meter. Unlike most homiletic verse, which circulates in relatively small groups of people and is commonly seen primarily as poetry, the *mawlid*, entirely poetic in composition, is nevertheless recited at mass gatherings of various kinds. There are numerous other poetic translations of Islamic poems and prayers originally in Arabic, usually composed in the *ukawafi* or *inkishafi* meter.

Finally, there is the *Hamziya*, a translation done around 1749 in Swahili verse by Idarus bin 'Uthman of a poem in Arabic called *Umm al-Qura* by Muhammad b. Said al-Busary, written in praise of Prophet Muhammad. Each verse is made up of fifteen syllables, with a caesura usually between the sixth and seventh and also between the tenth and eleventh syllables. We might note, in passing, that verses in the *wajiwaji*, *kawafi*, and *hamziya* have similar divisions and a like number of syllables in each line. The first poet to use such divisions and syllable numbers was Fumo Liyongo, the great poet-warrior-hero and the first of the known Swahili poets, who established the pattern in his famous verses to his servant Sada. All Swahili poems are meant to be sung to specific tunes, hence the paramount importance of metrical compositions.

Conclusion

Throughout Swahili history, both prose and poetry have played major roles in people's daily lives, especially those of the northern Swahili Coast. Islamic literature has also played a prominent role. In reality, the bulk of secular poetry composed in Swahili far outweighs the volume of religious verse, although Western scholars have concentrated on the written religious aspects, for reasons summarized above. Even so, Swahili culture is saturated with ideas of piety and prosperity that are ultimately religious in character. In most principal forms of poetic expression, therefore, we find substantial verse of the homiletic kind. This of course applies much more to pre-modern times, but the use of religion in social and political life continues into the present.

Poetry in general and the *tenzi* form in particular are used where many other cultures tend to utilize a prose form. Once the Swahili discovered that they could easily compose hundreds of *tenzi* verses using perfect meter and rhyme, the *tenzi* became the formal means of telling stories, recording historical events, admonishing good behavior, and even instructing married couples on ways of improving their sexual lives in the privacy of their home. While oral prose has survived over the centuries and often plays the same role as the *utenzi*, prose is considered as an informal means of communication. This is shown by the fact that very little of the Swahili prose tradition survives in manuscripts written in Arabic letters.

Swahili poetry is a functional art. The idea of "art for art's sake" is practically alien to the society. It is a public performance tradition. Even written poems are designed to be performed by being either sung or chanted. Almost all important, life-addressing issues that need to be eloquently articulated are presented to society in poetic form.

Today, no Swahili politician running for office in the northern Kenya Coast can hope to win without the backing of the '*Ulamaa* (religious scholars), especially the Sayyids (descendants of Prophet Muhammad), and the poets. The most important part of the campaign is conducted not on platforms in mass rallies where the candidate speaks. It is the poets with their emotionally charged verses, usually in the *utenzi* form, that make the difference in a politician's success. These *tenzi* are recorded on tape and copied in large numbers for the listening pleasure of the electorate. After the familiar introductory verses invoking the many attributes of God, the poets begin with quotations of familiar verses of the Qur'an or stories of love and betrayal as experienced by the prophets. After they have charged the faithful listener with emotions, then they argue for their candidate, showing how much he resembles a famous and beloved religious hero of the past and is therefore the best choice, while candidates submitted by others are compared to evil personalities in history and are therefore declared unworthy of election. The *shairi* composition is also used, especially in poetic exchanges between individuals, in the same manner employed by earlier poets such as Bakari Mwengo and Sheikh Ali b. Saad. In these electoral campaigns, one can see the living proof of how the *utenzi* and, the *shairi* are used to combine the traditional religious framework with historical invocation and contemporary political purpose.

We thus see that the religious and the secular domains in Swahili poetry, as in prose, are not nearly as distinct as they are said to be, and that they come together most forcefully in a compositional form, the *utenzi*, which itself borders on both prose and poetry, having the directness of the one and the rhythm of the other.

Why, we may ask, has Islam come to find expression in prosodic forms — why were Islam and poetic arts joined? (After all, there is nothing that requires religious belief to find expression in prosody.) And what can we make of their marriage and the effect of each on the other?

On a technical level, the Swahili language has readily borrowed words from other languages, enriching its lexicon and, as we have noted earlier, it has an abundant supply of rhyming words. In addition, Swahili also has an innate linguistic structure that makes meter and rhyme — the two most pronounced technical aspects that distinguish Swahili poetry from prose — easily attainable. The Swahili realized this resource of their language and have exploited it for at least ten centuries. The art was so advanced by the turn of the nineteenth century that it became one of the major means of communication.

The intimate connection between poetry and Islam in past Swahili literature underscores the pervasive role of religion in Swahili culture. The question of morality assumes the single most important focus for the poet. In Islam, the most noble task for man, the most deserving of *thawab*, is to exploit his innate possibilities to the full in the service of Allah. In committing his art to the propagation of Islam, the Swahili poet was consciously ensuring himself a dual benefit. He was serving the Muslim community by supplying the pertinent ethical and religious knowledge required to facilitate the believers' rough path through this world and preparation for the hereafter. His reputation as an upright devotee and bearer of knowledge would bring him wider esteem during his life, and his laudable art would be assured of eternal life.

The choice of poetry as a tool for purposes of instruction appears to be a natural one in a society whose social code was highly regulated by religious dictates. It may be helpful to remember that in the absence of formal secular schooling, the Muslim population relied heavily on Qur'anic institutions for much of its spiritual as well as temporal knowledge. The Qur'an became the most important influence in literary expression in content as well as in style. Since in many respects the Qur'an reads like poetry, the Swahili poets discovered in their poetically inclined language a heaven-sent resource for the articulation of the most important issues in their lives, of which Islam was a principal part.

Notes

1. For complete texts of the poems, see Shariff 1988, 54, 89–92.
2. Swahili theologians and scribes produced manuscript copies of the Qur'an using local styles of illumination, calligraphy, and materials.
3. Thirteen Swahili prosodic categories as well as their historical roots and functions are discussed in greater detail in *Tungo Zetu* (Shariff 1988).
4. Al-Baury, Fumo ·Liyongo, manuscript given to me by Ahmed Sheikh Nabhany, Mombasa, 1983.

5. There are many manuscripts of the poem in existence. Similarly, a number of Swahili bards know the verses by heart. The poem has also been published by several editors. An excellent version appears in J.W.T. Allen's *Tendi* (1971, 55–75). The source I used is from a tape sung by Bibi Rukiya Muhammad al-Busaidy, Mombasa, 1966. Most traditionalists believe that the original poem consisted of 100 verses. In some versions verses are missing, while in others new verses have been added by other poets.

6. This translation was done by Jan Feidel together with the present author. For a more detailed version of this episode see Shariff (1978, 174–77) and for other commentaries, see Abdulaziz (1979, 84–86) and also Hichens (1940, 29–31).

7. This poem by Sheikh Ali bin Saad and the following one by Bakari Mwengo, were from two sources: (1) Ahmed Sheikh Nabhany, field-notes, Mombasa, 1976, and (2) Mazrui papers, given to me by Al-Amin M. Mazrui, Mombasa, 1976. This translation is by the present author and Jan Feidel.

8. Manuscript given to me by Ahmed Sheikh Nabhany in Mombasa, 1982.

9. This version is from a tape recited by Zena Mahmud Fadhil and a manuscript given to me by Nabhany, Mombasa, 1973.

References

ABDULAZIZ, MOHAMED H. 1979. *Muyaka*. Nairobi: Kenya Literature Bureau.

ALLEN, J. W. T. 1971. *Tendi*. London: Heinemann.

DALE, GODFREY. 1923. *Tafsiri ya Kurani ya Kiarabu*. London: Society for Promoting Christian Knowledge.

———. 1924. "A Swahili Translation of the Koran." Harrisburg, PA: *The Moslem World* XIV: 5–9.

DARROCH, R. G. 1943. "Some Notes on the Early History of the Tribe Living on the Lower Tana, Collected by Mikael Samson and Others." *Journal of the East Africa Natural History Society* 17.4, 5, 77–78: 244–54.

FREEMAN-GRENVILE, G. S. P. 1966. *The East African Coast*. London: Oxford University Press.

HARRIES, LYNDON. 1962. *Swahili Poetry*. London: Oxford University Press.

HICHENS, WILLIAM. 1940. *Diwani ya Muyaka bin Haji al-Ghassaniy*. Johannesburg: Witwatersrand University Press.

HORTON, MARK. 1987. "The Swahili Corridor," *Scientific America* 257.3: 86–93.

KNAPPERT, JAN. 1967. *Traditional Swahili Poetry*. Leiden: Brill.

———. 1971. *Swahili Islamic Poetry* Leiden. Brill.

MAZRUI, ALI A. 1986. *The Africans: A Triple Heritage*. London: BBC Publications.

MOHAMED, MWINYIHATIBU. 1977. *Malenga wa Mrima*. Dar es Salaam: Oxford University Press.

NASSIR, AHMED. 1971. *Malenga wa Mvita*. Nairobi: Oxford University Press.

ROBERT, SHAABAN. 1967. *Masomo Yenye Adili*. London: Nelson.

———. 1967. *Utenzi wa Vita vya Uhuru*. Nairobi: Oxford University Press.

ROLLINS, JACK D. 1985. "Early 20th Century Swahili Prose Narrative Structure and Some Aspects of Swahili Ethnicity." *Towards African Authenticity: Language and Literary Form*. Eckhard Breitinger and Reinhard Sander, eds. Bayreuth, African Studies Series 2. Bayreuth, W.G.: Bayreuth Univ.

SHARIFF, IBRAHIM NOOR. 1978. "Translating from Swahili Poetry," *Pacific Moana Quarterly*. Hamilton, N.Z.: Outrigger Pub. Ltd. 3.2: 164–178.

———. 1988. *Tungo Zetu*. Trenton, N.J.: Red Sea Press Inc.

Chapter 4

▼▼▼▼▼▼▼

Language, Poetry, and Power: A Reconsideration of "Utendi wa Mwana Kupona"

ANN BIERSTEKER

"Utendi wa Mwana Kupona" is one of the best-known Swahili poems. It is a poem frequently recited within Swahili communities (Sheikh Nabhany 1972 iii, Strobel 1979, 84), numerous editions of it are available,[1] and it is frequently cited by scholars writing about the Swahili (Le Guennec-Coppens 1980; Mulokozi 1975, 1982; Strobel 1979). Yet the poem's status within the Swahili literary tradition is puzzling. Ostensibly the poem was composed by a mother for her daughter. It is the only poem by a woman which is considered a canonical text in the Swahili literary tradition. It is a poem which, according to most commentators,[2] deals with a theme, "wifely virtue,"[3] less philosophical and religious than the obvious themes of other major Swahili poems. How has a poem written by a mother for her daughter, a poem about how to be "a good wife," become a canonical literary text in a literary tradition where such prosaic topics are not usually treated, in the literary tradition of a society frequently noted for its Islamic philosophy and its patriarchal ideology?[4]

This paper suggests that while "wifely virtue" is one theme of the poem, it is only one mode of access to the poem. While "wifely virtue" is the most obvious literal theme in certain sections of the poem, other more philosophical and religious themes provide structural, ironic, and metaphorical cohesion throughout the poem. The concept of "wifely virtue" provides access to the poem at only its most literal and obvious level. Consideration of structure, irony, and metaphor provide a clearer explanation of why this poem has the status it does within the Swahili literary tradition. Structural cohesion in the poem is provided by the ways in which concepts of "blessing" and "salvation" and "appropriate speech behavior" are explicated. The way in which irony is employed seems to suggest contradiction to this structural cohesion. Examination of metaphor clarifies what would otherwise seem to be pointless ambiguity and explicates the way in which the poem addresses central issues in Swahili and Islamic ideology.

The Structure of the Poem

The verses on "wifely virtue" comprise less than one-third of the verses of the poem. When viewed within the context of the other verses, other readings become more plausible than a reading focussed exclusively on the duties of a wife. The first section of the poem (verses 1–27) consists of general advice presented as religious and social instruction. This section is addressed to the daughter. In the first lines of verses 12–14 an ordered summary of the advice is presented:

12. La kwanda kamata dini	First, hold fast to (your) religion
13. Pili uwe na adabu	Second, you should have good manners
14. La tatu uwe sadiqi	Third, be trustworthy/ honest

Throughout this section of the poem, the daughter/addressee is advised concerning the nature of *radhi* (approval or blessing) and how to secure it:

7. Mwanangu twaa waadhi pamoya na yangu radhi	My child, accept an admonition together with my blessing
22. Mama pulika maneno kiumbe ni radhi tano	My dear, listen to the words for a person it's five blessings
24. Naawe radhi mumeo siku zote mkaao siku mukhitariwao awe radhi mekuwea	And he should approve, your husband all the days you live together the day you are called

                                he should approve being
                                indebted to you

25. Na ufapo wewe mbee	And if you die first,
radhi yake izengee	his blessing should be sought
. . . .	

The five *radhi* (approvals) which are mentioned are those of God, His Prophet, father, mother, and husband:[5]

23. Nda Mngu na Mtumewe	Of God and His Prophet
baba na mama wayuwe	father and mother you know
na ya tano nda mumewe	and the fifth is of your
mno imekaririwa	husband
	often it has been repeated.

The advice concerning *radhi* continues into the section of the poem that focuses upon the marital relationship:

45. Fuata yake idhini	Follow his authority
awe radhi kwa yaqini	so that he approves definitely
. . . .	. . . .

Radhi is also mentioned when the mother describes her marriage:

54. Yalipokuya faradhi	When his time came
kanikaririria radhi	he told me many times of his
. . . .	approval

The purpose of the advice given in both the first and second sections of the poem — the reason one should seek and obtain approval — is provided in verse 11:

11. Yangu utakaposhika	Mine (what I'm saying) when
mwanangu hutosumbuka	you grasp it
duniani utavuka	my child you won't be
na akhira utakia	troubled
	this world you will escape
	and to the hereafter you will
	cross over.

The emphasis here on avoiding both worldly and spiritual difficulties is continued throughout the poem. A primary means by which all three sections of the poem are unified is through repetition of the phrases that include the words *akhera* (afterlife) and *dunia* (this world). These repetitions occur in the following lines:

22. . . . .
ndipo apate usono	when she obtains rest (peace)
wa akhera na dunia	of the hereafter and the world

65. . . . .
utaona nafuuze	you will see its benefit
za akhera na dunia	of the hereafter and the world

75. . . . .
uwepulie na tama	keep them from trouble
za akhera na dunia	of the hereafter and the world

95. . . . .
musipatwe na zitunu	you shouldn't suffer from bitterness (dissatisfactions)
za akhera na dunia	of the hereafter and the world

It might be suggested, if one looked only at the first two sections of the poem, that the daughter is being advised upon the requisite behavior so that she will achieve both earthly and divine approval. Yet even on this reading of these two sections, it is clear that not just the husband's approval is treated. It is also evident that approval is not presented as an end in itself.

The final section of the poem (verses 66–102) does not provide advice, nor is it explicitly addressed to the daughter. It is rather a request for *kheri* (good fortune). This request takes the form of a *dua* (prayer) addressed to God. The section begins:

66.
Tamati maneno yangu	This is the end of my words
kukuusia mwanangu	instructing you, my child
sasa ntamuomba Mngu	now I will pray to God
anipokelee dua	so that he will grant me a petition.

In subsequent verses a series of requests are made. The first request is for acceptance and completion of the poem:

68.
Nakuombawe Manani	I request of you, God
unitilie auni	that on my behalf you strengthen
ninenayo ulimini	that which I've said
na yote nisoyatoa	and all that I have not said

69.
Yote nimezoyanena	Everything as I have said it
Rabbi taqabali minna	may God will agree with me

ya yasalieo tena   that which still remains (unsaid)
Rabbi Mola nitendia   May God say/do for me.

The second request is for the preservation and prosperity of the poet's children and relatives:

70. Niwekea wangu wana   Protect my children
    na umbu langu mnuna   and my younger brother
    yakue yao maina   may their names grow
    yenee majimbo pia   becoming known in other states also.

71. Rabbi waweke nduzangu   God protect my siblings
    na wana wa ndugu zangu   and the children of my siblings
    wenee na ulimwengu   may they become known in the world
    kwa jamala na sitawa   with goodness and prosperity.

In the next verse prosperity and happiness are sought for all Muslims:

72. Na jamii Islamu   And for all Moslems
    Mola wangu warehemu   God show mercy to them
    matakwa yao yatimu   may all their desires be realized
    na nyoyo kufurahia   and their hearts made happy.

Verse 73 is a request for care and protection of the poet's children, while 74 is a request for their salvation:

73. Ya Allah wangu wana   God, my children
    nimekupa ni amana   I have given to you in trust
    watunde Mola Rabbana   care for them, God
    siwate kuwangalia   Do not abandon your care of them.

74. Nimekupa duniani   I have given them to you in the world.
    watunde uwakhizini   care for them protectively
    unipe kesho peponi   and give them to me in heaven
    mbee za Tumwa Nabia   before the Prophet.

In the next set of verses, benefaction for the poet/addresser rather than others is sought. In the first requests of this set of verses, relief from illness, forgiveness, and deliverance are sought. The section is introduced by a verse in which the poet/addresser presents herself as one in need:

77. Nisimeme muhitaji	I stand as one in need
mjao nakutarji	one approaching to request of you
ajili bi'lfaraji	of healing/deliverance and
ya afua na afia	health/recovery

The word play in the final line is significant to the requests that follow. In this line *afua* and *afia* are contrasted. These words happen to be from unrelated Arabic roots. Yet they are contrasted here in the same way as verbs or nouns that are derived from the same stem and that suggest different (even contradictory) meanings, are contrasted in other poems. One finds, for example, in a poem by Muyaka (Abdulaziz 1979, 234–35):

iii. Msimboneni kuteka, kuteka sichi kiteko
   You should not see me laughing, laughing is not this laugh.

iv. Vuka kuvukoni vuka, sichino kivuko
   Cross at this crossing place cross, this is not a crossing place
   . . . .
   Sichelee kupinduka, kupindukia pinduko.
   Do not fear being capsized, even being capsized in a
       capsization.

Afua in verse 77 may mean either "deliverance/redemption" or "cure," and similarly "*afia*" may mean "health" in a physical or spiritual sense. Throughout the requests that follow, this ambiguity is maintained, as the poet requests both the curing of her physical afflictions and spiritual deliverance:

78. Nondolea ndwee mbovu	Take from me the wretched disease
yaloingia kwa nguvu	which has become a grievous affliction
dhambi zangu na maovu	my sins and errors
ya Rabbi nighufiria	God, please forgive me.
79. Kwetu yagawa mazito	Although for us it is a burden
Kwako wewe ni matoto	for you it is nothing
nepulia uvukuto	relieve me of my suffering
upuke mara moya	relieve me immediately
80. Nakuombawe Latifa	I request of you Gentle God
unondolee makhafa	take from me fear

| kwa yaumu 'lArafa | because of this day of Arafat |
| na idi ya Udhuhia | and Idi of Udhuhia |

81. Kwa siku hizi tukufu	Because of these holy days
za kuhiji na kutufu	of the pilgrimage and the Kaaba
niafu Rabbi niafu	cure/save me God cure/save me
unishushize afua	enable me to recover/be delivered

In the second series of requests seeking benefaction for the poet addresser, the benefits sought are relief from problems, completion of words and thoughts, good fortune, happiness, and goodness:

85. Nami mjao dhaifu	I am a weak person
mwenye nyingi taklifu	with many difficulties
nakuomba takhifu	I beg you for relief
Rabbi nitakhafifia	God, relieve me

86. Nakuomba taisiri	I request of you promptly
Mambo nisoyaqadiri	that which I have not thought of
ungeshe kulla kheri	you will bring to me every blessing
shari ukinepulia	difficulties remove from me.

87. Ya Rabbi nitimiliza	God, finish for me
mambo nisiyoyaweza	that which I cannot not
wala moyoni kuwaza	or in my heart think
kwamba yatasikilia	that it will be heard

88. Rabbi unifurahishe	God, make me happy
mambo mema unegeshe	bring good things to me
maovu uyagurishe	drive problems from me
tusikutane pamoya	so that I am not confronted with them

The final request preserves the poem's emphasis on both the physical and the spiritual, as both earthly preservation and personal salvation are sought:

89. Uniweke duniani	Keep me in the world
miongo ya wahusuni	among the blessed people
nifapo nende peponi	when I die may I go to heaven
makao ya hafidhiwa	the dwelling of the saved.

This last section of the poem, which contains the prayer, is related to the first two sections because in the first two sections the addressor/poet/mother demonstrates through the instruction she provides why she merits the benefaction she seeks in the final section. The explicit addressee of the first two sections is the daughter. The implicit addressee of these sections is God, who is asked to complete what has not been said. Just as clearly, while God is the explicit addressee, the daughter, still the scribe, is implicitly an addressee of the final section. The mother's final lesson is not provided through injunctions. It is rather a demonstration of prayer seeking benefaction. Even at the very beginning of the poem, the daughter is told to write:

5.	Ukisa kulitangaza	When you have made known
	ina la Mola Muweza	the name of God, the Almighty
	basi tuombe majaza	then let us pray for his bounty
	Mola tatuwafiqia	God will be pleased
		with/approve of us

Prayer and instruction are integrally linked in the poem. The poem, then, may have the role it has in the tradition, because it *does* have as central themes the religious and philosophical topics more obvious in other poems. Here the structure of the poem suggests these themes are the relationship between "approval" and "good fortune" in this world and the next, and the critical role of instruction and prayer in seeking "approval" and "good fortune" in both worlds.

This explanation of the poem's status is strengthened by considering the type of actions described and recommended in the poem. The type of behavior which is enjoined and described throughout the poem is appropriate speech behavior. In the first section of the poem the daughter is advised:

13.	Pili uwe na adabu	Second, you should have good manners
	na ulimi wa thawabu	and a skilled tongue
	uwe mtu mahabubu	so that you are a loved person
	kulla utakapongia	wherever you enter.
17.	Ifanye mteshiteshi	Make yourself affable
	kwa maneno yaso ghashi	through words which are not guileful
	wala sifanye ubishi	nor should you be malicious
	watu watakutukia	such that people will hate you.

In these two verses the advice given is that one's style of speech should be typified by gentility and amicability rather than by guile or maliciousness. The rationale provided for this speech style is that it will engender love rather than the hate that will result from deceitful or vicious speech. An amicable speaking style is also recommended in verse 18:

18. Nena nao kwa mazha	Speak with them through jest
yaweteao furaha	which will give them pleasure
iwapo ya ikraha	if it is something offensive
kheri kuinyamalia	it's best to suppress it

The last two lines of this verse and the next verse deal with what should not be said and types of speech behavior to avoid:

19. Wala situkue dhana	Nor should you express ideas
kwa mambo usoyaona	through concepts you do not know
na kwamba na kunong'ona	nor slander or gossip
tahadhari nakwambia	beware, I'm telling you

The next two verses may also deal with speech behavior but are somewhat more difficult to interpret.

20. Sitangane na watumwa	Don't be idle with slaves
illa mwida wa khuduma	unless there's an opportunity for assistance
watakuvutia tama	they will lead you into trouble
la buda nimekwambia	as perhaps I have told you
21. Sandamane na wainga	Don't go along with fools
wasoyua kuitunga	who don't know how to behave
ziumbe wasio tanga	creatures who are not well brought up
wata kuwaqurubia	you should not go near them.

The above verses all make recommendations concerning general speech behavior. Appropriate speech behavior is also the topic of verses in the "wifely virtue" section of the poem. In verses 28 and 29, silence and agreement are the recommended speech behavior when one's husband is the speech partner:

28. Keti naye kwa adabu	Stay with him politely

usimtie ghadhabu	don't make him angry
akinena simjibu	if he speaks, don't answer him
itahidi kunyamaa	try to be silent

29. Enda naye kwa imani — Go with him peacefully
    atakalo simkhini — do not refuse what he wants
    we naye sikindaneni — you and he shouldn't make
               protestations to each other
    ukindani huumia — protestations cause pain

A subsequent verse in this section advises that the husband be treated as one lacking the ability to speak:

35. Mtunde kama kijana — Care for him like a child
    asiyoyua kunena — who doesn't know how to speak

The wife as caretaker of her husband becomes the wife as spokesperson for her husband in verse 48:

48. Mume wako mtukuze — You should praise your husband
    sifa zake zieneze — so his reputation spreads
    wala simsharutize — but you should not insist of him
    asichoweza kutoa — that which he cannot produce

    Speech behavior is also central in the prayer section of the poem where God is asked to complete the poem and the poet's thoughts (see above, verses 68 and 87). Effective and appropriate use of language is a central theme in Swahili poetry.[6] Yet a more plausible explanation for the emphasis throughout the poem on appropriate speech behavior is provided when these injunctions are considered in relationship to the poem's structure as examined above. It seems quite plausible to suggest that an argument is being made in the poem that a primary means by which to secure and maintain earthly and heavenly blessing and benefaction is through appropriate speech behavior. In the poem's presentation of this argument, appropriate speech behavior aimed toward the achievement of blessing and benefaction should be evident in one's everyday interactions as well as in instruction and prayer.

Irony

Irony as it is employed in the poem might seem to contradict this explanation based on structure. Examination of word play and double entendre,[7] particularly in the "wifely virtue" section of the poem, suggests that the image of the husband presented may be less than completely flattering and that the recommended treatment of the husband perhaps should not be characterized as respectful. In addition, while none of the verses are in any sense explicit, some may plausibly be read as suggestive.

Verses such as 32 and 33 are certainly not sexually explicit. Yet because they are temporally situated at times of waking and sleeping, it is reasonable to assume the physical setting is the bed and/or bedroom. Likewise, although the care specifically recommended is "massage" and "bathing," since the physical context is the bedroom and the thematic context is *kumtunda muili/*"caring for his body," it does not seem unreasonable to assume that these verses may "suggest" other activities that might take place given these contexts:

32. Kivikia simwondoe	If he gets sleepy/(loses strength) do not leave him
wala sinene kwa yowe	or mention it by a cry
keti papo siinue	stay right there, don't get up
chamka kakuzengea	when he rouses he will find you
33. Chamka siimuhuli	When he rouses you shouldn't rest
mwandikie maakuli	provide him with sustenance/ (satisfy him)
na kumtunda muili	and care for his body
kumsinga na kumwoa	massage him, and bathe him

Verse 34 in Allen's edition appears to deal primarily with shaving and perfuming of the husband. This is, however, the verse with the most variant readings of vocabulary in the manuscript sources upon which Allen based his edition (1971, 73). Many of these readings could make the verse seem more suggestive, but it is probably best not to consider the variant readings of this verse in this analysis, since the number of variant readings makes any translation or interpretation suspect. Whether the verse is openly suggestive or not, it does clearly focus on physical care of the husband and continues this theme.

Verse 35 does not present these problems, but has previously usually been translated quite innocuously:

35. Mtunde kama kijana	Care for him like a child
asiyoyua kunena	who doesn't know how to speak
kitu changalie sana	the thing to which to pay great attention
kitokacho na kungia	is that which goes out and in

Allen translates the final line as "his digestive system" (1971, 63); and Harries as "the household expenses and income" (1962, 77). Only Shariff translates "kitu" as "thing" (1983, 209). "Kitu" is, of course, a rather vague term. The reference could, in other contexts, be to household expenditures, or to food. Yet these lines occur in a verse which specifically mentions physical care and within the context of a series of verses which deal with the physical care a wife should provide for her husband. Household locations are not mentioned, but sleeping, massaging, and bathing would not take place in public areas of the household. These verses deal with physical attention provided by a wife to her husband in the privacy of the bedroom. The aspect of this care emphasized in the final lines of this verse involves "something that moves out and in," and it is said "great attention" should be devoted to this physical, i.e., non-abstract object. Within the conventions of the poetic tradition and those of academic explication, more specificity than this should not be required.

The first two lines of this verse also merit consideration. Here the husband is specifically referred to as a child. In other verses the soothing care recommended might also be that provided for a child:

31. Kilala siikukuse	If he sleeps/is resting,
	you should not move
	in a disturbing way
mwegeme umpapase	hold him so as
	to fondle him gently
na upepo asikose	with a breeze he should not lack
mtu wa kumpepea	someone to fan him

Indulgence toward the husband is certainly being recommended in these verses, yet the indulgence advised is very much like the care which would be recommended for infants.[8] The image of the husband presented here is not that of someone respected or honored. It is rather of someone indulged and spoiled. Within the context of the poem's emphasis on appropriate speech behavior, this already negative image seems even more unflattering. It becomes explicitly so in verse 35:

| 35. Mtunde kama kijana | Care for him like a child |
| asiyoyua kunena | who doesn't know how to speak |

Kijana (youth) is distinguished from *mtoto mchanga* (infant) by the ability of *kijana* to speak and understand (Johnson 1939, 115). The image here could then be of a large stupid child—one the age at which children normally speak, but who does not yet know how to speak. A third meaning of *kijana* is *mtu wa makamo mwenye nguvu* (a person of status who is strong) (Johnson 1939, 115). Even this meaning in context is negative, in that the husband is to be treated as someone powerful who is incapable of speech. The husband is to be regarded as lacking even the ability to speak and the daughter is advised to keep him this way. Line 36 is usually translated:

> 36. Mpumbaze apumbae   Amuse him so that he is amused.

It could also be translated:

> Render him stupid/speechless,
> so that he remains
> stupid/speechless

or

> Delude him so that he remains
> deluded

Such imagery and double entendre might seem an even less likely basis for explaining the poem's status, yet erotic double entendre is also a feature of other "classic" Swahili texts,[9] and ambiguous, if not clearly ironic imagery is also essily identified in many other poems.[10]

The poem may well be ambiguous on the issue of whether sexual or infantile physical pampering is recommended in this section. Given the context of the emphasis throughout the poem on speech behavior and the lines in this section that present the husband as speechless and the wife as spokesperson, it could even be argued that verbal pampering and indulgence are being recommended. What is not ambiguous is that the husband is presented in the poem as potentially powerful (through his ability to provide *radhi*) yet also controllable and vulnerable to manipulation. Similarly unambiguous is the recommendation that the means available to the wife for control of the husband are verbal skill and physical care.

Metaphor

Consideration of metaphor reconciles the apparent contradiction between the literal, structural, and ironic readings discussed above. Early in the poem the daughter is told she is being given a *"hirizi"* (amulet, line 8) in the form of a *"kidani"* (necklace, line 9). As noted by Allen (1971, 59), the poem as necklace is a typical conceit in Swahili poetry. Other examples are found in "Dura Mandhuma"[1] and "Inkishafi."[12] Line one of verse 9 is:

9. Nikutungie kidani   Let me compose a necklace for
                                     you

Kutunga (the infinitive form of *nikutungie*) can, of course, refer to
other types of composition. Its use within a poem, to refer to non-
poetic composition (stringing a necklace), within an extended
metaphor referring to poetic composition, is not atypical of the kind
of word play found in the poem. The daughter/addressee/scribe is
an apprentice poet. She is enjoined *kutwaa* (to take) the *waadhi*
(admonition, line 7), the *radhi* (approval/blessing, line 7), and the
"*hirizi*" (amulet as necklace and poem, line 8). *Kutwaa* is, of course,
much stronger than synonyms such as *kupokea* or *kuchukua*. It can be
used in the sense of military or sexual conquest. She is, then, being
given admonitions, blessings, and an amulet/necklace/poem and at
the same time being told to take control of these.

As an apprentice poet, she is being taught how to achieve
"approval" and "good fortune" in this world and the next through
using language eloquently and seductively as a poet. She is being
taught how to provide instruction, how to pray, how to soothe,
how to charm, and how to amuse and control through use of poetic
language. The instruction is provided through admonition, examples,
and demonstration, but all of these are provided through the medium of
poetry. The apprentice poet is being taught how to address, through
poetry, others in her community, her husband, her children, her
mother, and God. If the husband, who is always a topic never an
addressee, is not taken to be a literal husband, but rather a person
with political power, the poem might even be read as providing
guidance on how those with verbal power can manipulate and control
those with political power.[13] Such a reading would explain the
poem's status in the tradition. As the poem empowers young women
by guiding them in the use of their verbal skills, so too it empowers
the ethnic Swahili whose history for the last two centuries has been
characterized by external domination.

This is a poem about seductive verbal eloquence, i.e., a poem
about the power of poetry to affect action and behavior. This is, of
course, not an uncommon topic in Swahili poetry given the tradition
of poetic competition and poetic dialogue (Shariff 1983; Abdulaziz
1979). It is, however, a topic that has not been extensively discussed.

Conclusion

It could be argued that the four alternative readings given above indicate that the poem may not be "about" a prosaic topic, but rather alludes to a range of topics central to the Swahili literary tradition. It is, in fact, possible to argue that the poem is not "about" any one or any group of these topics. Rather, it is a poem which has been carefully constructed to elicit and manipulate a range of sometimes apparently contradictory, yet ultimately complimentary readings.

Yet quite obviously readings focussed on seduction or even the seductive power of poetry are not completely unrelated to readings which look only at "wifely virtue." Similarly, readings that look at relationships between prayer and instruction in the quest for earthly and spiritual blessing and deliverance are not unrelated to those that consider power imbalances between those who seek and those who bestow "approval." It is equally plausible to argue that the poem does disambiguate itself when the four possible readings are considered in terms of their inter-relationships. The four readings discussed about suggest:

1. There is an overt theme of "wifely virtue" presented in one section of the poem. This section has been read by various writers to suggest that women should be submissive to men and providers of pleasure to men.
2. The structure of the entire poem presents an argument that a primary means by which to secure and maintain earthly and heavenly blessing and benefaction is through instruction, prayer, and appropriate speech behavior in everyday interactions.
3. The ironic reading of the "wifely virtue" section of the poem indicates that this section mocks rather than flatters "husbands," whether those "husbands" are literal spouses or political rulers who are intellectually limited.
4. Further consideration of metaphor in the poem indicates that poetry is presented to be the most appropriate way to outline and explicate contradictions and a most appropriate means of praying and providing instruction.

The poem thus affirms through structure, metaphor, and language certain tenets of Swahili Islamic ideology:

1. the significant role of prayer, instruction, poetry, and appropriate speech behavior in seeking and obtaining divine and worldly approval, good fortune, health, and deliverance, for oneself and one's community, and

2. the role of prayer, instruction, and poetry in the Swahili language in obtaining the above.

Through ironic subversion the poem questions a belief that some have held to be fundamental to Swahili Islamic ideology, the belief that a woman must be submissive to her husband to obtain his approval for her entrance to paradise. Yet what the poem most clearly asserts through metaphor and irony would seem to be a political rather than a religious proposition: that through skilled use of language those who are otherwise powerless can manipulate those who are powerful.

"Utendi wa Mwana Kupona" is, then, a poem composed to "beguile" the unwary, be they young daughters, naive husbands, scholars, or other outsiders anticipating straightforward cultural messages in Swahili poetry. It is in this respect that this poem is a central text in the Swahili literary tradition — a tradition characterized by its "literariness," not by its "literalness." The reader who would rather be pleasurably "seduced" than be rendered a fool when reading this and other Swahili poetry must first accept the literariness of the tradition. "Utendi wa Mwana Kupona" is a poem composed *kuvuta* ("to entice") even the wary who anticipate ambiguity and complexity in Swahili poetry. It is not a poem composed to be explicated in prose. It was very likely not composed to transmit messages. It probably was composed to elicit the production of other poetry. Swahili poetry does embody the ideology of Swahili society, but it does so through its presentation of the contradictions and ambivalences within Swahili Islamic ideology and the sheer delight of play with words and respect for their power. Questions of the relationship of language and power are central to Swahili ideology, to Islamic philosophy, and are also central to Swahili poetry. It is these questions and the ways in which they are posed to which subsequent study of Swahili poetry might be usefully addressed.

Notes

1. The edition upon which this paper is based is the scholarly edition of J. W. T. Allen in *Tendi* (1971). In the preface to his edition, Allen lists the other editions which are available, and notes the manuscripts versions on which the editions are based. In writing this paper I have also consulted the editions and/or translations of Nabhany, Hichens and Werner, Harries, and Shariff.

   I have extensively consulted Ahmed Sheikh Nabhany and Ibrahim Noor Shariff concerning possible, probable, and unlikely interpretations of lines and passages in this poem. Their contributions have been considerable and are gratefully acknowledged. I also wish to thank Debra Amory for her many useful criticisms of an earlier version of this paper. I have incorporated most of her suggestions and very much appreciate her support of this project. Any errors in translation or interpretation should be attributed to me. The translations provided here are generally literal; for more poetic translations see Allen and Shariff.

2. Harries calls this section "the main argument of the poem" (1962, 72).

3. To use Hichens and Werner's title, *Advice of Mwana Kupona upon the Wifely Virtue* (1934).

4. Mulokozi says that the poem reflects a "feudal mentality" in which "the woman is not only subordinate to the man, she is a thing, a toy, a tool for the satisfaction of the man's desire" (1975, 54). In another article he states that the "image of the woman we are given by Mwana Kupona is that of man's submissive servant and a petty sensuous object" (1982, 43). Margaret Strobel says of the poem:

"A didactic poem, 'The Advice of Mwana Kupona upon the Wifely Virtue,' comprehensively depicts the model wife. Composed on her deathbed in the late 1850's by the wife of the sheik of Siyu near Lamu, this poem was passed on orally and in manuscript to generations of young girls being prepared for wifehood. Important as the clearest statement of the east African ideal of wifely virtue, the poem's popularity indicates how extensively patriarchal ideology infused the lives of women of upper class families" (1979, 84–85).

5. A search of *A Concordance of the Qur'an* under "r d y" identified many passages in which God's *radhi* is mentioned, but none in which approval by the father, mother or husband is mentioned. The most relevant passage found was:
    "the reward of these *shall be* paradise, gardens of eternal abode, which they shall enter and *also* whoever shall have acted uprightly, of their fathers, and their wives, and their posterity" (George Sale, trans., 242).

6. See, for example, the first two lines of Muyaka's poem "Moyo":

Moyo wanambia, "Kwamba, jambo la mt'u usambe!"
Moyo wanambia, "Omba, kitu cha mt'u siombe!"

My heart tells me, "Speak, but concerning others you shouldn't speak!"
My heart tells me, "Request, but things belonging to others should not be requested!"

(Abdulaziz 1979, 188–89)

Another example is found in Shaaban Robert's "Kiswahili":

Katika maamkizi, mepesi sana na mema
Lugha zote haziwezi, nyingine kudai kima
kama kile azizi, kwa Kiswahili kusema

In greetings, delicate and virtuous
No other language, could claim itself
to be like that wonder, Swahili spoken

(Shaaban, 1966, 28)

7. The suggestion to consider this topic was made by Ibrahim Noor Shariff, who also assisted by verifying examples in this section.
8. This insight was provided by Ibrahim Noor Shariff.
9. In his introduction to "Utendi wa Masahibu," Allen comments:

> sailors all over the world seem to think of nothing but seamanship and sex and have time to think out tortuous ways of describing either in terms of the other. My attention has been drawn to one passage in which the double entendre is complicated enough for Aristophanes and it is possible that I have missed the point elsewhere. (1971, 130–31)

> Other excellent examples are found in poems such as Muyaka's "Panda" (Abdulaziz 1979, 190–93), which plays upon four meanings of the verb *kupanda* ("to mount sexually," "to climb literally," "to plant," and "to climb socially").

10. See, for example, the political dialogue poems discussed by Shariff (1983) and the political poems of Muyaka which are discussed by Abdulaziz (1979).
11. See the editions of Dammann, Werner, and Harries.
12. See Allen's edition of this poem by Sayyid Abdalla bin Ali bin Nassir.
13. This is suggested by the repetition of the term *kijana* (youth) in the first line of verse 92:

92. Nina kijana muinga	I have a foolish youth
Napenda kumuusia	I wish to affect

References

ABDULAZIZ, MOHAMED. 1979. *Muyaka.* Nairobi: Kenya Literature Bureau.

ALLEN, J. W. T., ed. 1971. *Tendi: Six Examples of A Classical Verse Form with Translation and Notes.* New York: Africana Publishing House.

DAMMANN, ERNST. 1940. "Die aufgereihte Perle." *Dichtungen in der Lamu-Mundart des Suaheli.* Hamburg: Friederichsen, de Gruyter, 328–34.

HARRIES, LYNDON. 1953. "Strung Pearls: A Poem from the Swahili-Arabic Text." *Bulletin of the School of Oriental and African Studies* 15: 145–56.

———. 1962. *Swahili Poetry.* London: Oxford University Press.

HICHENS, WILLIAM, and ALICE WERNER. 1934. *Advice of Mwana Kupona upon the Wifely Virtue.* Medstead, Hampshire: Azania Press.

JOHNSON, FREDERICK. 1939. *A Standard Swahili-English Dictionary.* Nairobi: Oxford University Press.

KAMUSI YA KISWAHILI SANIFU. 1981. Nairobi: Oxford University Press.

KASSIS, HANNA E. 1983. *A Concordance of the Qur'an.* Berkeley: University of California Press.

LE GUENNEC-COPPENS, FRANÇOISE. 1980. *Wedding Customs in Lamu.* Lamu, Kenya: The Lamu Society.

MULOKOZI, M. M. 1975. "Revolution and Reaction in Swahili Poetry." *Kiswahili* 45:2: 46–65.

———. 1982. "Protest and Resistance in Swahili Poetry." *Kiswahili* 49:i: 25–54.

NASIR, SAYYID ABDALLA BIN ALI. 1977. *Al-Inkishafi,* translated and annotated by James de Vere Allen. Nairobi: East African Literature Bureau.

ROBERT, SHAABAN. 1966. "Kiswahili" *Pambo la Lugha*. Nairobi: Oxford University Press. 27–31.

SHARIFF, IBRAHIM NOOR. 1983. "The Function of Dialogue Poetry in Swahili Society," Ph.D. thesis, Rutgers University.

SHEIKH, AMINA ABUBAKAR, and AHMED SHEIKH NABHANY, eds. 1972. *Utendi wa Mwana Kupona na Utendi wa Ngamia na Paa*. (Sanaa ya Utungo, I.) Nairobi: Heinemann.

STROBEL, MARGARET. 1979. *Moslem Women in Mombasa, 1890–1975*. New Haven: Yale University Press.

TAASISI YA UCHUNGUZI WA KISWAHILI, CHUO KIKUU CHA DAR ES SALAAM. 1983. *Kamusi ya Kiswahili Sanifu*. Dar es Salaam: Oxford University Press.

The Koran, trans. by GEORGE SALE. 1909. London: Frederick Warne.

WERNER, ALICE. 1929. "An Alphabetical Acrostic in a Northern Dialect of Swahili." *Bulletin of the School of Oriental Studies* 5.3: 561–69.

Chapter 5

▼▼▼▼▼▼▼

Of Poets and Sheikhs:
Somali Literature

ALI JIMALE AHMED

In traditional Somali society, forums are part of the structure through which a wronged individual can get redress. The members of the community assemble under one large tree to witness and participate in the procedure of dispensing justice, carried out by a council of men. The council, which is the judge and juror in one body, is appointed only after the consent of the litigants involved in a case is secured. Once before the council, the plaintiff is first heard; then the accused is given a chance to refute or accept the charge. No council reaches its verdict without following such a procedure as the validity of a *caveat* is taken to heart by the elders of the community. The "tree" referred to above is the *geedka xeerka* (the tree of customary law). The council entrusted to dispense such justice consists of *heerbeegti*, men well-versed in customary laws. The Somali poet is more often than not a revered member of that council. But there is another "tree" that dispenses justice. This is called *geedka haqqa iyo hukunka*, the tree of truth and (by implication) Islamic jurisprudence (Samatar 1982, 28).[1] The chief dispenser of this form of justice is the *sheikh qadi* (Islamic jurist). By virtue of their status, the sheikh and the poet belong to the indigenous intelligentsia of Somalia. It was this recognition of their powers that prompted the second president of the First Republic, the late Abdirashid Ali Shermarke, to remark that Somali culture was firmly based on a dual structure: Islam and Somali poetry (Samatar 1982, 8). For the president to equate the two indicates the value the Somalis attach to their poetry.

Islam is a unifying force in Somali society. Like poetry, it cuts across clan lines. But the peaceful co-existence of the two forces within Somali culture also attests to the power of syncretism in African traditions. The synthesis that results is not that of a victor and a vanquished foe. The two, sheikh and poet, wield tremendous power and influence in Somali society. As members of the elite, they share among other things a desire to consolidate their power vis-a-vis the non-elite majority. Thus their interests sometimes converge.

At other points, however, their interests diverge. As each works to carve his own sphere of influence, he seeks to destroy the credibility of the other. In the pages that follow, we will delineate where their interests converge, where they collide, and what each one of them does to lure the public to his side.

Islam is a way of life, an all-encompassing system that pervades the social, economic, and political structures of its believers. For centuries, Islam has been one of the two pillars of Somali tradition, the other pillar being poetry. Somalia has been called a "nation of bards" (Burton 1984; Laurence 1964; Andrzejewski 1964). Somali poetry contains a significant body of cultural knowledge. In order that this knowledge be conserved and passed on to posterity, poems make great use of alliteration, which is known for its mnemonic quality. This is a quality which is pivotal for Somali tradition, since a great deal of their experience is kept in the bardic memory. This storing of experience rests upon the existence of a pool of memorizers, and a constant repetition of "the word" for its survival.

The Our'an, Islam's holy book, also presupposes memorization and recitation for its survival. The Qur'an has its own mnemonic quality which thrives on poetic and rhetorical devices, such as end rhyme, metaphor, and simile. In fact the word *qur'an* itself is a derivative of "the consonant root cluster QR', which conveys the sense of reciting" (Nelson 1985, 3).[2] The reasons for reciting the Qur'an at the embryonic stage of the Islamic movement included the shortage of literate persons, and the scarcity and impermanence of written materials.

The Qur'an and Somali poetry depend on rote memorization and recitation for preservation and dissemination across time and space. It is therefore obvious that the close affinity between performer/reciter and audience is lost when written forms come into use. The sheikhs and especially the Somali poets capitalized upon this loss in their effort to ward off literacy campaigns. Their fears could also be interpreted as the deep fear embedded in some members of the indigenous intelligentsia that with literacy comes death; their prominent roles in society would become obsolete, for "literacy short-circuits seniority as the way to wisdom" (Maxwell 1982, 2). Yet the reactions of these people are couched in terms that, at a surface level, reflect the concerns, anxiety, and consternation of other members of the community. The guardians of tradition are not without subterfuge in dissuading people from becoming literate. The famous Somali oralist, Mohamed Haji Hussein, "Sheeko Hariir," succinctly summarizes traditional reluctance to resort to writing: "Haashi dowr, haafid ma noqdo" (Samatar 1982, 33). [He who looks at a paper never becomes a memorizer.] The implication is that the literate person becomes too dependent upon paper, i.e., the written word. Such a dependency is to be feared since written items can get stolen, lost, or burned, while the oral word is engraved in a person's memory. (That the memorizer himself could die is ignored by them). The reasoning becomes meaningful when one considers the historical instances in which books were either thrown into a river or burned completely. The burning of books was not only a symbolic act of defeat, but one way of ensuring the final demise of a society. To early Muslims, this threat was real.

The prominent role of rote memorization and its recitation in Somalia could also be explained by the ecology of the Somalis. In Somalia, the nomadic way of living necessitates the orality of Somali poetry. The poet wanting to be heard in places far away from his homestead craves a spatial extension that allows his poems to travel to places he never dreamed of. He finds justification in the Somali proverb, "dhagax meel dhow ayuu ku dhacaa, dhawaqna meel fog." [Sound travels further than a stone (when it is thrown).]

In the riverine areas of Somalia where life is relatively sedentary, Sheikh Uways Mohamed wrote poetry in Arabic script, but it is not certain if his use of script really increased his readership among his peasant audience. Most Somalis, peasants or pastoralists, are sent to Qur'anic schools to learn to memorize the Qur'an, but the Somalis are not native speakers of Arabic, although they revere the language of the Holy Book. Nonetheless, there are Somali sheikhs who had composed original poetry in Arabic, including Sheikh Uways, Sheikh Mohammed Abdulle Hassan, Sheikh Abdulrahman, Sheikh Omar, and Sheikh Mohamed Hassan. Their poetry, overtly didactic, was memorized by disciples who continue to recite it on treasured occasions. The survival of these poems in a land where Arabic is not the mother tongue could be attributed to what Ibrahim Noor Shariff, elsewhere in this volume, calls "*thawab*, heavenly credit." Muslims believe that the repetition of a good word which propagates the faith results in rewards from Allah. Such rewards are mostly enjoyed in the life hereafter.

The oral culture of the Somalis could not preclude the co-existence of the two genres, for orality and literacy can live contiguously with each other, as had been the case for centuries. In Somali oral literature, the poetry is replete with Arabic words indicating a close affinity between the two cultures and the two genres. The existence of a people who haven't heard of literacy is unlikely and as Jack Goody explains:

> At least during the past 2000 years, the vast majority of the peoples of the world (most of Eurasia and much of Africa) have lived ... in cultures which were influenced in some degree by the circulation of the written word, by the presence of groups or individuals who could read or write .... It is clear that even if one's attention is centered only upon village life, there are large areas of the world where the fact of writing and existence of the book has to be taken into account even in discussing traditional societies. (Finnegan 1977, 161)

No place attests to the truth of that statement more than Somalia, where the people have been Muslims for centuries. It is therefore hard to imagine that there is a Somali who has not seen or heard of the Holy Book of Islam. Yet the Somalis have remained illiterate over the centuries. While most Somali sheikhs can read and write in Arabic, with the exception of a few who transcribed their poetry in Arabic script, no sheikh has ever endeavored to create a writing system for transcribing Somali oral literature. The reluctance of the Sheikhs to devise a script for Somali lies not only in the orality of the people of the area, as suggested by John Johnson in his *Heelooy* (12), but in the relationship of the sheikhs toward the laity. The sheikh in Somali tradition is a keeper of "the word," and as such has a tendency to monopolize his possession. In short, he does not want to expand the base of those with access to the tree of knowledge. This is not unique to Somali peripatetic religious men, but it is characteristic of men in robes spanning time and space.

The poet has also built a fortress to avert any incursion onto the sacrosanct terrain of his field. A rigid form of alliteration, coupled with the use of archaic language, discourages most from attempting to become a poet. Many Somali scholars have written numerous articles decrying the rigidity of the form. They all called for a change of rules so that future poets could compose in free verse. Unfortunately, none of these scholars came forward with any plausible way of combining theory with practice, and the lack of any meaningful praxis has put an end to the discussion.[3] A similar crusade to prosify Somali plays has suffered a similar fate. Both sheikh and poet have been unwilling to educate the people in their different domains, lest their control slip away.

Their stance against the emergence of a new genre of love poetry, *balwo*, after World War II is a case in point. The *balwo* genre is a miniature form of the classical poem *gabay*. The *gabay* can run to hundreds of lines, each line broken into two hemistiches; each hemistich contains one alliterative sound, which is equally distributed in the poem. The new genre was supposedly started by one Cabdi Deeqsi, whose truck broke down somewhere near the ancient Somali town of Zeila (Andrzejewski and Lewis 1964, 50). He called this poetry *balwo*, a corruption of the Arabic word for catastrophe. The new form appealed to townspeople because it was brief, and because it interpreted reality from their standpoint. To townspeople who found themselves in similarly catastrophic situations in the burgeoning towns of Northern Somalia, the song was a source of solace. The new emigrés to towns, with no one to turn to for help, found themselves in a desolate place, both spiritually and materially. As a meeting ground for different subgroups from the interior, the town had to be a place for all. This meant that no single code of reference prevailed, and a new code of reference had to be created. It was easy for the formerly nomadic towndwellers to identify with the imagery of the *balwo*, which espoused themes relevant to and depictive of the *modus vivendi* of the urban dweller. Songs of this genre made their debut with the establishment of radio transmissions.

Popular poets despised the short form of the *balwo* and viewed the new genre as nothing more than doggerel. The sheikh objected to the new love poetry for a different reason. To the religious man, *balwo* was a subtle form employed by Christian missionaries in their effort to proselytize Somalis. *Balwo* is sung to a tune and not chanted like classical poetry, and thus the cleric's objections to it evoke the perennial controversy on the status of music in Islam.

The Art of Reciting the Qur'an demonstrates that Muslims shy away from music because of its original association with the *qaynah*, "a slave or freed woman trained in the art of singing" who performed for the wealthy and the elite (Nelson 1985, 34).[4] The *qaynah*'s position was coupled with the *muxannat*, the effeminate male singer. The role of the effeminate male singer was brought closer to home by male actors playing the role of women in the nascent Somali theater of the time. Just as musicians and singers worldwide are viewed with both envy and hatred, there is no love lost between the orthodox Muslim, including the rulers, and the singer in Muslim societies. Caliph al-Ma'mun is said to have shied away from appointing Ishaq Ibrahim al-Mawsili (767–850), a famous singer, to the position of a *qadi* (Islamic jurist) (Nelson 1985, 35). Yet the Qur'an clearly warns the believers to beware the evil influences of the poet and not the musician. The Somali sheikh, like his counterpart in early Islamic history, could not completely tarnish the image of the poet.

The Somali religious man is feared for his powers to cast a curse referred to as *asmo* on his enemies. This curse is the ultimate weapon in the arsenal of the religious man and is to be used only under strict conditions as when the sheikh's existence or that of his clan is at stake. The curse, like any ultimate weapon, can bring untold misery to both its user and the one it is directed against. Because of its potential to boomerang, it is used with prudence. The availability of such a potent weapon at the fingertips of the sheikh gives the religious man power to command awe among the Somalis. The heavens purportedly take up the sheikh's case swiftly and Allah punishes transgressors.

Similar powers are associated with poets who can cast another form of curse, *yu'asho*, on every mortal who troubles them. Yet none of their powers emanates from the usual source of power — the sword. The source of their strength lies in "the power of the spoken word [which] can effect reality in the consciousness of oral people" (Maxwell 1983, 2). It is because of this direct association between the spoken word and the result it can occasion in its hearer that Somalis avoid vituperative persons at *cir-gaduud*, the time of dusk or before dawn.

The poet and sheikh also have constructive roles to play in society, as they can mediate between warring factions. Their concili-atory words carry considerable weight, as they are deemed repositories of clan or national history. The sheikh's encouragement can lead warriors among clans to engage in internecine feuds, but for a clan his restraining voice can mean "a war without blessing." The magical power of poetry to exhort clan warfare abounds in Somali history.[5] The Prophet's words to Hassan Ibn Tabit, a poet of great stature during the early periods of Islam, epitomize the magical efficacy of poetry:

> Pour out [an incitement to] the raid against the
> Bani 'Abd. Manāf, for by Allah your poetry is
> more potent than falling arrows in the darkness of dawn.
>   (Nelson 1985, 38)

The poet is aware of his status in society and utilizes it to the utmost; at times he too begins to believe in the extraordinary powers of poetry. Indeed, one Somali poet, Qamaan Bulxan, attributes the swift dissemination of poetry to supernatural powers when he claims:

> Caliyow dabuub taada gabay, daayinkaa wadaye
> Dabaylaha xagaagii bafliyo, daafigaa sidaye
> [O Cali, the Everlasting One has driven on the words of your poem
> the rustling wind of the warm breeze has carried them].
>   (Andrzejewski 1985, 356)[6]

Qamaan's words bring out the whole irony. True Muslims believe it is the powers of the *jinn* and not Allah [the Everlasting One] that are the driving force behind the dissemination of poetry. Hussein A. Bulhan in his essay, "The Captive Intelligentsia of Somalia," interprets a contemporary poet's words, which do not sound any different from Qamaan's in the early part of the twentieth century. Hussein's poet claims:

> The clouds await my lyrics
> Never raining a drop without my song. (1980a, 28)

This reveals one of the sources of intense rivalry between the sheikh and the poet: their competition for intercessionary powers.

The allusion to the poet's control of "the clouds"—in effect calling himself a rain-maker—is not lost on Somalis living in a region where rain or its lack can cause prosperity or famine. During droughts, it is the sheikh's succor that is sought. Both the sheikh and the majority of the populace believe that droughts are brought on by sin. To cleanse the community of evil deeds, the sheikh leads a procession of *roob-doon*, a prayer for rains. Such a prayer acknowledges the sheikh's eminence within the society. He is tacitly given intercessionary powers by his compatriots.[7]

The poet's assertion, "the clouds await my lyrics," suggests *shirk* (idolatry) in two ways. First, it refers to a tradition in pre-Islamic history, commonly referred to as *casril jahiliya* (the era of ignorance), whereby propitiatory acts were made to appease deities. The implication that Allah can be cajoled with lilting lyrics into delivering rain lowers the divine power of the Creator to a human level. Secondly, with his boasts, the poet abrogates for himself a divine status.

In the poet's claims can also be seen an intention to de-fetishize the sheikh's rain-seeking processions. The poet evidently does not agree with the sheikh's thesis that environmental catastrophes such as droughts are a manifestation of the human contravention of divine laws, or with the conventional wisdom of the Somali proverb "caado la burriyaa Caro Allay leedahay" (an abandoned custom brings forth the wrath of Allah). With a few lines then, the poet can fulfill several aims, yet leave much unsaid, ambiguous.

The ambiguity of the poet's words is deliberate. It gives him a maneuvering ground with which he can utilize the malleability of "the word." The elliptic form of poetry is what makes the word a double-edged scimitar. The Somalis equate this elastic quality of the word to sinews with all their flexibility, but:

> Malleability is one half of the dual nature of language — the half that permits us to use language the way a sculptor uses wet clay, making of it whatever we wish. (Norrman & Haarberg 1980, 6)

And herein lies the sheikh's suspicion of the poet's words. The Qur'an warns Muslims to beware of the deceiving words of the poets:

> Poets are followed by none save erring them. Behold how aimlessly they rove in every valley, preaching what they never practice. (Qur'an 26:227)

The insincerity alluded to in the last line reveals that truth and poetry are not necessarily viewed as compatible. It is against this proclivity of the poet to "wander about without any set purpose, and seek the depth (valleys) of human folly rather than the height of divine light" (Nelson 1985, 208) that Muslims react so negatively. The sheikh, like any true believer, must either utter the truth or keep silence.

More often than not, the sheikh is viewed as being understanding and forgiving. The poet, on the other hand, is considered vindictive and temperamental. This difference in disposition comes to the forefront when one examines the voluminous body of political poetry in

Somalia. Many poets have engaged in diatribes against their opponents. Ali Jaamac' Haabiil's poem against Sheikh Hassan reminds one of this type of conflict:

> But he [Mohamed Abdulle Hassan] wantonly lacerates the tendons of weary
> travellers and engorges their dates.
> He's battened on the weak and the orphan,
> Call ye this Italian-infidel a Mahdi?
> How puzzling the thought! (Samatar 1979, 290)

In the post-independence era, many poets had to appease different interests simultaneously.

But the dichotomy doesn't preclude the emergence of a poet who is also a sheikh, and vice versa. In the annals of Somali historiography one comes across a number of sheikhs who were great poets. These sheikhs were mostly known for their leadership of religious sects and/or for their patriotic role in the fight against colonial occupation. Sheikhs such as Mohamed Abdulle Hassan, his chief rival in the south, Sheikh Uways H. Mohamed, and Sheikh Ahmed Gabyow are among many whose poetic achievements are highly valued. For the sheikh-poet, the combination meant the consolidation of dual powers emanating from two different sources. It was to be expected that such an amalgam of powers was the sum total of diverse characteristics such as understanding, forgiveness, vindictiveness, and temperament. The diatribes that Sheikh Mohammed A. Hassan and Sheikh Uways Mohamed hurled at each other not only show that there was no love lost between the two, but that the sheikhly attitudes at times gave way to the pursuit of power and glory.[8] The unity of the usually separate powers in the hands of one man, some critics contended, was cause for worry. In the case of Mohammed Abdulle Hassan, Said Samatar writes, "The contradictory demands, it is argued, of these 'inner obligations' were responsible for the stormy, at times erratic, behavior that was to mark the later phase of his career" (1979, 6). That might be the case, if one could conceivably discern the existence of halcyon years in the lives of ambitious sheikhs who were bent on leaving their mark on history.

Notes

1. I have made slight changes in the nomenclature while sticking to the basic concept.

2. In fact, the first order to the Prophet was to "recite!" "Recite in the name of your Lord who created, created man from clots of blood" (Qur'an 96:1).
3. In the Arabic monthly, *Al-Hikma*, published in Sana', North Yemen, Somali novelist and critic Mohamed Dahir Afrah discusses the endeavors of one of the best Somali poets of the century to compose free verse. See Afrah 1987.
4. One Sheikh Mohamed Hassan composed "The Evils of the Balwo" in Arabic. The poem starts with "Oh my God, my God, have/ mercy on us and save us from the balwo" *Somali Poetry* (151). See Andrzejewski & Lewis 1964.
5. For a sample of this type of poetry, *geeraar* was employed for battle pledges (Finnegan 1978, 101).
6. Percy B. Shelley's "A Defense of Poetry" argues on similar grounds when he states that "Poetry is indeed something divine. It is at once the centre and the circumference of knowledge ..." (Forman 1880, 136).
7. Sheikh Aqib Abdullahi Jama is one of the best-known sheikhs who uses this type of prayer for rain. He composes his prayers in poetry form:
   Accepter of penance, who are wealthy, o God
   Gather water in rivers whose beds have run dry
   (quoted in Finnegan, 113).
8. Samatar records two poems (one by each sheikh) that epitomize the diatribe between the two (Samatar 1979, 184f).

References

AFRAH, MOHAMED DAHIR. 1987. *Al-Shakhsiya Al-turathiya fi Shi'r Al-Hadrawi Al-Hikma* (February) 135: 44−50.

ANDRZEJEWSKI, B. W., and I. M. LEWIS. 1964. *Somali Poetry*. Oxford: Clarendon Press.

ANDRZEJEWSKI, B. W. et al. 1985. "Somali Literature." *Literatures in African Languages*. London: Cambridge University Press. 356.

BULHAN, HUSSEIN A. 1980. "The Captive Intelligentsia of Somali." *Horn of Africa* 3: 1−28.

BURTON, RICHARD. 1894. *First Footsteps in East Africa*. London: Tylston and Edwards. 2 vols.

FINNEGAN, RUTH. 1977. *Oral Poetry: Its Nature, Significance and Social Context*. London: Cambridge University Press.

———, ed. 1978. *Oral Poetry*. London: Penguin Books.

FORMAN, HARRY BUXTON, editor. 1880. *The Prose Work of Percy Bysshe Shelley*. London: Reeves and Turner. 7:136.

JOHNSON, JOHN W. 1974. *Heelloy, Heelleellooy: The Development of the Genre Heello in Modern Somali Poetry*. Bloomington: Indiana University.

LAURENCE, MARGARET. 1964. *A Tree for Poverty*. Nairobi: Eagle Press.

MAXWELL, KEVIN, B. 1983. *Bemba Myth and Ritual: The Impact of Literacy on an Oral Culture*. New York: Peter Land Publishing, Inc.

NELSON, KRISTINA. 1985. *The Art of Reciting the Qur'an*. Austin: University of Texas Press.

NORRMAN, RALF, and JOHN HAARBERG. 1980. *Nature and Language: A Semiotic Study of Cucurbits in Literature*. London: Routledge and Kegan Paul.

SAMATAR, SAID S. 1979. "Poetry in Somali Politics: The Case of Sayyid Mohammad Abdule Hassan." Ph.D. thesis, Northwestern University.
———. 1982. *Oral Poetry and Somali Nationalism.* London: Cambridge University Press.
SHARIFF, IBRAHIM NOOR. n.d. "Islam and Secularity in Swahili Literature: An Overview." Chapter 3, this volume.

Chapter 6

▼▼▼▼▼▼▼▼

The Two-sided Image of Women in Season of Migration to the North

SONIA GHATTAS-SOLIMAN

A study of Sudanese literature must begin by acknowledging Islam as the primary cultural force. A cultural as well as a socio-religious institution, Islam is closely connected with the ideological systems of local Muslim societies. The Shar'ia (the law of Islam), the Qur'an and the Hadiths (the teachings and sayings of the Prophet Muhammad) are the foundations of the legal system in the Sudan and in the Middle East in general. Although Islamic law originated from one source, variations in interpretation caused a great diversity in its application. Consequently, Islamic beliefs and practice vary from one Islamic society to another. And, accordingly, the condition of women is subject to their local social structure and cultural milieu.

The Qur'an provides the Muslim with a set of laws, values, and principles that constitute a standard of conduct and a way of life. It proclaims the partnership of men and women and their equal rights. It also recognizes the existence of moral, spiritual, and human values of each sex. However, local customs and male ascendancy in society have put women under men's control. I intend to explain the causes of sexual inequality illustrated by Tayeb Salih in *Season of Migration to the North* and to explore the two-sided image of the woman as "the devil" and "the victim," as well as its impact on her life.

In Islam, the virtues of women are evaluated within the institutions of family and marriage. Asked about the best woman, the Prophet gave the following definition: "The best of your women, he said, is one who rejoices when her husband looks at her, who obeys him when he commands her, and who guards preciously his memory and his possessions when he is absent" (al-Ghazali 1951–52, 62, my translation).

Although the Prophet defended the rights of woman, such a prescription has the effect of causing her condition to remain static. In many instances, if the older male members of the community create their own set of beliefs and moral values, their given interpretations and applications of the Shar'ia will overshadow the principles and the ideals of Islam. And such practice undoubtedly leads to various forms of injustice and discrimination, as illustrated in Salih's novel. I will demonstrate how, in the name of religion, the central female character was physically and verbally abused even by the closest members of her family.

Hosna Bint (daughter of) Mahmoud is a Sudanese widow and a mother of two sons who, after her husband's death, decides to devote herself to her children and not to remarry. Still in her thirties, she is young, attractive, and the object of admiration of many young men. However, she turns down all proposals: "After Mustapha [her late husband], she says, I shall go to no man" (Salih 1970, 95–96). After three years of widowhood, Bint Mahmoud is forced by her father to marry Wad Rayyes, a married man in his seventies. For two weeks, "they lived together without exchanging a word." But since Bint Mahmoud refuses to have sex with Wad Rayyes, he resorts to one last alternative: rape. In an instant of rage, she kills her alleged husband, then kills herself.

The verdict is unanimous. All members of the community agree that Bint Mahmoud was "a hussy," "a sister of the devil," and "a mad woman. [S]he wasn't worth a millieme. If it wasn't for the sake of decency she wouldn't have been worth burying, says Mahjoub, one of the local leaders, we'd have thrown her into the river or left her body out to the hawks" (133).

This judgment not only represents the opinion of the community, but it also reflects the view of the Traditions, in which the woman is portrayed as an aggressive individual whose presence is a threat to society in general, and to man in particular. The Prophet warns man about a woman's fatal attraction and its potential danger: "When the woman comes to you, it is Satan who is approaching you. If one of you sees a woman and he is attracted to her, he should hurry to his wife. With her, it will be the same as the other one" (Ghazali 1951–52, 28, my translation).

According to Imam Muslim, the Prophet was referring to:

the fascination, to the irresistible attraction to women God instilled in man's soul and he was referring to the pleasures man experiences when he looks at the woman and the pleasure he experiences with anything related to her. She resembles Satan in his irresistible power over the individual. (Muslim n.d., 30)

This is the same "attraction" which possesses Wad Rayyes and takes over his life. The more unattainable Bint Mahmoud is, the more desirable she becomes. Sexual desire so controls Wad Rayyes's life that he slips from reality. For him, marriage is a way of expressing his sexuality; "The face is that of an old man, the heart of a young one, ... Almighty God sanctioned marriage and he sanctioned divorce, says Wad Rayyes, 'Take them with liberality and separate from them with liberality'" (Salih 1970, 77–78). Obsessed with sex, he escapes into fantasy while misquoting the Qur'an: "'Women and children are the adornment of life on this earth,' said God in His noble Book" (78). In fact, the verse should read "Wealth and Children." Blinded by his desires, Wad Rayyes goes against the teachings of Islam by proclaiming that "in any case, there's no pleasure like that of fornication" (78).

Islam, like other religions, condemns adultery, fornication, and all sexual vices. It teaches Muslims to moderate their natural inclinations and to control their sexual behavior: "And come not nigh to fornication and adultery: for it is a shameful [deed] and an evil opening the road [to other evils]" (Ansari 1973, 169). On a more positive level, Islam recognizes the natural character of sex. The Qur'an does not seek to suppress sexuality or to deny a healthy and satisfied sexual relation. Quite the reverse: satisfactory sex is the reward of the just on earth and in the hereafter. However, one of the main objectives of sex in Islam is the promotion and the preservation of the family, while satisfying one's sexual desires. On that subject, the Prophet said: "And in the woman's company, this relaxation chases sadness and pacifies the heart. It is advisable for the pious souls to divert themselves by means which are religiously lawful" (Ghazali 1964, 32).

However, relaxation and diversion are not guaranteed, as Wad Rayyes discovers too late. By marrying Bint Mahmoud, he unleashes destructive and sinful forces. Pain and deception are his share of that relationship. The sad evidence of his disrupted life confirms the validity of his friend's advice and proves the wisdom of the Traditions. In the face of happiness and fulfillment stands a warning against women: "God curse all women! women are the sisters of the devils . . . .

God rest your soul, Wad Rayyes . . . . He was a man without equal . . . .
If only he'd listened to me! To end up like that," said one of his
friends (Salih 1970, 123).

In the eyes of the community, Wad Rayyes is a victim whose
only guilt was to have underestimated Bint Mahmoud's will and
intentions. Both his friends' and the Muslim vision are in conflict
with his. He acted against the advice of Mahjoub, who asked him to
stay away from Bint Mahmoud: "This woman's a bringer of bad
luck. Keep away from her" (124). But Wad Rayyes yields to obsession.
Bint Mahmoud's very being incites him to a passionate response
while she herself remains passive.

The association of women with "bad luck" and "disorder" is a
reflection of the Prophet's view, who is reported to have said, "I am
not leaving a more harmful trial for men than women" (Khan, 69).
According to the Prophet, women are the source of destruction and
evil and the incarnation of the devil, because like him, they incite
men to wrongdoing and sin. Man, the potent aggressor, is unable to
resist or control their powerful charm. The aggressor becomes the
victim.

Wad Rayyes becomes Bint Mahmoud's victim when he allows
his feelings to take over his life. His potential power over her is
undermined; her independence is reflected in her disobedience. According to the traditions, the wife should ensure sexual satisfaction
for her husband; nevertheless, it is the husband's duty to satisfy her
sexually. The wife has the right to initiate divorce for lack of sexual
satisfaction as well as for her husband's impotence. The most serious
sin Bint Mahmoud commits is refusing sex to Wad Rayyes, for
constant obedience is demanded by the traditions in matters of sex.
The Prophet said, "When the husband calls his wife to his bed and
she does not come and he spends the night offended with her, the
angels keep cursing her through the night" (Khan, 68). Commenting
on the same subject, Al-Bayhami notes that:

> The greatest thing in which obedience is imperative is intercourse,
> which is the goal of marriage. It is the most important thing the
> man asks of his wife. It is not permissible for her to refuse it except
> for a legal purpose such as menstruation, sickness and child birth.
> For if she does, she commits sin . . . and God's curse will be upon
> her. (Al-Bahaymi, 23)

In other words, man is the incarnation of power and authority.
Social order is secured only when men are in a position of command.

Male supremacy has as its objective the protection of society from women's uncontrolled actions. It also represents the triumph of reason over unreason and order over disorder. The brutality of the murder and the images of death in *Season of Migration* are an example of this male perception of disorder and destruction: "Wad Rayyes had been stabbed more than ten times in his stomach, chest, face and in between his thighs . . . . We found her [Bint Mahmoud] lying on her back with the knife plunged into her heart" (Salih 1970, 127).

The general effect of Bint Mahmoud's actions is the corrosion of the social order and the immobilization of advancement and progress. Her crime reflects not only upon her family, but upon the whole village. Mahjoub describes the incident in these words:

> If it hadn't been for this . . . this calamity . . . on the day it happened we were preparing to travel in a delegation to ask for the building of a large hospital, also for an intermediate boys' school, a primary school for children, an agricultural School, said the Head of the National Democratic Socialist Party. . . . Suddenly, he broke off and retired into his angry silence. (121)

On a more personal level, Bint Mahmoud is a source of shame, sorrow, and pain to her family. She is guilty of challenging the authority traditionally held by the father. The honor of the family has been shattered and her father humiliated. The sociological and the moral impact of her action is deeply felt in the village: "Her poor father has been confined to bed ever since that ill-fated day; he never goes out, never meets anyone, said Mahjoub, . . . [he] almost killed himself with weeping that night—he was bellowing like an ox" (129).

The association of women with evil and the devil leads necessarily to Hell where, according to the Prophet, many of the women will land. According to a Hadith in Bukhari's *Sahih*, the Prophet is reported to have said:

> I was standing at the gate of Paradise. Most of those who entered were poor people while the well-to-do were detained at the entrance (for the squaring of their account), with the exception of those who deserved hell and who had already been taken there. I stood at the gate of hell. Most of those who entered there were women. (Sabbah 1984, 108)

Is Hell what Bint Mahmoud really deserves? Her late husband, who had an unbounded confidence in her and in her good sense, left her all his possessions saying, "My wife knows all about my property and is free to do with it as she pleases. I have confidence in her judgment" (Salih 1970, 65). This opinion is shared by her children's guardian, for whom "she is the sanest woman in the village and the most beautiful" (133). Are these biased views coming from two men who loved her, or was Bint Mahmoud the victim of a society dominated by men who rationalized the actions of one of their fellow men? In fact, Bint Mahmoud had no obligations whatsoever toward Wad Rayyes since her marriage to him was invalid.

After her husband's death, Bint Mahmoud made her intentions well-known. "After Mustapha Sae'ed," She said, "I shall go to no man" (95–96). She opted for celibacy. However, the position of Islam regarding celibacy is reflected in the Traditions, in these words of the Prophet: "There is no monasticism or celibacy in Islam" (Farah, 26). It is reported in a well-known tradition that the Prophet had asked Akhtaf al-Hilali if he were married, and when he said that he was not, the Prophet replied:

> Then you are one of the followers of Satan or one of the Christian monks. If so, go to them, but if you are one of us, then do as we do, for our *sunna* (practice) includes marriage. The most wicked among you are your celibates and the most ignoble among your dead are your celibates. (Smith 1928, 165)

According to the Prophet, marriage is a means of fulfilling one's religion and a way of overcoming one's passions. In a world of temptations and the abuse of human sexuality, Islam offers Muslims the unique opportunity to integrate their sexual desires and affections into everyday life. It is not only desirable that one marries; it is commanded. "Whoever marries safeguards half of his faith, let him fear God for the second half" (Ghazali 1951–52, 9; my translation).

However, this rule does not extend to the *ayyim* or women without husbands, either widowed or divorced. For the Qur'an declared that "If, they [the widows] themselves go away, there is no blame on you for what they do of lawful deeds concerning themselves" (Ali 1973, 103). That is to say that the widow has a choice in how to conduct her life, and her choice ought to be respected. If she is satisfied with her condition, then there should be no interference from her father or her guardian. Furthermore, a tradition confirmed by Muslim advances that "*Al-ayyim* has greater right to dispose of herself than her *wali* [guardian]" (Jones 1981, 118).

Marriage in Arabic is called a *mithaq*, an agreement, or a *nikah*, a union between two parties, the husband and the wife. It cannot be contracted without the consent of the woman whether she is a virgin, a widow, or divorced. Though the rule is often contradicted in practice, forced marriages are invalid according to Islamic law. "The widow shall not be married until she is consulted, and the virgin shall not be married until her consent is obtained" (Ali 1951, 271). "Until she is consulted" means "until she has given her approval" as illustrated by Khansa's annulment, discussed below.

Although Islam protects the rights of women mainly in matters of marriage, fathers and guardians often overlook the interest and personal choices of their daughters. Reporting the circumstances of Bint Mahmoud's marriage, Mahjoub said:

> He [her father] had given Wad Rayyes a promise—and they married her off to him. Her father swore at her and beat her; he told her she'd marry him whether she liked or not .... I talked to her father, added the leader, who said he wouldn't be made a laughing-stock by people saying his daughter wouldn't listen to him. (Salih 1970, 122)

It is well-known that Islam has accorded specific rights to the widow; however, in some Sudanese societies she is still not responsible for herself. The father of the widow is still her guardian; he holds the authority and the power, and his word should never be questioned. According to the Prophet, the father owes it to himself and to his daughter to examine the qualities of her husband to ensure that she is in good hands. It is his responsibility to secure her future. However, other considerations such as wealth, prestige, or family bonds take precedence over the woman's rights. The father who makes a bad choice commits a crime against his religion and exposes himself to the wrath of God. The Prophet is reported to have said, "Marriage is enslavement; let each one of you, therefore, be careful in whose hands he places his daughter" (Ghazali 1951–52, 66; my translation).

Unfortunately, Mahmoud (Hosna's father) was not careful. He did not take seriously her threats to kill Wad Rayyes and herself if forced to marry him; furthermore, he did not abide by her wish. By forcing his daughter to marry a man she did not want, Mahmoud confirmed the general belief that the choice of a husband is still dictated by the father. "Her father had charge of her and was free to act as he thought fit," said Mahjoub★ (Salih 1970, 132). Ironically, his best choice was a married man in his seventies. In reality, by

---

★ Please note that in translation this quote gives rise to all kinds of interpretations and does not adequately reflect the emphasis in the Arabic original of the authority of the father over his daughter.

denying his daughter the right to exercise her option, Mahmoud went against the spirit and the teachings of Islam.

Since Wad Rayyes's remarriage is the source of the community misfortune, it calls for a discussion of polygamy and its application, its justification, and its validity in the Muslim world and in the Sudanese society in general and in Wad Rayyes's situation in particular. Should a man marry more than one wife? This issue has often been debated and answered by Muslim commentators. However, the ambiguity of the Qur'anic verse produced different interpretations. The Qur'an says, "And if you fear that you cannot do justice to the orphans, marry such women as seem good to you, two, three or four, but if you fear that you will not do justice, then (marry) only one or that which your right hands possess" (Ali 1973, 187).

Some educated modernists such as Mohamed Abdou and his disciples advocate an exclusive point of view. According to them, monogamy is the only way of life, and if polygamy solved some social and moral problems when they occurred, this was an exception and not a rule. The clause in the Qur'an which gives the permission to contract four concurrent marriages is immediately followed by a restriction and it reads "If you cannot treat them with perfect equality in material things as in love and affection, then, marry only one." Since dealing equitably and justly with all of them is of the utmost difficulty, Abdou argues that the recommendation favors monogamy.

On the other hand, some exponents of Islam have interpreted the same verse as granting men the permission to have more than one wife. They note that under certain circumstances in the Muslim societies of the time (such as war when women outnumbered men), polygamy provided security and protection to women. They support their argument by using the Prophet as an example. With the exception of Aishah, all his wives were widows, and he married them in order to give them a home when no one else was willing to do so.

However, this situation is not applicable to Bint Mahmoud, who had been able to take care of her children on her own for three years. Her unwillingness to remarry was reflected in her refusal of all proposals, even from men younger than Wad Rayyes. As for her financial situation, Mustapha Sae'ed left her all his possessions:

> He left six acres, three cows, an ox, two donkeys, ten goats, five sheep, thirty date palms, twenty-three acacia, sayal and harraz trees, twenty-five lemon and a like number of orange trees, nine ardebs of wheat and nine of maize and a house made up of five rooms and a diwan and also a further room of red brick ... and

nine hundred and thirty pounds, three piastres and five milliemes in cash. (Salih 1970, 56)

Clearly, Bint Mahmoud's future was financially secure; she did not need Wad Rayyes's protection.

Polygamy is also defended by Muslim conservatives as being a solution to infidelity and to social misconduct. They would argue that it puts an end to adultery and prostitution. On a more practical level, it is seen as an answer to social problems such as a wife's sickness, sterility, or frigidity. This defense of polygamy is based on humanitarian and moral principles. But it is an exception and not a rule:

> What should a man do in this condition? they ask. Should he abstain for the rest of his life, and abstinence after marriage — as they say — is harder on the soul than before marriage? Should he divorce his sick wife and abandon her or expel her from the house in order to marry another? (Smith 1980, 73)

However, it seems that the Prophet himself was aware of the harmful and negative impact of polygamy on women, when he vehemently opposed his son-in-law's remarriage: "I will not allow Ali Ibn Abi Taleb, and I repeat, I will not allow Ali to marry another woman except under the condition that he will divorce my daughter. She is part of me, and what harms her, harms me" (al-Bukhari 1868, 453:67:109).

However, Ghazali provides an unique interpretation of polygamy, showing that it is no more than a selfish way of fulfilling men's desires. He holds that polygamy provides a man with a means of satisfying and indulging his sexuality, with no regard for the woman's feelings or needs. Wad Rayyes belongs to that category of people for whom polygamy is a means of gratifying his passions. His announcement of his marriage to Bint Mahmoud provokes mixed reactions. It is received with surprise and disbelief by Bint Mahzoub:

> What's come over you? Bint Mahzoub said to Wad Rayyes. For two years now, you've contented yourself with a single wife . . . . By God, the truth is Wad Rayyes, that you're past marrying again. You're now an old man in your seventies and your grandchildren have children of their own. Aren't you ashamed of yourself having a wedding every year? . . . (Salih 1970, 77)

But it is welcomed by a male friend who says, "Wad Rayyes is springily enough, and he's got money" (86).

In reality, no one can feel the psychological impact of Wad

Rayyes's remarriage more than his eldest wife, Mabrouka, for whom it represents an attack on her self-esteem and on herself as woman and a sexual being. However, she gets even with him by denouncing his vice and by becoming Bint Mahmoud's spokesperson:

> "Good riddance!" she said at the news of his death. When some women wanted to commiserate with her she yelled, "Women, let everyone of you go about her business. Wad Rayyes dug his grave with his own hands, and Bint Mahmoud, God's blessings be upon her, paid him in full." (128)

Hurt and humiliated, Mabrouka is the only member of the community to sympathize with Bint Mahmoud and to recognize her as a fellow victim.

Season of Migration is more than the story of a woman married against her will; it is also the denunciation of hypocrisy and authority in the name of Islam. The rationalization and the selfishness of the men of the community are obvious. "Let's suppose at the very worst, she [Bint Mahmoud] marries him [Wad Rayyes]," said Mahjoub, "I don't think he'll live more than one year or two and she'll have her share of his many lands and crops" (103).

The cynicism and the rationalization in this statement reflect the spirit in which an important decision such as marriage is made by Wad Rayyes and the leaders of the community. The essence and the purpose of marriage are lost in the midst of materialistic considerations. Furthermore, the teachings of Islam in reference to the woman's consent are overridden. The world Bint Mahmoud lives in is a hard place where understanding, compassion, and righteousness are second to pride and authority. Yet the sober realism of the story conveys the authenticity of its female protagonist. Bint Mahmoud is the victim of a father who is afraid of being ridiculed and of a man who is unable to control his sexual desires. Wad Rayyes insists on marrying Bint Mahmoud against her wishes. For him, it is accepted custom to marry a woman without her consent, a factor of secondary consideration. As for the other members of the community, her father's consent and not hers is all that is necessary:

> I shall marry no one but her, he said. She'll accept me whether she likes or not. ... You're not her father or her brother or the person responsible for her. She'll marry me whatever you or she says or does. Her father's agreed and so have her brothers. This nonsense you learn at school won't wash with us here. In this village, the men are guardians of the women. (97–98)

Wad Rayyes disregards the law and the Traditions for his own ends; he is aware that the marriage is not valid without Bint Mahmoud's consent, for, according to the Traditions, she would have the right to repudiate him, if she had been forced into an unwanted union.

On that subject, Khansa' reported that: "Her father gave her away in marriage and she was a thayyib [word which refers to both a divorcee and a widow] and she did not like it. So, she came to the Messenger of Allah and he annulled her marriage" (Ali 1951, 272).

If Bint Mahmoud is a victim *des autres*, as Sartre would say, Wad Rayyes is a victim of his own self-absorption and self-destructiveness. Imam Ghazali emphasizes the importance of self-control in these words: "If the desire of the flesh dominates the individual and is not controlled by the fear of God, it leads men to commit destructive acts" (Ghazali n.d., 28).

In Islam, references to discipline and self-control are numerous. If sexual desire in itself is not reprehensible, excessive desire is. Over-indulgence has a bearing on the individual; it overcomes reasoning and judgment and leads its possessor to perdition. According to Al-Ghazali, desire is an element which should yield to reason and to the Shari'a. Wad Rayyes, however, seeks the pleasure of the flesh, regardless of its harmful consequences. Since the Shari'a allows for sexual gratification with one's wife, Wad Rayyes opts for polygamy in the hope of legally satisfying his sexual urge, but according to Mahjoub, he was duped:

> For two weeks they remained together without exchanging a word .... He was in an indescribable state like a madman. He complained to all and sundry, saying how could there be in his house a woman he'd married according the laws of God and His Prophet and how could there not be between them the normal relationship of man and wife. (122)

Wad Rayyes justifies his position by using the Prophet's views on obedience; however, he fails to see the incoherence of his marriage and the precariousness of his situation. His failure to distinguish between the legal, moral, and religious implications of a mutual agreement and a forced marriage leads him to a brutal act that costs him his life:

> Wad Rayyes was as naked as the day he was born; Bint Mahmoud too was naked apart from her torn underclothes. The red straw was swimming in blood. I raised the lamp, said Bint Majzoub, and I saw that every inch of Bint Mahmoud's body was covered in bites

and scratches — her stomach, thighs, and neck .... The nipple of one breast had been bitten through and blood pored down from her lower lip. (127)

The violence and the cruelty of these images testify to the evil and the bestial nature of Wad Rayyes. Unable to control his sexual urge, he personifies the individuals who "are regarded by Al-Ghazali as having gone astray. [And] ignorant of the purpose of sexual desire, they surpass the lower animals in uncontrollable lust" (Abul Quasem 1975, 111). In consequence, Wad Rayyes received his punishment at the hands of his victim.

Salih's *Season of Migration to the North* is an analysis of Islamic teachings in reference to human sexuality, marriage, and polygamy. Behind the conciliatory tone, one detects a strong attack on conservative practices that conflict with the spirit of Islam. All manifestations of abuse — from excessive paternal authority to man's self-indulgence — are at the expense of woman and are denounced and condemned. In certain cases, traditional values do no more than perpetuate conditions that favor men. Salih emphasizes the importance of marriage as a central institution and as a guarantor of women's rights. For unless these ideals are upheld, woman will remain either the devil or the victim.

References

ABUL QUASEM, MUHAMMAD. 1975. *The Ethics of Al-Ghazali: A Composite Ethics in Islam.* Selangor, Malaysia: Published by the author.

ALI, MUHAMMAD MULANNA. 1951. Trans. *A Manual of Hadith.* Lahore: Anjuman Ishaat Islam.

———. 1973. Trans. *The Holy Qur'an.* Lahore: Ahmadiya Anjuman Ishaat Islam.

ANSARI, MUHAMMAD FAZL-UR-RAHMAN. 1973. *The Qur'anic Foundations and Structure of Muslim Society.* Vol. 2. Karachi: Zubair Printing Press.

AL-BAHAYMI, MOHAMMAD BIN SALIM. 1973. *Ustadh al-Mar'ah.* Cairo: Dar al Ma'arif.

AL-BUKHARI, ABU ABDALLAH MUHAMMAD IBN ISMAIL. 1868. *Kitab al-Jami' as-Sahih.* Leyden: Ludolf Krehl.

AL-GHAZALI, BU HAMID. n.d. *Ih'ya' Ulum al-Din.* Cairo: al-Mahtaba al-Tijariya al-Kubra.

———. 1951–52. *Ghazali: Le Liyre des bons usages en matière de mariage.* Trans. L. Bercher and G.H. Bousquet. Paris: Maisonneuve.

———. 1984. *Kitab Adab al-Nikah* (twelfth book of *Ih'ya' Ulum al-Din*). Trans. Farah, Madelain. *Marriage and Sexuality in Islam.* Salt Lake City: University of Utah Press.

———. 1964. *The Revivification of Religious Sciences.* Vol. II, Cairo: Dar al-Ma'arif.

HALL, MARJORIE, and BAKHITA AMIN. ISMAIL. 1981. *Sisters under the Sun: The Story of Sudanese Women.* London: Longman.

JONES, V. R. and BEVAN. 1981. *Woman in Islam.* Westport, Conn.: Hyperion Press.

MERNISSI, FATIMA. 1975. *Beyond the Veil: Male-Female Dynamics in a Modern Muslim Society.* Cambridge, Mass: Schenkman Publishing Company Inc.

MUSLIM, ABU-AL-HASAN. n.d. *al-Jami' as-Sahih.* Vol. III, Book of Marriage. Beirut: al-Maktab al-Tijari lil Tab'a wa Nash.

NAWAWI, IMAM. 1975. *Riyadh as-Salihin.* Trans. Muhammad Zafrulla Khan. *Gardens of the Righteous.* London: Curzon Press Ltd.

SABBAH, FATNA A. *Woman in the Muslim Unconscious.* 1984. New York: Pergamon.

SALIH, TAYEB. 1970. *Season of Migration to the North.* (2nd ed.) Trans. Denys Johnson-Davis. Malta: St. Paul Ltd.

AL-SHAHI, AHMED. 1986. *Themes for the Northern Sudan.* London: Ithaca Press.

SMITH, JANE I., ed. 1980. *Women in Contemporary Muslim Societies.* Cranbury, N.J.: Associated Press Inc.

SMITH, MARGARET. 1928. *Rabi'a the Mystic and Her Fellow Saints in Islam.* Cambridge: Cambridge University Press.

AL-SUHRAWARDY, ABDULLAH al-MAMUN. 1980. *The Sayings of Muhammad.* New York: Books for Libraries.

Part III

WEST AFRICA

Chapter 7

▼▼▼▼▼▼▼

An Approach to Islam in West African History

DAVID ROBINSON

In Yambo Ouologuem's *Bound to Violence*, Islam is an appendage to the state that helps to justify the slave-raiding, the harems, and the court's exploitation of the countryside and the commoner population. In Sembène's films, Islam becomes the basis whereby marabouts exploit the naïveté of children and their parents in the contemporary urban situation or destroy the legitimacy of a precolonial kingdom, as in *Ceddo*. For Camara Laye in *Dark Child*, on the other hand, Islam is part of the religious and social practice of Mandinka childhood, harmoniously integrated into the rhythm of the forge, farming, and initiation in Kouroussa. For Cheikh Hamidou Kane, Islam also has a positive connotation but in a sharper focus: it is, in the incarnation of Thierno, the soul of the society and the nation of the Diallobe under a siege of Westernization.

All of these images, and indeed many more, have their correspondence in the history of Islam in West Africa, or, to put it more accurately, the history of Muslims and Muslim societies in West Africa (see Hunwick, forthcoming). A sixteenth-century Timbuktu viewed by an author of Dogon background like Ouologuem, raised in colonial Soudan, is bound to differ from the portrayal of a native son of Futa Toro, like Kane, preoccupied with the cultural confrontation of an Islamic society and the French school.

These different Islamic realities — and their validity — have not been appreciated in the historical literature. Indeed, the literature on Islam in West Africa has three features that distort the appreciation of the variety of Islamic practice and belief. First, the literature has been dominated by an *orientalist* approach (see Triaud 1987),[1] in which philological and theological training are paramount. The commentator typically knows Arabic in order to read the relevant indigenous literature, and he should understand Islamic religious and doctrinal history. His task, as he moves from the center of the Islamic world to a periphery such as West Africa, is to discern and recount the spread of Islam and especially of Islamic orthodoxy, to the point where the peripheral region can be classed as a *dar al-Islam* ("the abode of Islam"). Once this point is reached—let us say in the eighteenth or nineteenth centuries for much of the West African savanna—the interest diminishes. This is reflected in the very underdeveloped history of Islam in the colonial period, in contrast to the accounts for precolonial times (see Robinson 1985a; Robinson 1985b, intro. and Ch. 9; Stewart 1986).

Second, the commentators strengthen the orientalist bias still further by limiting themselves to Arabic literature and traditions and especially to the legitimating documents of those who share their belief that the essential story is the progression of Islam and Islamic orthodoxy. The best case in point is the primary documentation created by the founders of the Sokoto Caliphate of Northern Nigeria and the secondary reinforcement created in the last thirty years by Islamicists on the basis of the primary material. The result is a very strong *received tradition* which makes it more difficult to reconstruct the history of religious practice in late eighteenth and early nineteenth-century Hausaland (e.g., Robinson 1985b, Ch. 2; Stewart and Adeleye 1987).

The third distortion comes from the colonial Islamicist tradition. The French and British colonial regimes became preoccupied in the early twentieth century with the control of Islamic societies and their leaders. To this end they trained and hired their own orientalists, at the same time and with the same intentions as they hired anthropologists to study the "pagan" and "stateless" societies of other regions. In both cases they worked from a kind of religious geography of West Africa, and in both cases their desire was to conserve and control. In the case of Islamic societies, which were more related to precolonial state-building traditions and military organizations, and which related to the larger Islamic world through the pilgrimage and a common doctrinal heritage, the colonial authorities watched closely at the territorial level but had little preoccupation with day-to-day practice. The best-known colonial Islamicist was Paul Marty, brought in from Tunisia by the Government-General of French West Africa in the 1910s to synthesize material that had been collected for some years on Islamic schools and marabouts (see Harrison 1988, Robinson 1988b, Robinson 1988a, Christelow 1987).

At the same time it is important to use the tools and concepts the historical literature provides. Islamic communities in West Africa can be divided between the more orthodox and the less orthodox, or between the more learned and the less learned; sometimes this division resulted in conflict, sometimes it led to war. The distinctions between the Islam practiced in the commercial centers and the rural areas, or between the Islam of the courts and that of the hinterlands of states, were significant. One has only to look at the attitudes in the early nineteenth century of Seku Amadu of Masina towards Jenne, or of Usman dan Fodio towards the Hausa capitals, to see one version of this division. Similarly, the distinction between militant and quietistic traditions in West African Islam has validity — witness the close association of many Fulbe scholarly communities with the jihad in the nineteenth century, at the same time that the Jakhanke network was holding just as firmly to a rejection of military means. But these divisions should not be reified in an ethnic hierarchy of West African Islam, as John Ralph Willis has done in the introduction to Volume 1 of the *Studies in the History of West African Islam* (1979).[3]

There is heuristic value in the three-level formula that many commentators have used for West African history, and which Fisher most recently formulated as quarantine, court, and reform (Fisher 1973, Horton 1971, Horton 1975). According to this perspective, Islam was initially practiced by small minorities primarily concerned with long-distance trade. The classical case of this is expressed in the account by the geographer al-Bakri of the twin cities of ancient Ghana in the eleventh century: the "pagan" capital and the Muslim trading enclave (see Levtzion 1973, Levtzion 1968). Islam then spread to the political capitals and ruling classes, and became a kind of imperial religion. The "classical" case here is usually the Empire of Mali, described by Ibn Battuta in the mid-fourteenth century (see Levtzion 1973).[4] Finally, in the third stage which was reached in the eighteenth and nineteenth centuries, Islam became the practice of rural masses, whether through the leadership of quietistic scholars or by the actions of more coercive leaders such as Uthman dan Fodio in Hausaland, who used the vehicle of jihad. Sufi brotherhoods, first the Qadiriyya and then the Tijaniyya, were vital to both the more quietistic and militant aspects of this stage. This scheme is useful in interpreting the broad outlines of change in practice. But it often does not work in the particular histories of societies, and it tends to equate Islamic development with state formation and centralization.

Islam and Society in the 18th and 19th Centuries

In the remainder of this paper I wish to focus on the period in which many West Africans began to think of their region — and I refer to the savanna (or Western and Central Sudan) and not the whole of West Africa — as part of the *dar al-Islam*. One could put this period in the sixteenth and seventeenth centuries, the period that Ouologuem treats and the time when Ahmed Baba, the renowned Timbuktu scholar, provided a kind of religious geography of Muslim and non-Muslim peoples, in an effort to explain situations in which enslavement and the slave trade were permitted and not permitted for Muslim elites (Hunwick 1985, Zouber 1977). However, the *dar al-Islam* of the sixteenth century reflects a rather limited time and space, specifically the structure established in the Songhay empire and oriented towards the central trans-Saharan trade from the Niger Buckle area.

A more permanent and widespread consciousness of Islamic identity came in the eighteenth and nineteenth centuries, through the quietistic and militant modes referred to above and connected to the third stage of the paradigm. The first pattern, the establishment of important networks that combined Sufi orders, scholarship, and long-distance trade, was launched principally by the great Kunta leader, Sidi al-Mukhtar, based in Arawan to the north of Timbuktu. Sidi al-Mukhtar trained a whole generation of leaders who fanned out into different regions of West Africa and in turn trained their own disciples (Brenner 1988, Stewart 1976b, Willis 1969). The heritage of Sidi al-Mukhtar was deep and broad; one has only to look at the number of his works that can be found in the main Arabic libraries of West Africa — in Northern Nigeria, southern Mauritania, or the Segu library which was transferred to Paris in the late nineteenth century (see Ghali 1985).

One of Sidi al-Mukhtar's most apt pupils was Sidiyya al-Kabir, who returned to southern Mauritania, established his own school and library at Butilimit, and then trained a new generation of learned Muslims who played important roles in the dissemination of Islam in the Western Sudan (Stewart 1973). These included persons who undertook reform, such as Cerno Brahim Kan of Magama in eastern Futa in the 1860s, or Cerno Mamadu Juhe, who created the Hubbu movement as an alternative to the Islamic regime of Futa Jalon in the

1850s, but it also included persons who became pillars of the status quo, such as Bokar Sada, *Almamy* of Bundu from 1855 to 1885, or the Wan of Mbumba in central Futa Toro (Robinson 1975a, Person 1987, Botte 1988).

This period was probably also the time when systems of Islamic instruction in indigenous languages were elaborated, in part by scholars associated with the same networks. Thanks to the work of Louis Brenner, we can now trace one such system, an esoteric form of instruction among the Fulbe, back to the eighteenth century (Brenner 1983, 79–86; Brenner 1985).[5]

The second instrument for the emergence of the *dar al-Islam* was the jihad. Beginning in the early eighteenth century with a movement in Futa Jalon, a series of Muslim communities organized to throw off what they considered pagan or nominal Muslim rule and establish Islam as the basis for governing society. In each case they lived on the peripheries of the pre-existing states, in each case they experienced the power of the state as exploitation rather than protection. The leadership and most of the constituency of these movements came from sedentary Fulbe. The result, by the mid-nineteenth century, was a virtual identification of *jihad* and "militant Islam" with the Fulbe community (see Robinson 1985b, Ch. 2).

The earliest movement occurred in Futa Jalon and required half a century to consolidate (ca. 1725–1780). The leaders created an Islamic state called the *imamate* or Almamate. It was a system that sought to balance central and regional power, to coordinate the roles of political, commercial, and scholarly leaders, to reinforce the control of a ruling class over a vast array of slave and serf producers, and to maintain a long-distance trading network and a highly influential educational system. Muslims from a large area of the Western Sudan and the Upper Guinea Coast went to Futa Jalon to study and then returned, in the manner of the pupils of Sidiyya al-Kabir, to their own home-lands to teach, preach, and mediate. Futa Jalon played a considerable role in the spread and cultivation of Islam in Sierra Leone, in the Kankan region of Camara Laye, and many other areas.

The reform movement of Futa Toro began in the late eighteenth century and achieved a temporary resolution more quickly than its predecessor in Futa Jalon. It then disintegrated under the impetus of internal and external opposition in the early nineteenth century. Almamy Abdul Kader, the first to institutionalize the regime, was assassinated in 1807, and with him died the hope of creating a strong central regime adhering to an Islamic code of conduct. However,

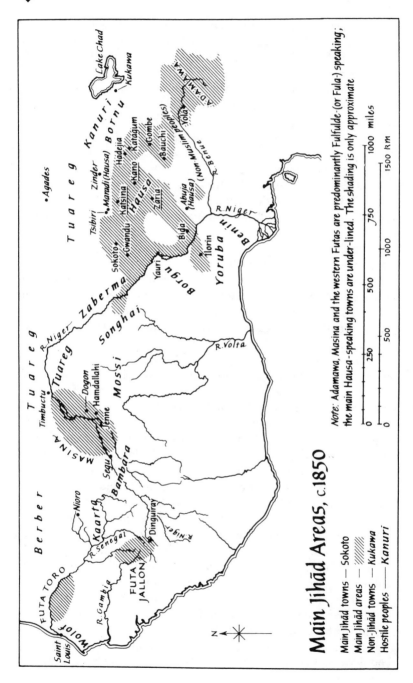

Main Jihād Areas, c.1850

Main Jihād towns — Sokoto
Main Jihād areas —
Non-Jihād towns — Kukawa
Hostile peoples —— Kanuri

Note: Adamawa, Masina and the western Futas are predominantly Fulfulde- (or Fula-) speaking; the main Hausa-speaking towns are under-lined. The shading is only approximate

0   250   500   750   1000   miles
0   500   1000   1500   km

Lake Chad

Agades

Kukawa

Timbuctu
Nioro
Dogon
Hamdallahi
Jenne
Segu
Dinguiray

Tsibiri
Zinder
Maradi (Hausa)
Katsina
Gwandu
Sokoto
Kano
Katagum
Hadejia
Gombe
Bauchi
Yola
Zaria
Abuja (Hausa)
Biga
Ilorin
Yauri

Saint Louis

Berber
Tuareg
Tuareg
Tuareg
Kanuri
Bornu
Hausa
Zaberma
Songhai
Mossi
Bambara
Kaarta
Masina
FUTA JALLON
FUTA TORO
Wolof
Borgu
Yoruba
Benin
Adamawa
(Non Muslim peoples)

R.Niger
R.Niger
R.Niger
R.Niger
R.Benue
R.Volta
R.Senegal
R.Gambia

many of the changes that he and his generation had instituted, especially the mosques and schools at the village level, remained and nurtured a strong Islamic identity throughout the middle valley of the Senegal River. It is this Islamic culture, and the nostalgia for an earlier day, which we see reflected in Kane's story of Thierno and Samba Diallo. Futa Toro, like Futa Jalon, had a considerable impact on the wider region, less through its example than through its native sons who campaigned for Islam abroad: al-Hajj Umar in western Mali, Ma Ba in the lower part of the peanut basin, and Amadu Madiyu in Jolof and Cayor (Robinson 1975b).[6]

The third Fulbe reform movement occurred at a slightly later time (ca. 1804–1812) in Hausaland. Usman dan Fodio, his brother Abdullah, and his son Muhammad Bello became the three key leaders of a movement that began in one corner of the state of Gobir and then expanded to the rest of Hausaland and beyond under the leadership of Uthman's followers carrying the banner of jihad. The triumvirate gave great attention to the justification and generalization of their actions, particularly under the impetus of a challenge from al-Kanemi, a Bornu-based scholar who contested the legitimacy of their jihad. The result was a literary effort that matched and in some ways surpassed that of Sidi al-Mukhtar, and that provided a resource and model for West African scholars who wished to pursue the "militant Islamic line" and establish Islam as the basis of governance in their own societies. One needs only look at the Sokoto community's works in West African libraries to form an idea of the breadth and depth of their contribution (see Ghali 1985, Mahibou and Triaud 1984).

The fourth movement in the series began as an offshoot of the Sokoto effort (Robinson 1985b, Chs. 8 and 9; Stewart 1976a). Seku Amadu, a Fulbe cleric based in a rural area near the old city of Jenne, sought a banner of jihad from Sokoto in about 1816. A few years later Seku Amadu established his own independent regime, built a new capital called Hamdullahi, and established his own Caliphate. He successfully altered most editions of the *Ta'rikh al-Fattash*, the chronicle written in Timbuktu in the seventeenth century, to provide a prophecy of his rule and to link his efforts to the reign of Askia Muhammad, the celebrated Songhay emperor (see Levtzion 1971). In the 1820s he consolidated the most thorough-going Islamic regime in West Africa: Fulbe nomads were forced to settle on the land and regularize the transhumance of their herds, the conduct of the economy was closely regulated, and the lives of cities like Jenne closely controlled. The Hamdullahi experiment was compromised by changes under Seku's grandson in the 1850s, and then came to an end when al-Hajj Umar, the *mujahid* from Futa Toro, conquered Hamdullahi in 1862.

The conquest provoked a Masinanke revolt, the decimation of most of the Umarian army and a painful civil war of twenty-five years duration in the Middle Niger. The struggle did great damage to Muslim Fulbe communities, the understanding of the Islamic state, and the commitment to *jihad*, and it informs the life and quest of another major contemporary literary figure, Amadou Hampâté Bâ, a descendant of both Umarian and Masinanke Fulbe families. Bâ has apparently completed the second volume of his *Empire du Macina*, but he will not publish it in his lifetime, because it deals with the epochal conflict between the two groups of Muslim Fulbe reformers. His divided background, and his reservations about the conflict, undoubtedly led him to the teaching of Tierno Bokar, an "Umarian" at Bandiagara who shared these reservations and was critical of the military jihad and the attitudes of superiority which Fulbe — Masinanke and Umarian alike — showed towards the Habe peoples such as the Dogon. Bâ has become the sole interpreter of Tierno Bokar's teaching, Sufism and spirituality, on the basis of the notes which he took at Bokar's feet in the 1930s (Bâ and Daget 1955, Bâ and Cardaire 1957, Bâ 1980, Brenner 1984).[7]

Al-Hajj Umar (ca. 1796−1864) put an end not only to the Hamdullahi experiment but also to the phase of successful internal Muslim Fulbe movements. His "imperial" jihad (1852−1864) marked a significant departure from the four "revolutionary" jihads that preceded it (Robinson 1985b, 365−70). He brought striking new credentials to Islamic politics in West Africa: he had made the pilgrimage to Mecca and he had been appointed as the *khalifa* or chief agent for the dissemination of the Tijaniyya order. The Tijaniyya made strong claims as a superior revelation and brotherhood, and it sharpened the competition for allegiance to Sufi orders in the Western and Central Sudan (Abun-Nasr 1965). Umar had personal links with each of the four preceding Fulbe movements and states. He grew up in Futa Toro, received an important part of his education in Futa Jalon, and launced his jihad there in 1852; he learned enormously from almost a decade of experience at the court of Sokoto in the 1830s, and witnessed the successes and failures of the radical Masina regime — well before embarking on the perilous conquest of that regime in 1862. He certainly saw himself as going beyond the achievements of the two Futas, and extending the experience of the Uthmanian regime.

Indeed, I would argue that in the early 1860s Umar conceived of his state, headed administratively by his son Amadu, as the counterpart in the Western Sudan to the Sokoto regime in the Central Sudan. The four preceding movements had created a widely held assumption that the savanna region was or was at least destined soon to become a *dar al-Islam* — to pass, in a sense, from peripheral to central status. The highest priority for the militant Muslim leader was the destruction of paganism, and especially those ruling dynasties who had gone against the tide of West African history by establishing "pagan" states and priesthoods in the eighteenth and nineteenth centuries. Umar took as his special obligation the destruction of the Mandinka state of Tamba, and the Bambara courts of Karta and Segu, which served as a stigma on the body of West African Islam. Much of the excitement among West and North African Muslims at the conquest of Segu in 1861 stemmed from the destruction of this capital of "paganism," and much of the respect Umar's son Amadu enjoyed during his reign in the late nineteenth century stemmed from the fact that he had built a capital of Islam on the cinders of the "pagan" center (Robinson and Hanson forthcoming). Sokoto, the capital of militant Islam in the Central Sudan, was a new city, which began as a military camp. Segu, the capital of militant Islam in the Western Sudan, was a transformed "pagan" site, whose national shrines had been publicly destroyed and where new Islamic palaces had been constructed (Robinson 1985b, Chs. 7 and 9).[8]

I would also argue that the Umarian conquest of Masina, which pitted Muslim Fulbe against Muslim Fulbe, caused great dissension within the growing *dar al-Islam* of West Africa, and it helped to undermine the legitimacy of jihad as an instrument of the extension of Islam. Umar did not intend to fight against Hamdullahi. His first target was Tamba, his second was Nioro, the capital of Karta, and his final goal was to be Segu, the capital of "paganism" on the Middle Niger. It was only the growing opposition of Amadu III at Hamdullahi, and the growing support of Amadu III for the Segu regime, that led Umar to formulate his justification, the *Bayan* (Mahibou and Triaud 1984), and ultimately to embark on a military solution. The *Bayan* was a well argued and thoroughly documented work, drawing on the experience of Sokoto and a classical Islamic tradition of dealing with apostasy from Islam, but it is unlikely that it persuaded many outside the Umarian camp of the legitimacy of the 1862 campaign. It created the conditions for massive revolt in 1863, and led the Kunta leader Ahmed al-Bekkay, successor to the tradition of Sidi al-Mukhtar, to abandon the lineage's traditional opposition to military operations and declare "*jihad* against *jihad*" in 1863. The rich Middle Delta was the scene of continuous conflict until the 1890s, between Kunta, Masinanke, and Umarian forces. The Umarians, ironically, were now constituted mainly by Habe and "stateless" Fulbe who had never been part of a Muslim state tradition (Robinson 1985b, Ch. 8).

This last Umarian campaign helped to cheapen the meaning of jihad in the Middle Delta and the Western Sudan. In the late nineteenth century jihad became any campaign against any foe for any reason. By this time the four Fulbe Muslim states routinely used jihad to describe any campaign, often directed at the smaller scale and more vulnerable societies, for purposes of securing slaves for production or exchange. At about this time Samori and other leaders were formulating their drive to power in terms of jihad in the southern Mandinka marchlands, while critics of the decline of Islam were trying to purify the faith by creating isolated communities of the faithful on the margins of the Muslim states (Person 1968–75, Ghali 1985, Mahibu and Triaud 1984).

Jihad in the late nineteenth century was no longer the monopoly of Fulbe scholars and communities, but the result was not the extension of the faith so much as the fragmentation of societies and the growth of violence. While the Central Sudan continued to function in a sense as one economic system with one recognized Islamic leadership, centered at Sokoto, the Western Sudan disintegrated into competing factions with no widely recognized Islamic leadership. The two most powerful and prestigious Muslim authorities, Umar's son Amadu and Samori, were often at war with each other and they did little to establish Islamic institutions (Oloruntimehin 1970).[9]

I would consequently argue that the savanna region had passed into the *dar al-Islam* by the late nineteenth century, at least in terms of the consciousness of many and perhaps a majority of its inhabitants, but that the two main parts of the region were poised very differently on the eve of European conquest and colonial rule. The Sokoto caliphate controlled and coordinated a significant portion of the Central Sudan, in political, economic, and religious terms. It provided a significant security for the practice and study of Islam, for the dispensing of justice and the arbitration of conflicts, and it served as haven and beacon for more disrupted areas to the north and east (Adeleye 1966).

The Western Sudan had no such central clearing house (see

Kanya-Forstner 1969). The older Kunta network had lost much of its luster in the cauldron of Masina, while the Jakhanke were divided over the jihad of Mamadu Lamin Drame (d. 1887). The Umarians still dominated the Tijaniyya Sufi affiliation, but they could not extend it much beyond the confines of the Umarian Fulbe community—given the sharpened ethnic-religious correlations of the time and place (see Marty 1921).[10] The Sidiyya maintained their network of relations through Senegambia, and the Fadhiliyya—especially under Saad Bu—developed a competing system in the same area, where potential adherents could choose Qadiriyya, Tijaniyya, or indeed other Sufi affiliations along with their basic Islamic education (see Robinson 1987, Robinson 1988). But there was no single umbrella under which the different traditions of Islamic education, Sufi affiliation, and the administration of justice could be practiced. The Umarian experiment in the destruction of "paganism" had not led to the establishment of an Islamic society.

Islam and Society in the Twentieth Century

The British conquest of the centerpiece of the Central Sudan led to the creation of a Native Authority system built around the emirates of the caliphate. The Caliph himself was reduced to the position of an emir of Sokoto, but he still enjoyed enormous prestige within Northern Nigeria: witness the influence of the Sardauna of Sokoto Ahmadu Bello, a member of the caliphal family, until his assassination in 1966. The British reinforced the police and judicial authority of the emirs, and the practice of Islamic law in many spheres of the society and economy. It is the continuity with the practice of Islamic law by the nineteenth-century Caliphate that gives such strength to the demands for the full implementation of the Sharia in Nigeria today (see Christelow 1987, Paden 1973).

The French, who conquered the peripheries of the Central Sudan and virtually all of the Western Sudan, faced a much stronger opposition from the pragmatic state of Samori than from the more self-consciously Muslim authorities such as the two Futas or Amadu's dwindling territories at Segu and Nioro (see Kanya-Forstner 1969, Hanson 1989). The French, often saddled with an anti-Islamic label, in fact took advantage of the fragmentation of the Western Sudan, opposed proponents of the Islamic state, and supported the anti-jihadic orientation favored by groups like the Sidiyya and Saad Bu. They avoided sending missionaries into areas that were demarcated as Muslim in the religious ethnography of the time, and they did

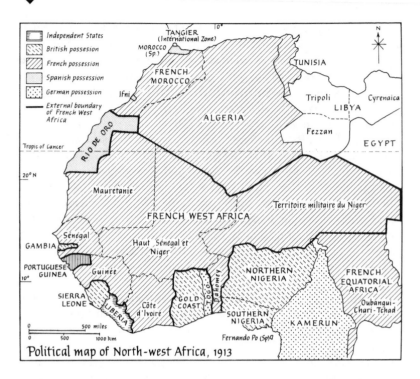

Political map of North-west Africa, 1913

formulate arrangements for non-intervention in Islamic family law; in this they practiced the same pattern as the British in Northern Nigeria. Indeed, they created a kind of indirect rule in the peanut basin of Senegal that rivalled the famed British version; the leadership of the Murid brotherhood, of the Tijaniyya of Malik Sy and of Abdullay Niass — differentiated clearly in colonial Senegal from the Umarian Tijaniyya — worked closely with the regime from the time of the First World War (Robinson 1988b, Robinson 1987a). What distinguishes the French regime most clearly from the British is the clearly enunciated secular state, the variety of arrangements with Muslim societies, and especially the rearrangement of space in the territories that became the Federation of French West Africa.

The new colonial space corresponded very little to the configurations of precolonial times. To some extent precolonial space had been organized along north-south lines, to take advantage of the differential potential of desert, sahel, savanna, woodland, and forest. The centerpiece of this sytem was the trans-Saharan trade, which took slaves, gold, and other products north and brought salt, weapons, and other goods south. Many of the important scholarly families built their prestige and wealth on this commerce and their ability to arbitrate disputes connected with it — the Kunta of Arawan, Timbuktu, and the Hodh, and the Sidiyya and Fadhiliyya in today's Mauritania. Under the impact of the Atlantic trade, this north-south orientation was considerably weakened, but it still functioned and controlled the mind-set and career patterns of many people in the interior zones of the Western Sudan (see Newbury 1966).

The European conquest of Africa, and especially the French conquest of North and West Africa, dramatically altered the equation. The French conceived of and practiced their empire in compartments — beginning with the Maghreb, on the one hand, and French West Africa on the other. Algeria functioned under the Ministry of War, Morocco and Tunisia under the Ministry of Foreign Affairs and subsequently the Colonial Office. French West Africa had a variety of civilian and military regimes until the Government-General took over in Dakar in the early twentieth century. Even then the configurations changed in the area of Haut-Senegal-Niger, which included the territories of today's Mali, Burkina Faso, and Niger. The trans-Saharan trade did not survive such a conquest and compartmentalization, albeit under the same imperial authority. The Sahara became the southern hinterland of the Maghreb colonies and the northern hinterland of French West Africa (see Kanya-Forstner 1960, Anene 1969).

In Senegal, under the impact of growing peanut cultivation in the late nineteenth century, the center of gravity shifted to the west central regions inhabited by the Wolof and Serer, redefined in the twentieth century as the peanut basin. The older focus had been the river region, which was the center of grain and gum production and the main avenue to the interior, and which was dominated by the Tokolor, Fulbe, and Soninke (Moitt 1984, Searing 1985). The middle valley of the river was also the site of Senegal's most ambitious experiment in creating an Islamic society — Futa Toro, or the Diallobe country of *Ambiguous Adventure*. The northern bank of the river became part of Mauritania, a territory which the French defined as a predominantly *beydane* or "white" territory — the consequences of which are evident today. The current rhetoric about re-establishing the centrality of the river zone to solve the economic problems of Senegal and Mauritania only underscores the decisiveness of the previous change.

In the mid-nineteenth century the area of Mali was still organized in north-south terms. The Umarian conquest, in contrast, created a strong west-east orientation, to obtain the sources of recruits and weapons necessary to sustain control over the Bambana (Bambara) and other indigenous populations. The French reinforced the west-east pattern. They established their capital in the south at Bamako and tied it by rail to Senegal (Roberts 1987). They projected a vast development called the Office du Niger, but they were never able to realize the enormous potential of the Middle Niger Delta, the old hub of the region. Timbuktu was even more peripheral to colonial Soudan, isolated from the southern center of gravity and cut off from its natural hinterland in the desert, Niger, and Upper Volta. These traditional Islamic centers in the northern areas became quite marginal to the new colonial society.

The reconfiguration of space also holds true for the other territories of French West Africa. Futa Jalon and to a lesser extent the Mandinka zone of Kankan had dominated the economy and society of the zone that became colonial Guinea. The new French territory featured Conakry and the coast, while the rail linked Conakry to the east but bypassed the populous Futa. Again the more important zone for the cultivation and dissemination of Islam was marginalized in the new colonial space (Georg 1986). In Ivory Coast the result was the same: Abidjan and the coast were emphasized, to the neglect of the areas like Kong and Odienne in the north, where Samori's regime had operated and where Muslim merchants and scholars had long plied their trade. Niger was organized around Niamey in the southwest, and made tributary to Upper Volta and Ivory Coast; its more natural ties were to the north, along the Niger River and up into the desert, and to the south and the cities of northern Nigeria.

The reorientation of space led to a decline in rewards for traditional Islamic scholarship. It was not that the French sought to undermine an Islamic system, but that they took the fragmented societies they had conquered and grouped them in new configurations. Most of the surviving institutions of the Islamic states of Futa Toro, Futa Jalon, and the Umarian domains of colonial Soudan disappeared. Koranic schools and Islamic higher education continued to train students, but the jobs their graduates might have filled within the precolonial states and economy, or in connection with trans-Saharan commerce, simply ceased to exist. Access to the positions within the new colonial bureaucracy and economy was acquired in a different way, through the limited but influential French educational system (see Kelly 1983, Kelly 1984, Robinson 1988b).

The sequence of Koranic followed by French education developed rather quickly and has become standard in francophone West Africa. The part that was left out, and soon forgotten, was Islamic higher education, the kind of training that the Samba Diallos of the twentieth century would have received had they not been pulled out of the Islamic system and sent to the French school. Most of the Muslim francophone authors have different degrees of the Koranic experience coupled with extensive French education. For them, as for many West Africans, the Koranic educational experience was part of a crucial Islamic socialization, and it is often remembered with nostalgia, but it did not and was never intended to lead to what we might call an Islamic profession — something that might very well have been the case a century before.

This is not intended to deny the creation of colonial Islamic institutions and a kind of colonial Islamic clergy. The practice of Islamic family law in several areas required judges and assessors trained in Islamic law, and this was provided in turn by a number of *medersas*, or Franco-Arabic schools, established both in the old pre-colonial centers, such as Jenne and Timbuktu, and the colonial centers like St. Louis, in the early twentieth century. Some of the teachers in the *medersas* came from North Africa, but others were recruited from local families with traditions of Islamic scholarship (see Marty 1921, Marty 1917).

The pilgrimage to Mecca was allowed most of the time, especially after the dismantling of the Ottoman state and the "Ottoman menace" in the course of World War I, and it even became an important instrument of colonial Islamic policy (see Robinson 1988b, Robinson 1987b). The pilgrimage allowed West African Muslims to broaden their horizons, re-establish contact with West African communities who had settled in the Near East (often in order to escape some of the realities of European conquest and colonial rule), and to contemplate the possibilities for obtaining Islamic higher education abroad. These educational opportunities were not seized upon nearly so much as they are today, in the era of the petrodollar and the scholarship, but they were exploited by a small number of West Africans who might then return home and try to sustain the older standards of learning.

Another feature of colonial Islamic policy was the packaging of knowledge about Islamic societies. This was carried out particularly by the Service of Muslims Affairs, established under the new Government-General of Dakar and run initially by Robert Arnaud and Paul Marty, orientalists who had been working in the colonial Maghreb and who were seconded to the West African bureaucracy to help with the administration of "more primitive" and fledgling Islamic societies. The files compiled on Muslim marabouts throughout French West Africa became the basis for Marty's volumes on Islam, published during the First World War. The knowledge they contained, however distorted, was sufficiently accurate and detailed to reduce the administration's fears of Islamic revolt and pan-Islamism which had plagued it in previous years. By the 1920s the French were using the term *Islam noir* to describe the societies of West Africa and to emphasize the differences with the ostensibly more orthodox Islam practiced in North Africa and the Near East (see Harrison 1988, Robinson 1988b, Cruise O'Brien 1967).

French colonial rule did, nonetheless, encourage the spread of Islam. The reasons for this have not been seriously explored, but it is possible to venture some hypotheses. The most obvious answer is that the French depended upon Muslims of all kinds to carry out colonial administration. They had more understanding of and confidence in Muslims, and indeed they had worked with Senegalese Muslims in particular in their commercial and political activities throughout the nineteenth century. This pattern of collaboration was replicated in Soudan and the other areas brought under French rule, both in the sense of the large participation of Senegalese in conquest and colonial rule in the new territories and in the sense of finding local indigenous collaborators who fitted the same mold.

It was also true that Muslims moved more quickly to take advantage of the limited opportunities provided by colonial rule. A case in point concerns the customary law courts, instituted by the Government-General in 1903 with a great flourish. The impulse was to determine the various mixes of Muslim and non-Muslim custom prevailing in the different regions and then to use that in a new court system to arbitrate disputes concerning land, marriage and divorce, and inheritance. After a few years of operation, it was obvious to French observers that it was the Muslim subjects with some experience with colonial rule who were taking advantage of the courts and providing the assessors. They helped created an ambience in which "pagan" subjects felt intimidated by Muslims or indeed presented themselves as Muslims (Geismar 1933, Meunier 1914, Robinson 1988a).

At a broader level, Islam provided a kind of cultural identity for West Africans that balanced the strong ethnocentric superiority of the French. Becoming Muslim did not necessarily mean submitting to the cultural or political hegemony of a Futa Jalon or an Umarian state; one could find a marabout or master of one's own ethnic group, one could migrate to a new area, one could find a variety of Qadiriyya and Tijaniyya affiliations — in short, one could fashion an Islam of one's own choosing. These Islamic sub-cultures functioned not only for those who repudiated the new options of colonial rule, or remained isolated from them, but also for those who followed the earlier patterns of collaboration and seized upon the new possibilities. A Koranic school education and faithful Islamic practice provided a kind of anchor for those who entered the colonial arena (see Clarke 1982, esp. Ch. 7; Gouilly 1952, Hiskett 1984, esp. Ch. 17; Stewart 1986).

The British administration of northern Nigeria differed sharply from colonial rule in French West Africa, but not necessarily because of different intentions or some special proclivity towards indirect rule. Rather, the British found in place a large state and social system, the Sokoto Caliphate, an established economy that was affected but not undermined by the decline of the trans-Saharan trade and the boundary compartmentalization of West Africa, and an established and somewhat homogeneous system of Islamic socialization. Confronted with the same reality, the French might very well also have taken advantage of existing structures for colonial administration.

The result in Northern Nigeria was that the new colonial space did not dramatically alter the precolonial arrangements. The Sokoto Caliphate was larger than the Upper North of Nigeria, but all of its principal capitals and large population centers fell within the new colonial entity. The caliphal family was reduced to the status of emirs of Sokoto, but still received preferential treatment at public ceremonies. The emiral dynasties remained in power, and they exercised significant police, judicial, and taxation functions as Native Authorities under the surveillance of the British Residents and District Officers. Because of this many of the Islamic "professional" positions survived, albeit in a somewhat transformed state, into the colonial era, and they provided rewards for those who persisted in the traditional Islamic educational system. A school for training colonial cadres was established at Katsina, and then Kaduna, and it provided an effective transition for the local elite from the exercise of power within a precolonial framework to its practice in the colonial arena. The British used many of the Muslims trained in administration in the Upper North to staff their administration of the "pagan" societies of the Lower North. Their system of indirect rule in the north became a model for colonial administration in other parts of the British African empire (see Dudley 1968, Lugard 1922, Lugard 1970, Watts 1983). In summary, the new colonial space in northern Nigeria was a revision of the Sokoto caliphate, and not a new creation.

What this analysis has left out, of course, is a discussion of Islam in the societies of the woodland, forest, and coast of West Africa, which comprise Southern Nigeria, Benin, Togo, Ghana, Ivory Coast, Liberia, Sierra Leone, and the two Guineas. In general, the "quarantine" form of Islam persisted in these regions well into the twentieth century; the description Levtzion provided for the hinterland of Ghana (Levtzion 1968) might well have some relevance today. Islam did not become the religion of the state and did not spread in significant ways to the rural population. Two exceptions to this generalization would be the southwestern or Yoruba part of Nigeria, where the jihad and state of Uthman dan Fodio played a significant role in the downfall of the Oyo Empire in the early nineteenth century, and Sierra Leone, whose large Muslim population has been tied to the economy and educational system of Futa Jalon for at least two hundred years. Apart from these areas, it is probably accurate to say that Islam is not a dominant theme in the literature of most authors from this region.

It remains to try to identify some Islamic sub-cultures that functioned in West Africa during the colonial period and that are relevant to the formation and imaginations of novelists and film-makers. I would first identify a theocratic form, by which I mean a situation in which Islam is pervasive and the pre-eminent socio-political authorities are what we might call Muslim professionals. The Islamic state in the traditional and precolonial sense obviously no longer exists, but it has been replaced to a substantial degree by influential and powerful arbiters of standards and performance. I have in mind here the Upper North of Nigeria, inheritors of the Sokoto Caliphate in the form of Native Authorities, and the peanut basin of Senegal where the authority of the leaders of the Muridiyya, the Tijaniyya of Tivaouane and the Tijaniyya of Kaolack holds sway. I would include in this the memory of the culture of Futa Toro, as it is expressed in *Ambiguous Adventure* — the idea that Islam should rule the hearts and minds of the Diallobe.

This theocratic sub-culture can be treated critically as well as positively. Sembène Ousmane has a particularly negative reaction to the Islamic "establishment" in Senegal, whether he portrays it in the form of the marabout in the city sending the children out to beg for him, or the marabout who gains excessive and corrupting influence at the precolonial court in *Ceddo*. Ouologuem might be assimilated to this critical position as well.

Another sub-culture might be called the syncretic, where Islam appears as an inextricable part of the fabric of socialization. Islamic authorities take their place alongside blacksmiths, village chiefs and other authorities, but they do not exercise overall control and they are not in a position to determine behavior. Here I have in mind the Islam of the Mandinka societies portrayed by Camara Laye; the Islamic presence was ancient but confined principally to the commercial sphere, and French colonial rule prevented the establishment of an Islamic state.

Finally, one might cite a mystical sub-culture, expressed particularly by Amadou Hampâté Bâ in his treatment of Tierno Bokar. He makes an implicit criticism of the theocratic version and offers an esoteric vision in which Islam begins to join the other "universal" religions in a kind of eternal wisdom of numbers and signs (see Bâ 1969, Bâ and Daget 1955, Bâ and Cardaire 1957, Bâ 1980). This sub-culture is perhaps the least changing, and can be found at least as far back as the seventeenth century.

Notes

1. I am not necessarily espousing the point of view of Edward Said in using this term; in some ways the study of Islam in West Africa has suffered from the *absence* of a strong orientalist tradition.
2. Marty's words were published in the *Revue du Monde Musulman* in separate volumes between 1913 and 1922.
3. Willis (1969), for example, puts the Tokolor or *torodbe* Islam at the top of the hierarchy.
4. One could also choose an example from the Songhay empire of the fifteenth and sixteenth centuries, as enshrined in the *Tarikh al-Fettash* and *Tarikh al-Sudan* (O. V. Houdas, ed. and trans., 2nd ed., 1964) or from other "medieval" West African states or indeed the states of Hausaland just before the Islamic movement organized by Uthman dan Fodio at the beginning of the nineteenth century.
5. The Muslim states created by Fulbe leaders in the eighteenth and nineteenth centuries also played a major role in the development of Islamic pedagogy.
6. One might add Malik Sy of Tivaouane and Amadou Bamba Mbacké of Mbacké and Touba to this list; both were descendants, on the patrilineal side, of Futanke clerical families.
7. Also my interview with Bâ in Abidjan, September 18, 1976.
8. The novelist Maryse Conde (in *Segou*), and the historian Adam Konare Bâ (in *L'Epopée de Segu*, 1987), represent the "traditionalist" point of view: that the values of indigenous African civilization were lost with the conquest and forced Islamization of the Bambara capital and kingdom.

9. Oloruntimehin (1970) tries to make the case for collaboration in resistance to French conquest, but the evidence is thin. The leaders make feeble attempts to unite at much too late a date.
10. The main exception was the passage of the Futa Jalon elite to the Tijaniyya persuasion in the late nineteenth century, under conditions that have not yet been documented, but here the ruling class had little allegiance to the Umarian leadership.

References

Abun-Nasr, Jamil. 1965. *The Tijaniyya: A Sufi Order in the Modern World.* London: Oxford.

Adeleye, Remi. 1966. *Power and Diplomacy in Northern Nigeria.* London: Longman.

Anene, J. C. 1969. *The International Boundaries of Nigeria.* New York: Humanities Press.

Bâ, Adam Konare. 1987. *L'Epopée de Segu. Da Monzon: un pouvoir guerrier.* Paris: Favre.

Bâ, Amadou Hampâté. 1969. "Jésus et Hasdu." *Bulletin de l'IFAN*, Series B, 31.3.

———. 1980. *Vie et enseignement de Tierno Bokar. Le Sage de Bandiagara.* Paris: Présence africaine.

Bâ, Amadou Hampâté, and Jacques Daget. 1955. *Empire peul.* vol 1. Paris: Mouton.

Bâ, Amadou Hampâté, and Marcel Cardaire. 1957. *Tierno Bokar.* Paris: Présence africaine.

Botte, Roger. 1988. "Révolte, pouvoir, réligion: Les Hubbu du Futa-Jalon (Guinée)." *Journal of African History.* 29.3.

Brenner, Louis. 1984. *West African Sufi: The Religious Heritage and Spiritual Quest of Cerno Bokar Saalif Taal.* Berkeley, CA: University of California Press.

———. 1985. *Reflexions sur le savoir islamique en Afrique de l'Quest.* Bordeaux: Centre d'Etudes d'Afrique Noire.

———. 1988. "Concepts of Tariqa in West Africa: The Case of the Qadiriyya." In *Charisma and Brotherhood in African Islam*, edited by D. Cruise O'Brien and C. Coulon. Oxford: Clarendon Press.

Brenner, Louis, and Murray Last. 1985. "The Role of Language in West African Islam." *Africa* 55.

Christelow, Allen. 1987. "'Orientalism': Islam and Colonial Rule in Algeria and Northern Nigeria." Paper delivered at Fall 1987 Annual Meeting of the African Studies Association.

Clark, Peter. 1982. *West Africa and Islam.* Ch. 2. London: Edward Arnold.

Conde, Maryse. 1984. *Ségou.* Paris, Robert Laffont.

Cruise O'Brien, Donal. 1967. "Towards a French 'Islamic' Policy." *Journal of African History* 8.

Dudley, Billy. 1968. *Parties and Politics in Northern Nigeria.* London: Frank Cass.

Fisher, Humphrey. 1973. "Conversion Reconsidered: Some Historical Aspects of Religious Conversion in Black Africa." *Africa* 43.

GEISMAR, L. 1933. *Receuil des coutûmes civiles des races du Sénégal.* St. Louis (Senegal): Imprimerie du Governement.

GEORG, ODILE. 1986. *Commerce et colonization en Guinée, 1850–1913.* Paris: L'Harmattan.

GHALI, N. et al. 1985. *Inventaire de la Bibliothèque 'Umarienne de Segou.* Paris: Editions du CNRS.

GOUILLY, ALPHONSE. 1952. *L'Islam dans l'Afrique occidentale francaise.* Paris: Editions Larose.

HANSON, JOHN. 1989. "Dissent, Revolt and the Umarian Era in Karta." Ph.D. thesis, Michigan State University.

HARRISON, CHRIS. 1988. *France and Islam in West Africa 1860–1960.* New York: Cambridge University Press.

HISKETT, MERVYN. 1984. *The Development of Islam in West Africa.* Ch. 17. London: Longman.

HORTON, ROBIN. 1971. "African Conversion." *Africa,* 41.

———. 1975. "On the Rationality of Conversion." *Africa.* 45.

HUNWICK, JOHN. Forthcoming. "Muslim Africa: Reflections on Some Research Agendas for the 1990s." In *African Futures* edited by C. Fyfe.

HUNWICK, JOHN, ed. 1985. *Shari'a in Songhay: The Replies of al-Maghili to the Questions of Askia al-Hajj Muhammed.* New York: Oxford University Press.

KANYA-FORSTNER, A. S. 1969. *The Conquest of the Western Sudan.* London: Cambridge University Press.

KELLY, GAIL. 1983. "Interwar Schools and the Development of African History in French West Africa." *History in Africa,* 10.

———. 1984. "The Presentation of Indigenous Society in the Schools of French West Africa and Indochina, 1918–1938." *Comparative Studies in Society and History* 26.

LEVTZION, NEHEMIA. 1968. *Muslims and Chiefs in West Africa: A Study in the Middle Volta Basin.* Oxford: Clarendon Press.

———. 1971. "A 17th Century Chronicle by Ibn al-Mukhtar: A Critical Study of the Ta'rikh al-Fattash." *Bulletin of the School of Oriental and African Studies* 34.

———. 1973. *Ancient Ghana and Mali.* London: Methuen.

LUGARD, FREDERICK. 1922. *Dual Mandate in British Tropical Africa.* London: Frank Cass.

———. 1970. *Political Memoranda 1913–1918.* Ed. A. Kirk-Greene. Totowa, N.J.: Biblio Distribution Center.

MAHIBOU, SIDI MOHAMMED, and JEAN-LOUIS TRIAUD. 1984. *Voilà ce qui est arrivé. Le Bayan d'al hajj Umar.* Paris: CNRS.

MARTY, PAUL. 1917. *Etudes sur l'Islam au Sénégal,* 2 vols. Paris: Ernest Leroux.

———. 1921. *Etudes sur l'Islam au Soudan,* 4 vols. Paris: Ernest Leroux.

———. 1921. *Islam en Guinée.* Paris: Ernest Leroux.

MEUNIER, PIERRE. 1914. *Organisation et fonctionnement de la justice indigène en Afrique occidentale française.* Paris: Challamel.

MOITT, BERNARD. 1984. "Peanut Production and Social Change in the Dakar Hinterland: Kajoor and Bawol 1840–1940." Ph.D. thesis, University of

Toronto.

NEWBURY, C. W. 1960. "The Formation of the Government General of French West Africa." *Journal of African History*, 1.1.

———. 1966. "North African and Western Sudan Trade in the 19th Century: A Re-evaluation." *Journal of African History* 7.2.

OLORUNTIMEHIN, B. O. 1970. "Anti-French Coalition of African States and Groups in the Soudan, 1889—93." *Odu*, 3.

PADEN, JOHN. 1973. *Religion and Political Culture in Kano*. Berkeley, CA: University of California Press.

PERSON, YVES. 1968—75. *Samori. Une révolution Dyula*. Dakar: IFAN, 3 vols.

———. 1987. "Futa Jalon and the Southern Savannas." In *History of West Africa*, Vol. 2. Ed. J. Ajayi and M. Crowder. New York: Longman.

ROBERTS, RICHARD. 1987. *Warriors, Merchants and Slaves: The State and the Economy in the Middle Niger Valley, 1700—1914*. Stanford, CA: Stanford University Press.

ROBINSON, DAVID. 1975a. *Chiefs and Clerics: Abdul Bokar Kane and the History of Futa Toro*. Oxford: Clarendon Press.

———. 1975b. "The Islamic Revolution of Futa Toro." *International Journal of African Historical Studies* 8.

———. 1985a. "L'extension, la métaphore et l'intensité de l'Islam Ouest Africain." *Annales ESC*, 40.

———. 1985b. *The Holy War of Umar Tal. The Western Sudan in the Mid-Nineteenth Century*. London: Oxford University Press.

———. 1987a. "Brokers and Hegemony in Senegal." Paper presented to 1987 Illinois Conference on "New Perspectives on Colonial Africa."

———. 1987b. "Umarian Emigration in the Late Nineteenth Century." *International Journal of African Historical Studies* 20.

———. 1988a. "Colonial Law and Ethnography in Senegal." Paper given at 1988 Stanford Conference on Colonial Law in Africa.

———. 1988b. "French 'Islamic'" Policy and Practice in Late Nineteenth Century Senegal." *Journal of African History*, 29.3.

ROBINSON, DAVID, and JOHN HANSON. Forthcoming 1991. *After the Jihad: Maintaining the Islamic State in West Africa*. East Lansing: MSU Press.

SEARING, JAMES. 1985. "Accommodation and Resistance: Chiefs, Muslim Traders and Politicians in Colonial Senegal, 1890—1934." Ph.D. thesis, Princeton University.

STEWART, CHARLES. 1973. *Islam and Social Order in Mauritania*. London: Oxford University Press.

———. 1976a. "Frontier Disputes and Problems of Legitimation: Sokoto-Masina Relations, 1817—37." *Journal of African History*, 17.4.

———. 1976b. "Southern Saharan Scholarship and the Bilad al-Sudan." *Journal of African History*, 17.

———. 1986. "Islam." In *Cambridge History of Africa, vol. 7: 1905—1940*. New York: Cambridge University Press.

STEWART, CHARLES, and REMI ADELEYE. 1987. "The Sokoto Caliphate in the Nineteenth Century." In *History of West Africa*. J. Ajayi and M. Crowder, vol. 2. New York: Longman.

TA'RIKH AL-FETTASH. 1964. Ed. and trans. O. Houdas. Paris: Adrien-Maisonneuve.

TA'RIKH AS-SOUDAN. 1964. Ed. and trans. O. Houdas. Paris: Adrien-Maisonneuve.

TRIAUD, JEAN-LOUIS. 1987. "Les Etudes en langue française sur l'Islam en Afrique noire. Essai historiographique." *Lettre d'information de l'association française pour l'etude du monde arabe et musulman.*

WATTS, MICHAEL. 1983. *Silent Violence: Food, Famine and Peasantry in Northern Nigeria.* Berkeley; CA: University of California Press.

WILLIS, J. R. 1969. "The Western Sudan from the Moroccan invasion to the Death of al-Mukhtar al-Kunti (1591–1811)." In *The History of West Africa*, I. Ed. J. Ajayi and M. Crowder. New York: Longman.

ZOUBER, MAHMOUD. 1977. *Ahmed Baba de Tombouctou, sa vie et son oeuvre.* Paris Maisonneuve et Larose.

Chapter 8

▼▼▼▼▼▼▼▼

Can a Single Foot Follow Two Paths?
Islamic and Songhay Belief Systems in the Timbuktu Chronicles and The Epic of Askia Mohammed

Thomas A. Hale

In his research on the Songhay belief system (Stoller 1987, 1989), anthropologist Paul Stoller often cites a proverb with deep meaning for those people in western Niger who still maintain a strong attachment to a pre-Islamic view of existence: *ce follo si fonda hinka gana* (a single foot cannot follow two paths). One cannot embrace both systems of belief, Songhay and Islamic, and expect to reach one's goal in this life or the next. The proverb's message underscores the tension that exists between the two belief systems. The purpose of this study is to show how two different forms of narrative about the past convey these sometimes competing views of the metaphysical world, and what meaning we may draw from them for understanding contemporary Sahelian societies.

Given the growing importance of Islam in the Sahel, those who assert that there is only one path for the Songhay might appear at first to be a diminishing minority of believers seeking a form of salvation they do not find in the nearly official Islamic religion of the country. But both medieval written and more recent oral sources that interpret the Songhay past, as well as current religious practices described by Stoller and others, suggest that the Songhay belief system has not given way completely to the advance of Islam over

131

▼

the centuries. There are some indications, in fact, that these deeply rooted beliefs continue to serve the needs of modern Songhay in Niger even as Islam increases its impact on society today. To understand this phenomenon, and, in a broader sense, the complex nature of other cultures in the region marked by the same historical forces, we shall look at verbal evidence describing the introduction of Islam in the region. In particular, we shall focus on the growth of the religion under the leadership of the Songhay ruler Askia Mohammed in the late fifteenth and early sixteenth centuries, and then link that period to the present via the oral tradition and the work of Stoller. In both cases, we shall draw from texts in which the line between literature and history does not always appear distinct.

But first, let us look briefly at the sources. Much of what we know about the rise to power of Askia Mohammed comes from what we shall term the Timbuktu chronicles, long narratives in Arabic written by Africans who were near to centers of religious and political power in the region, the cities of Djenné, Timbuktu, and Gao on the Niger river in present-day Mali. The two best-known of these documents, the *Tarikh el-Fattâch* (Kâti 1913) and the *Tarîkh es-Sudan* (Es-Sa'di 1898–1900), which we shall refer to as the *TF* and the *TS*, amount to more than 800 pages of narrative in French, the only translations into a Western language easily available to scholars who do not read Arabic. These texts in their different forms, Arabic and French, suffer from a variety of defects: errors in the transcription of African terms into Arabic by the earliest narrators, the mixing of marginal notes with the texts themselves by later copyists and interpreters, ambiguity about the authorship of the *TF*, modifications, in the case of the *TF*, by a nineteenth-century ruler and, finally, errors in the translation from Arabic to French (Hunwick 1969, 1973, Levtzion 1972, Dramani-Issoufou 1982, Robinson n.d.).

They are, then, hardly static documents fixed in the past, but constitute instead many layers of interpretation that continue to evolve in the present as contemporary scholars undertake new translations and annotations based on rereadings of existing manuscripts and analysis of variants. The texts, like many West African epics, are also multi-generic (Johnson 1986). They contain genealogies, prayers, letters, passes, prophecies, legal documents, legends, eye-witness accounts, and many other genres. Finally, the diverse information available in the many forms and layers of these narratives appears filtered through a perspective that is heavily Islamic. The narrators, Muslim holy men, frequently interject prayers, praises to Allah, and condemnations of those who are not Muslim. For example, the opening of what the French translators term the *doxologie* in the *TF* begins with the phrase "Praise be to God" and ends with the warning "Those who obey them (the Prophets, the Caliphs, and other leaders of Islam) are on the right path and will be rewarded; those who stray from them will be lost and disappointed" (Kâti 1913, 6).

Like the written tradition of the chroniclers, oral narratives recorded in the twentieth century offer us another view of the past. But it is more difficult to identify the changes that the narrators and their ancestors have introduced over the centuries. What we hear on the tape and read in the transportation is a modern interpretation of the past, a product of what has been handed down and in some ways a response to the expectations of society today. We cannot tell to what extent the oral version of the past has been influenced by the written, and vice versa. But we may conclude that each has evolved over time, and each represents a world view that differs somewhat from the other. Nowhere is this more evident than in the way they portray the two dominant belief systems in the region, Islamic and Songhay, especially as these appear in the story of Askia Mohammed, the ruler who brought the Songhay empire to its apogee.

In the Timbuktu chronicles, as well as in the correspondence between the North African theologian Al-Maghili and Askia Mohammed (Hunwick 1985), we find a highly positive description of Askia Mohammed, who governed from 1493 to 1528. He appears as a great defender and propagator of the faith across the Sahel. After overthrowing a descendant of the "evil" Sonni Ali Ber (Bâ 1977), a ruler responsible, according to the chroniclers, for the deaths of thirty virgin daughters of the religious and intellectual elite in Timbuktu, Askia Mohammed makes the pilgrimage to Mecca, undertakes a holy war against the "infidel" Mossi people, and conquers vast areas of the region. If the narrators of the chronicles take great pains to describe Askia Mohammed's role in the spread of Islam, we find, on the other hand, very few references anywhere to the pre-Islamic system of belief maintained by his people. We do learn that the Mossi, who fall under Songhay control, worship a tree as an idol and that Askia Mohammed destroys it by simply declaring that there is no divinity other than God and that Mohammed is His prophet (Kâti 1913, 134–35).

The correspondence with Al-Maghili also reveals a denunciation of a people who appear to be extremely resistant to Islam. The reference to guidance from a fox, suggests Hunwick, indicates that they are most likely the Dogon. After overthrowing Sonni Ali Ber, the new ruler reports to Al-Maghili that these people he has freed continue to believe in both Islam and their own pre-Islamic practices:

> Then I released everyone who claimed that he was a free Muslim and a large number of them went off. Then after that I asked about the circumstances of some of them and about their country and behold they pronounced the *shahada*: "There is no god save God. Muhammed is the Messenger of God." But in spite of that they believe that there are beings who can bring them benefit or do them harm other than God, Mighty and Exalted is He. They have idols and they say: "The fox has said so and so and thus it will be," and "If the thing is thus then it will be so and so." They venerate certain trees and make sacrifices to them. They have their shrines and they do not appoint a ruler or undertake any matter either great or small except at the command of the custodians of their shrines.
>
> So I admonished them to give up all that and they refused to do so without the use of force. (Hunwick 1985, 77)

The portrayal in the Arabic-language texts of Askia Mohammed and the Islamic values he defended gives a broad and often highly detailed view of the rise of the religion in the region. But the chroniclers are not the only ones to describe the spread of Islam in the Sahel. Another type of wordsmith, the oral narrator, known regionally as a griot and locally by a variety of terms that define more accurately his or her role in society, offers a parallel, complementary, but somewhat different view of the way Islamic and Songhay beliefs co-exist in the Sahel.

In the 1,602-line oral epic of Askia Mohammed I recorded from the griot Nouhou Malio in the town of Saga, Niger, in December and January 1980–81, Askia Mohammed, known as Mamar Kassaye, appears fully committed to the spread of Islam. Although the epic is much shorter than either of the chronicles, the griot takes pains to describe clearly how the ruler forces people to adopt the new belief system. He travels from village to village, sending advance men to teach the inhabitants how to lay out the foundations for a mosque. The ruler's army burns any village that refuses to accept Islam.

0276. In each village where he stopped during the day, for example, this place,

If he arrives in mid-afternoon, he stops there and spends the night.

Early in the morning, they pillage and they go on to the next village, for example, Liboŕe.

The cavalier who goes there,
He traces on the ground for the people the plan for the mosque.
Once the plan for the foundation is traced,
The people build the mosque.
It is at that time,
Mamar Kassaye comes to dismount from his horse.
He makes the people —
They teach them verses from the Koran relating to prayer.
They teach them verses from the Koran.
Any village which refuses, he destroys the village, burns it,
    and moves on.
In each village where he arrives,
The village which he leaves in the morning,
The horses ride ahead,
They build a mosque before his arrival.
When he arrives, he and his people,
He teaches the villagers prayers from the Koran.
He makes them pray.

0296. They—they learn how to pray. (Nouhou Malio in Hale, 1990,
    p. 201).

The griot's account does not differ in substance from that of the chroniclers who describe Askia Mohammed's conquests of various peoples throughout the region. The contrast in the two portrayals of the past lies instead in some of the details and in what is left out of the chronicles.

In the epic, we find a variety of references to the Songhay belief system, beginning with the ancestors of the hero. The chroniclers mentioned briefly the parents of Askia Mohammed. His father was probably of Soninké origin (Hunwick 1974) and his mother was the daughter of a governor of an island 40 kilometers upriver from Timbuktu. But the griot offers another view which, though clothed in Islam, reflects a Songhay view of the spiritual world. In the oral narrative, Askia Mohammed's father appears as a spirit who is chief of a town under the river. The inhabitants of the underwater world are all good Muslims, adds the griot, to emphasize the similarities between their ways and those who live on land.

149. Under the water there are so many cities, so many cities, so
    many cities, so many villages, and so many people.
  It is his father too who is the chief.

151. They too get themselves ready, they go out to go to the prayer
    ground. (Nouhou Malio, in Hale, 1990, p. 193)

The reference to people living under the river links the hero's
heritage to a complex network of spirits familiar to the Songhay
along the Niger River. Beneath a surface similarity to the Islamic
notion of *djinn*, we discover that the father is a *holey* (spirits who
appear as humans). There are 140 of them in Songhay pantheon.
They "control the forces of rain, wind, fire, thunder, clouds, sickness
and sometimes death" (Stoller 1989). According to Jean Rouch, they
have human qualities, dress, and customs. They are normally invisible.
One of the most important figures is that of Harakoy Dikko, chief
spirit of water. Today, for many Songhay living between Gao and
Say, the Niger River is the home for a vast array of these spirits. To
many modern Songhay listeners, there does not seem to be a paradox
here in the griot's account of Muslims who live under the river. One
can be a believer in Islam without denying the existence of a more
deeply rooted set of beliefs.

The differences between the two ways of interpreting the metaphysical world appear again after Askia Mohammed assumed power
and made the pilgrimage to Mecca. During a battle against the
Bargantché people in northern Benin, both the chronicles and the
oral narrative report that Askia Mohammed found himself in a
military situation with no possibility of victory. After he and his
sons become cut off from the main body of the army, the chronicles
portray him as facing east and seeking salvation by addressing a
prayer to Allah:

> O my God, I implore you in memory of that day when I stood
> next to the head of your messenger in his mausoleum and when I
> asked you to come to my aid in all the difficulties which I would
> experience; I beg of you, o my lord, to help me as well as my
> children and to make us escape safely from the hands of these
> people. (Kâti 1913, 133)

Whether it is thanks to Allah or the force of their counterattack,
Askia Mohammed and his sons escape from the Bargantché and
rejoin the retreating Songhay army without further casualties.

In the oral narrative, however, when Askia Mohammed encounters difficulty, he sends a *sohanci*, a Songhay sorceror, flying
through the sky to request assistance from his mother, Kassaye,
hundreds of kilometers upriver in the capital city, Gao. Kassaye, the
sister of the ruler Askia Mohammed overthrew and the ancestor of

sorceresses in western Niger today (Stoller 1987), provides the necessary devices for her son to escape from the near-defeat at the hands
of the Bargantché.

436. Now, she took some cotton seeds in her hand and said.
     "Take."
     She took an egg, a chicken egg, and she said to him, "Take."
     She took a stone, a river stone, she told him, "Take,"
     "If you go," if he goes to the Bargantché,
     If the Bargantché chase him,
     He should put all his horses before him and he should be the
     only one behind.
     He should scatter the cotton seeds behind him.
     They will become a dense bushy barrier between him and them.
     If they chop it down,
     This dense bush will not prevent anything.
     They will clear the bush in order to find him.
     If the bush does not help at all,
     This time, if they are still hunting him,
     He should put all his cavalry before him.
     He should throw the stone behind him.
     It will become a big mountain which will be a barrier between
     them.
     And when they chase him again,
     He should put all his cavalry in front of him again,
     Leaving himself in the rear.
     He should throw the egg behind him.
     The egg will become a river to separate them.
     The river cannot — they will stop at the river.
459. The egg will become a river which will be a barrier between
     them. . . .

468. He escaped from the Bargantché, the Bargantché who live
     along the river.
469. He never again fought against them. (Nouhou Malio, in Hale,
     1990, 211–213)

Later in the epic, at the time of the battles against the Moroccan-
led soldiers who invaded the region, Askia Mohammed's descendants
rely on three toorey, or spirits, incarnated in a python, a hen, and an
ox, for protection against the guns of the enemy. Each day, thanks
to these spirits, the city of Gao maintains its invulnerability.

1246. In Gao, it is to these toorey that they appeal.
It is with these things there that they have protected
the city of Gao from all surprises.

But a young woman who fraternizes with the attackers reveals
the secret of the city's protective spirits.

1275. "At the first cock crow,
"The entire city goes up in the air.
"Everything you do, with your guns, it is on the ground that
you shoot.

1278. "The city moves up above." (Nouhou Malio, in Hale, 1990,
257, 259, 261)

The epic, then, appears to be a syncretic portrait of two systems
of belief, an interpretation of the past that, on the surface, seems to
accord with many views of Islam in the Sahel today. But there is
more to these examples of Songhay belief in the epic. They reflect
not simply the coexistence of the two ways in the past, but the
survival, often in an atmosphere of some tension, of a pre-Islamic
perspective on the world beyond the real. The appearance of spirits is
not simply entertainment for the sake of the story, but, in fact, the
manifestation of a cosmogony which still concerns Songhay today.

The evidence for this interpretation of the oral narrative comes
from recent research on the Songhay by Stoller. Since independence
in Niger in 1960, and particularly during the rule of Seyni Kountche
from 1974 to 1987, Islam took on a more official character in the
country. With the support of some Arab nations, an Islamic university
was built in Say, a regional focus of Islamic activity 50 kilometers
downriver from Niamey. At the same time, however, new manifestations of adherence to traditional beliefs began to rise. No longer
were these seen as simply the domain of a small minority tied to the
past. Stoller, who served an extended apprenticeship in Tillaberi
with the late *sohanci* Adamu Jenitongo, gives examples of civil servants
and those with a Western-style university education who seek out
priests and sorcerors for help with contemporary problems — mental
illness, disease, and interpersonal conflict.

Stoller does not argue that there is a revolution in belief in Niger
today. But he suggests that the traditional Songhay world view,
rooted in at least a millennium of cultural activity, has never fully
given way to the more recently arrived Islamic religion. Islam will
continue to develop along several paths that include the integration

of elements of the traditional belief system. But if Islam remains the dominant religion in Niger, there appears to be greater freedom of religious expression now than at any time since independence. For much if not most of the thirteen years of the Kountché regime, those who wanted to hold a possession dance or other activity related to the Songhay belief system had to obtain permission from the police. With the death of President Kountché and the peaceful transfer of power to Ali Seibou, a leader open to a more pluralistic society, this requirement has been dropped. The most striking example of this new openness, according to colleagues in Niger who work on the oral tradition, is that soon after the new president took office, he invited delegations from many different groups in society to meet with him, including not only the Muslims but also the traditional healers known as *zimas*.

The co-existence of the two religious systems, most evident in the oral narrative but also in some syncretic features of Islam, does not mean that there is no conflict between the two. Stoller (1989) gives a striking example of a protest demonstration organized by Songhay priests outside the residence of the rector of the Islamic University. The priests blame the problems of the country on the expansion of Islam into the region. It is doubtful that such a protest will stop the spread of Islam in an area whose Islamic roots date at least to the time of Askia Mohammed. But as griots, priests, and sorcerors all interpret the past to listeners in the present, the Songhay proverb about the difficulty of following two paths takes on new meaning. In fact, it calls forth another proverb to support the notion that the Songhay belief system is likely to continue to survive beneath the surface layer of new religious practices: *nda boundou ga te giri zangoun harora, a si té caré*: if a log spends 100 years in the water, it will not become a crocodile.

Five centuries after Askia Mohammed ranged through the Sahel spreading the word of Islam, it appears that keepers of the traditional Songhay belief system are continuing to maintain their own identity and to meet the needs of a broad spectrum of society. To understand the roots of what each system means to its believers — often one and the same person — we can do no better than begin with those narratives, oral and written, that describe how Islam arrived in the Sahel.

References

Bâ, Adam Konaré. 1977. *Sonni Ali Ber*. Etudes nigériennes no. 40. Niamey: Institut de Recherches en Sciences Humaines.

DRAMANI-ISSOUFOU, ZAKARI. 1982. *L'Afrique noire dans less relations internationales au XVIe siècle: Analyse de la crise entre le Maroc et le Sonhrai.* Paris: Karthala.

ES-SA'DI, ABDERRAHMAN BEN ABDALLAH BEN 'IMRAN BEN 'AMIR. 1898–1900. *Tarîkh es-Soudan.* Trans. O. Houdas. Paris: Ecole des Langues Orientales Vivantes, 2nd ed. Paris: Adrien-Maisonneuve, 1964.

HALE, THOMAS. 1990. *Scribe, Griot, and Novelist: Narrative Interpreters of the Songhay Empire. Followed by the Epic of Askia Mohammed Recounted by Nouhou Malio.* Gainesville: University of Florida Press, 1990.

HUNWICK, JOHN O. 1969. "Studies in the *Ta'rikh al-fattash,* I. Its Authors and Textual History." Centre of Arabic Documentation; *Research Bulletin* 5: 57–65.

———. 1973. "Songhay Material in Arabic Sources: The Case of Songhay (Sonrai)." *African Languages Review* 15: 51–73.

———. 1974. "Al-Maghili's Replies to the Questions of Askia al-Hajj Muhammed. Edited and Translated With an Introduction on the History of Islam in the Niger Bend to 1500." Ph.D. thesis, University of London.

———. 1985. *Shari'a in Songhay: The Replies of al-Maghîlî to the Questions of Askia al-Hajj Mohammed.* New York: Oxford University Press.

JOHNSON, JOHN WILLIAM, and FA-DIGI SISÒKÒ. 1986. *The Epic of Son-Jara: A West African Tradition.* Bloomington: Indiana University Press.

KÂTI, MAHMOUD. 1913. *Tarîkh el-Fettâsh ou chronique du chercheur pour servir à l'histoire des villes, des armées et des principaux personnages du Tekrour.* Trans. O. Houdas and M. Delafosse. Paris: Ernest Leroux.

LEVTZION, NEHEMIAH. 1973. *Ancient Ghana and Mali.* London: Methuen. 2nd ed. New York: Africana, 1980.

ROBINSON, DAVID "The Imperial Tradition in Mali and Songhay," unpublished paper.

ROUCH, JEAN. 1960. *La religion et la magie songhay.* Paris: Les Presses universitaires de France.

STOLLER, PAUL. 1989. *Fusion of Worlds: An Ethnography of Songhay Possession.* Chicago: University of Chicago Press.

STOLLER, PAUL, and CHERYL OLKES. 1987. *In Sorcery's Shadow: Memoir of an Apprenticeship Among the Songhay of Niger.* Chicago: University of Chicago Press.

Chapter 9

▼▼▼▼▼▼▼▼

Amadou Hampâté Bâ and the Islamic Dimension of West African Oral Literature

GABRIEL ASFAR

Amadou Hampâté Bâ is best known for the numerous collections of Fulani and Bambara oral literature he has published, and for his instrumental role in establishing archives in order to help preserve some of the great oral literatures of West Africa in the transliterated Fulani or Bambara oral idioms, and in French renditions or adaptations, including such tales of religious and social initiation as *Koumen* (1961), *Kaïdara* (1968), *L'Éclat de la grande étoile suivi du bain rituel* (1974), and *Njeddo Dewal* (1985).

Hampâté Bâ's works also include writings that have a specific bearing upon religion and society in West Africa. These writings frequently elucidate Islamic esoterism in the oral literature, particularly in tales of an initiatic or didactic nature. In *L'Empire peul du Macina* (1962), he traces the development of Islamic religious authority before and during the period of French colonization in the early nineteenth century. In *Vie et enseignement de Tierno Bokar* (1957, 1980), he celebrates his great mentor and spiritual guide, who played a central role in the growth of the Tijaniyya and Hamalliyya Sufi orders in Mali in the 1930s. In *Aspects de la civilisation africaine* (1972), he offers a detailed inquiry into Fulani culture, relating it to other West African religious traditions, and stimulating much useful speculation on the underlying connections between Islamic doctrine, traditional religions, and West African oral literatures (Brenner 1984, 128–32).

Hampâté Bâ directs his analysis to the ethnic, traditional religions of his native Mali. He discusses peoples such as the Fulani, Bambara,

Dogon, and Malinke — inhabitants of the former colonial territories of the French Sudan. He notes that the advent of Islam among these groups may be considered a fusion, and not a clash, with traditional belief and practice. Indeed, strong compatibilities may be shown to exist between Islam (particularly the Tijaniyya and Hamalliyya Sufi confraternities) and the tenets of traditional African religions, whose cosmogony lies at the heart of traditional oral literatures in West Africa. Affirming that traditional religion survives in Africa "despite the blows struck against it by the religions and the technological and philosophical civilization of Western colonization," Hampâté Bâ asserts that Islam took hold and grew in sub-Saharan Africa upon the foundations of traditional religion (Hampâté Bâ 1972, 138).

Of all of Hampâté Bâ's writings on West African traditional society and on oral literature, the most pertinent to our subject is the chapter, "Réflexions sur la religion islamique," a text identified in a footnote as a "dialogue with students from Niger," in *Aspects de la civilisation africaine*. Hampâté Bâ's reflections on Islam in Africa serve to identify his own strict Muslim traditionalism as a Sufi of the West African Tijaniyya confraternity; they serve also to identify the specifically African role of the *waly* ("saint and sage of God"), as represented in the tales of Fulani and Bambara initiation that Hampâté Bâ has published and commented upon at length in the copious annotations that accompany the tales. In the dialogue, the students ask Hampâté Bâ why it is that all prophets come from Palestine or Arabia, and why there are no Black prophets. Hampâté Bâ's response is to outline the hierarchy of Muslim orthodoxy concerning the embodiment and transmission of Islam according to three categories of "men of God": the *rassoul*, the *nabbi*, and the *waly*.

The *rassoul*, literally a "messenger" of God, or Grand Envoy, is chosen, as are the others, by an act of divine grace, "to be the instrument of a major holy revelation, destined for the multitude, if not for all of mankind" (Hampâté Bâ 1972, 49; my translations throughout). Islam recognizes six Grand Envoys: Adam, Noah, Abraham, Moses, Jesus, and Muhammad. Hampâté Bâ refers to them also as Legislator Envoys, "because each received a new Law, adapted to the necessities of the time." These, Hampâté Bâ concludes, are known also as prophets, and with the advent of prophets, new religions have appeared, "though in reality they all teach a single eternal religion, that of God the One the Eternal" (50).

The *nabbi*, whose name also means "prophet" in Arabic, is the beneficiary of a revelation identical to that of the *rassoul*, but the audience of disciples now is restricted, secret, hidden, perhaps even absent. Where the Grand Envoy is always manifested, the *nabbi* may not be. Also, the *nabbi* brings with him no new law, but follows that of the *rassoul* preceding him. Among the *nabbis* in Hampâté Bâ's hierarchical conception are the Old Testament prophets, and he notes a figure of 124,000 *nabbis* in Islam alone.

Finally comes the *waly*, or "saint of God" in Hampâté Bâ's terminology, one who is "close to God, joined with him, and living in his Love." He adds that *walys* are innumerable, "they are of all times and all races." Hampâté Bâ asserts that the qualities of *waly* are inevitably part of the qualities of the *rassoul* and the *nabbi*, and that the *waly*, in his role as a transmitter of the Holy Word to humanity, is the living interpreter of divine law on earth. The *waly* is descended spiritually from all the *rassouls* and *nabbis*: and the *waly*'s revelations as well as the language he possesses and seeks to transmit are rooted in the monotheistic cosmogony of Abraham. "The quality of the *rassoul* appears at the very heart of the quality of the *waly*, saint and sage of God, living by and for the Love of God, in the mysterious circle of divine proximity. Thus the quality of *waly* knows no limits in time or in space." Hampâté Bâ concludes that "Africa has always been a land rich in *walys*" (52).

We recall here the important role, in the process of such transmissions, of the ancestral figure among the Fulani and the Bambara. The ancestor figure, as invoked long before the advent of Islam in Africa, could thus be considered a potential *waly* whose knowledge was measured in terms of the oral texts he had possessed and transmitted during his lifetime. "En Afrique, un vieillard qui meurt," in Hampâté Bâ's celebrated phrase, "c'est une bibliothèque qui brûle." [In Africa, every time an elder dies, a library is destroyed] (1972, 21). But in the ancestral figure, and in the oral narratives that constitute remembrance of the ancestor, a seemingly irreversible loss is reclaimed through language, asserting ritually and repeatedly the primacy of the Word.

Hampâté Bâ establishes, in outlining the hierarchical order of monotheistic revelation, one of the key features of the traditional, pre-Islamic African oral literatures: that of a central figure who engages in an elaborate quest for a source of illumination, and for the confirmation of a revelation, a revelation intricately bound with a sense of divine authority that is destined to bring order and harmony where chaos and conflict have appeared on the earth. Thus each initiate in the didactic tales comes eventually to be considered a supplicant for the authority of a *waly*.

In the cycle of *Kaïdara*, *L'Éclat de la grande étoile*, and *Njeddo Dewal*, which form a trilogy of Fulani tales of initiation, the central or key figures appear in each others' quests, and attain a common and ongoing revelation that marks each work. Thus Hammadi, the protagonist in *Kaïdara*, appears in *L'Éclat de la grande étoile*; and Bagoumawel, the protagonist of *L'Éclat de la grande étoile*, appears as a miraculous child, "young and old at once," in *Njeddo Dewal*. Indeed, we find strong similarities, not only among these central figures, but between them and the notion of *waly* in Muslim West Africa. In the Fulani trilogy of initiation cited earlier, *Kaïdara* may be said to represent the quest for knowledge, *L'Éclat de la grande étoile* the quest for wisdom, and *Njeddo Dewal* the quest of one who has attained knowledge and wisdom for a resolution to the conflict between good and evil.

Such a profoundly philosophical subtext constitutes the moral framework of the tale of initiation, with its "questing" protagonist, and with the elaborate natural and supernatural events of his quest, all bound up with representations of ordinary human life. The questing tales, or tales of initiation, are thus profoundly didactic in nature. Throughout each of these quests, a similar revelation of divine order occurs, and the central figure's task is to test that revelation in the world, a world not only of mysterious natural and supernatural forces, but also a world filled with the turmoils and vicissitudes of human society. The protagonist in such tales may thus be said to fulfill, in essence, the functions of a *waly*; indeed, the protagonist in a quest tale may be said to affirm, in a pre–Islamic, traditional African context, the central tenets of Islamic monotheism.

In his writings on religion and in his annotations of numerous examples of Fulani and Bambara oral literature that have been transcribed and published, Hampâté Bâ reveals a strong adherence to the teachings of the great Sufi sage of Bandiagara, Tierno Bokar, who was probably, for Hampâté Bâ, the great model of the *waly*. Tierno Bokar was a Sufi leader of the Tijaniyya confraternity, which was the principal branch of Islam in Mali in the early twentieth century. The Sufism of Hampâté Bâ and of Tierno Bokar bears a strong resemblance to the "path of initiation" discovered and disseminated by each of the central figures in the Fulani cycle of *Kaïdara*, *L'Eclat de la grande étoile*, and *Njeddo Dewal*. The Sufi "assumes God's presence" in the world. For Hampâté Bâ, the Sufi who lives "far from the hubbub and temptations of ordinary life" is considered "less accomplished" than the one who "succeeds in maintaining the same quality of internal spirituality while leading an ordinary life among human beings." Just as in the tales of initiation, the ideal of Islam, according to Hampâté Bâ, is "not to reject the world, but to integrate it in the divine presence." The role of the Sufi (as of the *waly*, and of the protagonist in various Fulani quest tales) is "not to renounce life, but to sanctify it in each act, to connect it to God in some manner, and to order it according to the laws of divine revelation" (1972, 54).

In this context, it is useful to cite Trimingham's observation in *The Sufi Orders in Islam* that, "All the theist orders claim the Law as the starting-point, a basis for further progress in either the directed or illuminative life" (159). Such a fundamental starting-point in Islamic law is evident in all Hampâté Bâ's writing on Islam.

Hampâté Bâ terms such divine revelation a "primordial echo" perpetually forgotten by mankind; thus he posits the important role of the Muslim *dhikr*, the ritual of "remembrance" or "memory of God" at the heart of the tales of initiation, a memory that forms the basis of the attributes of moral knowledge sought by the petitioner in the initiation tales — attributes of mercy, generosity, justice — all of which make up the moral lessons of the didactic tale.

Hampâté Bâ asserts that the notion of a divine spirit, transcendent and immaterial, to be "absorbed" by the initiate, lies at the heart of Islam (based on the notion of "submission" to divine authority). The same is true of the quest tales. Indeed, the central figure in the tales of initiation, much like the Sufi, is one endowed with a limited freedom to make choices; it is a freedom limited by what Hampâté Bâ calls "the general predestination of humanity"; thus in Hampâté Bâ's metaphor, one can change position within the closed compartment of a vehicle whose destination remains the same (1972, 61). In other words, it's not where one is going that counts, but rather how one gets there. In this sense, the tales of initiation are stories of journeys, not so much in time and space, but within the spirit of the quester; they are the accounts, not only of the numerous trials and intense inner struggles of the quester after initiation, but also the accounts of how each protagonist emerges as an initiate, of the true outcome, that is, of an arduous process of purification.

In tracing the principal edicts of Islam as promulgated by the West African Tijaniyya Sufis, we find the "primordial echo" of divine authority with which the advent of Islam in Africa suffused Fulani oral literature. Hampâté Bâ enumerates the qualities fundamental to Islam: the profession of faith, prayer, almsgiving, fasting, and the holy pilgrimage (the five Pillars of Islam), followed by the acceptance of the existence of God, of a day of resurrection, of the power of "angels" and of "messengers," of revealed writings, and of the concept of *maktoub* (literally, "that which has been written") — that is, of fate — and of the powerful primordial links between the notion of fatality and the power of language. We note in particular the etymologically identical concepts represented in classical Arabic by the words "fate" and "written."

In an essay on "The Traditional Relationship of the African with God" (113–40), Hampâté Bâ outlines just such a common ground, enabling us to see how closely linked are the cosmogonies of the two main branches of West African religious life. Hampâté Bâ begins by affirming the existence, behind the various traditional deities of pre-Islamic Fulani literature (what he terms "a plurality of gods"), of a "supreme and non-definable being" at the center of each of the quests that constitute the object of traditional tales of initiation. Though the names of this "plurality of gods," or pantheon, may differ between ethnic groups, or indeed within the same group, their attributes clearly anticipate the monotheism of Islam. Named variously as Maa Ngala (Master of All) or Masa Dembali (Uncreated and Infinite Master) by the Bambara, and Gueno (The Eternal One) or Dundari (The Supreme One) by the Fulani, such a divinity is regarded as the creator of the universe. Thus the advent in West Africa of Islam, with its monotheistic doctrine of an omnipotent, omniscient, and omnipresent God, was a reaffirmation in Africa of the Bambara doctrine of Sebaa Mansa Kolibali, the Omnipotent king, and of the Fulani doctrine of Kaïdara the Omnipresent. Hampâté Bâ shows that these concepts of a universal creative force are related, and together constitute the foundations of Islam in West Africa (120–21).

At the root of traditional doctrine, with its many intermediary gods, however, lies the conviction that such a supreme deity is beyond the reach of ordinary mortals; hence man's relationship to God is established indirectly, via the teachings of the initiated, that is, of the *waly* or "messenger," whose task is to reaffirm and bring alive, as it were, the presence of the deity, and to assert such a presence at the risk, if need be, of the *waly*'s own mortal life. Thus the protagonist of the tale of initiation may be considered as an agent of Islamic monotheism. "This manifestation of the sacred through the intermediary of an agent other than the supreme being, an agent holding spiritual power delegated to him by the supreme being," writes Hampâté Bâ, "is part of the earliest origins of the diverse secret religious confraternities" in Africa (116). Hampâté Bâ names several gods of the traditional religions of Mali: Ntomo, Nama, Komo, Nya, Nyawrole, Jarawera, among others: "Each is but a sacred agent governing its allotted share of supreme divine authority." Such traditional agents may be divided, furthermore, into two categories: one is revealed, public, ordinary; the other is hidden, secret, occult. Hampâté Bâ thus echoes the two principal dimensions, one public or exoteric, the other occult or esoteric, of all revealed religions, and particularly those of Islam. Maa Ngala, the "supreme being" of Bambara tradition, for example, "may be incarnated as animal, vegetal, or mineral, or in a natural or supernatural form," writes Hampâté Bâ. These aspects of Maa Ngala, and those of Gueno and Dundari in Fulani tradition, are the precursors of Islam in West Africa.

In an article on "Muslim Influences on West African Literature and Culture," Simon Battestini notes that "the considerable influence of the Hispano-Moroccan culture on Europe" in the tenth and eleventh centuries "had a symmetrical and not less important impact on West Africa" (Battestini 1986, 477). He notes that "the contact of the Hispano-Moroccan world with the West African Savannah was not only religious, economical, and political, but also cultural and, thus, literary" (477). Battestini points to the traditional Fulani tale of initiation, *Koumen*, as an example of the fundamental thematic and rhetorical compatibility of traditionalist and Islamic literatures in West Africa, a compatibility that facilitated the synthesis of traditions Hampâté Bâ describes in his expository writings on the Fulani. Battestini describes *Koumen* as a narrative that "traces a . . . hierarchical program of knowledge which the future initiate has to acquire progressively, finally reaching the 'last clearing,' the twelfth and supreme stage, illuminated by the 'light of lights' as total knowledge" (493). He links this traditional text, in its didactic aims and methods, directly to Hispano-Moroccan education. According to Battestini, traditional initiatic narratives such as *Koumen* "took up the question of Greco-Arabic values and borrowed elements from religious and profane sciences. The contemporary whole has a neo-Platonic goal that science and God, immanence and transcendance, 'finally' unite" (493).

Hampâté Bâ has elaborated at length on the didactic aims of the initiatic tale, and notes that the notion of a single supreme deity characterized by mercy, generosity, and justice is found in West African Muslim religious practice, as well as in the oral literature, particularly the Fulani and Bambara epic tales of initiation. Here again, Hampâté Bâ attributes to the spoken language, "la Parole," the single great task of bridging the gap between the Godhead and mankind, a task that the language of the tale of initiation seeks precisely to fulfill. The Godhead, rigorous and terrible as it is, is susceptible to pleas and to the language of prayer. Here enters the protagonist in the tale of initiation: his role is to make an arduous journey of enlightenment and to implore the divinity to mercy upon the ways of mankind.

Hampâté Bâ writes that "the secret motive of every ritual is in the *Word*, which constitutes the foundation, the magic, the *active agent* of all ritual" (Hampâté Bâ 1972, 117). Thus language itself comes to serve the intermediary role of "messenger" between the word of God and mankind. Hampâté Bâ stresses the commonness of "intermediary language" in African life, citing the practice of expressing wishes or desires indirectly, through an intermediary. "Many colonials who have lived in French West Africa know that the cook always goes through the houseboy to ask the boss for something, and the other way around," writes Hampâté Bâ, adding, "It is this social relationship that has endowed the 'interpreter,' an intermediary official between the administered and their boss, with a decisive role in colonial administration." Hampâté Bâ refers to the Bambara interpreter as "Répond-bouche" ("answering mouth" or "mouth answerer"); "Every king has one; every god has one" (117). Hampâté Bâ thus points to a feature common to traditional African regligions and to Islam: the text itself, be it spoken in the oral literatures, or written in holy scripture, is the crucial intermediary between divine authority and the faithful. Hampâté Bâ points out that traditional African religions share with Islam a belief in the presence of the sacred in all things. "The African attributes a soul to each thing" (120). Such a force resides, as we have seen, in Nommo, the Word, whose principal objective is to confront the profane in human life and, through a process of initiation and purification replete with setbacks and pitfalls (and occasional failures), to replace it with the sacred.

Among the traditional professions of traditional societies, Hampâté Bâ mentions the weaver, the potter, the blacksmith, the farmer, and the shepherd. These professions, as illustrated by numerous characters in the oral narratives, are not merely the pro-ducers or manufacturers of the utilitarian ornaments of human life, but are also reflections, in their rituals and forms, of the presence of the sacred in everyday life. Thus the craftsman, the artisan, and the cultivator are each a consecration and actualization of divine authority in human society. Hampâté Bâ considers that, in harmony with the tenets of Islam, traditional religious ritual is "the repetition of a primordial act inspired by Masa Dembali, the uncreated and infinite Master, and transmitted by the charn of initiated ancestors" (125). Hampâté Bâ continues: "Man can do nothing that does not come from Masa Dembali. Man invents nothing; he can only discover or rediscover that which existed before him; man can only reveal it; and only when Masa Dembali chooses" (126).

As Hampâté Bâ points out at length, the traditional religions of West Africa and, arguably, those of sub-Saharan Africa in general, proved to be entirely hospitable to the advent of Islam, and this amalgamation and eventual fusion of the two was no doubt hastened by the singularly hostile attitude of Western colonialism toward the traditional religions and ritual practices of West Africa. "The empire of Islam in Africa established itself, I shall not say upon the ruins of animism—for it survives still, despite the blows that were struck against it by the religions and by the technological and philosophical civilization brought by Western colonization—but upon the foundations of animism" (137–38).

Hampâté Bâ thus considers traditional religions as the matrix of Islam in sub-Saharan Africa, citing the "great principles" that the two traditions share in common: the quest to "replace the profane with the sacred in everyday life"; the sentiment of "solidarity with a whole encompassing a universe of human communities"; "the existence of a supreme being, transcendent yet immanent by its force in all things and in all places" (138). The conclusions drawn by Hampâté Bâ on the ancient (and, one might say, permanent) connections between traditional African religions and the tenets of Islam contain an expression of regret only concerning Western colonization, which has represented an interference with the socio-religious underpinnings of West African traditions, and which has marked, according to Hampâté Bâ, the single greatest schism between modern Africa and its traditional past.

References

Bâ, Amadou Hampâté. 1955. *L'Empire peul du Macina*. Ed. J. Daget. Paris: Mouton.

———. 1957. *Tierno Bokar, le sage de Bandiagara*. Ed. M. Cardaire. Paris: Présence Africaine.

————. 1961. *Koumen: Texte initiatique des pasteurs peul.* Ed. G. Dieterlen. Paris: Mouton.

————. 1968. *Kaïdara: Récit initiatique peul.* Ed. L. Kesteloot. Paris: Julliard.

————. 1970. *Inventaire du fonds Amadou Hampâté Bâ, répertorié à Abidjan en 1969.* Ed. Alfa Ibrahim Sow. Paris: Klincksieck.

————. 1972. *Aspects de la civilisation africaine.* Paris: Présence Africaine.

————. 1974. *L'Éclat de la Grande Etoile, suivi du bain rituel.* Ed. L. Kesteloot, C. Seydou, A. Ibrahim Sow. Paris: Armand Colin.

————. 1978. *Kaïdara.* Abidjan: Nouvelles éditions africaines.

————. 1980. *Vie et enseignement de Tierno Bokar, le sage de Bandiagara.* Paris: Seuil.

————. 1985. *Njeddo Dewal, mère de la calamité: Conte initiatique peul.* Abidjan: Nouvelles éditions africaines.

BATTESTINI, SIMON P. X. 1986. "Muslim Influences on West African Literature and Culture." *Journal of Muslim Minority Affairs* 7 (July): 2, 476–502.

BRENNER, LOUIS. 1984. *West African Sufi: The Religious Heritage and Spiritual Search of Cerno Bokar Saalif Taal.* Berkeley: U of California Press.

TRIMINGHAM, J. SPENCER. 1971. *The Sufi Orders in Islam.* London: Oxford University Press.

Chapter 10

▼▼▼▼▼▼▼▼▼

Kaïdara: *Islam and Traditional Religion in a West African Narrative of Initiation*

DENISE ASFAR

The quest tale is found among the basic forms of initiatic narrative of many cultures. In such tales, the protagonist sets out in search of a material or spiritual goal, and, in the process of the quest, is initiated into the social and religious order. The physical and spiritual tests to which the protagonist must submit represent the natural and supernatural forces he must come to understand as a responsible adult in his society. The quest tale lies at the heart of the Fulani narratives of initiation, which constitute an important part of their religious and literary tradition.

In research on Fulani literary forms, a basic distinction is made between the *taalol*, which are exclusively oral forms, and the *janti*, which have their basis in a corpus of written narratives. The *taalol* comprise shorter narratives, such as humorous anecdotes and animal fables. The *janti*, which allow for longer and more complex narration, comprise the tales of initiation. The word *jantol* derives from the Fulani verb *janngitude*, meaning to study again or to reread. The etymology of the genre underscores the didactic function of the narratives that fall into this category: They are intended to be retold and studied again and again, each time leading to deeper understanding and to revelation of yet another layer of hidden meaning (Bâ 1978, 7; my translations throughout).

The *janti* have for centuries been recorded in Arabic and *ajami* (the transcription of the Fulani language in Arabic letters); because the key details in the *janti* have sacred significance, it has been essential for them to be faithfully recorded from one storyteller to another. Thus, the act of writing is more an act of transcription than of creation, and the *jantol* remains, like the other Fulani forms of oral literature, fundamentally a performance literature; that is, its creativity derives from the performance, or recreation, from initiator (or storyteller) to initiate, of orally transmitted narration. While the story line and essential details remain the same, the style, embellishments, narrative asides, and (for the poetic versions) the rhymes all may vary from one storyteller to another.

The traditional storyteller typically recites the *jantol* in fragments, before a public that includes adults as well as children; he may adapt the narrative, giving an abridged version to non-initiates or to children, and reserving the complete version, with its esoteric mysteries and revelations, only for the initiates (7).

The narratives of initiation are performed by the religious or spiritual master; of those who seek initiation into the arcane teachings of the master, only a small number will succeed. The master speaks almost exclusively in images, symbols, and paradox; the disciples' degree of commitment to reflect on these teachings, as well as their ability to grasp the complex and abstract teachings, will determine which ones are initiated into the small circle of adepts.

An examination of these initiatic narratives reveals a profoundly Islamic dimension, common to many oral literatures of the Muslim peoples of West Africa. The coexistence of Islamic and traditional religious practices among the Fulani today is the result of centuries of Islamic diffusion into West African cultures. The steady Islamic influence that resulted from the activities of traders and scholars with traditional religions who were hospitable to Muslim doctrine facilitated the mutual assimilation of the two traditions, but it may well have been the underlying compatibility of these traditions that ensured their continuing intermingling beyond the rise and fall of the savannah states and throughout the eastward migration of the Fulani people. Indeed, it has been noted that "the Islamization of Africa was paralleled by the Africanization of Islam" (Boahen 1986, 12).

In much of sub-Saharan Africa, the confraternities of Sufis were the principal vehicles of Islam and remain today the central organizational structure of Muslim communities. During the nineteenth century, the period of the Fulani jihads and imperialist expansion, sects such as the Tijaniyya and Qadriyya spread among the peoples of West Africa as part of a general resurgence of Sufi influence (Nicolas 1981, 175, 184–85). Just as Islam may be considered among

West African peoples an assimilated rather than an imposed religion, so the local branches of the confraternities among West African Muslims have largely maintained their local character and traditions, as established by their own spiritual leaders (Coulon 1981, 152).

The Fulani are among the most thoroughly Islamized peoples of sub-Saharan Africa. The quest tales of Fulani initiation provide strong evidence of the confluence of Islam and traditional African religion. *Kaïdara*, the first in a trilogy of Fulani initiatic narratives, gives what may be the most obvious illustration of the structural and rhetorical elements of the quest tale; moreover, it is the convergence of two initiatic traditions: that of Sufism and of what Hampâté Bâ calls "pre-Islamic animism." (The fact that Hampâté Bâ remains the sole accessible interpreter of the pantheistic teachings of Tierno Bokar, while underscoring the need for additional biographical and historical research in this area, has little bearing on the discussion of Sufi ideology in the tale of *Kaïdara* presented here.)

The tripartite narrative structure of *Kaïdara* loosely parallels the three stages of Sufi initiation described by Milson in *A Sufi Rule for Novices*: "The beginning of Sufism is learning (*'ilm*), the middle is praxis (*'amal*), and the end is grace" (Milson 1975, 35).

In the first phase of *Kaïdara*, three travelers (Hammadi, Hamtou-dou, and Dembourou), set out on a journey through the underworld of the genie-dwarfs, in search of Kaïdara, god of gold and of knowledge. They pass through a series of trials, and view eleven unexplained mysteries, before their confrontation with the god. Each symbol is in fact an incarnation of Kaïdara, for Kaïdara is both the teacher and the lesson — the god of knowledge and knowledge itself, the path and the destination. The travelers are given gold as a reward for their journey, but they are warned to use it wisely, for Kaïdara's power over the gold is linked inextricably with that of knowledge. He leaves the travelers with the teaching of the Arab alchemists, that gold should be sought only for its value as a metaphor of knowledge. In *Kaïdara* the proverb reminds us, "Gold is the pedestal for knowledge, but if you confuse knowledge and the pedestal, it will come tumbling down and crush you" (Bâ 1978, 93).

In this first phase of their initiation, the questers have played a passive role, like the Sufi disciple in his first stage of learning. Their trials have been physical ones, resulting from the rigors of the journey. They have been presented lessons, and they all seem eager to master them; but true understanding of these lessons cannot be achieved until they prove themselves worthy of a later stages of initiation.

This occurs in the second phase of the narrative, the period of "praxis."

At the heart of each Fulani initiatic narrative are the dual searches for self-knowledge and self-discipline. Though the goal of the questers may be stated explicitly in material terms (in the case of *Kaïdara*, a physical journey or a search for gold), the quester comes to realize by the end of the tale that the true goal all along has been self-knowledge. If self-knowledge is the ultimate destination of each quester, then self-discipline is the path. These dual concepts may be identified by their Koranic models of *tasjid* and *jihad*, which, as described by Chevalier in *Le Soufisme*, are also fundamental to the Tidjaniyya doctrines espoused by Hampâté Bâ. *Tasjid* and *jihad* refer to the progressive process of assimilating ever-deeper levels of awareness as one seeks self-perfectibility, and the physical and spiritual *jihad* (or "holy war") for mastery over oneself that is necessary to achieve this goal (Chevalier 1984, 8).

Although the travelers to Kaïdara have all passed the physical trials, their most difficult test involves the jihad, the inner war, or moral trials, against their worldly desires, which are stirred up by their acquisition of the gold. In the second phase of *Kaïdara*, the travelers return to earth for another kind of trial — to prove themselves worthy, by their use of the gold, of the gifts of Kaïdara. Hammadi alone uses the gift to acquire knowledge; he alone remains master *of* the gold, and is never mastered *by* it, using it only as a means to seek knowledge.

On their return from Kaïdara, the travelers meet an old ascetic, whom Hammadi alone recognizes as a *silatigui*, an initiate and spiritual leader of traditional religion. (Later we learn that this *silatigui* is also an incarnation of Kaïdara, the archetypal initiator.) The ascetic offers three pieces of advice, but the questers must pay for each one with one of the hoards of gold. Hammadi alone is so eager for knowledge that he gladly divests himself of the hard-won fortune in exchange for the counsel. This demand for payment is mistaken, by Hamtoudou and Dembourou, as rapaciousness on the part of the ascetic; in fact they are falsely ascribing to the holy man their own base motives. The initiator demands payment not for the sake of the payment itself, but rather in order to assess the value the disciple places on the lesson. Before accepting payment, however, the initiator must ascertain that the money has been earned and is the rightful property of the disciple; similarly for the Muslim, "if one wishes to encounter Khadrou, the Muslim initiator, one must have earned the wealth that one pays him" (Bâ 1978, 14). According to Islamic esoteric tradition,

Khadrou is the initiator of all the prophets, including Moses; in the introduction to *Kaïdara*, Hampâté Bâ notes the similarity in the names of the archetypal initiator of Fulani tradition (Kaïdara) and of Islamic tradition (Khadrou), to underscore his assertion that the Fulani tales of Kaïdara predate the Muslim penetration of West Africa.

One requirement common to Fulani and Tijaniyya Sufi initiation is blind obedience to the master's word; obedience is related to the Islamic concept of submission to divine will (the Arabic word *Islam* means "submission"). Thus in *Kaïdara*, it is the obedient quester, Hammadi, who is rewarded, while his disobedient companions are destroyed. He is the only one of the travelers to Kaïdara that pays for and follows the ascetic master's advice. Although Hamtoudou and Dembourou refused to pay for the advice, Hammadi nonetheless shares it with them; still, though receiving it freely, they refuse to heed it, mocking the gravity with which Hammadi obeys his spiritual master. The faithless companions are therefore destroyed, after respectively violating the first and second of the ascetic's commands.

The warning to the travelers in the first phase of *Kaïdara* — "if you confuse knowledge and its pedestal (gold), the pedestal will tumble down and crush you" — clearly foreshadows the demise of the two unworthy disciples. Hamtoudou shows himself tyrannical and intolerant in his desire for power; Dembourou shows his selfishness in rejecting traditional ways in favor of material pleasures. Though in the first phase of their story, Hamtoudou and Dembourou are in awe of Kaïdara, by the end of the second phase, they become so absorbed in their own desire for power and wealth that they scorn the old ascetic who will prove himself (to Hammadi alone) to be an incarnation of the god. Only Hammadi sees gold not as an end but as a means to knowledge, which is the ultimate wealth. Respecting the traditional order and values, and seeking neither wealth nor power, he becomes nonetheless king of his land, rich and powerful. Hamtoudou and Dembourou, however, fail the test: in viewing gold as an end in itself, prizing only power and luxury, they prove themselves unworthy.

In each case, behavior determines destiny: Hamtoudou and Dembourou are both destroyed, according to Kaïdara's prophecy. Hammadi alone is rewarded, in the third phase of the story, by the revelation of the meaning behind the eleven mysteries — an exegesis of certain natural phenomena that symbolize the complementary positive and negative aspects in man's nature. In this final phase of the narrative, Kaïdara gives a double explanation for each of the symbols—the exoteric, profane meaning, and the esoteric, divine revelation—recalling what Martin Lings describes as the dual perspective of the Sufi (1977, 14).

Initiation is a ritualized form of socialization—an affirmation of traditional values through dedication to understanding the nature of the social and religious order. Hammadi lives the exemplary life of an initiate, honoring his parents and his elders, valorizing his family, and following the traditional laws that his fellow travelers had ignored. He is therefore rewarded in the final phase of revelation represented by Kaïdara's visit; finally he achieves divine grace, the third stage and ultimate goal of the Sufi disciple.

Although the journey to Kaïdara and the eleven symbols would seem to constitute the spiritual journey of a formal initiation, this is only the first stage, the beginning of learning; it takes Hammadi over twenty years to return home from his journey, to put into practice the precepts he has learned, and to enjoy his reward of divine enlightenment and grace. All three travelers pass the tests posed by the physical challenges of the journey to Kaïdara, the first phase of the narrative. It is the moral tests that decide, in this part of the narrative, the destiny of the travelers. Only Hammadi, demonstrating faith and obedience, and eschewing material wealth in his search for knowledge, passes the moral tests of the journey home from Kaïdara. It is only after showing that he can live an exemplary life—one of charity, faith, good judgment, obedience, abnegation, and the continual quest for revelation, only after Hammadi passes the test of "praxis"—that Kaïdara again appears; the state of grace brings Hammadi divine revelation, in the form of an exegesis of the eleven symbols and still other mysteries, which makes up the third and final phase of the narrative. This phase corresponds to what Trimingham refers to as "mystical gnosis," or *ma'rifa*, that is, the direct perception of God, which "enables those so favored to unveil the secrets of the unseen world of reality and contemplate the mysteries of being" (1971, 140). These "unveilings" in the initiatic narrative serve a function similar to the Sufi stages of purification.

This final state of illumination and divine grace means, for the Sufi mystic, that God is present in the initiate; this requires the initiate to be absent from the world and from himself, thus opened to the divine presence. The words of Abu Yazī al-Bistāmī, a thirteenth-century mystic—"Oh absent one for whom God is present" (Stoddart 1982, 83)—seem to be echoed in *Kaïdara* by each of the eleven symbols, which all refer to "the distant Kaïdara, the one close by." In his final revelation to Hammadi, Kaïdara explains: "I am the distant because I am without form, and not everyone has the ability to know me, to receive my teaching and to benefit from it. I am Kaïdara the one close by because there exists neither object nor distance between others and myself" (Bâ 1978, 177).

Asceticism is among the central themes in *Kaïdara* that reflect Fulani as well as certain Sufi initiatic traditions. The initiate is an ascetic engaged in a *jihad*, a holy battle for self-mastery in the process of spiritual purification. As we have seen, it is also an ascetic who functions as an initiator in Hammadi's journey, and who proves to be an incarnation of Kaïdara. In the first phase of the narrative, hunger, thirst, and fatigue are among the physical trials that the travelers face on their journey to Kaïdara. At one point in the journey, when the travelers grow hungry and weary, they are mysteriously renewed: "A moment later, their hunger had disappeared. Their thirst was quenched, they were refreshed; all fatigue left them" (Bâ 1978, 55).

This *jihad* of purification is "the greater holy war" of the Sufi, a holy war against the baseness of one's own soul (*nafs*). Sufi tradition warns that "the worst enemy you have is between your sides"; the Koran warns the faithful to fear the place of the Lord and hinder the soul from lust" (*Sura* 79:40). The Koranic expressions referring to the blameworthy soul (*an-nafs al-ammara bi's-su'*, "the soul commanding to evil," *Sura* 12:53) as well as to the blaming soul (*an-nafs al-lawwama*, *Sura* 75:2) point to this internal battle between the nobler and baser instincts that leads to the purification of the initiate (Milson 1979, 59, Schimmel 1975, 112–14).

Kaïdara is presented as the archetypal initiator, directly revealing himself to Hammadi as God did to the Prophets. The description of his incarnation as an ascetic is reminiscent of the description of Muhammad in *Sura* 53 of the Koran, the section entitled "The Star" (*an-Najm*). The old ascetic is found motionless, "turned to the East, his face lifted, and without the least shudder, watching the sky. Thus, he seemed to be waiting for the appearance of a star or of any other celestial thing." The stillness of the ascetic's gaze in anticipation of a heavenly apparition recalls that of Muhammad's gaze. According to Hampâté Bâ, Sufi mystics interpret the fact that "his (Muhammad's) sight did not rove" as indication of the Prophet's absolute concentration on God, and they aim to emulate such motionless contemplation as part of their spiritual and physical discipline (Bâ 1978, 87).

Just as each Sufi confraternity may have its own holy places as the destination of additional pilgrimages, so we may see the physical journey to Kaïdara as a kind of *haj* (or "pilgrimage") on the path to purification. The journey to the god of gold and knowledge is, like the Muslim pilgrimage, a journey into the self: the object is a mystical union with the deity and divinely inspired knowledge. Appropriately, the questing tale of Fulani initiation involves a physical journey as well. The travelers to Kaïdara make their journey on foot, the most trying means; walking also brings them in closer contact with the earth, the source of the gold and the mysteries it hides. At one point in their journey to Kaïdara, the three travelers journey by night, while others are sleeping; Hampâté Bâ explains the initiatic concept that systematically doing the opposite of what is customary (going against one's natural tendency, as it were) is a means of reaching the underside of reality, hence the esoteric truths (69). In Sufism, the main concern is the inner mystical aspect of religion, the esoteric "true reality" (*haqiqa*) rather than the exoteric, written law (*shar'ia*) (37).

Mental discipline is an important complement to the physical discipline the initiate learns to achieve in his "holy war" against the soul. Each of the eleven symbols the travelers encounter holds its own secret, which encourages patience among the three characters — as well as among the disciples who are listening to the narrative as part of their own initiation. When Dembourou begs the scorpion (the third symbol along the journey) to reveal its mystery, the vision responds, "When you will be able to wait to know, you will know" (57). When Dembourou later complains and again impatiently asks for an explanation of the symbols, a sylph explains that the travelers must be even more patient than a smith's assistant (117).

Fulani tales of initiation also contain an element of predestination (*maktoub*, "it has been written"), another precept of Tijaniyya Sufism that Hampâté Bâ discusses in his writings. In *Kaïdara*, for example, the names of the three travelers already foreshadow the way in which we will expect them to behave, even before their journey begins. We know that Hammadi is the only one who will behave in a noble manner, for his name indicates that he was born a son of nobles. Hamtoudou and Dembourou, on the other hand, are names of captives (captives of Hammadi and Demba, respectively), and so it is as if they were destined to behave less nobly.

Almsgiving, one of the five Pillars of Islam, appears as an important theme in *Kaïdara*. The oarsman who takes Hammadi back to the land of daylight requires gold for his service; he then tells the invisible guardians of the realm of the genie-dwarfs, "The tithe that must be paid by those who remove your gold has been rendered." A popular Fulani saying warns, "If the poor man is not given a part of the fortune, that fortune will dissolve and return to the earth" (45). The fifth symbol along the journey to Kaïdara is that of a water hole that seems to refill itself with an inexhaustible supply of water. In the exegesis of the eleven symbols that makes up the final phase of the narrative, Kaïdara likens the image to a man who, filled with compassion, shares all he has with the poor: "He who gives from the heart always finds something more to give" (79).

Before his final revelation to Hammadi, Kaïdara appears as a beggar sent from Guéno, the Supreme Being. Again, we are reminded of the Sufi *murid*, or spiritual disciple; the Arabic means, literally, the "wanter" or "beggar." Although the servants try to appease him with some rice, the beggar insists on dining with the king. Hammadi respects the Fulani tradition that requires that one never refuse a messenger sent from Guéno. So the beggar dines at the king's table, and Hammadi is eventually rewarded by Kaïdara's revelation. (In modern fiction, we are reminded of the role of the Black beggar in Camara Laye's *Le Regard du roi*, which has been compared to that of the *murshid*, or spiritual guide, in the protagonist Clarence's quest (Harrow 1983, 149).)

Hammadi learns that the proper use of wealth is in the quest for knowledge; Kaïdara tells him that the virtuous will find the ladder symbolizing the search into the self and the inner secrets of esoteric knowledge. When Hammadi begs Kaïdara to explain to him the eleven mysteries the travelers saw on their journey, the god responds: "Use well the gold I have given you. If your deeds are good, you will find everything in it, even the ladder that leads to the heavens and the stairs that lead to the center of the earth" (Bâ 1978, 31). This image of the ladder and stairway is reminiscent of the Sufi concept of the "ladder of perfection" (*suluk*), which is the path to mystic illumination, as well as the "ladder toward heaven," which symbolizes the Sufi master's role as mediator in bringing divine revelation to his disciple (Schimmel 1975, 237). This image is concretized in *Kaïdara* in the nine-step stairway which led the travelers to the underworld of the genie-dwarfs, when their journey to Kaïdara began. Again, we are reminded of Islamic esoterism, which associates a descent of nine steps with the ascetic path of purification that leads to mastery of the nine senses (Bâ 1978, 31).

Indeed, throughout *Kaïdara* we are reminded of the significance of numerology in Islamic and traditional African esoterism. In both traditions, for example, the number eleven has especially powerful symbolism. Eleven is the number of symbols that confront the travelers on their journey to Kaïdara, and whose exegesis makes up the final phase of Hammadi's initiation presented in the tale. These eleven symbols appear at eleven distinct phases of the journey, which correspond to the eleven layers of the earth through which the travelers must descend before reaching Kaïdara, god of knowledge and of gold. The number three and multiples of three are also found throughout the narrative. The three travelers set out on three routes; they are each rewarded by three hoards of gold; Hammadi receives three pieces of advice from the ascetic. While it is true that the number three is commonly found in many oral literary genres, virtually every page of *Kaïdara* contains an allusion to numerological symbolism; the abundance of these references is all the more striking given the relative scarcity of numbers found in Fulani references to worldly matters. Brenner's discussion of numerology in Tijaniyya tradition and, in particular, in the teachings of Tierno Bokar focuses on its underlying principles of analogical analysis, and thus helps to explain the seeming inseparability of numerology from the symbolism of Fulani initiatic narrative:

> The methodology of analogical analysis and demonstration was a logical derivation of the Muslim hierarchical vision of the cosmos: all existence is interrelated because it shares a common source in God, the Creator .... By studying what is observable and by employing the principles of analogy, one can gain greater understanding of what is not observable. During the classical period of Islamic scholarship ... the one discipline which seems to have gained and retained prominence among Muslim scholars in West Africa was numerology, because of its fundamental importance to all the other sciences. (Brenner 1984, 93)

We may compare Hammadi's role as archetypal initiate/initiator in *Kaïdara* to that of Islam's *waly*, "saint and sage of God, living by and for the love of God, in the mysterious circle of divine proximity" (Bâ 1972, 52); for Hammadi is directly chosen by God to be the instrument of revelation. At the end of *Kaïdara*, the god of knowledge bids his primordial initiate to transmit his knowledge to new initiates. Among Kaïdara's parting words is the following command: "Keep well what you have just learned, and transmit it, from mouth to ear, down to your grandchildren. Make of it a tale for the heirs to your power." Thus Kaïdara gives divine authority for the archetypal initiate to himself become initiator, and so sanctify both familial order ("transmit it to your grandchildren") and political order ("for the heirs to your power") (Bâ 1978, 177).

This chain of initiation corresponds to the Sufi concept of the "chain" (*silsila*) that links the initiator to earlier Sufi masters and to Muhammad himself (Trimingham 1971, 149–50); thus, the transmission of Sufi teachings through each link in the chain is imbued with the divine authority of the Word of God Himself, as revealed through the Prophet. The authority of the god Kaïdara, like that of the Koran, is also transmitted through the word, i.e., the spoken words of the storyteller/initiator. "Make of it a tale" is Kaïdara's final command, to his initiate Hammadi, to continue forging the chain of initiation.

Like the questers in *Kaïdara*, the Sufi disciple must pass through several stations on his spiritual journey. In the initiation into Tijaniyya Sufism, it is only after the disciple passes all the tests that his master reveals the secrets of esoteric knowledge (*ma'rifa*) and invests him with the invisible power of the blessed state (*baraka*), as Kaïdara does to Hammadi in the final stage of the story. Once the Sufi disciple is in a state of divine grace, he moves from the role of initiate/disciple (*murid*) to that of initiator/master (*murshid*); similarly, Hammadi returns to participate in the initiation of his grandson, in *Laaytere Koodal*, the second in the trilogy of Fulani initiatic narratives (Bâ 1978, 17).

For the initiate who hears the tale of Kaïdara, as for the disciple being initiated into Tijaniyya Sufism, it is the contemplation of the master's spoken word that ultimately leads to divine knowledge and grace. With an image reminiscent of the Sufi master as "the mirror whom God puts before the adept and who teaches him the right behavior" (Schimmel 1975, 237), Hampâté Bâ summarizes the function of the Fulani initiatic narrative as a means of entrance "into the center of one's being"; so he concludes in *Njeddo Dewal*, the last narrative in the initiatic trilogy, "a tale is a mirror where everyone can see his own image" (Bâ 1985, 9).

References

Bâ, Amadou Hampâté. 1968. *Kaïdara: Récit initiatique peul*. Ed. L. Kesteloot. Paris: Julliard.

———. *Aspects de la civilisation africaine*. 1972. Paris: Présence Africaine.

————. 1978. *Kaydara*. Abidjan: Nouvelles Editions Africaines.

————. 1985. *Njeddo Dewal, mère de la calamité: Conte initiatique peul*. Abidjan: Nouvelles éditions africaines.

BOAHEN, ADU, J.F. AJAYI, ADE, and MICHAEL TIDY. 1986. *Topics in West African History*. London: Longman.

BRENNER, LOUIS. 1984. *West African Sufi: The Religious Heritage and Spiritual Search of Cerno Bokar Saalif Taal*. Berkeley: University of California Press.

CHEVALIER, JEAN. *Le Soufisme*. 1984. Paris: Presses universitaires de France.

COULON, CHRISTIAN. 1981. *Les Musulmans et le pouvoir en Afrique noire*. Paris: Karthala.

HARROW, KENNETH. 1983. "A Sufi Interpretation of *Le Regard du roi*." *Research in African Literatures* 14.2: 135–64.

LINGS, MARTIN. 1977. *What Is Sufism?* Berkeley: University of California Press.

MILSON, MENAHEM. 1975. *A Sufi Rule for Novices*. Cambridge: Harvard University Press.

NICOLAS, GUY. 1981. *Dynamique de l'Islam au sud du Sahara*. Paris: Publications orientalistes de France.

SCHIMMEL, ANNEMARIE. 1975. *Mystical Dimensions of Islam*. Chapel Hill, N.C.: University of North Carolina Press.

STODDART, WILLIAM. 1982. *Sufism: The Mystical Doctrines and Methods of Islam*. Northamptonshire, England: The Aquarian Press.

TRIMINGHAM, J. SPENCER. 1971. *The Sufi Orders in Islam*. London: Oxford University Press.

Chapter 11

▼▼▼▼▼▼▼▼▼▼

Islam in Senegalese Literature and Film

MBYE B. CHAM

In few other places[1] in the creative traditions of sub–Saharan Africa is the factor of Islam more prominent and influential than in Senegal. Manifested in form and subject matter and spanning a wide cross-section of talent in both the traditional and modern media of creative expression, this prominence and influence can be attributed to a number of factors ranging from the artistic maturity, religious sensibility, intellectual astuteness and ideological orientation of individual artists, to the more general impact that Islam as a dominant religious force is perceived to have had on secular life in Senegal. These factors to a large extent determine the various ways in which individual Senegalese artists define themselves and their art *vis-à-vis* Islam in particular and society in general. These definitions are creatively translated into choice of form, thematic focus[2] and, to use a cliché, 'message'.

Two opposite sets of equally militant and mutually irreconcilable attitudes constitute the polar extremes that bracket the range of Senegalese artists' creative response to Islam. On the right pole is that ensemble of attitudes shaped by a zealous embrace and vigorous advocacy of Islam as the best, indeed the only, legitimate and effective vehicle for the integration of the individual and society; while the left pole posits a fundamentally materialist ideology and artistic creed which portrays Islam as colonial in nature and, therefore, an impediment to secular individual and social fulfilment. Between these extremes is a range of artistic responses which share an acceptance of the basic ideals of Islam yet are separated here by less zeal and didacticism, there by a constant alternation between reverence and mockery of Islamic holy men, and there again by a strident iconoclasm which indicts religious charlatans and distorters of Islam and its institutions.

Although constructed principally on the basis of religious attitude, this spectrum of Senegalese artists' creative response to Islam is also correlated with certain criteria of language and artistic form. Poetry — both oral and written — in Arabic and African languages is the privileged genre among the 'traditional promoters' on the right extreme, while the 'apostates' on the left end of the spectrum use fiction in French and film in African languages as the preferred media. The less zealous and less didactic 'modern promoters' use fiction (the novel) in French, while oral narrative (the folktale) in African languages or reworked in French constitutes the principal medium for the 'irreverents'. As for the 'iconoclasts', their most prominent vehicles are both fiction in French and film in African languages.

The Traditional Promoters

Although Islam arrived in Senegal as early as the eleventh century (Amar Samb, 1968: 629), it was only with conversion of the Damel of Cayor, Lat Dior Diop, in the latter half of the nineteenth century that the bulk of the Wolof converted to the new religion. In the wake of the advent of Islam and with the development of religious education there arose an indigenous elite versed in the teachings of the Koran and literate in Arabic language skills which were to constitute an important role in their efforts to proselytize and establish relatively independent centres of religious and secular power. From this elite came also the pioneers of creative writing in both Arabic and Wolof (the latter system referred to as 'Wolofal', that is, writing in Wolof using the *a'jami* script). This phenomenon continues to this day, coexisting with other forms of creative expression, both oral, literary and cinematic. Some of the more celebrated figures in this category include El-Hadji Abdoul Aziz Sy, El-Hadji Ibrahima Niasse, Moussa Ka, El-Hadji Ahmadu Bamba M'backe and Khali Madiakhaté Kala (see Bamba Diop, n.d.: 66–70, and Amar Samb, 1968, 1971, 1972).

Because Islam and the Arabic language are so closely identified,[3] literary expression in Arabic and Wolofal among Senegalese Muslim clerics and scholars becomes a religious undertaking. Hence the preponderance of themes clustering around Islamic hagiography, religious virtue and duty, and the dependence on formal and technical norms and conventions drawn primarily from the Koran and Arabic creative traditions. Amar Samb's study on this aspect of literary creativity among the Wolof Muslims is invaluable, and this section of my essay owes much to his findings. The formal and thematic dependence of part of Wolof literary creativity on Islam is succinctly captured by Samb when he makes the following observation:

> Que doit la poésie 'Wolof' à la religion musulmane? C'est avant tout la metrique, le cadre, la technique de la grande quasida ou ode. Tous les thèmes classiques que traitent les poètes arabes sont cultivés par ceux dont on a précédement évoqué le nom [i.e. Moussa Ka, El-Hadji Abdoul Aziz Sy, etc.]. [Amar Samb, 1968: 634.]*

Although one may take exception to Samb's attribution of the ode to Arabic sources—does not the Wolof have the *tagg* or praise poem/ song which is pre-Islamic?—details of this dual allegiance leap to the surface when one takes a look at a representative sample of works created in this tradition. In evidence are not only panegyrics to the Prophet Mohammed, religious masters, history of the prophets and expositions on Islamic eschatology, but also an impressive array of Arabic metrical patterns—*mutaqārib*, *basït*, *madïd*, *rajaz*, etc—and poetic formulas.

It is hardly surprising, then, to see a praise poem by El-Hadji Abdoul Aziz Sy composed in Arabic and Wolof, as can be seen in the following extracts from the poem dedicated to his elder brother, Abu Bakr Sy, the first *khalifa* of the Tijani brotherhood at Tivavoune:

1
Hamdan lirabinn Kariimin Khassanaa Tyilubir
Tyiây gnönêêlammitakh may dyog difentati woy
Abaal-Habiibi wa rabba-l-ardi
Yaa dyara woy

3
Khaliifatu sheikho wa-l mukhtaaru
Yaa fi di mbör
Yaa fii fêgal diina ay daanam
Te nyêpp lowar

5
Tyoos lên! te bakako
Bil—Amdaahi mooko yayoo
Daan sadyo gaangi
Te tösbit moodi
Mbor—mi ko-dyar

* Translations by the editor of French extracts are provided at the end of the chapter.

6
Minal — basiiti, maddidin
Kaamilin, ramalin,
Wa waafirin, rajazin,
Banye — de tamaak sabar

[Samb, 1968; 636—7]

Translation:

1
Glory to the Generous Master who has no doubt authorized me
To get up and compose a song in praise of his merits
O Father of Habib, O Lord of the earth!
It is you who are most worthy of praise.

3
O Calife, O Master, O the chosen one!
It is you who are the champion here
It is you who protect the religion against the evil of its enemies
Even though this is our duty all!

5
Move, exhalt him with praises
They are his due
Here is the invincible champion!
Lift up a leg to exhalt him
He who is the champion

6
(Praise him) in basiit, madiid,
Kaamil, ramal
Waafir and rajaz
Instead of using *tama* and *sabar*[4]

The interlinear use of Arabic and Wolof (line 1 in stanzas 1 and 3, and lines 1, 2 and 3 in stanza 6 are in Arabic, and most of the rest is in Wolof) is a procedure typical of this creative tradition in Senegal, and may in some way be expressive of a similar process within the larger context of the contact between Islam and Senegal.[5] Ironically, however, the poet seems unbothered by or unaware of the contradiction, evident in stanza 6, in his advocacy for the use of Islamic/ Arabic metre and poetic convention over supposedly 'pagan'/un-Arabic *tama* and *sabar* while much of the language of the poem — Wolof — belongs to the same cultural universe as the *tama* and *sabar*.

Moussa Ka, the celebrated Wolof poet and discipline of Amadou Bamba, the founder of the Muriddiyya brotherhood, whose poetic creations in Arabic he translated into Wolof, also makes creative use of Arabic — such as *Fā'ilum mafā'ilatun* — to cast the rhythmic patterns of his compositions, many of which carry the end rhyme *Ya-Allahi* (Amar Samb, 1968: 634). Just like his mentor and peers, he uses his imaginative skills to propagate the word of Allah while at the same time employing the praise mode to exalt the glory and saintliness of revered individuals, such as Amadou Bamba, and their devotion to the ideals of the religion. His diwan (oeuvre) entitled *Barzakh* (Amar Samb, 1968: 634), together with that of his master, Amadou Bamba, form a significant part of the ensemble of the poetic repertoire of the Muriddiyya in particular and the other Islamic brotherhoods in general, a repertoire characterized by a 'courant de religiosité' and 'un merveilleux inspiré par la mystique de la saintété ...' (Bamba Diop, n.d.: 106). These elements are quite pronounced in Moussa Ka's poem *Ma dyêma burati* ... ('I'll try to uplift myself again ...') (Ka, 1968).

Written much earlier but translated and published only in 1968 and too long to reproduce here, *Ma dyêma burati* stands out as one of Wolof's poetic masterpieces, remarkable not only for its refined religiosity and erudition but also for its fine artistry. In eighty lines of classical Wolof, each of which ends with a trill *r* rhyme, Moussa Ka makes skilful use of Islamic hagiography and the device of repetition effectively to convey some of the more salient aspects of Islamic eschatology. An ode to humility, piety and devotion, the poem recreates the history of many saints of Islam, as conveyed in the Koran, as a mechanism for underscoring the ephemeral nature and mortality of human existence. The death of the Prophet Mohammed is held up to be the prime confirmation of this fact:

Ndegam ka takh Yalla bindoon mo ming ne mes
Andaak Sahaaba ya, mbôôlôô moo fi gis dana far

[Ka, 1968: 848]

Since He [i.e. Mohammed], in whose honour God created, is no longer here,
As well as His companions, everyone you see here, will also go.

The poem continues along these lines, alluding to the glory and feats of saints like Sulayman (... *ki môômoon dend bepa* ..., *Daan war ngelaw* ... — 'Who was Master of all the universe ..., who used to ride the wind . . .'), Ayooba (*Yonent ba daan muny ba fatte diabar* — 'the prophet whose enduring patience and self-denial made him overlook a wife') and Issaa Ibn Maryama (*Di soopi yêfórya mbaamal-la, bunyu ko moyaan* — '. . . the one who transformed disbelievers into swine, because they refused to follow his way') who also died in spite of their virtues and greatness. Much of the poem also expounds concepts of heaven and hell and the conditions for entering one or the other. The thrust of the principal message of this poem is the need for a clean pious life in order to avoid the hot fires of *Dyanama* (hell) and gain access to *Tuuba* and *Firdawsi* (two places in paradise) under the guidance and protection of Serigne Touba, Ahmadou Bamba M'backe (see lines 77–80 of the poem).

Space does not allow a more detailed analysis of this poem and of the works of such other Wolof poets as El-Hadji Ibrahima Niasse and his daughter Rokhaya Niasse of the Kaolack School, who see their creative activity as an extension of their devotion to Islam even when their work is based on current secular reality. Their conception of Islam as an integral part of the Senegalese sociocultural patrimony and as the only effective guide for meaningful individual and social thought and action has left its imprint on many levels on their artistic products. Islam, for these individuals, is supreme. A similar disposition is echoed, albeit in modified form, in the creative work of the next group of artists on the spectrum.

The Modern Promoters

Products of African, Arab-Islamic and Euro-Christian education, Cheikh Hamidou Kane (1962) and Aminata Sow-Fall (1979) have had to come to terms with the conflicting values of all these systems which have played a role in shaping their life-worlds. Their efforts to synthesize or resolve these conflicts have invariably resulted in a wholesale embrace of the African and the Islamic, integrated into one indivisible whole in the case of Kane especially, and a rejection of the Euro-Christian, portrayed as a powerful intruder, the harbinger of destabilization and death in all senses of the word.

Outside their creative work, the staunch belief in Islam and its Africanness on the part of Kane and Sow-fall is equally unequivocal. Vincent Monteil quotes Kane, whom Wole Soyinka labels as 'a diligent expositor of the Faith' (Soyinka, 1976: 81), arguing that

> Si l'Islam n'est pas la seule religion de l'Afrique occidentale, elle en est la première par importance. Je veux dire aussi qu'il me semble qu'elle est la religion de son coeur. [Monteil, 1964: 42]

In the same vein, Aminata Sow-Fall, one of the rising female literary figures in Africa today, also expresses her faith in Islam and its place in contemporary Senegal. In response to an invitation to react to the controversial feminist anthology of her compatriot, Awa Thiam (1978), she offers the following guidelines for any liberation action, feminist or otherwise:

> ·... nous souhaitons ... que la femme se libère ... non pas à coups de slogans, mais dans la dignité et le respect de notre personalité et ... religion, ... l'Islam qui n'a jamais fait de la femme une esclave. [Sow-Fall, 1976: 53]

This word view permeates their creative works.

Less didactic and slightly more secularly oriented than the poetry of the Wolof Muslim poets, the novels of Kane and Sow-Fall embrace Islam with equal enthusiasm as the most effective antidote to the Western Christian colonial culture of the Senegalese experience.

Such a view is projected symbolically in *L'aventure ambigue* in the form of a structure of polar opposites which, when juxtaposed in conflict, reveals the superiority of one over the other. Diallobé Islamic mysticism is contrasted and brought into conflict with Western materialist individualism, and this drama, which is played out in the person and experience of Samba Diallo, results in death. But his death, far from implying the defeat of Diallobé Islamic doctrine, vindicates its view of the ephemerality of mortal existence and the primacy of the spiritual. Soyinka's assessment of Kane's novel reinforces this point when he observes that in *L'aventure ambigue*,

> The victor is not traditional Diallobé society, nor the West which was responsible for the weakening of Diallo's spiritual roots, but the doctrine of death; the Teacher: the Word of Islam. [Soyinka, 1976: 85]

Kane's interest is not so much in reconstructing the penetration of all external forces, both Arab-Islamic and Euro-Christian, into Senegal (as is the case with Ousmane Sembene's *Ceddo*) as exploring the disintegration of an already established Islamic society. In other words, Kane's historical account of culture contact and conflict is aborted at the point of the Western intrusion into Senegal, and it does not go back any farther to consider the process by which Diallobé society came to acquire its Islamic character. For him Islam is Diallobé and Diallobé is Islam. Hence the portrayal of the West and its materialist and individualist credo as the antithesis of Diallobé spiritualism and communalism. This dialectic accounts also for the philosophic intensity of Kane's fiction which, in its own way, becomes one of the most glowing panegyrics to Islam by a contemporary Senegalese novelist in French. His glorified account of the mystic purity and commitment of the Teacher of the Text, and of the principles and process of Islamic-Koranic education, stands out in sharp contrast to the more critical account of the same process offered by Mahama Traoré (1974) in *Njangaan* and A. Samb (1971) in *Matraqué par le destin ou la vie d'un taàlibé*. *L'Aventure ambigue*, like Aminata Sow-Fall's *La Grève des battus*, does not allow even the slightest touch of irreverence towards Islam.

Despite its lack of a philosophic and mystical aura, as seen in *L'Aventure ambigue* and in spite of its more pronounced secular orientation. *La Grève des battus* constitutes a significant part of that body of Senegalese creative works that come across as defending Islam. While the sphere of scrutiny in Kane's work is wide and almost epic in scope, *La Grève des battus* limits itself to a fictional exploration of one of the five pillar principles of Islam, *zakat* (alms giving) at work in real life. In this novel irony and outright denunciation of the distortion of this principle by individuals become the devices used by Aminata Sow-Fall to underscore the importance of respect for the true ideals of *zakat* if individual and society are to attain fulfilment in Senegal.

La Grève des battus is the story of Mour Ndiaye; Director of Public Health, whose efficient (officially) yet inhumane removal of beggars, the traditional recipients of alms and sacrifices, from the city in the interest of tourism thwarts his hopes of being appointed to the newly created post of Vice-President of the country. The novel also details the disarray of individuals like Mour Ndiaye who see the beggars' strike (that is, their refusal to accept alms in the city) as the bane of their selfish objectives.

In exploring the divergence between the principle and practice of *zakat* in Senegal, Aminata Sow-Fall strongly indicts society's obsessive materialism which fosters a psychology of dependence easily exploited by charlatans masquerading as venerable marabouts. Deviation from the true altruism of *zakat* bastardizes its moral intent, leading one of the beggars lucidly to observe that people no longer give out of the goodness of their heart but out of an instinct for self-preservation and improvement:

> ... ce n'est ni pour nos guenilles, ni pour nos infirmités, ni pour le plaisir d'accomplir un geste désintéressé que l'on daigne nous jeter

ce que l'on nous donne. Ils ont d'abord soufflé leurs voeux les plus chers et les plus inimaginables sur tout ce qu'ils nous offrent. ... Et quand ils nous invitent gentiment devant des calebasses fumantes et parfumées de *laax*, pensez-vous que c'est parce qu'ils ont songé que nous avons faim? Non, mes amis, ils s'en foutent. Notre faim ne les dérange pas. Ils ont besoin de donner pour survivre ... Ce n'est pas pour nous qu'ils donnent, c'est pour eux. [Sow-Fall, 1979: 52−3]

This account of the distortion of zakat is contrasted with that of the real essence of *zakat*. Significantly, Sow-Fall entrusts the latter task to the mouth of Serigne Birama, Mour's main marabout, who functions in the novel as the principal watchdog of true Islam. He spells out the nature of *zakat* thus:

Il est toujours bon de faire un sacrifice. C'est une façon de remercier le Créateur qui t'a confié ce que tu offres aux pauvres pour les aider à supporter leur misère. C'est bien que chaque fois tu le peux, il faut donner. La fortune n'a pas de domicile fixe, Dieu ne l'a pas attribué d'une manière définitive. Il ne fait que la prêter. Cela, il faut toujours y penser.

The consistency with which Serigne Birama imparts this ideal of altruism throughout the novel reinforces Sow-Fall's preoccupation with the social, political and moral implications of the distortion of zakat for her society. She is quite aware of the all-embracing hold that Islam has on this society, and, like Kane, her interest lies not in challenging this religious domination but in reaffirming its legitimacy and potential by thoroughly indicting its profit-minded detractors. In *La Grève des battus* these exploiters of Islam are to be found in all segments of society, even though the spotlight is on Mour Ndiaye, a representative of the bourgeoisie. Sow-Fall's criticism does not in any explicit way focus on the serigne-marabout. Here concern is with the hypocritical attitude of the monied Westernized elite in particular towards the *serigne-marabout*, who is revered and vilified according to their needs. As in *L'Aventure ambiguë*, there is no room for religious irreverence and deviation in *La Grève des battus*. These spell death, but of the kind that reaffirms the principles and ideals of Islam. The death of Mour Ndiaye's vice-presidential ambitions strips away the obstacle to a true spiritual and moral vision of life. Only at this point is he able to begin to think clearly about the real meaning of his obligations and responsibilities as a public official and a devout Muslim, especially in his dealings with the less fortunate such as the beggars.

The Irreverents

If the Wolof Muslim clerics of Cheikh Hamidou Kane and Aminata Sow-Fall present religion and religious figures with an aura of deep reverence, popular oral traditions tend to poke fun at them but without questioning either their legitimacy or power. The surface irreverence of the oral traditions *vis-à-vis* the *serigne-marabout* is but a thin veil for their deep allegiance to Islam. Parallels can be drawn here with other creative traditions such as Afro-American oral traditions which are rich in satirical narratives about the foibles and shortcomings of respected religious figures, especially the preacher; and this despite a profound belief in Christianity.

Wolof satirical narratives about the serigne-marabout temporarily rob this sacred figure of certain trappings of sanctity, reduce him to the level of an ordinary mortal person, and thus laugh at his weakness as well as his strength. Among the more frequently encountered images are those of the greedy and dishonest *serigne* who falls victim to these moral deficiencies (Equilbecq, 1915: 252−6), the *serigne* who becomes the butt of the practical jokes and tricks of his *taalibé* who finally ditches him into a well (Copans et Couty, 1976: 177−8); the serigne who journeys to visit his disciples in another country, but who nearly starves to death on account of miscommunication due to language differences (Birago Diop, 1961: 137−40); the charlatan Serigne Fall who takes undue advantage of the faith and kindness of his host to freeload off him, but who gets kicked out of the house one evening because his host sees him eating biscuits after dinner (Birago Diop, 1958: 39−47); the *serigne* trickster who outwits a thief (Birago Diop, 1963: 208−15), a madman (ibid, 114−22); and another who tricks a man into confessing that he repudiated his wife after arguing at first that he did not (Birago Diop, 1961: 21−30).

The use of sex as a means of demystifying and mocking the Islamic holy man is quite prominent in Wolof oral narratives. The main motif here is the inability to resist sexual temptation of one kind or another and the inadvertent revelation of sexual misconduct by the holy man in the midst of prayer, meditation or reading the Holy Koran. One such narrative (Copans et Couty, 1976: 103−4) tells the story of the false marabout who, in his zeal to impress the people of his piety, decides to set up house outside the village under a tamarind tree in order to shun the company of women in particular. A young woman, having heard about this very holy man, vows to unmask him. All dressed up, she sets out to the marabout's outpost to find him deeply engrossed in the Koran. She approaches him and asks, 'Where is the road to Misirah?' to which the marabout glibly replies, 'Houn, houn, go on further ... and someone will show you the way to Misirah,' momentarily lifting his eyes from the Koran to catch a fleeting glimpse of the young woman. After a short while this young woman returns to the marabout, prettier and more provocative. Lifting her *pagne* (wrapper) to reveal a glimpse of her *beeco* (underwear), she asks the marabout the same question: 'Where is the road to Misirah?' This time the marabout looks up and says, 'As for the road to Misirah ... ra ... ra, wait a minute ... I'll show you.' Then he flings the Koran aside and jumps on the young woman and proceeds to make love to her, telling her, 'My good woman, this here is the road that leads to Misirah.' In popular lore among the Wolof, Misirah (the Wolofized form of Misr — Egypt) sometimes stands in a metonymic relation to the Holy Land and, by extension, to paradise or happiness. In this narrative, the performer skilfully plays on this word effectively to unmask and poke fun at this imposter who readily renounces the religious path to paradise in favour of a sexual one.

Another popular story — more like a joke — on the sexual foibles of the Islamic holy man mocks the imam whose extramarital affair with the wife of a member of his mosque by the name of Malick is inadvertently revealed by the imam himself. Each time he leads the congregation in prayer he gets stuck reciting the fatiha, and the point at which he falters is after '*bismilaahi rahmaani rahiim* ...' At this point he always turns round to the congregation and asks, 'What is the name of Koumba's husband? to which some answer, 'Malick,' which then is the prompt to continue the fatiha with '*maaliki yoomi diin* ...'

Also prominent in this tradition are stories spun round the adventures and pranks of the *taalibé* on his rounds of begging (Copans et Couty, 1976: 102–3), and the 'fast tongue' of that other human symbol of Islam, the *naar* (Moor), whose perceived inability to keep the smallest of secrets has inspired the popular labelling of a tattler among the Wolof as 'a person who has a *naar* squatting in his/her stomach (Birago Diop, 1961: 13–19).

The use of animal characters as metaphors for exploring human reality occurs frequently in the Wolof, as in many other oral traditions. Thus, it is no surprise that certain animals become invested with Islamic religious attributes. Among the Wolof the cat (called *muus* in Dakar and *woundou* in St Louis) is believed to be Muslim but, this religiosity notwithstanding, he still remain a cat, selfish, artfully deceitful and greedy. In fact the term *muus* in Wolof is also used as an adjective to mean wise, and *woundou*, as a noun, designates a trickster.

The narrative, 'Woundou El-Hadji', retold by Birago Diop (1963: 123—30), effectively captures this duplicity to expose religious hypocrisy and the unscrupulous use of religion for selfish interests. Deeply disturbed by the fact that all of his fellow villagers — Jinax-the-Mouse, Kantioli-the-Rat, Sindax-the-small-Lizard, Ganar-the-Chicken, etc. — consciously shun his company, even though he is known to be a Muslim, albeit a selfish one, because of the reputation of cats as predators, Woundou-the-Cat decides to go on a pilgrimage to Mecca in the hope that returning an El-Hadji would change the perceptions of his fellow villagers. Having no means of generating an income — unlike the fishermen of Cayor or the Peulh cattle herders of the Ferlo — to pay for the journey, Woundou decides to make the journey on foot, just as many did in old times. On his way to Mecca Woundou encounters the same kind of reaction to his presence everywhere he goes. Small creatures run away at the sight of him; his appearance at a mosque in Djakouma causes a stampede and, because he goes there on a moonless night, he is accused of 'taking the Moon away!' (now part of the folklore of Djakouma). Woundou finally reaches Mecca and undertakes all the religious rites for the pilgrimage and then sets out on his return journey now in full El-Hadji attire with a heavy chaplet around his neck. In his absence his fellow villagers bask in complete freedom and revelry and their vigilance is at an all-time low. Woundou returns in grand style, bringing back with him the customary holy water from the Zem-Zem well, chaplets, other small gifts and, seemingly, more wisdom and piety. A huge crowd gathers to listen to Woundou recount his journey to the Holy Land in a calm, composed tone and language, peppered here and there with lofty, nice-sounding religious phrases, all exuding piety and humility. Soon Woundou's narration begins to lose its cadence and the rhythm of counting his beads beings to falter as his eyes begin to focus more and more on his fellow villagers, most of whom now appear more plump and juicy. The crowd begins to get restless and, before long, a sudden stampede for safety as Woundou flings aside the chaplet, the turban on his head, the rest of his El-Hadji attire and the sheepskin on which he is sitting to go after his traditional prey, affirming that 'La Mecque n'a jamais changé personne.' A spoof on the hajj,[6] especially on the artificial glow of respectability and veneration it beams instantly on any returnee from Mecca, the narrative satirizes the El-Hadji who comes back from a pilgrimage to the Holy Land only to revert back to his old evil selfish ways, aptly captured in Woundou's own argument that 'La Mecque n'a jamais changé personne' which he craftily uses to justify his inability to resist jumping on the succulent prey (the rats) in front of him. This narrative is, in many respects, similar to the one discussed earlier ('The Young Woman and the False Marabout'). Their light-hearted tone and irony mask a popular indictment of religious Tartuffes in society.

Although the oral narratives mock these and other religious personalities, the Prophet Mohammed, the Islamic saints and the venerable leaders of the various Muslim sects in Senegal are sacrosanct and, therefore, not the subject of any such narratives (see Copans et Couty, 1976: 36).

The influence of Islam on the formal properties of these narratives is minimal since they are basically pre-Islamic. What influence is there can be discerned primarily in the area of lexical and idiomatic borrowings from Arabic. It is not uncommon to encounter oral narrative performers substituting *bissimilahi rahmaan* ... for the traditional Wolof formulaic opening of narratives, *leboon* ('there was a story'). The Islamic background of the milieu is suggested by the use of Arabic words and allusions to the Koran and related religious matters. The ability of these pre-Islamic art forms to incorporate themes and styles from Islam is a testimony to their versatility and flexibility.

The Iconoclasts[7]

Equally versatile and flexible, film offers the Senegalese artist yet another medium for creative engagement with his experience as well as that of his society, and the predominance of Islam in the latter has made religion a salient theme in his work. The film *Njangaan* by Mahama Traoré provides a good example of such a work.

In spite of his professed belief in Islam, Traoré uses this film to launch a severe attack on the Senegalese *serigne-marabout* as the prime guardian of the first phase of Islamic education. However, like the other artists in the previous categories, his targets are the selfish detractors of Islam rather than Islam itself: 'Je précise que je ne m'attaque pas à la religion en tant que telle mais à ceux qui la détournent de ses objectifs pour opprimer le peuple en le trompant' (in Hennebelle et Ruelle, 1978: 140). As such, the film, whose title means *taalibé* or student, takes a jaundiced look at the dara (the Koranic school) and its headmaster, the serigne-marabout who is part of that group of people Traoré labels as 'les plus gros bourgeois du Senegal contemporain' (ibid., 140).

Set in the rural countryside against the background of a drought, *Njangaan* relates the tragic story of a six-year-old boy, Mame, who is sent away from his village to be educated at the famous *dara* of Serigne Moussa in Rip, just as his father had been educated there by Serigne Moussa's father. But Mame ends up in Dakar as *taalibé* of Mahtar, Serigne Moussa's son, driven from the land by drought and hope of a better life in the city. On one of his begging rounds Mame is hit and killed by a chauffeur-driven Mercedes Benz.

Traoré critically examines the system of education by ordeal common in the dara. Unlike Kane, whose idealized portrait of the system in *L'aventure ambigue* radiates beauty, erudition and mysticism, Traoré lays bare the crudeness, insensitivity and cruelty of a system whose abuse of the physical being of the *taalibé* far outweighs, in Traoré's view, the potential mental and spiritual benefits to be gained from it. The ideal of a healthy balance between intellectual pursuit and physical labour for wholesome education is, in the case of Serigne Moussa, warped and manipulated, producing a disequilibrium in which the physical (because it produces immediate material benefits) becomes primary.

Thus, in *Njangaan*, begging no longer functions as a means of instilling a sense of humility in the *taalibé*. Instead, it is transformed into a meal- and money-producing activity for the benefit of the *serigne* and his family. In the *dara*, Mame and his fellow *taalibé* not only give up their food and money received from begging, but they are also required, under pain of severe flogging, to fill a daily quota. It is on one of his attempts to accomplish this task in the city that Mame loses his life.

Physical labour also combines with begging to further discredit the system in Traoré's eyes. Ideally, because of its rural base, the dara aims to foster a sense of hard work and self-reliance by requiring the *taalibé* to labour in the fields. However, the application of this ideal has too often resulted in the *taalibé* serving as free labour to work long hours on the fields of the serigne. Traoré denounces this exploitation of child labour in the case of Serigne Moussa.

The complete control and freedom of action Serigne Moussa enjoys over the *taalibé* raises the issue of instructor and parental responsibility and obligation towards the child. Mame's father is portrayed as a victim (although a willing one) of his faith in Serigne Moussa. Unconcerned about the change in era, Mame's father's determination to continue tradition obliges him to deliver him to Serigne Moussa with instructions to mould him into a good Muslim or turn him into ashes. It is this unconditional transfer of parental authority in the name of religion to the *serigne* that Traoré questions in *Njangaan*, for such 'abdication' absolves the *serigne* of any responsibility whatsoever. The prevalence of excesses of physical abuse, malnutrition and dangers to which the *taalibé* are exposed are attributed partly to this mentality. Thus, Mame's father never questions the circumstances of his son's death. Serigne Moussa's religious rationalization of his demise is enough: Mame was made by Allah for a reason and placed in this world temporarily, and now that He needs him He has decided to take him back. Serigne Moussa then gingerly walks away with the gifts of expensive cloth just given to him by Mame's father securely tucked away under his arm. Traoré's challenge to this view of life sets him far apart from Kane, who seems to glorify such a perspective in *L'aventure ambigue*.

Again, the divergence between the true positive principle of Islam and its negative selfish practice and interpretation constitutes the focus of *Njangaan*, as it is also is Sow-Fall's novel and the narratives in the oral traditions. But *Njangaan* differs from these in its extremely irreverent presentation of the *serigne-marabout* as a child abuser and heartless exploiter of the religious faith and credulity of staunch believers. Traoré himself offers the following assessment of Islam and the *serigne-marabout* in Senegal:

> l'islam a eu un double rôle au temps du colonialisme: d'un côte il a été un rempart contre la pénétration étrangère, d'un autre côte il a été aussi manipulé par l'occupant à ses propres fins. La France a acheté les marabouts pour mieux asservir le peuple. En surface, ces marabouts ne faisaient (et ne font) pas partie des structures industrielles et commerciales, ils n'appartenaient qu'à l'ordre spirituel, mais en fait, il suffisait que le colonialisme leur donne des ordres: ils les appliquaient. Aujourd'hui la situation n'a pas fondamentalement changé et le maraboutisme joue toujours un rôle mystificateur. Les marabouts actuels disposent d'un main d'ouvre gratuite et de moyens de persuasion plus forts que ceux des hommes politiques qui parlent à la radio ou dans des meetings. Ils sont les plus gros bourgeois du Senegal contemporain. [In Hennebelle et Ruelle, 1978: 140]

Hence Traoré's fundamental distrust of religious intermediaries, especially of the type of Serigne Moussa. Traoré does not explore artistically the details and implications of this dual role of Islam and the *serigne-marabout* in any other work besides *Njangaan*; it is to the literary and cinematic oeuvre of Ousmane Sembène that one has to turn to for the most consistent and radical examination of these issues.

The Apostate

The bulk of the work[8] of Ousmane Sembene (1960, 1962, 1963, 1965, 1968, 1970, 1971, 1973, 1977) reads like a dissertation on religion, and on Islam in particular, and its impact on secular thought and action in Senegal. Like his predecessors and contemporaries in the first category of artists, Islam forms the dominant theme in his work, but from a diametrically opposed perspective. And just as the narratives in the oral traditions and the film *Njangaan* focus on the distortion of certain principles of Islam by individuals such as the *serigne-marabout*, so too does the work of Sembène. But, unlike them, his work takes a radical step and goes much beyond the misdeeds of the individual to project and ultimately reject Islam itself as *the* obstacle to the true integration of individual and society in Senegal. The very first image of the very first film of Sembène, *Borom Sarrett* (1963), is a full shot of a mosque and, on the sound track, the voice of a muezzin issuing the call to prayer. The last image of the last film (to date) of Sembene, *Ceddo* (1977) is a woman blasting away the testicles of an imam with a shotgun. In these two images Sembène gradually and symbolically captures the hegemony of Islam in Senegal on the one hand, and his own atttitude towards it on the other. The dialectic manifested by these two images, separated by a fourteen-year time span, is the most persistent feature in Sembène's work.

In *Les bouts de bois de dieu*, the management of the railway is quietly aware of the power of the religious elite whose active help it seeks in its efforts to crush the worker's strike. Sembène contrasts the collaborationist tendencies of this elite with the defiance of the women who support the demands of the workers for a better deal. Many of the short stories in the collection *Voltaïque* (1962) also set up similar kinds of opposition in which Islam comes out on the side of oppression and, therefore, is contested. This is the case in the story entitled 'Communauté' (ibid.: 117–21) which echoes a similar story referred to in our previous discussion of oral traditions.[9] Here, the crafty Inekieve, the rat, sees through the religious smokescreen of the imam, El-Hadji Niara, the cat, and works out a plan with his fellow victims to thwart the real intentions of El-Hadji Niara and his tribe of cats. Another story, 'Mahmoud Fall' (ibid.: 127–38), details the punishment meted out to individuals who hide behind Arab-Islamic religious and secular symbols to extort money and material profit from believers. And in 'Souleyeman' (ibid.: 139–56), a woman and an elderly cynic team up to advocate a popular logic which makes a mockery of Islamic law regarding women, divorce and child custody.

This dialectic also underpins the very structure of *Borom Sarrett* (1963) which sets up an opposition between the cart owner who relies inordinately on his juju and on the mercy of Allah and the '*grands marabouts*', on the one hand, and his wife who puts more faith in her own actions, on the other. *Emitai* (1971) repeats this opposition, but here the focus is on traditional religion instead of Islam. In *Tauw* (1970) Sembène juxtaposes the image of the Koranic teacher (who sits back and sends his students out to beg or perform physical labour for money which they hand over to him) with the image of women busy at work in the market and of other men working or actively seeking work. The notion of *aaté yalla* ('the will of Allah' in Wolof) which informs the world view of the devoutly religious, such as Adja Awa Astou, and which favours the rich and the powerful in *Xala* (1973), is contrasted with the realistic vision projected by the beggars and the physically disabled who see the El-Hadji Abdou Kader Beyes of their society as the people mainly responsible for their socioeconomic condition. Hence their action against El-hadji. In *Ceddo* this dialectic is at its most extreme with the contending and conflicting ideologies of the Muslims and the *ceddo* brought into sharp focus. Here Sembène commits the ultimate sacrilege when he sets up a woman as the prime challenger to the credo of Islam.

The artistic resolution of the conflicting opposites invariably projects the triumph of the material over the spiritual in different ways. A function of his declared atheism and Marxism (Hennebelle et Ruelle, 1978: 114, 120), Sembène's rejection of Islam is firmly rooted in a materialist interpretation of its impact on the world view of the Senegalese and their approach to the real problems of their society. A brief look at *Borom Sarrett* and *Ceddo* will help outline the main contours of these issues.

The first fiction film by Sembène, *Borom Sarrett* (1963) can be regarded as an overview of his entire oeuvre, in that we find here the rudiments of the themes and styles that Sembène was to take up again and develop in subsequent full-length features. More especially, *Borom Sarrett* offers the first succinct cinematic definition of Sembène's attitude towards Islam. Religion is here shown to be powerless in the face of practical problems of hunger, poverty and the law of the state which seems to be on the side of the educated and the rich. The cart owner's incessant invocation of the mercy and protection of Allah and the *grands marabouts* fails to shield him or provide relief from his miserable condition, so that by the end of his day which the film documents not only does he lose his only means of livelihood (the cart and his tools of trade) when he is lured into a zone of the city forbidden to the likes of him, but he is also stripped of his sense of manhood and self-esteem when forced to switch roles with his wife. And all this in spite of the loyal services of a horse named Al-Bourah.[10] The assemblage of bones in the emaciated skeleton of the cart owner's horse, which he significantly baptizes Al-Bourah, is at once a parody and irreverent negation of the splendour, the grace and the beauty of its more famous mythical namesake. Sembene resorts to such kinds of symbolism to ridicule aspects of Arab-Islamic belief and folklore held in reverence of Senegalese Muslims.

Borom Sarrett contrasts two different methods of dealing with socioeconomic challenges. The first one represented by the cart owner, focuses on Allah and the *grands marabouts*, while the other one, represented by his wife, places a premium on the concrete actions of human beings. The cart owner's profound sense of religious piety is portrayed as a handicap which not only renders him vulnerable to exploitation but also inhibits actions deemed imperative by Sembène for solving his pressing problems. His decision to venture into the forbidden (to him and his cart) plateau area of Dakar is a function of his naïve belief in the power of his prayers to Allah and the *grands marabouts* to work miracles and keep the police away. Of course, these powers remain silent and impotent *vis-à-vis* the power of the Western-style police who confiscate his cart and send him back to the Medina,[11] emasculated and accompanied by a hungry, malnourished, overworked and humiliated Al-Bourah. Should one see in this return to his familiar, more wholesome, neighbourhood (as opposed to the decadence of the Western-inspired plateau) a parody of the journey from Mecca to Jerusalem and then to the Dome of the Seven Heavens by the Prophet Mohammed?

By contrast, the wife's determination and her promise to feed the family that evening are presented as more realistic and promising in terms of their efforts to satisfy their basic material needs. Although the film ends with the wife handing over the child to the husband and leaving the compound, thus letting the audience speculate as to what she will do to feed the family — prostitution? — the important issue for Sembène is the potential for change implied in her action. She is the embodiment of Sembène's essential belief in man as the only force capable of solving practical problems of the kind portrayed in the film.

The opposition between the spiritual and the material laid out in this first film becomes one of the basic building blocks of each of Sembène's subsequent works. The artist systematically undermines the reign of the religious, which he clearly links to secular systems of exploitation, while at the same time glorifying the virtues and promise of practical human action, individual as well as collective. This orientation is worked out in details and from various perspectives in *Mandabi* (1968), *Tauw* (1970), *Emitai* (1971) and *Xala* (1973). In these works Sembène reinforces the Marxist notion of religion as the opium of the people by realizing subtle portraits of a society in the octopus grip to Allah, *grands marabouts* and traditional gods, a society held hostage by the *serigne-marabout*, real and charlatan, whose piety is, in Sembène's view, at once a mask for material gain and the reins holding back meaningful social progress. The origin of this hegemony of Islam in Senegal is what Sembène attempts to spell out in his last film, *Ceddo* (1976), which has taken a long time to receive official clearance for showing in Senegal for reasons that will shortly become apparent.

Unlike the majority of his fellow Senegalese artists who subscribe to Islam's claim to indigenous antiquity in Senegal, Sembène presents Islam as one of the forces — the other being Euro-Christianity — responsible for what Soyinka refers to as Africa's 'enforced cultural and political exocentricity' (Soyinka, 1976: 99). Thoughts and practices hitherto taken as Senegalese or African by these artists and by the society at large are re-examined and shown to be of Arab-Islamic origin. Moreover, the process through which these Arab-Islamic thoughts and practices came to take root in Senegal is presented as insidious and violent, not unlike the ways in which Euro-Christian slavery, colonialism and imperialism made inroads into Senegal. Thus, for those artists who see culture conflict in Senegal only in terms of Africa (that is, Africa with Islam as indigenous) and the foreign West, Sembène offers in *Ceddo* an enlarged framework of conflict in which Arab-Islam and Euro-Christianity are cast as foreign, intruding violently into an indigenous Africa with the aim of clearing and cultivating fertile ground to sow their own cultural and religious seeds. The foreign and, especially, the indigenous vehicles of this violent acculturation process are singled out as opportunists to be administered their own medicine of violence. *Ceddo* is, therefore, the most irreverent attack on Islam by a Senegalese artist. It reconstructs its history in Senegal from a diametrically opposite perspective to Kane's account in *L'aventure ambigue*, and the result is the shattering of the Islamic myth espoused and so eloquently conveyed in the work of the Wolof Muslim clerics.

The image of Islam portrayed in *Ceddo* is not a beautiful one at all. Muslims come across as scheming violent fanatics with little regard for the principles of self-determination and religious freedom. Their belief in the supremacy of Islam is translated into a series of highly studied moves which systematically eliminate the Christian mission, the traditional secular power structure and a significant mass of the *ceddo* and their 'pagan' beliefs. This plan culminates in the establishment of a rule based on principles of Islam with the imam as head.

The designs of the imam on the society are quite clear from the very beginning. His initial litany of verbal attacks on the persistence of 'paganism' among the *ceddo* is indirectly pointed at the Wolof secular authority, the king, now a convert, yet who tolerates the presence of such infidels in his society. These attacks become more pointed as the militancy of the Muslims intensifies and as the imam's vow to undertake a jihad against all non-Muslims in the society looms closer to execution. To the king's question as to why the imam never addresses him by the title 'King', the imam replies, that, for him, there is only one King, and that King is Allah. To the *ceddo*s' complaint about the growing harassment from the Muslims and to their question as to whether religion is worth a man's life, the imam, usurping the duty of the king, shouts blasphemy and renews his threats against them. This attitude captures the relationship of the imam to the society around him, and it sets the stage for embarking on a jihad to bring about the rule of Allah. The Muslims burn down the Christian mission and kill the white missionary, their principal rival for the soul of the *ceddo*. Next the news is announced that the king has died on the same night from a snake bite (a Muslim snake?), and the *ceddo* are then subdued and forcibly converted to Islam. Into this power vacuum steps the imam.

The imam's accession to power marks the beginning of what Sembène conveys as one of the most radical processes of cultural transformation in Senegalese history. The imam lays down new rules of spiritual and social conduct hitherto adhered to by only a minority, albeit a powerful one. Among the *ceddo* prohibited practices are the consumption of alcohol and the reproduction of human forms in art and weaving. The *griot* of the erstwhile royal court together with his cronies is unceremoniously replaced by Koran-toting disciples of the imam, and the regime of five daily prayers, the shahada (profession of faith) and Koranic education becomes mandatory. The high point of this process of change comes in the mass conversion sequence of the film where the *ceddo* have their heads shaved clean before undergoing a new baptism, receiving new Arabic-derived names such as Momadou, Sulayman, Baboucar and Ousmane. The music on the sound track of this particular sequence, Arthur Simms's 'I'll Make It Someday', combines with the visuals effectively to echo similar experiences of Africans elsewhere in Africa and the Americas.

Historical reconstruction in *Ceddo*, then, aims to explode a deeply ingrained myth in Senegalese society. Sembène's own attitude towards this myth is most graphically defined in the final scene of the film when Princess Dior, heiress apparent to the throne of the now-dismantled secular kingdom, kills the imam with a shotgun in full view of his disciples and new converts.

Ceddo may be unique in Senegalese artistic perceptions of Islam in terms of its tone, tenor and uncompromising view of the religion, but it is indicative of a growing current of thought in African literature and film in general. One is reminded of the equally caustic savaging of Islam in Yambo Ouologuem's *Le devoir de violence* (1968), Ayi Kwei Armah's *Two Thousand Seasons* (1973) and, elsewhere, in Chancellor William's *The Destruction of Black Civilisation* (1974).

His patent rejection of Islam notwithstanding, Sembène's work is saturated with Arabic terms, idioms and religious symbols which he skilfully integrates into the fabric of each work. Artistic conventions demand this, for he is representing a fictional milieu in which these predominate. One of the most common transition shots in many a Sembène film is the mosque, and the passage of time is usually marked by reference to the five daily prayers. Like his colleagues, he makes creative use of lexical and idiomatic items culled from Arabic for characterization and quite often for satire and irony.

Conclusion

This brief survey has attempted to show the coexistence and interaction of multiple vehicles of artistic expression in Senegal, vehicles which serve to convey individual ideologically oriented assessments of the impact of Islam in a country with a population of approximately six million, 90 per cent of which is Muslim. Vacillating between extremes of reverent apologia and uncompromising agnosticism, with reformist orientations in between, these assessments all convey the almost absolute hegemony of Islam in Senegal. Whether from the right, the middle or the left, the works of the artists examined here converge on at least two counts. First, they project the same overall image of Euro-Christianity and Western culture as villain — for different reasons, of course — vis-à-vis African and Senegalese culture. The same cannot be said for the Arab-Islamic image where there is a conspicuous absence of any such consensus. Secondly, these works are united by a common concern for the health and future direction of Senegal and the Senegalese individual. As such, they form a very important part of the efforts of Africans to come to terms with the myriad forces that have historically shaped and influenced the character of contemporary Africa.

Notes

1. Cf. northern Nigeria among the Hausa and the Fulani, and northern Sudan.
2. For more detailed discussion of the influence of religious sensibility on literary technique and theme, see Johnson (1980) and Amar Samb (1968, 1972).
3. Cf. Mamadou Dia's remarks: 'L'Islam, ce n'est pas seulement une doctrine religieuse. C'est aussi une pensée, une culture et une institution', and '... L'Islam, c'est d'abord une pensée, une culture qui doit beaucoup à la langue arabe, langue du Coran ...' (Dia, 1975: 35).
4. *Tama* and *sabar* are two kinds of Wolof drums. The translation of the poem is mine and is based on Samb's French translation of the original.
5. See Amar Samb (1972: 213–41).
6. See the highly sexually oriented spoof of *zakat* in Copans et Couty (1976: 103–4).
7. Because of space limitation and because of its close thematic kinship with *Njangaan, Matraqué par le destin ou la vie d'un taalibé* is not discussed here. Other works of fiction in this category include *Kaala-Sikkim* (1975) by Mbaye Gana Kebe and *Le marabout de la secheresse* (1979) by Cheikh N. Ndao.
8. Only *Bòrom Sarrett* and *Ceddo* will be discussed at length in this section.
9. See pp. 454–5 of this essay.
10. Al-Bourah (Wolof rendering of the Arabic Al-Buraq) is the winged horse (animal?) which carried the Prophet Mohammed first from Mecca to Jerusalem and then on his ascent to the Dome of the Seven Heavens.
11. Medina is the name of the slum area of Dakar where the cart owner and other people like him live.

French Translations

Page 165: What does Wolof poetry owe to Islam? Above it, it is the entire meter, the frame, the technique of the great "quesida" or ode. All the classical themes that Arab poets treat are cultivated by those who have already been involved (i.e., Moussa Ka, El-Hadji, Abdoul Aziz-Sy etc.).

Page 168: If Islam isn't the only religion of West Africa, it is the first in importance. I also mean that it seems to me that it is the religion of its heart.

Page 169: We wish ... that woman should be freed not through slogans but in the diginity and respect of our character and ... religion ... Islam which has never made a slave of woman.

Page 170: It's not because of our rags or our infirmities or for the pleasure of making a generous gesture that they design to toss us their charity. Beforehand they've breathed their dearest and most fantastic wishes on everything they offer us, and when they kindly invite us to partake from their steaming, scented bowls of laax, do you think it's because they care about whether we're hungry? No my friends, they don't give a damn. Our hunger doesn't disturb them. They need to give in order to survive ... they don't give for us but for themselves.

Page 171: It's always good to make a sacrifice. It's a way of thanking the Creator who has given you what you offer to the poor to help them bear their misery. It's good that everytime you can, you give. Good luck doesn't have a fixed residence; God hasn't dispensed it definitively — it is only on loan. That's something to think about.

Page 177: At the time of colonialism Islam had a double role. On the one hand it was a rampart against foreign penetration; on the other it was also manipulated by the occupier for his own ends. France bought off the marabouts in order to subjugate the people better. On the surface these marabouts didn't (and don't) belong to the industrial and commercial structures, they belong to the spiritual order; but in reality, all that was needed was for the colonialists to give the orders, and they carried them out. Today the situation hasn't fundamentally changed and maraboutism still plays a mystifying role. The actual marabouts enjoy free manual labor and have stronger means of persuasion than politicians who speak on the radio or at meetings. They are the biggest bourgeois of contemporary Senegal.

References

COPANS, J., et COUTY, P. 1976. *Contes Wolof du Baol,* Paris: Union Générale d'Editions.

DIA, M. 1975. *Islam, sociétés africaines et cultures industrielles.* Dakar: Nouvelles Editions Africaines.

DIOP, BAMBA M. n.d. *Lat Dior et l'Islam suivi de la doctrine sociale de Mouhamadou Bamba.* Bruxelles: Les Arts Graphiques.

DIOP, BIRAGO. 1958. *Les nouveaux contes d'Amadou Koumba.* Paris: Presence Africaine.

———. 1961 (first published in 1948). *Les contes d'Amadou Koumba.* Paris: Presence Africaine.

———. 1963. *Contes et lavanes.* Paris: Presence Africaine.

EQUILBECQ, F. V. 1915. *Essai sur la littérature merveilleuse des noirs suivi de contes indigènes.* Paris: Ernest Leroux.

HENNEBELLE, G., et RUELLE, C. 1978. 'Les cinéastes d'Afrique noire', *Afrique littéraire et artistique,* 49 (numéro spécial).

JOHNSON, L. 1980. 'Crescent and consciousness: Islam orthodoxies and the West African novel', *Research in African Literatures,* 11 (1): 26–49.

KA, MOUSSA. 1968. 'Ma dyêma burati ...', *Bulletin de l'IFAN,* Sér. B., 30 (3), 847–60. Transcrit et traduit en français par Bassirou Cissé.

KANE, C. H. 1962. *L'aventure ambigue.* Paris: Julliard.

MONTEIL, V. 1964. *L'Islam noir*. Paris: Seuil.

SAMB, A. 1971. *Matraqué par le destin ou la vie d'un taalibé*. Dakar: Nouvelles Editions Africaines.

SAMB, AMAR. 1968. 'L'influence de l'Islam sur la littérature "Wolof"', *Bulletin de l'IFAN*, Sér. B. 30 (2): 628–41.

———. 1971. 'Essai sur la contribution du Sénégal à la littérature d'expression arabe', *Bulletin de l'IFAN*, Sér. B, 32 (3), 658–63.

———. 1972. *Essai sur la contribution du Sénégal à la littérature d'expression arabe*. Dakar: IFAN, Mémoire no. 87.

SEMBENE, O. 1960. *Les bouts de bois de Dieu*. Paris: Le Livre Contemporain.

———. 1962. *Voltaïque* Paris: Presence Africaine.

———. 1963. *Borom Sarrett* (film).

———. 1965. *Vehi Ciosane ou Blanche Genèse suivi du Mandat*. Paris: Presence Africaine.

———. 1968. *Mandabi* (film).

———. 1970. *Tauw* (film).

———. 1971. *Emitai* (film).

———. 1973. *Xala*. Paris: Presence Africaine. (Film adaptation 1974.)

———. 1977. *Ceddo* (film).

SOW-FALL. A. 1976. 'Africa donne la parole aux négresses', *Africa*, 111 (Mai): 53.

———. 1979. *La grève des battus*. Dakar: Nouvelles Editions Africaines.

SOYINKA, W. 1976. *Myth, Literature and the African World*. Cambridge: Cambridge University Press.

THIAM, A. 1978. *La parole aux négresses*. Paris: Denoel/Gonthier.

TRAORÉ, M. 1974. *Njangaan* (film).

Chapter 12

▼▼▼▼▼▼▼▼▼▼

Women, Tradition, and Religion in Sembène Ousmane's Work

EDRIS MAKWARD

There was a time, now fortunately almost all forgotten, when the imported linguistic and cultural polarity, English–French, with all its distinctive intellectual, educational, and even ideological implications, was considered a stimulating theme for discussion by African and Africanist scholars. Now, a reading of post-independence African fiction such as Yambo Ouologuem's *Le Devoir de violence* (1968) or Ayi Kwei Armah's *Two Thousand Seasons* (1973), in the light of a memorable address given in 1979 by Wole Soyinka, makes one wonder whether the polarity had not already begun to shift from the linguistic to the religious level. And this new polarity could very well be characterized as an indictment on the one hand, or a defense on the other, of Islam in Black Africa.

In his address, Soyinka started by eloquently praising Sembène Ousmane for his sharp criticism of Islam and Islamic influence in Senegal in his novel *Les Bouts de bois de Dieu* (1960), while denying Cheikh Hamidou Kane the merit of authenticity because of his positive treatment of Islam in *L'Aventure ambiguë* (1961), as an integral part of his people's heritage rather than an alien religion imposed through the sword, and through intense social and political pressure.

In *Two Thousand Seasons*, Armah seems determined to show how the outside world was instrumental in the destruction of Africa, and how in this deplorable work of destruction, the Europeans, "the actual destroyers," were preceded by "the predators," the original Muslims, that is, the Arabs. For Armah—in this novel at least—

"Muslim" and "Arab" are almost always interchangeable aliens in Black Africa. The narrator is explicit:

> We are not so warped in soul, we are not *Arabs*, we are not *Muslim*, to fabricate a *desert god* chanting madness in the wilderness, and call our creature creator. That is not our way. (Armah 1973, 4–5; my emphasis)

This negative depiction of Islam and Muslims echoes the more vivid and picturesque portrayal by Yambo Ouologuem in *Le Devoir de violence:*

> With the support of the sheikhs, emirs, ulemas, he (Saïf) formed a union of the aristocrats and notables throughout the empire who, setting aside their lemon-yellow babouches at the doors of the mosques, practiced Islam with great humility and converted the fetishist populace who were beginning to be dismayed at the blackness of their souls. This made it still easier to hold down the people and exploit them. And the Evil One shall be driven out. (1971, 22)

Both Armah and Ouologuem treat Islam in their works from an uncertain historical standpoint and not as it is lived and experienced today in any given Muslim African community. Moreover, both novelists are non-Muslims and their descriptions of Islam and its mark on the lives of millions of Africans tend to be either all too sweeping or indeed superficial.

Religion, in general, and Islam in Black Africa in particular, does not exist in a vacuum and should not be examined in isolation from its cultural and social context. This paper will attempt a discussion of Sembène Ousmane's treatment of religion and tradition in his fiction.

It is appropriate here to refer to the genuine bewilderment of Ibn Battuta, who could hardly believe his eyes and ears at observing a West African Muslim community with its distinctive cultural traits regarding women, marriage, and inheritance, some 650 years ago:

> Their women are of surpassing beauty, and are shown more respect than the men. The state of affairs amongst these people is indeed extraordinary. Their men show no signs of jealousy whatever; no one claims descent from his father, but on the contrary from his mother's brother. A person's heirs are his sister's sons, not his own sons. This is a thing which I have seen nowhere in the world except among the Indians of Malabar. But those are heathens; these people are Muslims, punctilious in observing the hours of prayer, studying books of law, and memorizing the Koran. Yet their women show no bashfulness before men and do not veil themselves, though they are assiduous in attending the prayers. (Battuta 1935, 320–321)

Thus, a fourteenth-century Muslim scholar and traveler from North Africa was confronted with an African society that, in spite of what he saw as its staunch adherence to Islamic precepts, still had its own conception and its own practices and traditions regarding the role of women in society and the rules governing lineage and inheritance.

The people whose customs are described above with obvious ethnocentrism by the renowned "Traveler of Islam," who covered 80,000 miles in a lifetime of travels in Asia, Africa, and Europe, are referred to by the author as belonging to the Massufa tribe whose principal town was known to him as Iwálátan. They are described as Black, Muslim, affluent, and handsome, but of amazing behavior and conduct in the eyes of their Arab observer from the North.

Ibn Battuta was equally baffled at the way the inhabitants of Mali expressed what he viewed as their servile submission to their sovereign, and he quickly generalized about the "negroes' abject behavior" before their king. He described with obvious disapproval the practice of prostration in front of the king by his subjects as well as the style of performance of the traditional poets or griots (Battuta 1935, 327–29).

It goes without saying that Delafosse's remark that most of these customs as described by Ibn Battuta (1935) more than 600 years ago (Delafosse's invaluable elucidation of the Ibn Battuta material dates from 1912) are authentically African, is still valid today (Battuta 1935, 381). While Delafosse's remark was probably based on his own observations made some seventy years ago and applying to the countries then identified as constituting the Western Sudan and now more commonly designated as the Sahel, that is, Mali, Senegal, Niger, and Burkina Faso, etc., it is remarkable to note the similarity of some of these descriptions with say, Wole Soyinka's own childhood observations as they appear in his recent autobiographical novel, *Ake, the Years of Childhood* (1981).

While Sembène's avowed commitment to progress, development, and justice in Africa, regardless of race, ethnic origin or identity, religion or sex, is unequivocal, he remains nonetheless profoundly respectful of those elements of culture and traditions that are part of his upbringing and that do not necessarily conflict with his basic values. Thus his denunciation of societal abuses does not generally amount to a sweeping condemnation of tradition or religion, but comes more often as a result of a discriminating evaluation of specific individual or communal behaviors and practices.

Thus, he writes in his introduction to the short novel *Véhi-Ciosane (Blanche-Genèse)* that: "racial solidarity did not prevent murders, illegal detentions, political imprisonments by the ruling dynasties of today in Black Africa" (Sembène 1966). The story itself starts with the statement that while the village of Santhiu-Niaye had nothing distinctive about it and was not a place of pilgrimage for Christians or for Muslims, its residents were indeed true believers in the precepts of Islam: "ils croyaient ferme, sincèrement, usant leur peau frontale, leurs genoux à la prière: cinq fois par jour" [they were firm believers, wearing out the skin of their foreheads, their knees, at prayer, five times a day] (Sembène 1966, 22).

Ngoné War Thiandum, the grandmother of the illegitimate child whose name Véhi-Ciosane gives the story its title, is a devout, docile Muslim in this very Muslim community. But there are doubts in her mind. She herself does not know whether the long internal monologue that goes through her mind while she lies on her bed, unable to sleep, is a prayer or a list of complaints addressed to Allah.

Moreover, at the outset, the narrator of *Véhi-Ciosane* does not mince his words: Things have changed; the pride of yesteryears, the *sakhe*, the granary-treasury, which was once the true savings bank for the family, is now empty; and the young people desert the countryside for the city where life seems easier, more attractive. The reader is not told the source or origin of this movement that is destroying the village at the benefit of the city; and while Islam is not said to be responsible for this decadence, it is clearly seen as a kind of pillar of stagnation against which the elder men can lean safely in their terror of an unknown future:

> They subsisted on *adda* ... (custom, tradition) and on the hypothetical promise of a choice place in paradise. The paradise of Allah was as a nail standing at the center of their brain, the cornerstone of all their day-to-day activities, reducing, chopping at their capacity to think out their future. They had reached a stage where they could no longer feel the desire (to live) and where they enclosed themselves in the old adage: "Life is nothing." (Sembène 1966, 23)

Although he is not questioning here the truth of Islam, Sembène Ousmane seems to be blaming it for its spirit of fatalism and its inherent message of inertia and passivity.

For her part, Ngoné War Thiandum is rethinking her life as an illustration of an oppressive tradition:

> women this; women that; faithfulness, limitless assiduity, total submissiveness body and soul, so that the master-husband after

Yallah will intercede on her behalf for a place in paradise. A woman's role thus became that of a listener. Apart from her house-work responsibilities, she was given no opportunity to express her point of view or formulate her opinion. She had to listen and apply only what her husband said. Ngoné War Thiandum had come to the conclusion that what the man said had more sense than her tortuous ideas. As a woman — among all women, she thought — she had never had a good idea. (Sembène 1966, 31)

Though this and other such passages in Sembène's work lend themselves to obvious feminist reading, for my part I see Ngoné as an individual woman confronted with a specific trying experience, namely, the incestuous actions, in her own respectable family, of her "devout Muslim master-husband after Yallah, Djibril Guedj Diob."

As can be expected, Ngoné's heretofore harmonious reality begins to fall apart and she consequently makes an astonishing discovery; namely, her capacity to assess events on the basis of her own sensitivity: "à partir de son moi de femme" [beginning with her identity as a woman].

Naturally, the shock of this realization is brutal and Ngoné, as a result, detaches herself somewhat from her everyday reality, and loses interest in the familiar components of the ordinary life of a traditional African woman, in order to take charge of the situation and react responsibly to it, rather than accept the dictates of another individual, namely her husband.

The tragedy of incest within the noble Diob family and their attempts to cover it up constitute the main plot of *Véhi-Ciosane*, and the dénouement is tragic: the grandmother, Ngoné War Thiandum, unable to bear the shame and despair, commits suicide; and her husband, the infamous Guibril Guedj Diob, the incestuous father, is murdered by his own mentally disturbed son, Tanor Ngoné Diob, a veteran and victim of World War II and of French colonial wars in Indochina and Algeria.

However, this short novel is above all an eloquent plea for the necessary transfer of power and leadership and the renunciation of the traditional hierarchical structure of society in the face of abuse and corruption. Sembène speaks unabashedly for change and for confidence in the future through the other hero of *Véhi-Ciosane*, Déthyè Law, a man of modest origin — "un homme de caste inférieure" — a griot and a leather-worker, but definitely now the most credible and most qualified voice in the community to speak for honesty and justice. It is indeed very clear that even though this community seems hopelessly doomed, the continued faith and practice of Islam remain unquestioned for both those few who cannot yet face the uncertainties of immigration to *Ndakarou* (Dakar) and those who leave. Sembène conveys the image that life here will continue to revolve around the five prayers of the day and around all the other basic tenets of Islam. But as the traditional supremacy of the husband, the head of the family, is hesitatingly questioned by Ngoné War Thiandum, the traditional foundation of Wolof society based on the age-old and still pernicious caste system and its inherent implications of prejudice of all sorts are unequivocally challenged by the representative of those so-called lower castes, Déthyè Law, who also doubles as the best muezzin in the community:

> the very foundation of our community is now very shaky. If no one says it now, someone will someday. You are not a leader. You are the murderer of your brother, and our community is no longer what it used to be ...: Griot is not synonymous to servility .... (Sembène 1966, 100–101)

Naturally, not all his listeners agree with him. Some do, however, and he leaves the community with the respect and the blessings of some of his friends who are still influential and respected members of Santhiu-Niaye. The latter fact is naturally meant to give more credibility and weight to Déthyè Law's prophetic words. And his help and support to the young mother, Khar Madiaga Diob, and her daughter (symbolically named Véhi-Ciosane, "White-Genesis") also convey the same faith in the future: "it was a page in their lives. A new one is beginning, which depends on them" (Sembène 1966, 108).

In *Le Mandat* (1966), another short novel which is also the subject matter of Sembène's second feature film, Islam is again portrayed as the way of life of the people; and the morality and relevance of its precepts are certainly not questioned throughout the painful trials of the hero Ibrahima Dieng who, in the end, joins his faithful peers at the mosque after his bitter quarrel with the shopkeeper Mbarka. There he is greeted with the conciliatory words: "Amine! ... Amine! ... Voilà ce qu'on appelle des musulmans. Etre simple, plein de son prochain. Que Yallah nous maintienne sur cette voie" (Sembène 1966, 183). [Amen! ... Amen! ... This is what is called being a Muslim. Simplicity and mutual love and consideration. May Yallah keep us on the right path.] Interestingly, the film version ends differently, with a confrontation between Dieng and the postman introducing a call for social change.

Sembène's second novel, *O Pays, mon beau peuple* (1957), tells the story of Oumar Faye, a World War II veteran, who returns to his native Casamance in southern Senegal to work the land with his people and end their exploitation by the French colonials. Oumar Faye is an unusual "been-to" who comes home not with a head full of book knowledge and an idealistic vision of the motherland, but with a great deal of common sense acquired the hard way as a soldier fighting in a deadly war and as a factory worker, not as a privileged university student. He is determined to confront prejudices from either end; from the bigoted white colonials as well as from the traditionalist members of his family who resist social change. His weapons are his confidence in himself, hard work, and the support of his own people. Oumar's father, Moussa, is a devout Muslim and a respected man of his community:

> For him, everything was said in the Koran and it was in the holy book that he would draw all his judgments and his advice. He had the reputation of being severe, harsh even, but he was loved by all and he was often called upon for advice at the local tribunal. In the eyes of the faithful he was even more venerable because of his three wives. (Sembène 1957)

As can be expected, there is a real gap between father and son here. But although Oumar can hardly conceal his bewilderment on learning that his father, in his eagerness to make the holy pilgrimage to Mecca, had disposed of property that was Oumar's through inheritance from his maternal grandmother without consulting him, he refrains from open confrontation with his father, in the name of tradition. And while he confesses to both father and mother that he has no desire to visit Mecca for the holy pilgrimage, "the dearest hope of every true Muslim," he does not interfere with Moussa's plans for the Haj.

Thus, here, too, the hero's concern is change and progress for the benefits of all. His dream is of a world of:

> popping tractors pulling ploughs from morning to evening across the plain; all around, the crowd of those who were not yet initiated watching with eager eyes .... In three days, three fields had been ploughed and sowed .... The marshes had been sweetened, the rice fields irrigated, the bush cleared for miles and miles, the ponds filled ... (Sembène 1957, 178, my translation)

Oumar knows that this dream cannot occur miraculously without important changes in people's behavior and attitudes to life, but he seems also aware that some reasonable amount of patience is necessary.

He shows this in his dealings with "Papa" Gomis, the older African trader whose cooperation and support he and his young partners are seeking. This awareness is also apparent in the discussion with his French wife, Isabelle, and a friend, Agnès, regarding the touchy question of excision or female circumcision among the Diola of Casamance.

In the short story, "Ses trois jours" (Sembène 1962, 43–71), the injustices inherent in a polygamous marriage are revealed. There is also a reference to the desire for change among some women. Naturally, this is not seen with a sympathetic eye by the male protagonists who find unacceptable the demands by a group of Bamako women that polygamy be abolished.

It is significant, however, that although the main character here, Noumbé, does ask herself the important question: "Pourquoi acceptons-nous d'être le jouet des hommes?" (Sembène 1962, 61). ["Why do we accept being the toy of men?"], we are still told that "this desire to escape from the circle of polygamy . . . was rather like a moment of aberration on her part" (Sembène 1962, 61). Moreover, when Noumbé finally revolts openly against her polygamous husband and in the presence of his friends, it is not to denounce the institution of polygamy itself, but more specifically to protest her husband's failure to abide by the "rules of the game," in particular the "three days" rule (les "trois jours").

The short story "Souleymane" is also (139–56) about polygamy. It deals with Souleymane, the caretaker of the village mosque and husband of three wives already, who lusts for a fourth, much younger woman. Here, too, the abuses of the institution are revealed, and the aging lustful Souleymane is even ridiculed, but the institution itself is not questioned by the men or the women. Yacine, the young wife who is said to be a Muslim believer, but not a saint, takes a lover, and when she gets pregnant a second time, the dispute is taken to an eccentric *cadi* (a Muslim customary judge), who argues that the death of a husband does not prevent a pregnant woman from giving birth; therefore, nobody is really sure that Souleymane is the true father of Yacine's two sons . . . (Sembéne 1962, 155–56). Thus, while the lustful Souleymane is ridiculed in public, the institution of polygamy is not really questioned in this story.

Xala, one of Sembène Ousmane's more recent films also based on one of his short novels (1973), is the story of corruption and of base venality among a relatively newer class of *nouveaux riches* in contemporary Africa, the successful businessmen. The hero, El Hadji

Abdou Kader Bèye, is an influential member of the newly Africanized Chamber of Commerce of Dakar. He must translate his new success into the only terms he knows, the "acquisition" of a new wife, his third; as with Souleyman's fourth, she is much younger than his first two. But as he is about to savor his "victory," he is struck by a cruel blow of destiny: he has the *xala*, he is impotent!

In addition to denouncing corruption and the abuse of power by the new ruling classes, *Xala* develops a strong case against polygamy, excessive materialism, and the lingering power of superstitions and charlatanism among so-called modern Africans who have not yet completed a true synthesis of two cultures. Kader Bèye and his friends are the representatives of that class of Africans. He is thus described as having "a bourgeois European education and a feudal African education," but we are also told that the fusion, the synthesis of the two was incomplete.

Les Bouts de bois de Dieu, (*God's Bits of Wood*, 1960), Sembène Ousmane's universally acclaimed novelistic masterpiece, can be said to be as much the story of the historic 1947−48 Dakar−Niger railway strike under colonial rule as it is an eloquent account of the strength, courage and foresight of women − not educated or aristocratic, but ordinary, illiterate womenfolk of modest origin and rank in society, including a prostitute and a common blind woman beggar. Characteristically, the book is dedicated to men and women: "A mes frères de syndicat et à tous les syndicalistes et à leurs compagnes dans ce vaste monde." (To all my trade-unionist brothers and to all the trade unionists of the wide world and their women). It is also of significance to note that about one-third of the book centers around women, their preoccupations and their participation in the strike; and the chapters are titled after the names of some of the most visible women characters in the novel, such as "Maimouna," "Penda," "Mame Sofi," "Ramatoulaye," "Houdia Mbaye" or "la marche des femmes."

Four generations of women are represented in the novel: the old Bambara grandmother, Niakoro-la-vieille, who speaks for the continued respect of tradition; the wives of railway workers from the three major cities in which the action takes place, Dakar, Thiès and Bamako; the adolescent high school student, N'Dèye Touti; and little Ad'jibid'ji, who exasperates her grandmother with her spontaneous use of French words and phrases. While no chapter is named after N'Dèye Touti, she is truly the representative of the African woman of tomorrow, literate, independent-minded, and uncompromising on the question of polygamy. She naturally admires the central hero in the novel, the trade union leader, Bakayoko, who also rejects polygamy and is for progress and change, but who warns her on several occasions against the servile and indiscriminate imitation of Western culture (Sembène 1960, 108; 1970, 114).

While Islam is not directly criticized here, its most dignified leaders, Sérigne N'Dakarou (the marabout of Dakar) and El Hadji Mabigué, represent an old-fashioned leadership always ready to play the colonial masters' game of exploitation and oppression.

Another recent novel by Sembène, *Le Dernier de l'empire* (1981), provides some very humorous glimpses of contemporary Senegal, but on the whole is a disjointed and mostly anecdotal picture of a hopelessly corrupt neocolonialist government of Senegal. Here, under the leadership of a Christian president, Léon Mignane, and a younger prime minister, Daouda, the presence of the one and only woman cabinet minister, Madame le ministre de la Condition Féminine, Nafissatou, does not suggest progress or improvement of any kind in the condition of women. She is doubtless only a showpiece.

Le Dernier de l'empire does not compare favorably with Sembène Ousmane's earlier works. It is sketchy and the plot is diffuse, centered as it is around the strange and apparently deliberate disappearance of the venerable president. This disappearance is well thought out to allow the previously docile and hesitant prime minister to succeed his mentor legally in accordance with the recently amended national constitution. Many of the episodes are so close to current events in Senegal and other parts of Africa at the time of publication that it is often almost impossible to draw a line between satire, jest, double entendre, or plain reality.

In *Ceddo* (1980), a more recent film, Sembène treats Islam in an historical context for the first time. He gives a vivid and spectacular portrayal of Islam as a new religion that came from the outside and imposed itself over the traditional religious and political institutions, first insidiously, and then very forcefully and overwhelmingly. *Ceddo* is indeed the first work in which Sembène depicts Islam not as a fully integrated part of his people's everyday life, or even as a spiritual power concerning itself extensively with the salvation of the soul, but rather as a powerful institution whose adherents strive to establish a towering and comprehensive control over the people's lives, and above all, aspire without any doubts whatsoever to impose a lasting new ruling class through its ambitious leadership. To use Lemuel Johnson's words, *Ceddo* is indeed "Sembène's most comprehensive attack on God's saints and governors, and their effect on the African past and present" (1980, 40).

What is important here is not the veracity of the historical details or the accuracy of the chronology, but the compelling execution of the author's intent to remove the untouchable aura of Islam in his country by portraying its implantation in his society as the result of a merciless struggle for political control between the weakening, age-old traditional royal institution led by *Buur* (the king) and the intruder, that is, Islam under the leadership of the marabout. In this struggle, Sembène shows that while the winner is undoubtedly Islam, a brave and defiant princess can find in herself the willpower to stand up and avenge her father's disguised assassination by shooting the Imam (*ilimaan*) himself.

Ceddo is undoubtedly a very powerful and timely statement on a very touchy subject in Senegal, that is, the religion of the majority of the national population. It boldly asseses an institution that sought to dominate the entire lives of the people, and that was ready to bring to an end the traditional political institutions that initially allowed it to infiltrate the society and that now appeared to stand in its way.

Naturally, Sembène is dealing here with the past, and more specifically with the Senegalese past. It goes without saying, however, that the interpretation of those past events in contemporary terms is unavoidable. And it is doubtless because of the seriousness and the immediacy of such a transposition, and because of all the political and social implications involved, that *Ceddo* had difficulty obtaining the Senegalese government's authorization to be shown to the general pubic in Senegal, and certainly not only as a consequence of any linguistic quarrel over the spelling of the title, as has been rumored.

Those elements that characterize Sembène Ousmane's best works are present in *Ceddo* — that is, the blunt honesty and courage of a committed artist who portrays his society at a significant turning point in its history, without any complacency. Despite the basic fundamental differences in the psychological and temperamental make-up of their personalities, and in the nature of their varied callings, Sembène's main characters are all portrayed vividly and full-size, so to speak, and with very little shadings. Thus, the weak king, his colorful aides and the brave princes, the passionately resolute princess, the *ceddo* or pagan leaders, the *illiman*, or Muslim leader, the French missionary and the French trader with their dreams of past and future, are all dramatically convincing and unforgettable. Indeed, the Muslims are not portrayed as worse than their predecessors, the *ceddo*, the "pagans." Nor are they seen as necessarily better. Sembène's intention here is clearly neither to vilify nor to idealize. Rather, his purpose is to portray Islam as an institution that sought to establish complete control over all aspects of life in the society. Sembène is concerned with showing, above all, that Islam did not establish itself among his people only so as to save their souls. There always was and there still is the desire to wield more secular power.

While the position displayed in *Ceddo* is quite compatible with Sembène's religious skepticism, this work does constitute a definite break from his previously guarded criticism of Islam. The parallels between Islam and Catholicism in Senegal, as seen through the colorful pageantry of the Catholic pilgrimage of Popenguine, are a clear indication that as far as Sembène is concerned, the same lust for power and domination applies to the history of both Islam and Catholicism in his country. Moreover, it is certainly not just another gratuitous statement as to the equally foreign nature of Islam and Christianity in Black Africa. *Ceddo* constitutes Sembène's determined attempt to make his people re-evaluate their belief in the over-whelming capacity of their religion to correct the evils and failures of their society. It must be noted, however, that Sembène's stand is quite in agreement with his long-standing Marxist-Leninist leanings. For although Sembène has never before openly questioned the legitimacy of Islam and Islamic culture in Senegal in his writings and in his films, he has never hidden his free-thinking skepticism. His more modern heroes, Faye in *O Pays, mon beau peuple* and Bakayoko in *Les Bouts de bois de Dieu* are fictional incarnations of that stand. Likewise, his tendency to bestow on his pre-Islamic ancestors an unflinching sense of freedom, courage, and independence, has been a characteristic trademark, decades before the making of *Ceddo*. But between the young advocates of change and revolution — the Oumar Fayes, the Mamadou Bakayokos, and the N'Dèye Toutis — and the representatives of the old Muslim establishment — the El Hadji Mabigués, the Moussa Fayes, the Sérigne N'Dakarous — there was seldom any real confrontation.

Thus, *Ceddo* indicates more boldness in the treatment of Islam. There is here a definite intent to demystify by portraying symbolically the advent of Islam in a given community in Senegal as the subjugation of one system of control — political, social, and religious — by another. But, even in *Ceddo*, there is no overt attempt to attack the divine spirit and practices of Islam, and, in fact, Sembène's harsher portrayal of Islam has to be seen more as an understandable urge to broaden the perspective of his viewers with regard to their history than as a sudden bold disaffection with the religion of his forbears. The sense of urgency of his endeavor may indeed have been increased by the appearance of the first tentacles of the hydra of Muslim fundamentalism in Senegal and in other parts of Muslim West Africa in the late 1970s.

Lastly, neither *Ceddo* nor any of Sembène Ousmane's other works so far can be equated with the harshly condemnatory frescoes of Islam found in some of Armah's earlier work and in Ouologuem's only novel. Nor should they be read as illustrative indicators of a new polarity in Africa along religious lines.

References

ARMAH, AYI KWEI. 1973. *Two Thousand Seasons*. Nairobi: East African Publishing House.

BATTUTA, IBN. 1935. *Travels in Asia and Africa, 1295—1354*. London: George Routledge and Sons.

JOHNSON, LEMUEL. 1980. "Crescent and Consciousness: Islamic Orthodoxies and the West African Novel." *Research in African Literatures* II, 1: 26—49. (Also Chapter 16 in this book.)

KANE, CHEIKH HAMIDOU. 1961. *L'aventure ambiguë*. Paris: Julliard.

OUOLOGUEM, YAMBO. 1971. *Bound to Violence*. New York: Harcourt Brace Jovanovich.

OUSMANE SEMBÈNE. 1957. *O Pays, mon beau peuple*. Paris: Le Livre contemporain—Amiot Dumont.

———. 1960. *Les Bouts de bois de Dieu*. Paris: Le livre Contemporain.

———. 1962. *Voltaique*. Paris: Présence africaine.

———. 1966. *Le Mandat, précédé de Véhi-Ciosane*. Paris: Présence africaine.

———. 1970. *God's Bits of Wood* New York: Doubleday.

———. 1973. *Xala*. Paris: Présence Africaine.

SOYINKA, WOLE. 1981. *Ake, The Years of Childhood*. New York: Random House.

Chapter 13

▼▼▼▼▼▼▼▼▼

Mouridism in Senegalese Fiction

DEBRA BOYD-BUGGS

Muslim brotherhoods have considerable political and economic influence in Senegal and this influence is reflected in fictional portrayals of Senegalese society. There are two dominant brotherhoods in Senegal, particularly among the Wolof: the Tidjaniyya and the Mouridiyya or Mourides.[1] The founders of these brotherhoods are considered to be saints or *waliyu* in Wolof. Novelists never criticize them. Certain saints, especially Cheikh Amadou Bamba, the founder of the Mouride sect, are given nearly equal status with Allah and the Prophet Mohamed, since their lives are shrouded by popular beliefs about their supernatural powers. Although the Mouride founder, also known as Serigne Touba,[2] is considered to be a saint and is highly respected by writers, Mouridism itself comes under attack by most of the novelists who address it, even by those writers who profess to be Mouride. If Cheikh Amadou Bamba is never criticized in the Senegalese novel, the same is not the case for all of his teachings or for the basic concepts of Mouridism. In novels there is a conflict between the writers's respect for Serigne Touba and their "mise en question" of certain aspects of Mouride doctrine.

Amadou Bamba Mbacké (ca. 1857–1927) was a pious Muslim, a scholar in the Sufi tradition, peace-loving and ascetic, a man whose life was devoted to the improvement of his own religious knowledge and to some extent, that of his followers. Mouridism, as conceived by Amadou Bamba, is characterized by a general militancy, by the importance of the marabout or Muslim spiritual guide as an intermediary between God and the believer, and by a belief in the value of work; as Amadou Bamba himself declared, "le travail fait partie de la religion" (Dumont 1975, 115) (work is a part of religion). He also strongly endorsed the sanctity of the marabout by encouraging the new convert to submit himself to "the necessary guidance of a cheikh like a corpse in the hands of the washer of the dead" (326). These concepts are not documented in the Koran. The innovational force of Mouridism derives from the Mouride marabout's attitude toward work and discipline rather than any emphasis on prayers and litanies. For example, Amadou Bamba's most famous disciple, Cheikh Ibra Fall, would neither fast nor pray, but he did display an exuberant devotion to hard physical labor on Amadou Bamba's behalf. Through Fall's efforts, Mouride disciples were organized into hard-working production units and became some of the largest producers of peanuts in Senegal. As a result, the Mourides have maintained a strong economic and political base.

During the French colonial regime, the Mouride order attracted numerous followers of colonial resistance leaders such as Ma Bâ Diakhou (1809–1867), Lat Dior Diop (1842–1886), and others. Amadou Bamba's brotherhood was feared by the French from the outset since Bamba's father had been a counselor to the warrior Ma Bâ and had married the sister of Lat Dior, who was the last *damel* or king of the Cayor region. In 1886 Lat Dior also led the last major resistance to the French in that area. Thus the colonial authorities watched Bamba carefully throughout his career, and on two occasions when rumors circulated that Bamba had plans to overthrow the French, they deported him. When Bamba was finally allowed to return to Senegal, he was denied permission to settle in Touba, his chosen religious center. Instead, he had to remain in Diourbel, the nearby administrative center until his death in 1927. Bamba's periods in exile, which serve as the basis for popular legends about his life, added to his reputation and drew a large following from those who felt alienated from the French. The theme of Mouridism in Senegalese literature evolves in part around the sainthood of Cheikh Amadou Bamba and the lauding of his role as a militant Black leader.

In his semi-autobiographical novel *Matraqué par le destin, ou la vie d'un talibé* (1973), Amar Samb, himself a Mouride, documents many of the miracles that Cheikh Amadou Bamba is believed to have performed. These accounts of Bamba's activities take place in Touba during the Magal or the annual pilgrimage of Mouride believers and other Muslims to the holy city in honor of the marabout's return to

Senegal after seven years of exile. In Samb's novel they are narrated by a marabout-griot named Bara Niang. Such stories help explain why the Mourides consider Serigne Touba to be *may u Yalla* or divinely elected.

In one of Bara's stories, Serigne Touba and several other marabouts were betrayed to the French. When the colonial governor ordered them to renounce their faith or be shot, the others complied, but Amadou Bamba, prompted by his constant companion, the angel Gabriel, refused to abjure his faith. As a result, the French ordered him into exile. The Serigne's first miracle occurred when his jailers served him a dish of roast dog. As soon as they had set it in front of him, the meat started barking angrily. On another occasion, they took him to Dakar and put him in a cage with an enormous lion. As in the biblical account of Daniel in the lion's den, when the authorities returned the next day, Serigne Touba had tamed the ferocious animal. Cheikh Amadou Bamba is also believed to have demonstrated an ability to walk on water while saying his prayers. When a captain who was anxious to rid the French of the venerated marabout tried to prevent him from praying on the ship, Amadou Bamba threw his lambskin on the waves, stood upon it, and prayed. The entire crew was amazed at the sight. In still another incident, the marabout and the man who betrayed him are both left on an island where a ferocious monster devours humans. But when the creature threatens Bamba, Gabriel appears with an army of angels, saves the marabout, and puts the terrible monster to death in the twinkling of an eye. (This angelic army was the same one that had once helped the Prophet Mohamed fight against the forces of hell.) After this miracle, Bamba and the other prisoner were reportedly transported through the air from the island to the port of Dakar. The authorities in Dakar then arrested the extraordinary marabout who had arrived in Dakar two months before the ship reached port there. At first happy in the conviction that he had rid the French of an African troublemaker, the ship's captain committed suicide when he learned that the marabout had arrived at Dakar before him. At this point, the French banished Serigne Touba to Gabon, but seven years later in 1902 he was granted permission to regain his homeland.

While Bara Niang vividly imparts details about Cheikh Amadou Bamba's life, the people shout, clap their hands, and throw money on the rug in front of him (Samb 1973, 145–147). Cheikh Amadou Bamba is a symbol of national pride in that he resisted the foreign invaders in his own way, not by natural force but by supernatural means. The people believe these accounts of his life and they receive inspiration from them; this indicates that Bamba's influence is even greater after his death. Serigne Touba, to quote the poetess Mame Seck Mbacké, "vit dans les coeurs de ses disciples" (lives in the hearts of his disciples).[3] Instead of thanking Allah and His Prophet, which is what most Muslims do, the Mouride thanks God and Cheikh Amadou Bamba. Novelists who depict Mouridism provide considerable documentation for this practice.

In *Matraqué par le destin*, when the character Uncle Tolé is asked about his health, he thanks God, Serigne Touba, and his personal marabout (29). In Ibrahima Sèye's *Un Trou dans le miroir* (1983), Mamour Diop thanks God and Cheikh Amadou Bamba that his business is doing well; he believes that Cheikh Amadou Bamba is in perfect harmony with God, a claim that he feels should be reserved for saints (1983, 16, 103). Adja Déjuène Fall, another character in Sèye's work, claims that Serigne Bamba, who has no equal, is also her marabout, although she is merely using Mouridism as a pretext to approach Mamour as a possible future husband for her niece.

Mamour's son Doudou, the hero of the novel, regards Cheikh Amadou Bamba in a somewhat different light, for he credits him with having provided the previous generation with a Black leader who helped them retain what remained of their dignity during the disorganization caused by the white colonial presence:

> I can't even begin to tell you all that we owe to Cheikh Amadou Bamba, especially us, the "young people of today," he said gravely, while seating himself in front of Serigne Ablaye. My father and his generation had an image right there in front of them that they could relate to in order to save themselves from the disorganization caused by the white invader. They found a true black leader who helped them to recuperate collectively what dignity they had left. (113)

But Doudou also recognizes that those who want to continue Bamba's work face a difficult task. First of all, they are not saints; they are ordinary humans. Next, they live in a world full of pitfalls even more prevalent and more complex than those that Bamba had to avoid. Lastly, marabouts are confronted with young people who are far more distressed than their grandfathers were.

However, when one turns from the glorious portrayal of Amadou Bamba to examine novelists' perceptions of the basic concepts of Mouride doctrine, one finds Mouridism serving as a basis for attacking the maraboutic superstructure. It is viewed as having established a system of domination and exploitation in which a religious elite distorts Bamba's teaching, abusing their privileges vis-à-vis their *talibés* or disciples for their own personal gain. The implication of the societal problems provoked by Mouridisim appear early in the Senegalese novel and more recent novelists have also addressed the issue. It's important to note, however, that the abuse of the marabout-*talibé* relationship is not seen as unique to the Mourides, who have influenced the other brotherhoods. Nonetheless, the predication of the necessity of the marabout in the salvation of the soul is a key aspect of Mouride doctrine, though such teaching is not based on the Koran.

In *Karim* (1948) Ousmane Socé suggests that Mouridism converts illiterate and naive but strong, muscular men into submissive peanut workers. On a visit to Diourbel Karim meets a young man who fits the above description:

> At Diourbel, Karim met a "mouride," the boatman Médoune Dieye, totally illiterate, over six feet tall, defined pectoral muscles like spread out fans, long arms and legs with powerful muscles. He was employed to carry heavy sacks of millet or peanuts weighing at least two hundred twenty pounds. In spite of his prodigious strength, he was simple-minded and naive, so naive that it made him likeable. (1948, 133)

Médoune takes Karim on a tour of the landmarks of Mouridism. He also tries to persuade Karim of Amadou Bamba's sainthood by speaking of the popular beliefs surrounding the day of Serigne Touba's death. Afterwards Karim, contrasting life in the cities with life as he perceives it to be in Diourbel, communicates what is essentially Socé's definition of Mouridism. According to him, Mouridism offers an existence similar to that of a vegetable: work, self-preservation, and a salvation from hell that is achieved by giving all of one's excess wealth to the chief of one's religion. From this perspective Mouridism has two main elements: work and submission to the marabout. Socé sees little necessity for any independent thinking (1948, 125). Whatever impression was made upon him, Karim gives no indication that he is personally interested in Mouridism as a way of life, and he quickly returns to the city. Socé's hero would obviously prefer the excitement of urban living to the vegetable-type existence and exploitation which he sees in Mouridism.

Ibrahima Sèye carefully outlines various aspects of Mouridism in his novel *Un Trou dans le miroir*. The story centers around a marabout-father who uses Mouridism as a pretext to emasculate his own son.

Like Socé, Sèye emphasizes the notions of domination and exploitation. Even though Mamour has been in the city since adolescence, he has scrupulously followed the *ndiquel*, the charge or order of his marabout who had told him to "go, work, pray, and read the Koran" (Sèye 1983, 31). Attempting to instill the principles of Mouridism into his son, he regrets having allowed the boy to attend school, and he tells Doudou that, if he could turn back the hands of time, he would have a peanut field in the country and Doudou would have a field of millet. According to this dream, Doudou would have worked the peanut field in the morning and in the afternoon he would have cultivated his own millet. In Mamour's division of labour, Doudou would not only do his work, he would also do the marabout's work. The implication is that Mamour would do nothing. Uneducated and unskilled, Doudou would have no choice but to do as he was told.

Doudou is viewed by all as the black sheep of the family because he has not followed in his father's footsteps. But Doudou's behavior is not inexplicable. When Doudou was a child, Mamour restricted him. Doudou was not allowed to play with other children, and he was forbidden to laugh. Even after he started secular school, Mamour forced him to study the Koran night and day. Doudou's mother convinced her husband to let him attend the university, but Mamour still made the boy continue simultaneous studies in Islam and Mouride teachings. Although all appeared well on the surface, Doudou was actually undergoing a crisis. At the university, he had met and fallen in love with a girl of the *teugg* or jewelers' caste.[4] Displeased, Mamour ends by humiliating Doudou and forcing the young man to leave school to take a job. Not only is he Doudou's father, he is also the marabout who enforces his authority on a spiritual level. Mamour controls Doudou's earnings by exploiting the Mouride teaching, according to which a disciple owes total submission to his master. He tells Doudou that the true disciple must work for his master until the master tells him, "Go! I'm pleased with you; I bless you." It is only then that he can enjoy the fruit of his labor in solitude. Furthermore, whoever has not received the blessing of his marabout will never succeed in life (Sèye 1983, 31). In essence what the novelist does in this passage is to call into question the teachings of Cheikh Amadou Bamba, who stressed the importance of the marabout as fundamental to the salvation of the soul. According to Serigne Touba, truth lies in one's love for his cheikh. The talibé should obey his master's orders always and everywhere; he should never put up any resistance, not even in his inner feelings. One has to renounce his own free will because the cheikh's thoughts and actions are beyond question (Bara-Diop 1981, 276). In an attempt to assert his manhood, Doudou revolts against the system represented by his father. He quits his job, isolates himself, and neglects the Koran in favor of secular books. Unable to stand up to his father and openly challenge the stigmas of the old caste system, he loses his girlfriend, who marries someone else. Frustrated, Doudou deteriorates morally and succumbs to a life of alcohol, drugs, and illicit sex; eventually he becomes emotionally and mentally disturbed. Mamour decides that the only way to help Doudou is to place him in the hands of another marabout.

The reader is baffled to find a young man who has attended the university and studied the Koran all of his life being led by the hand back to the *daara* or Koranic school. By using Mouride Islam as a reason for denying his son the right to individual freedom, Mamour becomes the author of his son's dilemma. Doudou realizes that he is lost. He cannot adopt his father's characteristics so he finds himself facing "un trou dans le miroir" (a hole in the mirror). When Doudou looks into the mirror, he cannot see his own reflection; instead he finds a hole in place of his identity.

In pure Mouridism, then, one's individual freedom is surrendered to the marabout, who thinks for his followers. The individual should not even attempt to think on his own, because Satan inspires the thoughts of isolated individuals. As Amadou Bamba once stated, "celui qui n'a pas de cheikh pour guide aura Satan pour cheikh, n'importe où qu'il aille" (Bara-Diop 1981, 276). (He who has no cheikh to guide him will have Satan for his cheikh no matter where he goes.) Novelists like Sèye document the reality of Mouridism and the conflicts that this philosophy creates for protagonists who live in a modern world where the individual is encouraged to work first of all to realize his or her personal desires, to act on one's own behalf. In the Mouride marabout-*talibé* relationship, the master receives all the terrestrial benefits, while all the talibé can do is hope for celestial rewards. These notions of work and submission to one's marabout, as one writer has documented them, are still being preached by those who preside over the Mouride brotherhood at the present time.

In *Matraqué par le destin ou la vie d'un talibé*, Amar Samb renders honor and praise to Cheikh Amadou Bamba, but repeatedly criticizes Mouride marabouts who abuse the faithful. Samb even attacks the Grand Cheikh of the Mourides, an actual marabout and the successor to Cheikh Amadou Bamba. The reader's attention is first drawn to the fact that Cheikh Mbacké's enormous wealth derives from contributions given by people who are very poor. During the Magal, these contributions swell the marabout's bankroll to the point where he can easily be considered a multimillionaire. Pilgrims desire to profit from his *baraka* (or ability to impart divine blessings), since he is believed to have inherited his father's *baraka*. However, this marabout's *baraka* is not free. People wait in long lines to kiss his hand and to leave as much money as possible for the privilege of having done so.

Next, according to Samb's depiction, the grand Cheikh is also politically powerful. He heads the second largest brotherhood in Senegal. All the dignitaries in Senegal, including the governor, make their appearances at the Magal. Past and present government authorities recognize the political and economic power of the Mourides' chief marabout, who has the power to mobilize votes and the wealth to buy whatever de desires. In this sense Cheikh Mbacké is a political leader as well as a religious one.

When the Cheikh of the Mourides makes his appearance in Samb's novel, a great ovation breaks out. This charismatic marabout's appearance provokes hysteria. In a phenomenon that is more frequent among the Mourides than among other Muslim sects, the people break out in a spiritual frenzy that closely resembles "shouting" or "holy dancing" in the churches of Black Americans. Some Mouride devotees faint; others enter into states of ecstasy or trances; still others fall into the sand, shaking and screaming when they see the Grand Cheikh. In theory, the Mourides are not allowed to express their own thoughts, and it has been suggested that the emotionalism of this hysteria enables them to obtain some release from the tension created by the repression of what they feel under other circumstances.

In the portrait painted by Samb, Cheikh Mbacké is somewhat unorthodox in his approach to Islam. After he greets the dignitaries and the faithful, he begins his speech. First, he absolves the talibés of the need to go to Mecca. According to the marabout, the pilgrimage to Touba replaces the *haji* or pilgrimage to Mecca. In this way, he confirms the beliefs of followers who assert that Touba is more important than Mecca or Medina, because the Prophet is now in Touba (Samb 1973, 151). In this description, Samb confirms that the Mourides are the authors of unorthodox teachings that clearly distinguish them from other Muslims. The pilgrimage to Mecca is one of the five pillars of Islam, and no one has the authority to absolve a

Muslim of this responsibility. When the Grand Marabout of the Mourides attempts to do so, he is directly contravening the word of the Koran.

After his initial comments, the Cheikh of the Mourides continues by reemphasizing the principles of Mouridism. He urges them to work, because work is the only source of salvation; he exhorts them to practice their religion, because religion is the key to heaven; and he commands them to listen to their superiors and obey them without question. The highlights of Cheikh Mbacké's message are not centered around the pillars of Islam; no instruction is given as to how to live and no references are made to the Koran. As seen in Samb's fictional portrayal, the Magal represents a special time for Mouride believers, but the emphasis is placed on the accumulation of money and on the unanswered question about what the Mouride brotherhood actually does in return for the substantial contributions of its followers.

In Sèye's *Un Trou dans le miroir* there are two other Mouride marabouts, Serigne Ablaye and Serigne Gora. Like Cheikh Mbacké, neither is a mystic; the precepts of Islam do not appear to be their primary concern, and they both support the basic principles of Mouridism: work and submission to the marabout. However, they are strikingly different. Ablaye is an opportunist who had the good fortune of being born the son of a well-known marabout. He is a selfish man whose main interest is to work his way up to the rank of grand marabout for his own gain. Gora, on the other hand, is a type of traditional priest who uses Mouridism and his wits to obtain workers for his fields.

Gora's *daara* or koranic school is situated in the middle of his peanut fields. Mamour Diop takes his son Doudou to Gora with hope that this marabout can cure the young man of his mental instability. Doudou is subject to fits or periods when he loses touch with reality. Oddly, some of the revelations that Doudou receives during these moments shed light upon some of the problems in Senegalese society and seem to reflect insights that Doudou did not have the strength to share openly. When Doudou enters into one of his states in the presence of Serigne Gora, the marabout gives the young man a fistful of cowrie shells, which Doudou hands back to him. Gora casts and recasts the shells. But instead of a regular session of *tanni* or divination during which he would predict the young man's future or reveal what spirit is plaguing Doudou, the reader is astonished that Serigne Gora chooses this moment to narrate a fable entitled "the doe and the horse." The author uses this fable to satirize the Mouride work ethic.

The fable begins when the doe meets the horse, which is wounded and dying in the middle of the field. The horse tells the doe that hard work and age have caused his wounds. The doe sympathizes with the horse but feels that he is responsible for his own misfortune since there is grass all around and he could have eaten it instead of working so hard. The horse replies that he is not like the doe and explains that he only eats what his master gives him. In fact he admits that he is not free to do as he pleases because he is "under orders" of a man who had been his father's and his grandfather's master before him. Because they had enjoyed long lives, he agrees to accept his own state of servitude in the expectation of doing the same thing. After failing to convince the horse to come with him, the well-nourished and healthy doe bids the horse adieu and reflects upon how sad it is to have a master (Sèye 1983, 137). The implication here is that outsiders view the submissive lifestyle that the Mouride brotherhood imposes upon its followers as undesirable.

However, shortly afterwards the doe is wounded by a hunter. Ironically the horse, now the picture of health, comes by. According to the horse, his master came, fed him, bathed him, and caressed him while the others worked. Now that he is well, he works even harder, and the master gives him extra rations. The doe asks the horse to find him a master, but the horse is not certain that all creatures can have a master. This reversal superficially suggests that the Mouride work ethic has positive aspects. However, the reader obviously notices the possible motive behind the master's sudden interest in the horse which results in further exploitation. Also, the wounded doe is now willing to accept a master, but only out of desperation.

The irony of this story becomes apparent within the context of Doudou's experience under the tutelage of Serigne Gora, for his first task is to help the small children organize the dead wood they had gathered from the fields. A university-trained young man is being ordered to repeat Koranic primary school. He is being sent back to the *daara*, as if he were to blame for the education that he had received — the education that had rendered him incapable of discovering and maintaining the equilibrium necessary for day-to-day existence. As a nonviolent, mentally ill person, Doudou is being entrusted to a marabout who is actually a traditional priest using Mouridism as a means to an end. Gora does not pray with his guests nor does he share verses of the Koran with them. Instead he shares a story, which reveals that he expects work and total obedience from his talibés at all costs, a philosophy that paraphrases a previously cited quote from Cheikh Amadou Bamba.

In the religious system of the brotherhoods, disciples are expected to give gifts to their marabouts. Since the marabouts do not have to worry about their physical needs, they can presumably dedicate themselves to their spiritual mission. In return, the faithful benefit from the *baraka* of their masters. These gifts to marabouts are called *addiya* and are not the same as alms given to the poor, although they have the same goal: salvation. *Addiya* are offered to a holy person in hopes of obtaining some of his *baraka* or getting him to intercede in prayer. The *addiya* is not found in sacred texts, but in Senegal, it reflects an obligation that is greater than the alms recommended by the Koran. In principle it is not obligatory; in practice one cannot belong to a brotherhood and have recourse to marabouts without regularly offering them the *addiya* if one has the means to do so (Bara-Diop 1981, 301). Senegalese novelists frequently document this social reality and demonstrate how the *addiya* is essential to the marabout-talibé relationship.

Even though the *addiya* is different from the *zakat* (a basic tenet of Islam directing the believer to give alms), which is supposed to be offered to the poor, some marabouts also profit from the *zakat*. The Mourides, for example, give their *zakat* to their cheikh in the belief that he is in the best position to identify the deserving poor. Regardless of one's economic status, one is expected to share one's possessions with the marabout. Peasants often take the *addiya* off of the top of their sale of peanuts (Bara-Diop 1981, 301). If there is a choice about whom to pay, the marabout generally has priority, and he often exploits this attitude in order to amass a large personal fortune.

Only one writer, the poetess Mame Seck Mbacké, appears to consistently exalt Mouridism for its mystical concepts. In her short story "Mame Touba" (*Anthologie de la Nouvelle Sénégalaise*, 1978), the hero is a devoted Mouride whose wisdom is attributed to his having obeyed his marabout. Mame Seck Mbacké, a member by marriage of Touba's holy family, also makes numerous references to Cheikh Amadou Bamba, Touba, the Magal, and the principles of Mouridism in her book, *Le Froid et le piment* (1983), a collection of semi-fictional, tragic portraits of the lives of Senegalese immigrants in France. One of the underlying themes of her work is that the solution to the Senegalese cultural dilemma is a return to spiritual values. These values are linked to Mouride Islam. According to this author, Cheikh Amadou Bamba provided the banner of salvation and the reading of his poetry constitutes a temporal as well as spiritual balm for the ailing soul (Mbacké 1983, 117); Seck Mbacké defines the Mouride disciple as one who displays great courage, perseveres in work, refuses assimilation and is rooted in traditional values.

Part Three of *Le Froid et le piment* gives the account of the tragic exile of Youmané, a young girl who was raised in a Mouride home in the Baol region of Senegal. According to Yaye Peinda, Youmané's mother, the girl was born with a contrary spirit. Early in life she displayed a preference for what was considered to be masculine activities, such as sports and running in the fields. Flighty and impulsive, she is unable to perform well in school. Her preoccupation with material things and with her individual desires eventually leads her from the village to the city to work as a maid. In the city she is sexually abused and impregnated by a white employer. This situation dishonors her parents who had previously placed her in a secure environment. Despite Youmané's insensitivity to her parents' feelings, Yaye Peinda comes to the city to care for her mulatto grandson. However, Youmané again falls prey to a white suitor whom she marries and follows to France, again deceiving her mother. During this time she neglects her duties as a Muslim, fails to remember her religious upbringing, and seeks assimilation and acceptance into the white man's world. Youmané's initial experiences in Paris are marked with the joys of marital bliss with her husband, Gérard, and second child, but the love affair eventually ends when the husband turns to his own kind and abandons her. To feed her children, Youmané, who has only recently given birth to a third child, is ultimately reduced to prostitution and becomes gravely ill. She dies in France, alienated and exiled from her people and ignorant of the plight of the two children she has left behind.

Diara, Youmané's sister, was born with a feminine spirit and loves womanly chores such as keeping house. The spiritual-minded Diara was named after Amadou Bamba's mother, a pious woman who is said to have been dedicated to meditation and prayer. According to tradition one inherits several of the character traits of the person whose name one receives. Thus Diara loves to pray and to meditate. She has great respect for Serigne Touba and her parents take her to the Magal every year. Diara honors her mother and father. She dedicates her time to work and to the reading of the Koran and Bamba's poems. Accepting her role according to tradition, she marries one of her own people and remains in Africa where Allah graces her with a prosperous life.

The implication here is that failure to put spiritual values first in one's life, disrespect for tradition (represented in the story by Mouridism), insensitivity to one's parents, and the lack of pride in one's own culture will eventually lead to misfortune, or as in the case of Youmané, a tragic and premature death.

In *Le Froid et le piment* the Magal is described as a period of great spiritual fervor. Seck Mbacké's portrayal of this event underscores only its positive attributes and centers around the contributions that Cheikh Amadou Bamba made on behalf of the Senegalese people. However, she makes no reference to the Mouride work ethic as it applies to agricultural production. Nor does she discuss the gifts offered to the Mouride marabouts. Instead, her works focus primarily upon the human condition and the need for spiritual fulfillment.

Seck Mbacké uses the term "mystic" to describe Bamba's main disciple, Cheikh Ibra Fall, who is credited with establishing the Mouride peanut empire. However, certain historians, in particular Donal Cruise O'Brien, affirm that Ibra Fall displayed little or no inclination toward the duties of Islam and dedicated himself exclusively to work, even to the point of madness (Cruise O'Brien 1971, 141–158; 1975, 42–58). Fall's disciples, known as the "talibés Baye Fall" or disciples of Father Fall, appear frequently in the Senegalese novel. In the actual society as well as in fictional portrayals, these talibés go to great lengths to earn money for their marabout and are distinguishable by their behavior and manner of dress. They constitute the most eccentric group of the Mouride sect.

Both Mame Seck Mbacké and Amar Samb profess to be Mouride. However, their portraits of the Magal offer a sharp contrast. In an interview, Samb attributed his earlier negative attitude toward Mouridism largely to his own youthful rebellion against the faith.

The theme of Mouridism in the Senegalese novel revolves around the person of Cheikh Amadou Bamba and his teachings. Novelists honor Serigne Touba and acknowledge his sainthood. At the same time, some of these writers call into question the Mouride doctrine that the Muslim believer must submit himself to and work for a spiritual master in order to obtain salvation (a notion that is not supported by the Koran).

This contrast between the lauding of Bamba and the scrutinizing of his ideas suggests that writers, who are part of the Senegalese intellectual elite and most of whom are also Muslim, admire Serigne

Touba primarily for his role as an indigenous religious leader who sparked hope and pride in the hearts of the Senegalese people during French occupation. However, they attack those aspects of Mouridism that favor the domination and exploitation of one individual by another. At the same time, novelists imply that there is a disequilibrium between Mouridism's contribution to national progress in contemporary Senegal and to the genuine spiritual development of its followers.

Notes

1. Tidjaniyya and Mouridiyya are Arabic terms. For the purpose of this paper we will use the French equivalents, Tidjanes and Mourides.
2. "Serigne" is the Wolof term for master or teacher. "Touba," which means happiness, is the holy city of the Mourides and is also the site of the grand mosque and tomb of Cheikh Amadou Bamba.
3. Personal interview with Mame Seck Mbacké (Dakar, Sénégal), July 15, 1982.
4. In the hierarchy of the Wolof caste system, the "teugg" or metalsmiths are ranked as inferior. Members of this caste are traditionally believed to bring misfortune to a marriage with someone of superior caste.

References

BARA-DIOP, ABDOULAYE. 1981. *La Société Wolof.* Paris: Editions Karthala.

CRUISE O'BRIEN, DONAL. 1971. *The Mourides of Senegal.* London: Clarendon Press.

DUMONT, FERNAND. 1975. *La Pensée religieuse de Amadou Bamba.* Dakar: Nouvelles éditions africaines.

MBACKÉ, MAME SECK. 1983. *Le Froid et le piment.* Dakar: Nouvelles editions africaines.

———. 1975. *Saints and Politicians.* London: Cambridge University Press.

SAMB, AMAR. 1973. *Matraqué par le destin ou la vie d'un talibé.* Dakar: Nouvelles éditions africaines.

SÉYE, IBRAHIMA. 1983. *Un Trou dans le miroir.* Dakar: Nouvelles éditions africaines.

SOCÉ, OUSMANE. 1948. *Karim.* Paris: Nouvelles Editions Latines.

———. 1983. *Karim* Tr. Charles Oliver, Jr. Ann Arbor: University Microfilms International.

Chapter 14

▼▼▼▼▼▼▼▼▼▼

The Image of Islam in Selected Tales of Birago Diop

I. C. TCHEHO

The three volumes of tales published by Birago Diop[1] cover a vast area that spreads over the greater part of West Africa. To this area the author adds Mauritania, frequently referred to as "the North of the Great River"; it is incorrect to affirm without qualification, as Mohamadou Kane does in his work *Birago Diop* (1971, 209), that Mauritania is totally outside the spatial inspiration of the disciple of Amadou Koumba.

Birago Diop knew the West African territories especially well because of his wide travels as a veterinarian throughout the area known in the colonial period as French West Africa. This area, by all indications, is the home of Islam in Black Africa, and a good number of Diop's tales discuss one or more elements of Islam.

The purpose of this paper is to study the way in which Birago Diop, through his narrators, describes the components of Islam, and to discuss the perspectives from which such elements are presented.

The Tolerated Presence of Islam

The physical and spiritual features of Islam are brought into prominence by the narrator in various tales. At the levels of conception and design, as seen for instance in "Un jugement" (1961) there is no doubt that one is in the land of Islam. The holy ground for the main prayer, the mosque and its sandy yard, constitute the focal points in the narrative. While all the villagers' houses in Maka-Kouli are built of straw, the mosque is distinguished by its clay structure and its spire that dominates the whole area. A brief description of it is given in "Woundou El Hadji": "The spires, interspersed with tree trunks, displayed their grey towers against the shadow of the sky" (1963, 126).

Wherever it is practiced, Islam regulates the daily life of the people. The activities of the Muslim Wolof, Fulbe, Serere, and Bambara are organized according to the different prayer times programmed for the day: the "Fadjar" prayer, the "Yor-Yor," the "Tisbar," and the accompanying ablutions are observed by all the adherents. If a believer misses one of the ritual prayers, he will make up for it. Thus in "Le Prétexte," Mar N'Diaye adheres to this requirement.

> Once relieved of the preoccupations of the day, all his accounts made up, he had finished saying his evening prayer and was telling his beads to compensate for all the prayers he had not said because of the intensity of the daily toil. (1958, 45)

The Muslim feast days are equally observed in all respects. In fact, one of the tales in *Contes et lavanes* is entitled "La Tabaski de Bouki," about the "Aïd Kebir" or the Feast of the Ram. The "Tabaski" is celebrated with splendor. This is the occasion when the Muslims in the same tale vow to promote peace and harmony among the faithful in order to be saved.

> The Great Prayer having been said, the litanies having been intoned and the sermon having been conducted by the Imam, everyone went back home begging for forgiveness from neighbors, relatives and friends. (1963, 87)

The daily language also bears the imprint of Islam. It is made up of formulaic phrases frequently used by the believers. For instance, the mechanical mention of the name of the Prophet is always followed by the consecrated expression "Blessed be His Name";[2] the expression of a wish always ends with another ritual expression, "Inch Allah." One swears by "Bilahi! Walahi!" Common proverbs, or in some cases, proverbial phrases made up by Birago Diop himself, are fashioned out of images of the Muslim Moor. One such proverb opens the tale "Khary-Gaye" in *Les Nouveaux contes d'Amadou Koumba*; "that which is said by the Moor is learned under the tent" (1958, 83).

According to the storyteller in "Un Jugement," Maka-Kouli "looked like no other village." Desiring to keep their prayer grounds in a state of cleanliness befitting Allah and his Prophet, the people of Maka-Kouli sought to avoid any stain of "dog urine [which] annihilates the most fervent prayers." As for the cat, the mess it would hide within the sand in the Mosque yard would upset the faithful and reduce the effectiveness of the prayers: "That is why in Maka-Kouli there was neither dog nor cat" (1961, 26–27). Here Islam is equated with exemplary cleanliness.

The Muslims educate their children in Koranic schools, a typical institution of Islamic society. The Koranic schools mentioned in the tales are located in West Africa as well as "in the North," that is, in Mauritania. In the imagination of the people, the Koranic schools found in Mauritania are better than those in West Africa. In "Bouki et ses tablettes," Bouki's parents prefer a Mauritanian school:

> As fresh, pure water can only come from a limpid source, Bouki's parents had decided to send their offspring up there in the North of the Great River to grow in the shadow of a Moorish marabout. (1963, 68)

If their means permitted; other parents would have preferred to send their children to Morocco, Tunisia, or Egypt. Indeed, the commonly held opinion was that the Moors, and by extension the Arabs, as descendants of the Prophet were the true sources of the authentic Muslim faith.

The lessons taught in the Koranic schools are based on a substantial program centered essentially around sacred studies. The marabouts teach their disciples (or talibés) to memorize the "litanies, praises to the Lord and Saints of Islam." They also teach them "to recite the Koran from top to bottom and from bottom to top" (1963, 151). Furthermore, the talibés, who all come from countries or villages with an oral tradition only, are initiated into reading and writing the sacred texts — invariably in formal Arabic. At a higher level, they are taught to comment on the Holy Book, the Koran.

While the running of these Koranic schools may vary slightly from one country to another, the teaching program remains the same. For example, with the Toucouleurs where Thierno Torodo reigns, evening classes are provided for the less brilliant children (such as Bouki-the-hyena), who could not succeed in the normal day school. By contrast, in Mauritania the only provisions made for are the day schools, "the days being long enough in this land without shadow to leave ample time for instruction" (1963, 68).

School fees are paid in the form of manual labor carried out by the talibés for the benefit of the marabouts. Throughout his training, the pupil is expected to bring presents to his tutor; sometimes firewood or the like would be enough, or even "camel dung used as fuel to light the fire or keep it burning" (1963, 69) in Mauritania. Even after their stay in the Koranic schools, and practically for life, the disciples feel indebted to their former masters, and do not hesitate to offer them valuable presents. In *Contes et lavanes*, Serigne Khali receives from his former students "a sprinkle of gold powder, tiny pieces of gold, and gold ringlets for his wives and daughters" (1963, 211). The relationship between marabouts and talibés is characterized by respect and pious consideration.

The marabout is admired almost as a demi-god in his command of the Koran, the repository of supreme knowledge. He is the final point of reference with respect to knowledge itself and wisdom. He is sought by the people as both a religious head and as a judge in social matters. Thus one finds in *Les Contes d'Amadou Koumba* Demba (the husband) and Koumba (the repudiated wife) having recourse to the marabout Madiakate Kala after others had labored in vain to identify the guilty spouse with respect to a repudiation. Despite the general feeling that no solution could be found to their problem, Madiakate Kala cleverly devised a strategy to unveil Demba as the guilty spouse. In *Contes et lavanes*, the same marabout, subtle as usual, stops Malick Gaye from depriving the young orphan, Seydou Dali, of his father's heritage. The reputation of the marabout is enhanced and the storyteller underscores this point by affirming in conclusion, "The judgment of Madiakate Kala is still being talked about today" (1961, 162).

The marabout is at once teacher and guardian of social justice and of moral values. His wisdom derives from his faith in Allah and his mastery of the Koran, and not the reverse. That is why the storyteller hears the whisper of Allah in the pronouncements of his judgments: "The Creator often inspired the learned Master" (1961, 149–62), says the narrator about Madiakate Kala, after emphasizing that the latter "had made the pilgrimage to Mecca innumerable times" (1961, 27).

The reputation of marabouts like Madiakate Kala or Taiba Mbaye spreads far, and the schools and the villages where these masters are found become centers of Islam, almost branches of Mecca and Medina. People flock there from all over when they cannot go to Mecca, or even on their way back from Mecca. Maka-Kouli, the village of the celebrated Serigne Madiakate Kala, is a telling example in the tales of Birago. There the days are spent "in work and prayers." The marabout of the village holds the record for the number of pilgrimages to

Mecca, and his numerous devoted disciples live in an appropriate manner:

> Day in day out, in this village, it was only prayers, recitations of litanies, praises to Allah and his Prophet, readings of the Koran and Hadiths (1961, 26–27).

Here one is faced with a truly mystical Muslim society:

> The people bowed, the bodies bent, the foreheads touched the sand, which was as white as sugar, the heads raised again, the bodies followed and the genuflexions, modulated by sacred verses, succeeded one another. At the last one, the heads turned to the right and then to the left to greet the angel of the right side and the angle of the left side. (1961, 29)

Through its teaching, Islam seems to welcome everyone without discrimination. With the Toucouleurs, the storyteller in *Contes et lavanes* affirms that the marabout teaches the Koran to "the old and the young of the country" (1963, 64). In the same way, in N'Djour, according to the same narrator, everyone observes the requirements of Ramadan: "As good Muslims, the old and the young, men and women observed lent" (1963, 84). Their faith seems to be one in which class distinctions, age or sex divisions are attenuated, if not eliminated.

Were it only for these reasons, the contribution of Islam to West African societies would be wholly positive. When, inspired by the fundamental teaching of the Sacred Book, the marabout dispenses justice or unmasks a thief, the whole society benefits from the presence of Islam.

This does not mean, however, that in the tales of Birago Diop, people show no resistance to Islam. Different images of Islam indicate that its integration into West Africa is rather problematic. The storyteller often interposes positive and negative images of Islam. For this reason, it will be necessary to go back to some of the ideas enunciated above in the light of the narrator's insinuations, even when he is complimenting such noble characters as the marabouts and talibés.

A Problematic Presence

In the tales of Birago Diop, West African societies are characterized by racial heterogeneity: Blacks of different ethnicities and Arab Muslims constitute the principle groups. The latter are identified as Lebanese, Syrians, and Moors. They are described as "Whites" each time they appear on the scene. "Narr (that is to say the

Moor) still distinguished himself from the others by his white skin," says the narrator (1961, 15). And in *Les Nouveaux contes*, when the griot of King Bour is asked what Narr's complexion is like, he responds with great surprise: "But he is white like all true Moors, like the pure Moors" (1958, 88).

The repeated references to skin color when the Moor is brought to the fore are not always objective or gratuitous. More often than not, they are made by a storyteller or by black characters who do not look favorably on the presence of Moors (or Arabs in general) in West African communities. Whatever the advantages occurring from the coexistence of the local folk and Arabo-Moors, the presence of the latter and the religion they represent, Islam, is exasperating to the storyteller. That is why, in comparing the period before the arrival of Arabs and the present time, the narrator declares:

> In those days, one would not lend you two pence and get back three times as much. We did not have Lebanese everywhere, neither were there as many Syrians, and the number of Nor-ou-Gamar running shops was hardly noticeable. (1958, 24)

From such statements, the reader gathers that the storyteller sees the Arabo-Moors as invaders in West Africa. As the storyteller also lingers on their occupation as traders, it is implied that they have monopolized the local economy. Rarely in the tales does the reader come across an indigenous character occupied in trading. One is left with the impression that the Arabo-Moorish traders are guilty of plundering the territories they had invaded and transformed into a stronghold of Islam. While speaking thus on behalf of the people, the storyteller suggests that the latter were too naive in welcoming the foreigners without any awareness of the possible danger they could represent.

The storyteller occasionally points out that it is from the north (that is, Mauritania), the stopover to and from Mecca, that the West African people import their sheep. Yet, says the narrator, the exchange between the north and the south of the great river is more beneficial to the Arabo-Moors that to their West African counterparts.

The coexistence of the two communities also seems to have resulted in widespread fraud and usury. As already shown from the storyteller's declaration, two pence fetch six. Thus, there is a disturbing coincidence between a certain moral degradation and the arrival of Arabo-Moorish characters. As foreigners, the latter are suspected even openly accused, of being at the root of the decline of moral and human norms in society. From this perspective, the repeated references to the Moors as "people with white skin" or "people with white ears" often contain a good deal of xenophobia coupled with anti-Islamic innuendo.

In fact, the storyteller never mentions the Moor without making reference to Islam: the Moor, here, is necessarily the representative of the Islamic faith. He refers to himself first as the propagator and forerunner of Islam and is accepted as such. One might expect him to be a model. However, in some of the stories he turns out to be a believer whose behavior contradicts religious teaching he professes. More often than not, for example, his role as a trader tends to overshadow his role as a marabout. Sidi Ahmen Beidane is a case in point:

> Sidi Ahmen Beidane was at the same time a shopkeeper and a schoolmaster. He would sell all sorts of things to parents: food, condiments, drugs, material, utensils, and would teach rudiments to children. (1963, 204)

In this quotation the stress is put on the contrast between "all sorts of things" he sells and the "rudiments" he teaches to uncover the extent to which the Moor places other considerations above the very religion he is supposed to foster. It is equally noteworthy that Sidi Ahmed Beidane loses his sanity on discovering that a thief has emptied his shop. Being a "fervent" descendant of the Prophet, he should have been content with the only real wealth for a true believer, that is, the Koran. Instead, master of the Koran though he is, he sinks into madness, as if to show that spiritual wealth cannot match material wealth.

The storyteller portrays such a contradiction between the behavior of the Koranic teacher and his teaching that he must intend to expose the weaknesses inherent in Islam. This is all the more significant inasmuch as in most Muslim communities portrayed in the texts, "Any Moor from Ghanar was automatically regarded as a Sharif, a descendant of the Prophet."

In the tale entitled "Fari l'anesse," there is another Moor known as Narr-le-Maure. He seems to disturb the rest of the population with his ablutions. Citizens like Fari can be happy only when Narr is on pilgrimage to Mecca. Trouble begins as soon as he returns, because Narr, the Muslim, has a nasty flaw—he is an incurable gossip. He goes so far as to interrupt his ablutions and prayers to run and tell King Bour of his joy at having seen some beautiful women bathing in the open. The satire here is obvious: if Narr cannot end his prayer before indulging in gossip, he must be of doubtful faith.

In addition, as a consequence of his actions, the descendants of Fari "undergo severe beatings" (1961, 19).

Undoubtedly, by helping King Bour unmask false beauties hidden behind Fari's faces, Narr is doing a good turn. But the storyteller does not actually compliment him, for he thinks that the good turn is accidental; that it is the result of Narr's flaw.

The bad character is appropriately punished, as in most tales. When the she-asses are deprived of happiness forever, their first kicks in reaction to their condemnation break Narr's jaw. Narr receives punishment through injury to his mouth, which should have been used for the holy purpose of singing psalms and litanies to Allah.

Even when a Moor is sincere in his faith, he still does not earn the praises of the storyteller in Birago Diop's tales. Though Narr "was perhaps the only subject in the kingdom to practice the Koran sincerely" (1961, 15), this is not seen as "anything extraordinary, since he was in any case expected to be worthy of his ancestors" (1961, 15). And the same storyteller derives much pleasure from phrasing his criticism repeatedly in the form of a proverb: "It is said of a tale-bearer that he has swallowed a Moor" (1961, 15). An elaborate version of this anti-Moorish saying is further couched in the following terms:

> To entrust a hyena with meat, even with dried meat, and prevent it from tasting it? This was a goal more difficult to achieve than to make Narr-le-Maure with red ears keep a secret. One might as well forbid thirsty sand from swallowing the first drops of the first rain (1961, 94).

Similarly, in "Liguidi Malgam," as soon as it is discovered that Awa, a Senegalese woman, has a bad character, it is explained that she is of Beidane origin, "because until her old age she had never been able to keep a secret" (1958, 157).

To a large extent, the persistent criticism of the characters of Islamic origin, originates from the West Africans' resentment of the Arabo-Moors' domination of the local economy. Stories and anecdotes in which foreigners play the worst roles are frequently an outlet for the frustrations of the society for which the storytellers speak, providing the means to express with metaphors their deep-seated xenophobia and rejection of the foreign culture (or even religion). Furthermore, in many of Diop's tales, those who share the same religion with the Moor are portrayed in an equally satirical manner. The West African marabouts are no exceptions to this; neither are their disciples.

It turns out that the success of some marabouts is largely due to the ingenuousness of their believers. Sometimes they only need to move about with a kettle and beads, murmuring unintelligible prayers punctuated by the act of spitting into the hands and onto the heads of the profane to be taken seriously. The storyteller illustrates such a case of religious superficiality with the example of Serigne Fall. The latter claims to be a first class marabout, but in fact knows no more than five or seven Koranic chapters in addition to the Fatiha. Serigne Fall is a sluggard, one among many throughout the Muslim West African world. In the narrator's own bitter words,

> They are always similar in kind: outstanding in displaying mock religious fervor, unbeatable as parasites, unreliable, and addicted to wanderings. If you want to cover them, you will remain with your bottom totally uncovered. (1958, 41)

Their great number is a misfortune for Islam as a whole: such marabouts, ill-behaved as they appear to be, will probably generate more false Muslim believers. Furthermore, if one decides to rid the society of such marabouts in order to safeguard Islam, the end result might be genocide, given their great numbers. That seems to be the meaning suggested by the last part of the statement quoted above.

Thus Birago Diop looks at Islam with suspicion. In his view, it has weaknesses or ambiguities that can be easily exploited by wicked people for their own ends. He finds no other explanation for what he deplores, namely the proliferation of "small talibes of Koranic schools who beg in the morning, beg in the middle of the day, and in the evening" (1958, 40). This situation is encouraged (if not caused) by the Muslim principle that the faithful must give alms to beggars.

The relationship between the Serignes and their disciples is not always healthy. It is often based on a system that fosters the exploitation of one group by another. The marabout is always the beneficiary, especially when he is dealing with people who are as devoted as they are naive, shallow, or pretentious.

The marabouts are anxious to answer the invitations of their disciples, as these are occasions to acquire valuable presents. For instance, just one tour in Bambara land earns Serigne Khali, a marabout based in Senegal, an impressive collection of presents of untold value: a bag full of precious cloths, sprinklings of gold powder, and ringlets of gold. He has so many presents that he has to be accompanied by a carrier. The narrator reports with a touch of irony that the latter was the son of devoted Muslim parents whom Serigne Khali had to guide "on the harsh road to salvation." The marabout himself carries the most precious presents with much care:

> The bags full of gold were carefully put together with the sacred books of the marabout in the double bag dangling on the right side of the master. (1963, 211)

Putting gold powder and holy books in the same bag creates a striking association: the marabout's precaution indicates clearly the importance he attaches to earthly acquisitions and, consequently, to his (so-called) religious tours.

Birago Diop goes even further to call into question the power given to Islam by some of its followers. The ancestor of Woundou the cat gained initiation into Islam almost at the source, that is in Mauritania. Woundou himself goes on a pilgrimage to Mecca in the hope of replacing his hypocrisy and egoism with character traits worthy of a respectable man of faith. Yet the change is superficial: on his return from Mecca, where he has been made an al-Hadj, he entertains the idea of eating the rats and mice, his guests at a feast held in his honor. "Mecca has never changed anybody," the storyteller comments (1963, 130). Perhaps this is due to human nature; but it may also be interpreted as meaning that Islam embodies some doctrinal ambiguities which may lead even well-intentioned believers to expect miracles.

The latter hypothesis is substantiated by one or two cases in which the storyteller allows one Sa Dagga to speak in a blasphemous way and, through this character, to destroy the reputation of Sidi Ahmed Beidane, the marabout and trader. Sa Dagga questions the validity of the compulsory use of the consecrated expression, "Yalla le Bon Dieu." Following the storyteller's remarks, this expression makes some people uneasy, especially as "those who have just come back from Mecca or even from a lesser distance" would delight in showing off by quoting it day in day out. Yalla (or Allah), Sa Dagga claims, is also the cause of evil: "He jolly well kills," he says, before concluding in no ambiguous terms: "God (is) slippery, (it) is impossible to get hold of Him, to rely on Him as recommended by his representatives and mouthpiece, the Marabouts" (1963, 206).

To consider Allah a killer is a blasphemy, but here, it does not scandalize the storyteller; thus he stands apart from Islam and its believers. This satire of Islam is perhaps more amply conveyed by those tales in which the historical background of West African Islamization is depicted. Indeed, Diop's narrator re-reads local history to explain that Islam began with violence perpetrated all across West Africa by the "hordes of Islam." The local population, it is revealed, did not acquiesce to the process of Islamization. It was accomplished as the result of naked force. According to the story teller, wherever the "first men with white skin" passed, blood flowed profusely: rivers were reddened! The reader of the stories is made to travel from one corner of West Africa to another in order to measure the scale of the tragedy:

> Wars and corpses: corpses in such great numbers that the greediest of the crocodiles would have indigestion that would last seven times seven months. (1961, 52)

The Toucouleur seem to have singled themselves out in this venture, proving to be even more blood-thirsty than the Moors who initiated them. In "Maman Caïman," they appear on the scene, ransacking the places forgotten by the first batch of Islamic troops, seeking out the populations, cutting off women's plaits or beheading those who resist. Their leader makes it a point of honor to order the "fanatic talibés" to burn down the sacred forests of the animists. Here, it is obvious that the storyteller is against the killings and intolerance instigated by a dogma and carried out through the jihad.

In the name of Islam, therefore, massive destructions of human life and cultures occurred in West Africa. Still in the name of Islam, the economies of most societies in West Africa have been invaded by marabouts and traders of Arabo-Moorish origin. No wonder, then, that the storyteller, as the spokesman for these societies, speaks harshly of the followers of Islam and of Islam itself: as a universal rule, and in a cycle of reprisals, violence in history begets counter-violence in fiction (even in oral tradition).

In the tales of Birago Diop, positive and negative images of Islam are interwoven. Like parasites, the latter tend to develop at the expense of the former, almost stifling them. The effort of the story-teller to make this phenomenon an asymptotic one is noticeable. The role of positive images is to reduce the drastic effect of the negative ones. Nevertheless, the satirical goal of the storyteller turns out to be so powerful that the critical bias often escapes his control. Given the end result, it is difficult to disentangle the threads and to distinguish clearly between the questioning of Islam *per se* and the criticism of its deviant disciples.

Earlier critics have often analyzed these tales as reflecting a world of innocence. However, taking into account the fact that Diop's stock negative figures are invariably Muslims and characters of Arabo-Moorish descent, such a reading is clearly very limited. Diop's tales are a far cry from Hampâté Bâ's literature, in which the encounter of Islam and West Africa is harmonious. They contradict most critics who claim that Birago Diop is too sympathetic to Islam to be so critical.

Notes

1. This article is based on three collections of stories by Birago Diop: *Les Contes d'Amadou Koumba*, *Les Nouveaux contes d'Amadou Koumba*, and *Contes et lavanes*. All translations into English are mine.
2. "Bismilaï djani," in Arabic, pronounced with a Wolof accent in the tales.

References

DIOP, BIRAGO. 1958. *Les Nouveaux contes d'Amadou Koumba*. Paris: Présence africaine.

———. 1961. *Les Contes d'Amadou Koumba*. Paris: Présence africaine.

———. 1963. *Contes et lavanes*. Paris: Présence africaine.

KANE, MOHAMADU. 1971. *Birago Diop*. Paris: Présence africaine.

Chapter 15

▼▼▼▼▼▼▼▼▼

Islamic Elements in Camara Laye's L'Enfant Noir

ERIC SELLIN

In an interesting study of *L'Enfant noir* by Camara Laye, Jacques Bourgeacq writes: "Comme celle de ces confrères écrivains instruits dans les écoles de l'Occident, l'œuvre de Camara Laye tient à une double influence. Elle est le produit d'une tension entre deux sensibilités, deux visions, deux manières d'être, de saisir le monde" (Bourgeacq 1984, 8). ["Like that of his fellow writers educated in Western schools, Camara Laye's work entails a double influence. The work is the product of a tension between two sensibilities, two visions, two ways of being, of grasping the world."] Indeed, there is clear evidence of the two worlds, or visions, one African and one European, in Camara Laye's first novel, published in 1953. Numerous articles have listed the inventory of the two worlds and discussed their interaction, producing the tension of which Bourgeacq speaks. What is frequently overlooked in essays devoted to Camara Laye is the fact that the African component of the above-mentioned dichotomy is, itself, composed of a double influence: one in which we encounter a symbiotic relationship between traditional African cultural patterns and those more commonly associated with Islam.[2] Bourgeacq, for example, offers brilliant observations on the traditional cosmological associations of *L'Enfant noir*, and lists some of the autochthonous and foreign symbols of Laye's world, but he does not dwell on those equally concrete elements that reflect the presence of an Islamic sensibility or vision. This illustrates a fundamental distinction to be drawn between the Occidental and Islamic influences: as Bourgeacq has stated, the double African–Occidental influence produces "tension"; on the other hand the African–Islamic relationship is, for a number of reasons, one of more or less accommodating symbiosis, which J. C. Froelich attributes to a certain flexibility on the part of Islam and a certain selectivity on the part of the African culture: "Il y a eu imprégnation de l'Islam par l'animisme qui, à son tour s'est laissé imprégner par l'Islam" (Froelich 1962, 122). ["Islam became embued with animism which, in turn, let itself become embued with Islam."][3]

In *The Influence of Islam upon Africa*, J. Spencer Trimingham broadly places Guinea, Camara Laye's country of origin, in the "fourth belt" of the Islamization of West Africa, below the densest Muslim third belt along the Sahel; but, as he points out, there are pockets within the fourth belt that are characterized by a very high percentage of Muslims — one of these being the area around Laye's birthplace, Kouroussa. Additionally, Islam tended to have a far greater impact in urban than in rural areas.

The African conversion to Islam was, according to Trimingham, less abrupt, radical, or "violent" an experience than the conversion to Christianity; Islam and traditional African religions practiced a form of mutual accommodation, with the end result being not tension but a natural interfusion of practices, rituals, and beliefs. Trimingham discusses this accommodation in a key passage:

> Islam has been present in the Sudan belt for centuries and accommodated itself in such a way that it became a natural aspect of its environment. The difference between Islam as an impersonal and abstract system with a body of doctrine and a rigid legal code embracing, not merely ritual, but every aspect of life, and the diversified and complex African systems of life appears so profound that few points of contact seem apparent and the psychological shock of religious change to be so great as for an African converted to Western Christianity. This is not so in practice. The reason is that Islam in contact with Africans is characterized by a series of gradations which act as insulators passing on Islamic radiation gradually to animist societies. Aspects of Islam as cult and ethic are characterized by their individualistic form. All the forces of African conservatism would be arrayed against this, but in fact such individualistic elements as might undermine social structure are not stressed. Elements alien to the local genius were rejected and those adopted were moulded into conformity. Islam thus does no violent uprooting but offers immediate values without displacement of the old. It is not a question of either-or but of both-and. (Trimingham 1980, 41–42)

In *L'Enfant noir* there are a good many references to things Islamic, but I should like to stress three of the most interesting passages that underscore respectively: (1) the co-existence of African and Islamic traditions in the life sequence, or calendar; (2) the intersection of Islam and traditional African ritual in the adoption of Qur'ānic verses in amulets; and (3) a passage in which the all-pervasive presence of Islam is so clearly yet so unobtrusively stated that the translator has neglected to convey it in the standard English-language edition.

African and Islamic Traditions in the Calendar

Chapters IV and VII of *L'Enfant noir* open with descriptions of annual "feasts," one fundamentally African, the other Islamic. In Chapter IV, Laye finds himself in the rural setting of Tindican in December, the dry season, at the time of the rice harvest, which Camara Laye describes as a festival. As the narrator says: "Chaque année, j'étais invité à cette moisson, qui est une grande et joyeuse fête, et j'attendais impatiemment que mon jeune oncle vînt me chercher" (Laye 1953, 49). ["Every year I was invited to this harvest, which is a huge and joyous festival, and I waited on tenterhooks for my young uncle to come to get me."] This "fête" does not have a fixed date, depending rather on such factors as the climate: "La fête évidemment ne tombait pas à date fixe: elle dépendait de la maturité du riz, et celle-ci à son tour dépendait du ciel, de la bonne volonté du ciel" (49). ["The festival obviously did not fall on a set date: it depended on the maturity of the rice, and that depended in turn on the heavens, the good will of the heavens."] Although this "feast" is really a work detail, it is so romanticized, entailing consultation with divine forces, the beating of drums, and singing, along with glistening bodies and hearty appetites — reminiscent of the *coumbites* in Jacques Roumain's *Gouverneurs de la rosée* — that it emerges primarily as an occasion for joy for the young narrator. The fact that its date varies creates a resemblance, to a degree, to the Muslim feast mentioned at the beginning of Chapter VII.

The celebration preceding the month-long fast of Ramadan does not fall on a fixed solar date either, for it is predicated on a lunar calendar and thus retrogresses annually in terms of the solar calendar. It coincides, in the case of the reference in Chapter VII of *L'Enfant noir*, with Laye's entry into the pre-circumcision "association des non-initiés."

Le temps était venu pour moi d'entrer dans l'association des non-
initiés. Cette société un peu mystérieuse, encore que très peu secrète
(...) était dirigée par nos aînés, que nous appelions les grands
"Kondén." J'y entrai un soir précédant le Ramadan. (Laye 1953, 91)

[The time had come for me to join the association of the
uninitiated. This slightly mysterious, yet not terribly secret society
(...) was led by the older fellows, whom we called the big
"Kondéns." I joined the society one evening before Ramadan.]

Thus the Muslim holy day of Ramadan is intertwined with customs
attendant upon a ritual involved in an African's traditional coming of
age. Laye adds that it was the first time that he would be spending
Ramadan at Kouroussa instead of at Tindican and he is extremely
excited at this prospect. The suggestion is, indeed, that the festivities
at Kouroussa will be far more lively and elaborate than in the rural
setting at Tindican, and we are reminded that the devotion of people's
commitment to Islam seems to increase with the size of the city:
"Islamic culture was based on urban civilization and Africa had
relatively few towns and cities; and where no towns existed, as
among Bantu and Nilotic tribes, it could not penetrate at all. All the
same, Islam in Africa flourished where there was some basis of urban
culture, together with trading relations which ultimately stemmed
from the city" (Trimingham 1980, 3). Indeed, when Laye later arrives
at the capital city of Conakry, he observes that Uncle Mamadou,
whose life is "directed by the Qur'ān," is more devout than his father:

Il était musulman, et je pourrais dire: comme nous le sommes
tous; mais il l'était de fait beaucoup plus que nous ne le sommes
généralement: son observance du Coran était sans défaillance. Il ne
fumait pas, ne buvait pas, et son honnêteté était scrupuleuse. Il ne
portait de vêtements européens que pour se rendre à son travail;
sitôt rentré, il se déshabillait, passait un boubou qu'il exigeait
immaculé, et disait ses prières. (Laye 1953, 150)

[He was a Muslim, and I should perhaps add: as are we all; but
he was, in fact, much more of a Muslim than we generally are. His
observance of the Qur'ān was impeccable. He did not smoke nor
drink, and he was scrupulously honest. He only wore European
clothes when he went to work: once back home, he would take off
his clothes, put on a boubou, which he insisted be spotless, and said
his prayers.]

It is undoubtedly no mere coincidence that Laye's induction into
the pre-circumcision association of the "non-initiés" occurs during
the days of celebration customarily preceding a Muslim holy day. As
the two "feasts" we have discussed clearly indicate, there were essentially two kinds of calendar governing African life, the solar

agricultural calendar and the lunar Muslim calendar. A major element in Islamization is the adoption of the lunar calendar (Trimingham 1980, 65). The two calendars can, of course, co-exist, but the impact of the Muslim calendar was such that it tended to pre-empt some of the events associated with the agricultural calendar and to subvert the role and importance of the "pagan priest" in favor of the *imam* or Muslim cleric:

> The Muslim agriculturist follows two calendars, the Islamic for all that concerns its ritual cycle and the solar for the natural cycle of seedtime and harvest. After Islamization one is tempted to call them the religious and secular calendars, were it not that "secular" is hardly a word that fits in with any traditional African context, since the natural cycle retains its own ritual observances in spite of the adoption of Islam. The significant aspect is the role of the Islamic calendar in the attack on the old religion; it now becomes the official religious calendar and this undermines the old cycle of ritual observance which loses the position it formerly held in the life of the community. Frequently the Muslim cleric replaces the pagan priest in performing agricultural ritual and propitiating the spirits. (Trimingham, 1980, 65)

The Muslim call to prayer and the various holy days provided an armature for all events in African life, even those already established before the advent of Islam in the area (Trimingham 1980, 65). Thus the elders would no doubt deem it meet and propitious to select an auspicious day such as, say, that preceding Ramadan to effectuate a completely non-Islamic traditional event such as the induction to which Laye refers. Other factors presumably also entered into the timing: as Nuruddin Farah and others pointed out during the conference at which this and other papers were discussed (held at Michigan State University in 1989), the actual initiation and circumcision usually took place at a time when they would interfere neither with schooling nor harvesting. Thus Ramadan itself does not always fall at an appropriate moment but happened to be a handy and auspicious day at the time of Camara Laye's story.

The Intersection of Islam and Traditional Ritual

The traditional African interest and/or belief in divination, in *gris-gris*, in "propitiating the spirits," and the like, found natural links in Islam. The use of amulets, for example, that had existed before the arrival of Islam in West Africa, now utilized the holy words of the Qur'ān, believed by Muslims to possess their own unique sacrosanct

qualities. Furthermore, many references to magic and superstition —
such as the "evil eye" and evil "blowers on knots" — occur in the
Muslim scriptures and commentaries.[4] An amulet is the agent of
power, and so, by extension, is the pouch, necklace, anklet, or
whatever else contains the charm or agent. The amulet may also be a
potion.

One of the most interesting passages in *L'Enfant noir* is that
describing how Laye's mother has placed a bottle among his effects
when, at fifteen, he leaves home in order to continue his studies in
Conakry. When he asks what it is, she replies that he must be careful
not to break it and that he is to take a little sip from the bottle each
morning before going to class:

> "Est-ce l'eau destinée à développer l'intelligence?" dis-je.
> "Celle-là même! Et il ne peut exister de plus efficace: elle vient
> de Kankan!"
> J'avais déjà bu de cette eau: mon professeur m'en avait fait
> boire, quand j'avais passé mon certificat d'études. C'est une eau
> magique qui a nombre de pouvoirs et en particulier celui de dével-
> opper le cerveau. Le breuvage est curieusement composé: nos
> marabouts ont des planchettes sur lesquelles ils écrivent des prières
> tirées du Coran; lorsqu'ils ont fini d'écrire le texte, ils l'effacent en
> lavant la planchette; l'eau de ce lavage est précieusement recueillie
> et, additionné de miel, elle forme l'essentiel du breuvage. (Laye
> 1953, 137)[5]
> ["Is it the water destined to develop intelligence?" I asked.
> "That very one! And there is none more effective: it is from
> Kankan!"
> I had drunk such water: my teacher had made me drink some
> when I sat for my student certification examinations. It is a magic
> water that possesses a number of powers, notably that of developing
> the brain. The potion is made in a curious manner: our marabouts
> have little wooden boards on which they write prayers taken from
> the Qur'ān. When they have finished writing a text, they erase it by
> washing the board; the water from this washing is carefully collected
> and, enriched with honey, it constitutes the main part of the
> potion.]

This liquid amulet is especially powerful since it comes from
Kankan, a particularly devout Muslim town: "Acheté dans la ville de
Kankan, qui est une ville très musulmane et la plus sainte de nos
villes, et manifestement acheté à haut prix, le breuvage devait être
particulièrement agissant" (Laye 1953, 137). ["Purchased in the city
of Kankan, which is a very Muslim town and the holiest of our
cities, and obviously bought at a high price, the potion was supposed
to be particularly effective."] Laye's father, for his part, gives him a

little goat's horn containing talismans: presumably one of the little horns partially wrapped in leather — usually decorated with a cowrie shell, and containing, among other things, verses of the Qur'ān folded up into a little square — of the sort commonly found throughout West Africa.

Potions derived from washes of writings on Qur'ānic boards have been described by numerous scholars who point out the critical interaction of matter and words. Sometimes forms are drawn on — or Qur'ānic words spoken over — sand which is then sprinkled about or worn in containers; sometimes ink washed from paper or boards on which Qur'ānic names, words, and verses have been written is used to make a potion of "holy water" or "writing water," which René Bravmann describes in *African Islam* as "an amulet, a liquid suspension obtained by washing potent magical or Koranic verses that have been written on a wooden tablet" (1983, 32) and which is kept in a vial or wooden bottle to be appropriately sipped or rubbed on the body. Bravmann describes the prescription and preparation of amulets, both solid and liquid, given him by a marabout to allay his fears about a two-month trip to Marrakesh:

> Mamadou turned back towards us and (...) began a long and complex journey into the mysteries of his craft. He cast the cowries again and again, noting their configurations with pen and ink upon the board. Spreading sand upon his mat, he carefully aligned the eggs in patterns that seemed to correspond to those created by the shells. The mirror had been placed in such a manner that it reflected every detail of this complex procedure. Mamadou held the hawk's beak between the middle fingers of his left hand and used it to mark a certain rhythm on the lips of the gourds. Three times he opened the Arabic manuscript at specific places and nodded, apparently satisfied that each selection related well to everything else. (1983, 33)

Bravmann received "a small vial of dark liquid and what appeared to be a rectangular packet wrapped in cotton thread"; he was instructed to have the latter wrapped in leather and to wear it on his body during his trip, and to rub a bit of the liquid on his body or place a drop of it on his tongue whenever he felt apprehensive (1983, 34–35).

A Neglected Clue to the Presence of Islam

Finally, one of the most interesting, if least conspicuous, references to Islam will perforce have gone unnoticed by readers of the English translation. A brief but important exchange between Kouyaté and his father takes place when Kouyaté's nemesis at school, the bully Himourana, is invited to their home for a meal, designated as the malefactor, and beaten. The critical exchange occurs when young Kouyaté swears "by Allah" that Himourana is the culprit and the father says that if he swears by Allah, it must be true. Here is the passage in question:

> Himourana, après un coup d'œil sur les marmites, qui lui parurent lourdes de promesses et de succulence, fut s'asseoir parmi la famille et se rengorgea à l'idée des compliments qu'on allait lui adresser. Mais alors Kouyaté se leva brusquement et pointa le doigt sur lui.
> "Père, dit-il, voici le grand qui ne cesse de me frapper et de m'extorquer nourriture et argent!
> —Eh bien, eh bien, voilà du joli, dit le père de Kouyaté. C'est bien vrai au moins ce que tu me dis là?
> —Par Allah! dit Kouyaté.
> —C'est donc vrai," dit le père. (Laye 1953)
> [Himourana, having glanced at the cooking-pots, which appeared heavy with promise and succulence, sat in the midst of the family and gloated over the idea of the compliments he was about to receive. But then Kouyaté suddenly stood up and pointed at him.
> "Father," said he, "this is the big boy who never stops hitting me and forcing me to give him my food and my money!"
> "Well, well, that's a fine state of affairs." said Kouyaté's father. "Is what you are saying at least true?"
> "By Allah!" said Kouyaté.
> "Then it is true," said the father.]

The English translation of *L'Enfant noir* (*The Dark Child*, also issued under the title *The African Child*), by James Kirkup, makes no mention of Allah, omitting the last two lines of the above dialogue altogether, which from the viewpoint of this essay is an egregious omission, for the matter-of-fact acceptance of that oath tells us how completely and unself-consciously Islam has been integrated into the truth system in the world described by Camara Laye in his novel.

Notes

1. The translations throughout this essay are my own.
2. Of course not all critics have underplayed the importance of the role of Muslim thought in Camara Laye's *weltanschauung*. Kenneth Harrow, for one, has published several penetrating analyses of the subject, including "The Mystic and the Poet," *Africana Journal*, 13:1–4 (1982), 152–72; and "A Sufi Interpretation of *Le Regard du roi*," *Research in African Literatures*, 14:2 (Summer 1983), 135–64. In an article that deals briefly with Muslim practices in *L'Enfant noir*, Azim Nanji speaks of the narrator

Laye's Muslim upbringing and schooling and makes a tenuous link between the father's goldsmithing scene and "many a Qur'ānic verse" (1982, 104). He also points out the "intermingling of Islamic symbols, such as the feast of Ramadān, the role of the teacher (or 'Shaykh' to use the Sufi term), in the initiation and circumcision rituals" (105), which we discuss here, albeit from a different angle.

3. As Froelich elaborates, in his study on *Les Musulmans d'Afrique noire,* "La souplesse de l'Islam noir fut telle qu'il composa partout avec les croyances animistes et autorisa les manifestations des cultes archaïques, là même où les musulmans étaient en majorité; on a pu se demander si, lorsque l'Islam convertit des Noirs, ceux-ci, à leur tour, ne convertissent pas l'Islam; en effet, quand le Qorân est introduit dans une région, les éléments qui sont d'abord retenus sont ceux qui s'adaptent à la foi animiste et la complètent" (1962, 122). ["The flexibility of Islam in black Africa was such that it compounded everywhere with animistic beliefs and allowed for the manifestations of archaic cults, even where Muslims were in the majority; one could well ask if, when Islam converted the Blacks, the latter did not, in turn, convert Islam; indeed, when the Qur'an is introduced into a region, the first elements to be taken up are those which can be adapted to the animist faith and round it out."]

   An article entitled "L'Islam 'noir' ou les preuves d'une grande tolérance," published in Morocco's *Matin du Sahara* magazine (16–23 April 1989), has also emphasized this "syncretism": "En effet, l'Islam ne repousse pas un certain syncrétisme. Il ne s'oppose pas a l'animisme. Il compose avec lui. Animisme et Islam subsistent souvent dans le même individu. L'Islam impose des rites qui sont souvent facilement integrés par l'animisme (immolation rituelle des animaux, circoncision, gestes de prières, etc . . .)" (14). ["Indeed, Islam does not resist a certain syncretism. It does not oppose animism. It co-exists with it. Animism and Islam often exist in the same person. Islam calls for rituals which are often easily integrated with animism (the sacrifice of animals, circumcision, prayer gestures, etc.)."]

4. There were natural affinities. Traditional "animists" found elements to their liking in the Islamic rituals, as Trimingham points out: "Islam's most obvious signs are the prayer ritual, especially communal prayer, its death ceremonial, and its taboos. The question of power is also a consideration, and strong aspects attracting the animists are Islam's divining, magical and animistic practices . . ." (42). See also Samuel M. Zwemer, *The Influence of Animism on Islam,* 163–207, esp. 170–71. Sura 113 of the Qur'an, entitled *Al-Falaq* ("The Daybreak"), contains a plea for protection from, among other things, *al-naffāthāt,* "the blowers upon knots," generally interpreted as a reference to evil sorceresses. M. M. Pickthall, who normally translates quite literally, has preferred to translate *naffāthāt* as "malignant witchcraft."

5. In this passage, one word, "curieusement" ("Le breuvage est *curieusement* composé . . ."), takes on considerable weight. In this word, which acts almost as a disclaimer, we find Camara Laye, the adult narrator who is reminiscing, distancing himself to an extent from the alleged efficacy of such potions and thereby from the entire religious-philosophical system

of which it is a part. Elsewhere in *L'Enfant noir*, the narrator Laye says that he left home too early, before having been taught access to the secret ways and powers of his father.

References

BOURGEACQ, JACQUES. 1984. *"L'Enfant noir" de Camara Laye: Sous le signe de l'éternel retour*. Sherbrooke, Qué.: Editions Naaman.

BRAVMANN, RENÉ A. 1983. *African Islam*. Washington, D.C.: The Smithsonian Institution Press, and London: Ethnographica Ltd.

CAMARA LAYE. See Laye, Camara.

FROELICH, J. C. 1962. *Les Musulmans d'Afrique noire*. Paris: Editions de l'Orante.

HARROW, KENNETH. 1983. "A Sufi Interpretation of *Le Regard du roi*," *Research in African Literatures*, 14:2 (Summer), 135−64.

———. 1982. "The Mystic and the Poet," *Africana Journal*, 13:1−4: 152−72.

"L'Islam 'noir' ou les preuves d'une grande tolérance," *Le Matin du Sahara magazine* (16−23 April 1989), 14.

LAYE, CAMARA. 1953. *L'enfant noir*. Paris: Plon.

———. *The Meaning of the Glorious Koran*, 1953. Trans. Mohammed Marmaduke Pickthall. New York: New American Library.

NANJI, AZIM. 1982. "Ritual and Symbolic Aspects of Islam in African Contexts." In *Contributions to Asian Studies*, Vol. 17, *Islam in Local Contexts*. Richard C. Martin. Leiden: E.J. Brill, 102−09.

TRIMINGHAM, J. SPENCER. 1980. *The Influence of Islam upon Africa*. 2nd ed. London and New York: Longman and Librairie du Liban.

ZWEMER, SAMUEL M. 1920. *The Influence of Animism on Islam: An Account of Popular Superstitions*. New York: The Macmillan Company.

Part IV

COMPARATIVE APPROACHES

Chapter 16

▼▼▼▼▼▼▼▼▼

Crescent and Consciousness: Islamic Orthodoxies and the West African Novel

LEMUEL A. JOHNSON

I. Introduction: al-Mukhlit

Right at the beginning then, Mali was a province of the Bambara kings; those who today are called Mandingo, inhabitants of Mali, are not indigenous; they come from the East. Bilali Bounama, ancestor of the Keitas, was the faithful servant of the Prophet Muhammad (may the peace of God be upon him). Bilali Bounama had seven sons of whom the eldest, Lawalo, left the Holy City and came to settle in Mali; Lawalo had Latal Kalabi for a son, Latal Kalabi had Dumul Kalabi who then had Lahilatoul Kalabi.

D. T. NIANE, *Sundiata, Epic of Old Mali*

They called her the Most Royal Lady .... *The little white gauze veil clung to the oval of a face of full contours* .... *It was like a living page from the history of the Diallobe country. Everything that the country treasured of epic tradition could be read there* .... *An extraordinarily luminous gaze bestowed a kind of imperious lustre upon this face* .... *Islam restrained formidable turbulence of those features in the same way that the little veil hemmed them in.*

CHEIKH HAMIDOU KANE, *Ambiguous Adventure*

We are not so warped in soul, we are not Arabs, we are not Muslims to fabricate a desert god chanting in the wilderness, and call our creature creator.

AYI KWEI ARMAH, *Two Thousand Seasons*

As the title of this essay suggests[1], and as our introductory quotations confirm, the issue here concerns the role of Islam in its various Afro-Islamic manifestations as it affects structures and generates themes in selected African novels. We anticipate somewhat our conclusion by indicating at this point that thematic and narrative structures are more often resolved in syncretism and tension than in a return to orthodoxy. The reasons for such a tension parallel, and so may be deduced from, the general tendency in modern African literature to present religious phenomena primarily in terms of their contribution to crises of allegiance and identity. Thus, for example, Ferdinand Oyono's treatment of "cross" (Christianity) and consciousness in *The Old Man and the Medal* predictably results in a tension that is finally resolved in parody and violence. Oyono's orientation is not really surprising from our point of view. As I have put it elsewhere (1978, p. 20):

> His novel and those of our (other) authors are set in landscapes whose significance is deducible from the multifoliate cleverness of the title of Louis James's collection of essays on Caribbean literature. (These landscapes) are all "the islands in between." That is, they are zones of consciousness, temporal and spatial, which fall through the awkward interstices of orthodox evangelism. They are, as Césaire develops the motif,
>> Islands that are scars upon the water
>> Islands that are evidence of wounds
>> crumbled islands
>> formless islands.

These landscapes are certainly the norm in the literature that concerns us here. We are, as a result, in a world coded to be unorthodox, whether for epic, tragic, or satirical reasons. Orthodox, and formal propositions of dogma, imagery, and structure are set, modified or else ridiculed in the contexts provided by our "form-resisting" island. It is, however, primarily in Yambo Ouologuem, Ayi Kwei Armah, and Ousmane Sembene that the resistance to Islamic orthodoxy reflects the terms in which Christian orthodoxy, for example, is rejected. The tenor of that resistance is much given to ridicule. Writers like Cheikh Hamidou Kane, Camara Laye, and D. T. Niane in *Sundiata, Epic of Old Mali* give us a somewhat different perspective. Together, the two groups of writers determine the reading of crescent and consciousness that follows.

In a term of reference derived from Islamic counterheretical thinking, the Afro-Islamic context is, more often than not, an *al-Mukhlit* one. The term, which means "the mixers," is of course not theologically disinterested. Although its use throughout this study emphasizes aesthetic rather than theological issues, the term is, in essence, religious and inquisitional; it can therefore imply a purist concern with apostasy, heresy, and syncretism (Fisher, p. 128). Only in the near-pathological excesses of mortification and ecstasy in Cheikh Hamidou Kane's Thierno, teacher of the Diallobe (in *Ambiguous Adventure*), do we come close to such a concern in our texts. For our purposes, perhaps the clearest manifestation of the dual consciousness and of the calmer, though divided, allegiance involved in *al-Mukhlit* is to be found in Camara Laye's *The Dark Child*. We see this in the apparent equanimity with which it celebrates Kondén Diara and Malinke totemism, and Allah and Ramadan (p. 138):

> On the eve of my departure all the marabouts and witch-doctors, friends and notables, and indeed anyone else who cared to cross our threshold attended a magnificent feast in our concession.

The culture's magico-religious syncretism so clearly demonstrated by the Kankan "elixir" also reflects the same dual and even tempered allegiance (pp. 139–40):

> I had already drunk some of this liquid. My teacher had forced me to when I was taking my scholarship examination. It was a magic potion possessing many qualities and particularly good for developing the brain. It is a curious mixture. Our marabouts have small boards on which they write prayers taken from the Koran. When they have written down the texts they erase them with water. The washing water is carefully collected and, when honey has been added to it, the resulting mixture is the essence of the elixir. If it had been bought — and bought at a very high price — in Kankan, a strongly Mohammedan town and the holiest of our native places, it must be a particularly potent drink. The evening before my father had given me a he-goat's horn containing talismans. I was to wear it always as a protection against evil spirits.

I say "apparent equanimity" above because Laye nonetheless recognizes a strict, and so orthodox, *Shari'ah*; in effect, it is respect for a pure and fundamentalist tradition in Islam that determines the portrayal of *The Dark Child*'s Uncle Mamadou (pp. 150–51).

> He was a Mohammedan — as we all are, I may add — but more orthodox than most of us. His observance of the Koran was scrupulously honest. He neither smoked nor drank and was absolutely honest. He wore European clothes only for work. As soon as he came home he undressed and put on a *boubou* which had to be immaculate, and said his prayers. On leaving the Ecole Normale he

had taken up the study of Arabic .... It was simply his desire for a deeper knowledge of religion that had persuaded him to learn the language of the Prophet. The Koran guided him in everything.

Still, whatever tension there is in Camara Laye is a muted tension. Indeed, as we shall see in the next section, syncretism dominates the aesthetics at work in the religious world that Camara Laye gives us in his novels, especially in *The Dark Child* and *A Dream of Africa* [*Dramouss*]. In sum, whether the evidence comes from the impatience in Ousmane Sembene and Ayi Kwei Armah, from the exuberant Koranic inversions of Yambo Ouologuem, or from the Sufi dilemmas of Hamidou Kane, one clear premise may now be established. What we have, given the pressures of conflicting demands, is an unorthodox coincidence of self, place, and doctrine that simply cannot support established dogmas without mutation. As may be expected, that mutation is most outrageously and scandalously demonstrated in Ouologuem's *Bound to Violence*.

> "Don't be in a hurry to meet the Most-High," Saif said to them, "or He will punish you: a man can die of an itch for immortality. Therefore be good soldiers, fight and wait, for Heaven will not come to you until God has granted you salvation and given you His blessing. My gentle lambs, let us praise the Lord for the abundant favors and benefits He has heaped upon us by making us His devoted worshipers, so preserving us from evil. *Allahu akbar! wakul rabbi zidni ilman!*"
>
> Then Saif strode with measured step, preceded by drums, balafons, tom-toms, lambis, and trumpets, and his sorcerers sang that he was invulnerable. His guard carried long bulls' tails which, so it was said, diverted bullets. Kratonga, Wampoulo, and Yafolè, covered with fetishes and carrying roosters, walked behind His Royal Magnificence with Madoubo, murmuring sacrificial prayers.

Camara Laye is, of course, more charitable to the two cultures at work.

II. The Cora and the Koran

> "Fatoman, ask your witch-doctor to tell the one about the jealous man."
>
> I had heard this story always with great enjoyment I don't know how many times.
>
> ... Kessery the witch-doctor stood up ....
>
> "Moussa! Moussa! Moussa!" he suddenly shouted as if inspired. "Moussa, the jealous man, suffered deeply on account of his jealousy ...."

The witch-doctor, enthralled as much by the sound of his own voice as by the music of his cora, began his chanting.

CAMARA LAYE, *A Dream of Africa* [Dramouss]

The troubadour, called, with surprising inadequacy, a *witch doctor* in James Kirkup's translation of *Dramouss*, is, significantly, a *griot*. His *chantefable*, lasts for thirteen pages (pp. 98−121), adding up to more than half of the novel's "Kouroussa" chapter. The impression of the novel's narrative informality is thus further strengthened by the story of Imam Moussa, "adored human creature," and his sometimes comic, sometimes fantastic, but ultimately illustrative, encounter with a wife, Habibatou, who is passionate in her infidelity to him, and his Lord, "whom he called the King of Kings."

The narration of the *chantefable*, its principal actors, as well as the nature of its interpolation into the formal structure of the novel, illustrate rather well the many dimensions of a syncretist aesthetics at work. The tale is, quite clearly, of dual parentage. It allows for an exegesis derived from either *griot* or Islamic aesthetics. Better, and more logically, since we have already proposed that the Afro-Islamic perception is *al-Mukhlit* in consciousness, the exegesis of the tale of Imam Moussa may best be performed through *griot* and Islamic categories. The tale itself provides internal direction.

Imam Moussa is visited by an angel. "It was winged, and its great pinions of silver and diamonds sparkled like hosts of suns ... so impressively brilliant that the human eye could not behold its magnificence for more than thirty seconds without blinking" (p. 109).[2] This encounter between Islamic angel and *konianké* imam is especially relevant because "The angel was wearing a white *pipao*." As a footnote to the text points out, the *pipao* is a garment worn by Mohammedans of black Africa; but this time the Mohammedan "garment" clothes identities that are decidedly less orthodox than the *Shari'ah* or *Hadîth* values to which, we have already seen, *The Dark Child's* Uncle Mamadou subscribes. In *A Dream of Africa* Imam Moussa's encounter with the angel is clearly *al-Mukhlit* (p. 110)

> "Was it thou who didst call upon the King of Kings?" the angel demanded.
>
> "I don't understand!" babbled Moussa.
>
> For the angel had couched its question in literary Arabic, which the Imam did not understand, because he could not catch the meaning of all of the words.
>
> "Ah!" cried the angel. "Dost thou not speak Arabic? What tongue does thou speak? I speak all languages."

"I speak the konianké tongue."

"What can I do for thee?" the angel asked, speaking in the konianké tongue.

Thus, the tale is indeed *konianké*. It is told by a *griot* to *cora* accompaniment; it is also narrated and performed in such a way that it evokes participatory questions and interpolations by the audience. The tale's thirteen-page displacement of the novel's linear development of plot is also explainable in *konianké* categories. The traditional structure of the novel has, in effect, been reshaped by a *griot* virtuoso aesthetics. Time and plot development are necessarily more malleable quantities in virtuoso performances, especially those "with so many fine nuances, with so much eloquence."

In effect, though he is called a witch doctor, Kessery clearly belongs to that tradition of historical and aesthetic tradition out of which comes the voice recorded by Niane (1965, p. 1). "I am a griot I ... Djeli Mamadou Kouyate, son of Bintou Kouyate and Djeli Kedian Kouyate, master in the art of eloquence." It is therefore not surprising that the Imam Moussa *chantefable* ends in Malinke ritual and ecstasy. The audience role is recognizably dramatized in Bilali's emotional and practical response when, "radiant with happiness," he takes out of his pocket a thousand-franc note that he hands to the *griot* Kessery. "I was happy this evening, really happy to have heard the story of my ancestors. I had already heard it recounted by other witch doctors, but never with so many fine nuances, with so much eloquence. Thank you for the tale about Moussa." Bilali's response also points to the combination of oral archives and panegyric that we often find in the *griot*'s expression. Kessery's response, as the aesthetics demands, is at once praise poem, ecstatic chant, and business contract (p. 121):

> "*Ohon! Ohon!* N'diati Bilali! *Kante, Kante,* your ancestor Soumaoro would have done no less! *Kante, Kante!*" cried the witch-doctor. "Tomorrow I shall call upon you at dawn to receive from your noble hands my fine embroidered boubou."

The aesthetic tradition at work had, of course, been more fully and yet intimately and exquisitely demonstrated in Camara Laye's first novel, *The Dark Child*. We see it at work in that novel's illustrative encounter between praise-singer and goldsmith. Thus, in a reported *chantefable* integrated into the formal structure of the novel, the praise-singer, "whose business it was to register excitement, ... did not stop speaking faster and ever faster, increasing his tempo," throughout the metamorphosis of molten gold and charcoal into the spiral pyramid of a woman's trinket (pp. 38–39):

> For the praise-singer took a curious part—I should say rather that it was direct and effective—in the work .... He shouted aloud in joy. He plucked his *cora* like a man inspired. He sweated as if he were the trinket-maker, as if he were my father, as if the trinket were his creation .... And when my father, after having soldered the large grain of gold that crowned the summit, held out his work to be admired, the praise-singer would no longer be able to contain himself. He would begin to intone the *douga*, the great chant which is sung only for celebrated men and which is danced for them alone.

Griot and audience move to consummation in ritual and ecstasy. And so, though at a far more heightened level of both archetypal imagery and realism, Bilali and Kessery's celebration of their relationship is paralleled by the goldsmith's dance and the praise-singer's music (p. 39):

> At the first notes of the *douga* my father would arise and emit a cry in which happiness and triumph were equally mingled; and brandishing in his right hand the hammer that was the symbol of his profession and in his left a ram's horn filled with magic substances, he would dance the glorious dance.

An exegesis of the Imam Moussa tale in such categories as the above is legitimate, of course. It is, nonetheless, necessarily partial, given our postulation of Islamic and *konianké* aesthetic integration. The *chantefable* of Imam Moussa is, in its clear etiological function, a teaching fable, at one with, for example, John M. Chen's summary of the nature and significance of teaching stories in Saiyid Idries Shah (p. 34):

> Both *Reflections* and *Tales of the Dervishes* are collections of fables, legends, and teaching stories of the Sufis. Idries Shah has succeeded in presenting these in the English language in a manner that still preserves their thought-provoking nature. He has spent much time tracing these stories and in compiling them into his books. These tales are amusing and entertaining. Yet they challenge the reader, in many cases, to seek a deeper meaning. These fables also present a variety of illustrations on human nature.

It is thus of some significance that in *A Dream of Africa* Marie's request for the tale is "Fatoman, ask your witch-doctor to tell the one about the jealous man."

Additionally, the tale of Imam Moussa is in many respects made up of Islamic formulae. These range from the nature of the benign anticlericalism of the narration itself to *chahada* and liturgical rhythms which Laye gives us in "My Lord, praise be unto thee, Creator of heaven and earth, of angels and devils, of water and fire, Creator of all things, King of Kings, show me the light." There is the inevitable resolution of intensity in the scriptual formula *"Allahou akbar!"*

These formulae also encapsule two Islamic modes of perception. In one, the phenomenal world is bound and stabilized by a *shari'ah* perception of time, space, and purpose. "Soon the muezzin was summoning the faithful to the Mosque for the first prayers of the afternoon" (p. 105). In the other, reality is, as the Sufi insist, unstable, coalescing into iconographic correspondences that ultimately "soar directly into the stairway of heaven." The tale of Imam Moussa's fantastic ontology is readily explainable in such terms as these. Thus, the Imam enters into a mystical contemplation of and yearning for "the real baptismal name of the King of Kings" (p. 108). His contemplation provokes a "fantastic sound." He raises his head to find "that the ceiling was no longer there, that the roof of his house was no longer there either. And now the Imam's gaze soared directly to the stairway of heaven, was lost in the immensity of the starry vault . . ." (p. 113).

The prayer that follows this "vision" is formulaic in two ways, religious and generic. The prayer echoes the language and rhythm of Islamic mysticism and ecstasy. Its more secular tenor, however, suggests one of the modalities of the teaching story, that of comic fantasy. In effect, the prayer's mystical formulae totter and collapse into studied bathos — for, as Chen, above, has put it, the teaching stories are often amusing and entertaining. The imam's startled devotion is an apt one (p. 109):

> "Glory to Thee, my Lord!" he prayed, mastering his fear. "I am convinced that thou art the sole Master of the Universe and the Prophet Mohammed is thy chosen emissary!" Then he added: "I am convinced that the power thou dost wield, on high heaven and everywhere, is very great, is infinitely greater than the sign which thou has just revealed unto me. I know that this sign is as nothing, nothing but a symbol of the power thou dost wield and that is even more astounding, infinitely more astounding, than the vanishing of my ceiling and of the roof of my dwelling-place."

III. al-Wahdaniyya: Approximations

The element of mysticism in Camara Laye, especially as it is worked into the major themes of *The Dark Child* and *A Dream of Africa*, needs fuller and finer development. Since Laye's mysticism also demands an *al-Mukhlit* approach, I introduce a caveat at this point to temper the Sufi element in Imam Moussa. I have perhaps too unconditionally linked certain formulae in the tale of Imam Moussa to Islamic mysticism only. The mystical in Laye's works, however, is also a product of dual parentage, as is the tale of Imam Moussa itself; hence the caveat, which the following contrastive discussion of Kane will clarify.

The evidence is there, and in dramatic profusion, in all three of Camara Laye's novels that only a very finely hinged door of perception separates the world of phenomena from the world of immanent, ineffable essence. Very often a fundamental *liber naturael liber Dei* equation inspires or sustains such a perception. Nasrolla S. Fatemi's essay on Sufism provides illustration by way of the pantheistic formulation of the view in the following excerpt from a prayer of Dhu'l Nun (p. 51):

> O God, I never hearken to the voices of the beasts or the rustle of the trees, the splashing of water or the songs of birds, the whistling of the wind or the rumble of thunder, but I sense in them a testimony of thy unity [Wahdanyya, *sic*] and a proof of thy Incomparableness; that thou art the all-prevailing.

Dhu'l Nun's consciousness is, however, more graphic and lyrical in Kane's *Ambiguous Adventure* than portrayals in Laye's novels. In sum, Kane's Islamic vision and art are rather more concentratedly tidy than Camara Laye's. Thus, given the high-strung Sufi allegiance in *Ambiguous Adventure*, when the world of phenomenal reality is transfigured into an "incandescent next" it is manifestly a testimony to Allah's Wahdaniyya, to his unity, apprehended with exquisite and agonizing intensity (pp. 68 and 159):

> On the horizon, it seemed as if the earth were poised on the edge of an abyss. Above the abyss the sun was suspended, dangerously. The liquid silver of its heat had been reabsorbed without any loss of its light's splendor. Only, the air was tinted with red, and under this illumination the little town seemed suddenly to belong to a strange planet.
>
> On the horizon, the setting sun had dyed the heavens with a tone of blood-stained purple. Not a breath of air stirred the motionless trees. The only sound to be heard was the great voice of the river, reverberating from its dizzily steep banks. Samba Diallo bent his gaze toward this voice, and saw the clay cliff in the distance. He remembered that in his childhood he had believed for a long time that this immense crevasse divided the universe into two parts, which were united by the river.

Water imagery, river and sea, dominates the narration in *Ambiguous Adventure*. These images insist on fluid motion in a way that reflects Sufi ideas. In the light of Sufi thought, they are formulaic and iconographical representations of the *Wahdaniyya*, that is, of the ontological unity that defines the origin, medium, and object of mystical contemplation and consummation. As Martin Lings has it in *What is Sufism?* (p. 13):

> The Ocean is within as well as without; and the path of the mystics is a gradual awakening as it were "backwards" in the direction of the root of one's being, a remembrance of the Supreme Self which infinitely transcends the human ego and which is none other than the Deep towards which the wave ebbs.

It is obviously in similar imagery and style that Samba Diallo enters "the place where there is no ambiguity" at the end of *Ambiguous Adventure* (pp. 165-66):

> in the luminous arena of your duration man unfurls himself to infinity. The sea! Here is the sea! Hail to you, rediscovered wisdom, my victory! The limpidness of your wave is awaiting my gaze. I fix my eyes upon you, and you glitter, without limit. I wish for you, through all eternity.

The style is, at one level, fashioned by the language of *al-Wahdaniyya*, by the language of ontological unity ("duration," "*harden* into Being," "sea," "place"); but the vocabulary in the selection is also indicative of yet another Sufi understanding of God's unity, the supraontological *al-Ahadiyya* (therefore "glitter," "luminous," "without limit"). This state of supreme Unity, unknowable by creatures through distinctive cognition, is for the Sufi "the absolute indivisible Divine Essence, impersonal and supraontological" (ᶜAta 'illah, p. 71). Kane thus writes in full consciousness of a state of Oneness prior to and subsequent to its "hardening into Being"; his language echoes that of Islamic mystics.

In a more poetic shorthand, "the great Andalusian Sufi, Muyi 'd-Din Ibn ᶜArabi, used to pray a prayer which begins: 'Enter me, O Lord, into the deep of the Ocean of Thine Infinite Oneness'" (Lings, p. 11). The doors of perception are delicately hinged in *Ambiguous Adventure* — and necessarily so because, as Seyyed Hossein Nasr has it in *Sufi Essays* (p. 16), "In the Holy Quran God refers to Himself as the Outward (*al-zahir*) and the Inward (*al-batin*). Inasmuch as this world and all that is in it are reflections and theophanies of the Names and Qualities of God, all the realities of the world also possess and outward and an inward aspect."

The tidier theology at work in *Ambiguous Adventure* results in an effective structuring of the novel in accordance with the major postulations and imagery of Islamic Sufi thought. Narration therefore moves, imagistically, from the poverty of chapter one to the sea of the last chapter. The poverty can therefore be seen as an illustration of Nasr's claim that "The Sufi bears spiritual poverty (*faqr*) within himself even if he lives outwardly amidst the riches of the world. Sufism is in fact often called 'Muhammadan poverty' (*al-faqr al muhammadi*)." By the same token, the simultaneous extinction and affirmation of consciousness that we see in the last chapter's confluence of voice, sea, and face may be interpreted as a translation of what the Sufis term "externality after extinction" (*al-baga ba'd al-fana*). The thirteenth century Andalusian Sufi Shustari is exquisite in his poetic summary of the view (Lings, p. 88):

> After extinction I came out and I
> External now am, though not as I,
>   Yet who am I, O I, but I

Still, the peculiarity of Kane's place in the world, which, after all, provides the crisis in *Ambiguous Adventure*, causes modification of orthodox Sufi mysticism. The theology is still remarkably tidy; thus there really is no descent to syncretistic "untidiness" of the sort that will be found in Camara Laye below. The difference that arises in Kane is rather more psychologically projected. It manifests itself in the apocalyptic agony that infuses his Sufi ecstasy. The thematic frame of the first chapter and the last chapter, in itself optimistic, nonetheless encloses a perception that agonizes over the imminent disappearance of that kind of Sufi Master whose continued influence is an important aspect of the cosmic and ecological optimism implicit in *al-Wahdaniyya*. His absence, or crippling, is a threat to governance — as may be deduced from Al-Hujwiri's *Kashf al-Mahjub* (V. Monteil, p. 87).

> God has His saints whom He has singled out by His Friendship and whom He has chosen to be governors of His Kingdom, whom he has designated to manifest His deeds, and whom He has blessed with different miracles (*karamat*); whom He has purified of natural corruption and delivered from the bondage of their base instincts and their passions in such a manner that their thoughts come from Him and that they are intimate only with Him ... He has named the saints governors of the Universe; they have become entirely devoted to His cause and have stopped heeding their sensual attachments. By the blessing of their coming the rain falls from the skies; by the purity of their lives, plants surge from the ground; and by

their spiritual influence the Moslems win victories over the Unbelievers.

Historical and cultural consciousness in *Ambiguous Adventure* is, however, determined by an unhappy, even fatalistic view that is succinct and lucid in the Fulfulde saying, "The cleric (*tyerno*) begets a chief (*lamdo*); the chief begets an infidel (*kefero*)." The ecstatic lyricism and grim apocalypse of the "Night of the Koran" chapter is perhaps the novel's most agonized response to the threat of apostasy so clear-cut in the Fulfulde epigram just quoted. Stylistically, what results is a remarkable tension between the transfiguring incandescence of a Sufi reading of Koranic incantation and a distinctly non-Sufi consciousness of "Extinction" as finality (pp. 66–67).

> But he considered that it was important for him, more than for any of those who had preceded him, to acquit himself to the full on his Night. For it seemed to him that this Night marked an end. This scintillation of the heavens above his head, was it not the star-studded bolt being drawn upon an epoch that had run its course? Behind that bolt a world of stellar light was gently glowing, a world which it was important to glorify one last time. His voice, which had progressively risen as if linked to the thrust of the stars, was raised now to a pathetic fullness. From the depths of the ages he felt, springing up in him and breathed out by his voice, a long love which today was threatened. In the humming sound of this voice there was being dissolved, bit by bit, a being who a few moments ago had still been Samba Diallo. Insensibly, rising from profundities which he did not suspect, phantoms were assailing him through and through and were substituting themselves for him. It seemed to him that in his voice had become muffled innumerable voices, like the voice of the river on certain nights.
>
> But the voice of the river was less vehement, and also less close to tears. The voice of the river did not carry along with it this refusal which was now being cried out in the voice of Sambo Diallo.

It is true in Kane that the cleric still points out the Way (*Tariqa*) for "the only moments of enthusiasm that could be seen in him [Thierno, teacher of the Diallobe] were those in which, lost in mystic meditations or listening to the recital of the Word of God, he would stand erect, all tense, and seem to be lifted from the earth, as if raised by some inner force" (p. 6). But the physical (and cultural) reality is the awareness (or suspicion) that "The man was old, emaciated, withered and shrunken mortifications of the flesh" (p. 6), that (p. 26):

> the teacher was failing physically. More every day, his body emphasized this sorry propensity to remain glued to the earth. For

example, he no longer had confidence in the joints of his feet, which refused him all obedience.

The pervasive tension in *Ambiguous Adventure* thus assumes a form here that seeks relief in devotion and mortification: in "crippled prayer" (p. 156), in prayer that is "a grotesque and painful exercise" (p. 109), and in "broken prayer, this incongruous and tragic dumb show" (p. 155). The teacher thus reflects in an intensely physical form the cultural and spiritual crisis in Kane's novel: the Way (*Tariqa*) is locked in conflict with a secular and materialist need to "join wood to wood." It is now not the Most Royal Lady's agonized pragmatism that results; we have, instead, the knight's vision of an apocalypse (p. 64):

> At this point in his reflections the knight had something like an hallucination. A spot on our globe was burning with a blinding brilliance, as if a fire had been lighted on an immense hearth. At the heart of this fierce light and heat a swarm of human beings seemed to be giving themselves over to an incomprehensible and fantastic mimicry of worship. Emerging from all sides, from deep valleys of shadow, floods of human creatures of all colors were pouring in; and in the measure of their approach to the hearth, these beings took up, insensibly, the rhythm which had encompassed them, while under the effect of the light they lost their original colors, which gave way to the wan tint that filled the air roundabout.

The power of orthodoxy in *Ambiguous Adventure*, however, is such that the novel does not resolve its dilemma in apostasy, though a paradoxical *chahada* profession of doubt runs delicately through the novel. Still, it never rises to the pitch that we find, for instance, in Ousmane Sembene's Mohammedan character Sounkare. His prayer, in the face of the chaos that Thies projects and represents in *God's Bits of Wood*, is at once *chahada* (formulation of faith) and anti-*chahada*; it is clearly poised on the edge of apostasy. Colonial violence, economic deprivation, and physically precarious existence drove Sounkare to a special response to his faith; "a kind of prayer" had accordingly formed within him (p. 179):

> "Lord," he had said, "Oh Lord who loves me, I am alone on the only road I know. Having suffered as much as I have, I am still at the beginning of suffering. Does this mean that I am damned? Lord, what are You doing for me? You do not prevent the wicked from doing as they will, nor the good from being crushed beneath the weight of their misery, and by Your commandments You stay the arm of the just man when he would lift it to repair the evil. Do You really exist, or are You just an image? I don't see that You show Yourself anywhere. Lord, You are a God of goodness, and

You have given me Your grace; is it I who have failed? Forgive me, and help me, Lord, for I am hungry, I am very hungry. Do something in my behalf, oh Lord who loves me, for I am worthy of Your help."

For his own part, Sembene responds to deprivation with a materialistic dialectic of a far more decisive nature than Sounkare's volatile anxiety. Strikes, for example, are more likely to influence the forces of production than prayers. Sembene in his impatience with Islam differs markedly from Kane, or Laye for that matter. It is, for *God's Bits of Wood*, not as convincing or even comforting that "God has His saints whom He has singled out by His friendship and whom He has chosen to be governors of His Kingdom" as it is in that more orthodox vision that Monteil translates (above) from al-Hujwiri's *Kashf al-Mahjub*. Sembène insists that much remains to be done — especially because of "God's governors" (p. 279):

> A campaign to demoralize and undermine the unity of the strikers — and particularly of their wives — had been undertaken by the men who were their "spiritual guides," the imams and the priests of other sects. After the prayers and religious services all over the city, there would be a sermon whose theme was always the same: "By ourselves, we are incapable of creating any sort of useful object, not even a needle."

Sembene's latest film *Ceddo* constitutes his most comprehensive attack on "God's saints and governors" and their effect on the African past and present.[3] It is therefore not surprising that Kane's exquisitely fashioned and endured dilemma is brusquely dispensed with in *God's Bits of Wood* (p. 281).

> "It is the will of God." Arona said.
> "Oh shut up with your talk about the will of God!"

As we have seen, and as our conclusion will now further develop, Allah's will and Islamic liturgy are more patiently entertained in Camara Laye. We move now to a discussion of other reasons for this by focusing our attention on the mystical in Laye's works.

IV. Al-Mukhlit: Conclusion

The "flavor of mysticism" in *A Dream of Africa* and *The Dark Child* creates a kind of affinity with Islam. Though it is highly suggestive of *al-Wahdaniyya* in Sufi and in Kane, the finely hinged door of perception that separates the world of phenomenal reality from ineffable essence responds best to an *al-Mukhlit* key in Camara Laye. It is only in *A Dream of Africa* that the opening mechanism is directly attributed to Allah, and even there, while the attribution is proposed in Islamic terms, the symbols of its manifestation are non-Islamic.

In *The Dark Child*, as will be seen in the following sequence, there are three stages of perception — though it does finally become clear that they are to be considered as stages in a single mode. In the first selection the transformative power is invested, not in the supernatural, but in the "glad animal movements" (Wordsworth) of the young protagonist (p. 44):

> But I was hardly aware of the road, for all sorts of marvels lay along it.
> I say "marvels" for Kouroussa is actually a city and hasn't any of those country sights which a city child always finds marvelous. As we walked along we were likely to dislodge a hare or a wild boar; birds flew away at our approach, with a great beating of wings; sometimes we would meet a crowd of monkeys. Every time something like this happened I felt a small thrill of excitement.

The hypnotic intensity of the second stage in highly suggestive of the pantheistic; at this stage, however, it is a pantheism that avoids the *liber naturae/liber Dei* that we get in Dhu'l Nun and Hamidou. In Laye, an intensity at once physical and emotional results in the following: As the signal is given, a long line of reapers sets out to harvest. "The young men threw their sickles into the air and caught them as they fell. They shouted simply for the pleasure of shouting, and danced as they followed the tom-tom players" (pp. 56–57). Soon, there is a mesmerizing fusion of sickles flashing in the sun, spirited music, sweetness in the air, and the crescendo of tom-toms. "Everything is in flower. Everything is young" (p. 57). The mode of perception is luminous with the language of mysticism; the tense shift to the present (p. 57).

> everywhere, the country, which until now has been drenched with rain and dulled by heavy clouds, lies radiant. The sky has never been clearer nor brighter. Birds sing ecstatically. Joy is everywhere, erupts everywhere, and every heart is moved by it. This season, this beautiful season, stirred me deeply. And so did the tom-tom and the festal air that our march acquired. It was a beautiful season, and everything in it — what wasn't there in it? what didn't it pour forth in profusion? — delighted me.

The supernatural, though not yet Allah as in *A Dream of Africa*, is introduced in the third stage. Instead of Allah we see the supernatural made manifest in the ambiguities of the jinn phenomenon. The etymology of the word is, of course, Arabic; its culture is at once popular magico-Islamic and pre-Islamic. As Rene A. Bravmann's "Gyinna-Gyinna: Making the Djinn Manifest" has it (p. 46),

> Throughout the Islamic world, among both the clerical elite and the mass of believers, the concept of djinn is an everpresent feature. From Morocco through Islamized portions of black Africa, the Middle East, and as far afield as Southeast Asia, the mysteries and workings of the djinn form a central part of the scriptural, magical, and popular dimensions of the faith.

Jinn are as old as the faith itself. On the other hand, "many regard them as the nature spirits of the pre-Islamic Arabian world" (Bravmann, ibid.).

Their presence in African literature and their integration into *al-Mukhlit* narration are both ancient and of ambigous ancestry. Thus, shortly after that genealogical linking of Mali with Mecca in *Sundiata, Epic of Old Mali*, which opens this essay, we read (p. 2),

> Lahilatoul Kalabi was the first black prince to make the pilgrimage to Mecca. On his return he was robbed by brigands in the desert; his men were scattered and some died of thirst, but God saved Lahilatoul Kalabi, for he was a righteous man. He called upon the Almighty and jinn appeared and recognized him as king. After seven years' absence Lahilatoul was able to return, by the grace of Allah the Almighty, to Mali.

The jinn is here proffered as an extension of Allah and in formulae derived from Islamic liturgy. The epic, nonetheless, has other references that localize the phenomenon, making it a supernatural extension of the "Bright Country," that is, of Mali in its golden age and savanna brightness. Sundiata's invocation at the water's edge is thus steeped in ritual that suggests a non-Islamic ancestry (*Sundiata*, p. 71).

> "Oh jinn of the water, Master of the Moghoya-Dji, master of the magic water, I sacrificed to you a hundred bulls, I sacrificed to you a hundred rams, and I sacrificed to you a hundred cocks. You gave me the victory but I have not destroyed Kita. I, the successor to Kita Mansa, come to drink the magic water, the moghoya dji."

In Camara Laye the phenomenon appears to derive more of its values, as in Sundiata's invocation, from the Malinke totemism and ritual whose transfigurative powers are insisted upon throughout *The Dark Child*. Examples that come readily to mind, are, of course, the father-black snake and mother-crocodile ties, each one suggestive of degrees of metempsychosis and magic. The ancestral worship and totemism in those relations bring us closer to forces and agents that bridge the gap between the natural and the supernatural (p. 64):

> Above us the swallows were already flying lower, and although the air was a clear as ever, the end of day was near. We were happy as we entered the village, weary and happy. The geniis had taken good care of us: not one of us had been bitten by snakes dislodged when we trampled the field. The scent of flowers, awakened by the approach of evening, seemed to clothe us in fresh garlands. . . . Ah! How happy we were in those days!

When the jinn reappears in *A Dream of Africa* it does so, as we shall see, in a contest redolent of dark, Afro-Islamic occultism and conjuration.[4] Given the thematic orientations of the two novels, the change is hardly surprising. The nostalgic lyricism that tempers the phenomenal and the supernatural worlds of *The Dark Child* is absent in Laye's third novel. The *al-Mukhlit* consciousness in *A Dream of Africa* is rather more sharply engaged in eschatology and politics. The symbolism through which Laye now expresses his vision of the apocalypse is made up of Malinke icons: Dramouss, snake, hawk, Black Lion, and enormous cailcedra; it is, however, an Islamic Prime Mover, Allah, who gives unity and value to the symbols. The style in which Laye records the syncretism is cabalistic and yet orthodox in liturgy and moral vision, a predictable result of the use of jinn, Allah, conjuration, and prayer beads in *A Dream of Africa's* climatic statement.

It is thus in that prophetic high drama that ends *A Dream of Africa* that Laye shows us the most extraordinary and yet politically charged *al-Mukhlit* consciousness and depth. The scene is, of course, heavy with apocalypse and moral passion. As may be expected, the teaching tale of Imam Moussa had, in its political features, anticipated the conjunction of ritual, magic, religion, and the political process that the novel's coda will dramatize (pp. 115–16).

> "Behold your prince!" Imam Moussa cried. He was unable to finish the phrase, for the people, howling with joy, had drowned it with their massed shouts of happiness. The king himself could hardly believe his eyes. Overwhelmed with emotion, he began to weep. And he breathed a sigh of relief that, even should he be taken from the throne by death, nothing now could prevent the kingdom from continuing to enjoy royal sway.

Clearly, in the teaching story, the chaotic element in the Fulfulde proverb has been eliminated. The *tyerno* begets *a lamdo* and order is restored.

A darker conjuration takes place when the Imam Moussa nuclear fable is expanded in the novel's coda. There, the reality that must be exorcised is the chaotic element. For, "suddenly, out of the blue, a hawk which had been hovering above us for a moment plunged down on the concession . . . . When it swooped back into the sky we saw, to our dismay, that one of the chicks was clutched in its talons" (pp. 187–8). In a great surge of anger, Fatoman's father plunges his hand furtively into his caftan and brings out a string of beads that he brandishes in the direction of the soaring hawk (p. 188):

> "*Sala moûne gawlan mine Rabine Rahimine, adjib ly yâ Kachafa ya ilou, Wal Djini Alga Atou Bintou Maimouna.*" [God I call upon thee through the intermediary of Bintou, daughter of the Djinn Maïmouna and through his master the Rouhania Yâ Kachafa Ya ilou]
> My father uttered these words distinctly, one by one, each time a pearl in the chaplet passed through his fingers. He was seated, quite absorbed in his prayers.

Suddenly, even before the father has finished telling his beads, the hawk, as if stunned, swoops down to the ground level, beats its wings, then comes down to earth within reach of the father's hand. The hawk is grabbed and the chicken is released. "Then he picked up a bulrush — there are always some lying about our concession — and struck the hawk with it three times" (188–9).

As the novel ends, the meaning of the drama is centrally located and explained in categories that suggest a brand of cabala and Islamic mysticism:

> "Yes. Those words have a great deal of power. When one has spoken for the Lord, acted for the Lord, and lived alone in the wilderness for the Lord, as I have, in contemplation, and all for the Lord, then the Lord hearkens unto one when one prays to him."

Quite clearly, though at a more intense and profound level, Fatoman's father, like Imam Moussa in the teaching story, has after much contemplation reached out into "the real baptismal name of the King of Kings." He can therefore "soar directly to the stairway of heaven," for "God has His saints . . . . whom He has designated to manifest His deeds, and whom He has blessed with different miracles" — to return to al-Hujwiri's formulation. Appropriately, *A Dream of Africa* reformulates in *al-Mukhlit* categories. *A chahada*- like benediction ends the novel. The liturgical structure is Islamic and the vision of

the just future is incarnate in the recurrent Malinke Black Lion
(pp. 189–90):[5]

> "Yes, the heroic and infinitely wise Black Lion, whom you
> know as well as I. Law and justice shall return also. And then ye
> shall be reconciled, reconciled with yourselves and with others.
> Yes, even with that country, that other country over there whose
> tongue you speak. I say unto you: if such be the will of Allah,
> blessed be thy name!"
> "*Aminâ! Aminâ!*" I replied.

Camara Laye thus pronounces a benediction, at once orthodox
and unorthodox, upon the *al-Mukhlit* consciousness we have been
discussing. As should be clear by now, Laye occupies a middle
ground between Cheikh Hamidou Kane's agonized assumption into
a Sufi Paradise and Ousmane Sembene's exorcist pronouncements of
anathemas against saint, creed, and paradise. The view that we get
from Sembene's short story "White Genesis" is thus typical of his
unambiguous judgment of the "true believer" (pp. 9 and 10): "They
were wearing away the skin of their foreheads and their knees in
prayer, five times a day .... They sought comfort in the adda, the
tradition, and in the hypothetical promise of one of the best places in
paradise." It makes, finally, for the most disquieting union of crescent
and consciousness in this study of *al-Mukhlit* expressions (p. 10):

> Allah's paradise, like a nail in the centre of their brain, the cornerstone
> of every activity of their daily existence, weakened and breached
> their faith in the future.

Notes

1. The plural "orthodoxies" in the title is potentially problematical, given
   Cheikh Hamidou Kane's Sufi consciousness and the conflict between
   legalistic religion and mysticism. The fact that "official Islam shows little
   sympathy for a Moslem mysticism, and some even deny its existence"
   (Vincent Monteil, p. 88) is clear in the literature. It is also clear that Sufis
   and Sufi apologists reject this view as an attempt to reduce Islam in the
   words of Seyyed Hassein Nasr (pp. 16–17),

   > to the narrowest possible interpretation of the Divine Law or
   > *Sharîah* ... [but] if we mean by *al-islâm* the religion revealed
   > through the Holy Quran, then likewise the ... *tasawwuf* which
   > may be legitimately practised must be the one that has its roots in
   > the Quranic revelation and which we call 'Sufism' in the general
   > acceptation of this term. In any case a valid esoteric way is inseparable
   > from the objective framework of the revelation to which it belongs.

One cannot practise Buddhist esotericism in the context of Islamic *Sharīah* or vice versa.

2. Compare Jan Knappert, p. 74, *Traditional Swahili Poetry*,

> According to other traditions, Gabriel has six wings, which are made of emeralds, pearls and rubies. On his head he has a crown incrusted with pearls and other precious stones.

Knappert also records (p. 74) al-Isbahan's version of an encounter between the Prophet Muhammed and the Angel Gabriel. In response to the Prophet, "in a moonlit night, Gabriel appeared to him, and lo! He filled the sky from East to West. The Prophet swooned and fell down fainting. Gabriel lifted him up and said: 'Do not fear, I am your brother Gabriel.'"

3. Vincent Montiel's "Marabouts" in *Islam in Africa*, eds. James Kritzeck and William H. Lewis, provides variations in the terms of opposition (pp. 100—01):

> The objections come also from those who are shocked by certain excesses which appear hysterical, such as the behavior of Bay Fal, an unorthodox branch of the Murids. A film, *Pilgrimage to Touba*, made by Blaise Senghor in July 1961, shows one of these "mad Murids" being buried in a hole in which a fire rages .... He comes out unharmed .... In 1913 Paul Marty, speaking of Murids, used expressions such as "robbery," "extortion of funds," and "exploitation of the needy" .... In March 1963 in Dakar, a young Tokolor put on a satire, in French, called *Astuce mauresque*, of which the marabouts were the targets .... Sembene Ousmane (1962) compares marabouts to cats who "like to be fed without doing anything for it."

Additionally, the "Arts" page of *Africa* 86 (1978), 85, makes some pertinent observations about Sembene's *Ceddo*, the Film Censorship Board of Senegal, and Sembene's feeling that "Africans have been depersonalized by their conversion to Islam. It was forced upon them and they lost their traditional identity."

4. Charles Monteil's reading of the phenomenon (1969) is a somewhat reductive one. Vincent Monteil thus quotes him in "Marabouts," p. 97.

> Africans are avid for all aspects of magic. The pagans have limited means: Islam has brought them, on that score, the greatest satisfaction. All Sudanese, believers or unbelievers, are faithful clients of "men who tell hidden things" — fortune-tellers or marabouts, for them it's all one and the same. These are the practices that form the bridge between Islam and paganism; these magicians of all kinds, Moslems or pagans, form the liaison between the two religions. Geomancy is probably the form of magic which, thanks largely to the Moslems, has taken the deepest hold among the Negroes and is the most highly esteemed.

Jan Knappert is reductive and fierce when he pursue purity in Swahili poetry: "How far are we here from the ideals that seem universal in Africa: to have many wives, children and cows, and to conquer one's enemies. The terrible stain of the fear for witchcraft, the horror of evil spirits, is removed by Islam." Our texts and authors have, of course, the advantage of rather more intelligent and supple readings of cultural and religious ambiguities. Also, compare René Bravmann, in text and below.

5. Compare the following extract from Ibn Khaldun's Prolegomena in volume one of his *General History of the Arabs and Berbers*. The passage is in William Desborough Cooley, *The Negroland of the Arabs* (p. 62):

> The Mohammedans say that the first King of Málí was Baramindánah. He performed the pilgrimage to Mekkah, and enjoined his successors to do the same.
>
> But the great King of Málí who conquered the Súsú, and took their country, was named Mári Játah, which means, in the language of that country, Amír Lion, for Mári signifies an Amír, or prince of the blood royal, and játah means a lion.

It is this tradition that is conjoined in *A Dream of Africa* with that of the jinn and the "magical arsenal" of the Islamic faith. René Bravmann, p. 46, underscores the magical: "Muslim literature is replete with references to fairies, *djinn*, and spiritual forces that are either immical to mankind or that may serve individuals through positive and enlightened guidance." The appeal to Maïmouna's daughter Bintou is therefore an effective appeal to forces of enlightened guidance. *A Dream of Africa* thus ends with a strong affirmation of the magical arsenal of the Islamic faith.

References

ARMAH, AYI KWEI. 1973. *Two Thousand Seasons*, Nairobi: East Africa Publishing House.

ʿATAʾILLAH, IBN. 1973. *Sufi Aphorisms* [Kitab al-Hikam]. Trans. Victor Danner. Leiden: E. J. Brill.

BRAVMANN, RENE A. April 1977. "Gyinna-Gyinna: Making the Djinn Manifest." *African Arts*, 10, 3.

CHEN, JOHN H. M. 1973. "Literary Comparisons and Effects." In *Sufi Studies: East and West*. Ed. L. F. Rushbrook Williams.

COOLEY, WILLIAM DESBOROUGH. 1966. *The Negroland of the Arabs*. London: Frank Cass. Reprint of 1841 ed.

FATEMI, NASROLLAH S. 1973. "A Message and Method of Love, Harmony, and Brotherhood." In *Sufi Studies: East and West*. Ed. L. F. Rushbrook Williams.

FISHER, HUMPHREY J. 1969. "Separatism in West Africa." In *Islam in Africa*. Ed. James Kritzeck and William H. Lewis.

JOHNSON, LEMUEL A. In press. "Cross and Consciousness: The Failure of Orthodoxy in African and Afro-Hispanic Literature." *Studies in Afro-Hispanic Literature*.

KANE, CHEIKH HAMIDOU. 1974. *Ambiguous Adventure* [L'Aventure ambiguë]. Trans. Katherine Woods. New York: Collier.

KNAPPERT, JAN. 1967. *Traditional Swahili Poetry: An Investigation into the Concepts of East African Islam as Reflected in the Uter Literature*. Leiden: Brill.

KRITZECK, JAMES, and WILLIAM H. LEWIS, eds. 1969. *Islam in Africa*. New York: Van Nostrand-Reinhold.

LAYE, CAMARA. 1971. *A Dream of Africa* [Dramouss]. Trans. James Kirkup. New York: Collier.

―――. 1970. *The Dark Child* [L'Enfant noir]. Trans. James Kirkup and Ernest Jones. New York: Farrar, Straus and Giroux.

LEWIN, LEONARD, ed. 1976. *The Elephant in the Dark and Other Writings on the Diffusion of Sufi Ideas in the West by Idries Shab and Others*. New York: E. P. Dutton.

LINGS, MARTIN. 1975. *What is Sufism?* Berkeley: University of California.

MONTEIL, CHARLES. 1949. Unpublished Notes. In Vincent Monteil, "Marabouts."

MONTEIL, VINCENT. 1969. "Marabouts," In *Islam in Africa*, Ed. James Kritzeck and William H. Lewis.

NASR, SEYYED HOSSEIN. 1972. *Sufi Essays*, London: Allen and Unwin.

NIANE, D. T. 1965. *Sundiata: An Epic of Old Mali*. London: Longman.

OUOLOGUEM, YAMBO. 1971. *Bound to Violence* [Le Devoir de violence]. Trans. Ralph Manheim. New York: Harcourt Brace Jovanovich.

RUSHBROOK WILLIAMS, L. F., ed. 1973. *Sufi Studies: East and West*. New York: E. P. Dutton.

SEMBENE, OUSMANE. 1972. *The Money Order* with *White Genesis*. Trans. Clive Wake. London: Heinemann.

―――. 1970. *God's Bits of Wood* [Les Bouts de bois de Dieu]. Trans. Francis Price. London: Heinemann.

SHAH, IDRIES. 1964. *The Sufis*. New York: Doubleday.

TRIMINGHAM, J. S. 1965. *Islam in the Sudan*. London: Frank Cass.

―――. 1964. *Islam in East Africa*. Oxford: Clarendon.

―――. 1962. *A History of Islam in West Africa*. London: Oxford University Press.

Chapter 17

▼▼▼▼▼▼▼▼▼

Camara Laye, Cheikh Hamidou Kane, and Tayeb Salib: Three Sufi Authors

Kenneth W. Harrow

> *When his Lord said to him, "Surrender," he said, "I have surrendered me to the Lord of all Being"*　　　　　(Koran, II, 125).

Many of the dominant forms of Islam in the Eastern Sudan and West Africa, have been Sufi.[1] Trimingham's disparaging assessment that "(t)he orders in West Africa became ordinary non-esoteric religious associations ... [which] rarely have anything to do with mysticism," and that "the ordinary member knows nothing of the mysticism upon which his order is based" (1959, 92) finds its echo in Lewis's view that "their esoteric content is generally not strongly developed" (1980, 18). Nonetheless, the literary effusions of certain prominent African Muslim authors, like Camara Laye, Cheikh Hamidou Kane, and Tayeb Salih, would seem to find inspiration in a well defined, long-standing mystical tradition — which has had its own literary forms in addition to an ideological framework. This framework varies somewhat less than do the forms adopted by the authors: Laye's and Kane's fictionalized, autobiographical accounts would seem to be worlds apart from the folktale or romance, which share certain qualities with Salih's *Wedding of Zein* and Laye's *Le Regard du roi*, although the two models meet, curiously enough, in Laye's *Dramouss* and in Salih's *Season of Migration to the North*. Here we will not consider questions of genre, but will examine instead the Sufi components of Laye's *Le Regard du roi*, Kane's *L'Aventure ambiguë*, and Salih's *Wedding of Zein* while considering how the context accounts for the ideological differences between these vastly different authors.

Part I: The Sufi Way: *Le Regard du roi*

The allegory of the pilgrim begins with the individual soul, since it is only in the particular individual's life that the general truth can find its embodiment. Laye's pilgrim is a white man named Clarence whose quest begins with the determined desire to get to Africa, despite the impediments posed by the journey and the symbolic sand bars that stand in his vessel's way. Africa, and not Europe, must serve as a point of departure for Clarence. Indeed, Europe is never mentioned. Clarence strives to find his goal in Africa, vague though his notions are upon his arrival, but instead of terminating his journey, he finds it has only begun. As the quintessential white man in Africa, Clarence experiences all the fatuity we would associate with natural man on the first or lowest level as conceived by the Sufis. His white skin color, combined with the social history of the black continent, give him a false sense of superiority, further blinding him to his own inadequacies as well as to the virtues, strengths, or superior qualities of others. This leads him to misjudge or misunderstand the actions and people he first encounters, including particularly the beggar who becomes, in fact, his first guide.

Despite his limitations, Clarence is nonetheless portrayed as being on the "Way," as a pilgrim en route, albeit unconscious of his journey and its goal. He is as unilluminated as carnal or natural man is at the outset of his existence, but is still touched by the essential need or desire to pursue a path, symbolically expressed by his discontent with his lot and the urge to press forward. Laye's language is deliberately suggestive of this meaning as he opens with the image of Clarence attempting to advance: "Lorsque Clarence atteignit l'esplanade, il se heurta à une foule si nombreuse et si compacte qu'il désespéra d'abord de s'y frayer un passage" (1954, 9) ["When Clarence reached the esplanade he found his way blocked" (1971, 21)].[2] Clarence doesn't seem to be aware of exactly why he has come — "depuis plusieurs jours déjà, il n'avait plus de choix!" (1954, 9) ["he has had no say in anything for some days now!" (1971, 21)]. And, in the grips of this inexplicable compulsion, he attempts to force his way through the throng. The crowd constitutes an obstacle, the first of many that lie along his path, and as he pushes his way through he is acted upon, ostensibly by "une odeur de laine et d'huile" (1959, 9) [the odor of "warm wool and oil"] (wool, *suf* in Arabic), so that his senses are dulled and he enters into "une espèce de sommeil" (9) [a "kind of trance"]. The metaphors Laye uses to evoke this state — trapped as if in a "liquid that had suddenly congealed" or in "slowly-shifting sand" — combined with Clarence's somnambulance, give the effect of unreality, as if he were in a dream or having a vision. The reiterated "maybes" used by the narrator — "soit que l'odeur fût devenue moins forte, soit pour tout autre motif" (1954, 9) ["*maybe* the smell had become less strong, *maybe* there was some other reason" (1971, 22, my emphasis)] — contribute to reinforce the air of mystery and unreality with which the novel begins. The transition from an apparently realistic narration to an allegory is both subtle and pervasive, since Clarence bears the weight of a character presented as a real human being, and yet who is entering upon the *via misteriosa*. Not until the end of the novel does Laye let go completely of the level of everyday reality. But even here, at the outset, as Clarence continues to force his way forward, dream-like transitions intrude at each step: "les noirs devenaient plus grands, se transformaient insensiblement en géants" (1954, 10) ["the black men got bigger and bigger, growing imperceptibly to giant size"].

The reef, which we learn later Clarence had such difficulty in getting past upon his arrival in Africa, marked the boundary between ordinary existence and the liminal state of transition. In the scene on the esplanade that follows, Clarence, having entered on his path, is granted a glimpse of the goal — the king — so that he might be able to give direction to his yearning, to his efforts and travails. The dance establishes the frame, which is then filled by a great cloud of red dust, brilliant light, and a mass of devotees salaaming their mounted king. The dancers are responsible for the dust, "arrachée à la terre battue par les pieds nus" (10) [which they "threshed up from the bare earth" (1954, 20) with their naked feet] ... "ce nuage rouge et rayonnant" (1954, 19) [a "red and radiant cloud of dust" (1971, 30)] that hides the king from the view of the spectators. The impression of a dance of devotion, love, and spirituality is created, conveyed by the fineness of the dust, its lustre, and vastness. The dance is the first expression of devotion, and its concerted motions contrast with Clarence's undirected impulses and shoves, his viscosity and torpor. It is less an African dance than Sufi whirling here: the cloud comes not from a community of participants, as Laye describes the celebrants who dance at his initiation in *L'Enfant noir*. The cloud they raise is an "insignia of royalty"; the dancers, like dervishes, express their ecstasy through gestures which lead them to lose conscious control.

Noaga and Nagoa, the two aspiring dancers whom Clarence here encounters, have chosen to offer their services by learning to dance for the king. When later in the novel they and Clarence are lost in the maze of the Nabi's labyrinthine palace, they find the right way by spinning. "'Il y a un autre moyen,' dirent les garçons. Là-dessus, l'un d'eux se mit à tournoyer si follement qu'on ne put bientôt plus distinguer son menton de sa nuque. Subitement, il se laissa tomber. Sa tête indiquait très légèrement la droite" (1954, 159). ["'There *is* another way,' said the boys. Whereupon one of them began to revolve so fast that his face was soon just a vague blur. Suddenly he dropped to the ground. His head pointed ever so slightly to the right" (1971, 162).] This use of whirling is the most directly employed, specifically Sufi image in the novel. I cannot state categorically that Laye would have known such practices either in the Tijaniyya or Qadiriyya orders in Upper Guinea or abroad, but it is not inconceivable that Shadhiliyya practices, once well-known in the Futa Jalon, might have survived and influenced him, or that he learned of them elsewhere. Noago and Nagoa's spinning bears no obvious resemblance to any other tradition of mysticism apt to have influenced Laye.

The king, too, who makes his appearance on the esplanade, beats the traits of an African tradition, though only superficially. He is adorned with golden bracelets, and a white royal robe and turban — all attributes, his youth excepted, with which we expect to find African royalty cloaked. However, Laye's emphasis makes clear the mystic qualitity of each of these attributes, as well as of the royal figure himself. "Et ces ténèbres étaient absolues, plus profondes encore chez le roi que chez ses sujets" (1954, 22) [and these shadows were absolute, still more profound with the king than with his subjects]. It is a "midnight" of darkness that, in an inverse direction from white, Christian, European symbolism, is too profound and absolute to suffer human limits. Clarence recognizes in this purity and absoluteness the possibility to love, not in a "bestial" way, but in a way which "apportaient peut-être à l'amour sa fine pointe" (1954, 22) ["lift(s) love to its purest peak" (1971, 34)]. The king's smile reminds Clarence of an idol's face — "lointain, énigmatique ... le reflet d'une vie intérieure. 'Est-ce cette vie que je suis venu chercher,' se demanda Clarence" (1954, 22) ["remote, enigmatic ... the reflection of an inner life. 'Can it be the sort of life I have come here to find?' wondered Clarence"]. The king opens Clarence to the possibility of a true goal, a perfection of such magnitude that he feels "une sorte d'abîme ... devant lui" (1954, 22) ["an abyss open up under his feet"]. Even the gold worn by the king contributes to his spiritual being. His blackness is not a darkness of the inner being, but its opposite; his gold is not a sign of material wealth, but its opposite as well—pure love, which keeps the king from ascending to heaven directly. The basic Sufi vision of God, not as a remote and inaccessible being—though he appears so to Clarence at this stage—but as one whose love is given to operate through us, is here magnificently captured in an African guise.

In Islam, devotion is expressed through submission of one's will to that of God. The adoration and prostration of the crowd before their king is only the outward manifestation of that Muslim belief: when the beggar informs Clarence that "on ne devait plus respirer" (1954, 23) [one is "not allowed to breathe" (1971, 35)] when the king is making his salutation, he is expressing the absoluteness of its nature.

For the mystic, white is black and black is white: the world of appearance is deceptive, unreal vis-a-vis spiritual reality. The beggar whom Clarence encounters wears ragged clothes and has uncouth ways. Yet he can show Clarence the way to the path he is seeking, answers his questions, and acts as his guide. He is Clarence's first *murshid* or spiritual teacher, and from the start he takes it upon himself to explain the significance of what is happening. It is the beggar who tells Clarence he is not allowed to breathe when the king makes his salutation, and that the gold worn by the king is "l'un des signes de l'amour, si l'amour atteint à sa pureté" (1954, 21) ["one of the signs of love, ... the purest kind of love" (1971, 33–4)]. Clarence's thoughts are set in motion by the beggar's words, and he accepts the beggar's offer to represent him before the king. Soon the beggar tempers and corrects Clarence's inexperience and impatience as he explains. "Il y a toujours des obstacles" (1954, 25) ["There are always certain obstacles" (1971, 37)]. Although Clarence can see the king, he knows that "aussi ne s'était-il jamais trouvé plus éloigné du but qu'il ne l'était présentement" (1954, 24) ["never before had he seen so far from his goal as he was now" (1971, 36)]. Unable to cross the barriers between himself and the king, Clarence accepts the beggar's advice to seek the king in the South, and to allow the beggar to act as his guide. The journey thus begins with the basic Sufi elements of a Way or *tariqa*, a guide or *murshid*, and a goal of perfection to be won at the end in union with the divine.

Sufism stands in opposition to Muslim legalism. We might thus

expect Clarence's enlightenment to include overcoming the obstacle
of legalism. This is the basic theme established by the beggar whose
ideology is not to live according to his "merits" but by the undeserved
gifts or "favors" he can receive in accordance with his profession.
Clarence's mind always returns to his "rights" — the putative rights
of the white man in black Africa, the vaguely felt rights with which
he hopes to obtain a position with the king. Again the surface level
of meaning bears upon the external situation in which Clarence, the
white European, finds himself; the deeper significance lies in the
opposition of these rights to the beggar's favor in helping him: here
the white neophyte reflects on the irony of needing to rely on a black
beggar for favors, rather than simply demanding a position on the
basis of his rights: "Qu'importait après tout que ce fût une faveur,
quand cela aurait dû être un droit! Pouvait-il être question de droit,
dans un monde comme celui qu'il avait sous lex yeux?" (1954, 28)
["What did it matter after all that it was a favor, when it should have
been his by right? Could there be any question of 'rights' in the sort
of world he found himself in now?" (1971, 39)]. At the time that he
lays claim to non-existent rights, Clarence reflects on his unfortunate
situation and concludes that fortune is opposed to him, that he is
down on his luck and has been so since his arrival in Africa. He
doesn't just reflect in negative terms, he accepts notions of luck and
rights unthinkingly — exactly the condition of "natural" man at the
outset of his journey. The beggar is his teacher especially in this
regard, and as Clarence mentions disparagingly his right to only
poor living quarters, the beggar responds, "Je n'ai parlé que de
'faveur.' Vous vous trompez certainement en m'attribuant des propos
sur un 'droit' quelconque. Pour ma part, je n'ai jamais revendiqué
aucun droit, je me suis toujours borné à quémander" (1954, 42). ["I
spoke only of favors. You are quite wrong to think I said anything
about 'rights' of any kind. As far as I am concerned, I have never
claimed any kinds of 'rights.' I have always restricted myself to
soliciting favours" (1971, 52)]. Clarence finds it difficult to associate
the notion of a beggar, of one who merely "begs" favors, with this
peremptory, imposing, self-assured black giant, and so he expresses
reservations about what the beggar has told him. Yet he doesn't
hesitate to evoke his own bad luck in falling on hard times, whereupon
the beggar exclaims, "La chance! Vous ne cessez d'avoir ce mot dans
la bouche ou dans le coeur, et vous me reprochez de parler de
'faveur'!" (1954, 43). ["Good luck! You never talk about anything
else — it's always on your lips and in your heart, and you dare to

reproach me with talking about 'favors'!" (1971, 53—54).] As Clarence ponders this, he becomes ashamed of his former illogic, and, more importantly, comes to perceive the relationship between the two: "on l'obtenait ou on ne l'obtenait pas" ["either one received it or one did not receive it"]. Now, the idea of "receiving" a favor implies that someone is granting the favor. Perhaps no expression is more common in Islam than *inch'Allah*, "if God wills it." Clarence grows with the realization that even eating must be a favor, and with the awareness of the bizarre and "extraordinary folly" that he has "confié [son] sort à un mendiant" (1954, 45) ["put [his] fate in the hands of a beggar" (1971, 55)]. He has no real appreciation of the significance of this — his guide is still only a beggar in his eyes, and he is far from seeing beyond this. Yet, his unenlightened acceptance of the situation marks his debut on the guided path. The irony of the situation springs from Clarence's ignorant, unenlightened words of thanks to the beggar for guiding him to the inn — "Je ne sais comment je m'y serait retrouvé si vous ne m'aviez reconduit" (1954, 39) ["I do not know how I should have found my way if you had not guided my steps" (1971, 50).] Thus, when the beggar offers to guide Clarence south — "Je vous guiderai" (1954, 54) ["I'll show you the way" (1971, 64)] — Clarence thinks the beggar wants to sponge off him. Like a dervish, the beggar seems to be gifted with telepathy, and he tells Clarence that he will see to their food and lodging. The beggar's profession is begging, as he informs Clarence. But it must also be that of a guide, which is why he seeks to convince Clarence to accept his offer. Both are acting under compulsion, with the difference that Clarence is unaware of that fact, while the beggar is not.

Clarence remains in the dark, lost, or continually getting lost, bewildered, frustrated, and resentful as long as he remains in the North. The central episode in which all of these feelings emerge is the one in which he appears before the judge, in a surrealistic hall set in a labyrinth of rooms and corridors. Clarence finds himself lost in a maze of illogic, with "un dédale de pièces abandonnées et de couloirs déserts" (1954, 73) [a confusion of "empty rooms and deserted corridors" (1971, 83)]. Within this building, which serves as the hall of justice, piles of rubbish are littered everywhere. Clarence loses his way here, as he had earlier in the town, opening doors only to find himself back where he started from, attempting to escape but never finding his way through the puzzle. The ultimate nonsense of Clarence's claims are matched by the greater irrationality of the judge, and the rubbish and lost corridors represent the last repository of justice, the ultimate symbol for the dervish's rejection of the *'ulama*, or leaders of Muslim legalism. It is not morality itself that is called into question here, but the *human* attempt to arrogate the right to judge according to an absolute or sacred system. The beggar recognizes his need to obtain a less peremptory tone; how much greater the need of the white with his false pride to discover the virtue of humility.

Clarence is led by the beggar from the inn directly to the street. Here a mad-cap festival is under way, one in which "la face diabolique qui est dans tout fête, triomphât à présent" (1954, 61) ["the diabolical aspect that is found in all festivals, was in the ascendant" (1971, 70–71)]. The wild spirit of the celebrants is seen in the dancing women who "avançaient, hardiment, avançaient, la buste découverte et se précipitaient, ruaient à la danse, se livraient à nu à une trépidation et à une fureur" (1954, 60) ["advanced, bravely advanced, their breasts bared, rushing forward, throwing themselves into the dance, abandoning themselves, naked, to a quivering tempest"]. Clarence finds himself blocked, once again, unable to pass through the crowds and circles of dancers, and the beggar has to shake Clarence in order to wake him from his torpor. Into this atmosphere of uncensored sexual license Clarence finds himself plunged, his senses overwhelmed by the sensual. He is attracted to it, yet when immersed in a bath of sensation, he responds by losing all conscious control of himself. Here is the path, then, that he must follow: in order to rise to a level where he can present himself to the king he must first experience the full meaning of the life of the senses, of the natural or carnal man. That this, too, is a stage on the Path is demonstrated by the guidance offered to Clarence by one of the dancers (another dancer!). She attracts him with her beautiful breasts, and kindly leads him out of the maze of streets and through the halls of justice so that he can be launched on his journey South. The beggar is aware that until Clarence is fully plunged into this life he will be unable to pass beyond it. Thus he leads Clarence first to the street, the dance, the women, the palm-wine, and the life of intoxication, and eventually guides him to the South and to the life there as a male servant to the Naba, employed as the breeder in his harem.

Clarence's entry to the South is marked by a recasting and expansion of the encounters adumbrated in the North. The primary experience is that of the senses bombarded with odors, colors, and other stimuli. Clarence becomes a somnambulist. The forest presents itself to him as a wall, the paths through it a labyrinth again leading nowhere, or to further walls. Where he sees only obstacles and meaningless divagation, the beggar perceives all the paths, has travelled them often, and is able to lead Clarence unerringly to the village of the *naba*, the mark of the true guide. Thus, he tells Clarence, "Il y a des sentiers. Si vous ne les voyez pas—et pourquoi les verriez-vous?—n'accusez que vos yeux" (1954, 87). ["There are paths. If you can't see them—and why should you see them—you've only got your own eyes to blame" (1971, 95).] Throughout, the red, luminous colors, the solid wall of the forest, and a multitude of images reiterate those encountered at the king's palace and on the esplanade, reminding us of the ever-present significance of each step as ultimately guided and purposeful, of each obstacle or moment of darkness as referents within a larger system of meaning, governed by the oxymoronic coupling of sleep-walking, light-dark, radiant-opaque, clarity-confusion. Clarence enters the realm of the senses, of sleep, of total, helpless confusion. "Il avance en aveugle" (1954, 91) [He walks "like a blind man" (1971, 99)], feels "l'immonde torpeur l'engluer" (1954, 91) [an "unclean and cloying weakness stealing over him"], succumbs helplessly, and allows himself to be led docilely: "il tend docilement la main" (1954, 91) ["he holds out his hand docilely"]. But in the dullness of his mind he keeps alive the hope for his "delivrance, jusqu'à la venue du roi chez ses vassaux du Sud" (1954, 93) ["day of deliverance . . . the day the king comes on a visitation to his vassals in the South" (1971, 101)].

Clarence's descent is experienced as a dissolution of his spirit. The odor which first put him to sleep on the esplanade now is used by the *naba* to subdue his conscious mind at night while his body is used for breeding purposes. Yet Clarence continues to question, to wonder in his brief moments of awareness, about the beggar, and where he is being led. The beggar's own abilities to drink, his tendencies to lasciviousness, are indications that he knows of the loyalty to the Way as well as to the permanence of his pursuit of the Way. Clarence becomes helpless in his hands—signifying the beginnings of the self-abandonment or self-negation, which must precede the granting of favors.

Part II begins with Clarence sunk in the heaviness of the body, of the night without dawn. Again and again he awakens, groggy, trying to throw off his torpor. His senses are drugged, but now he struggles against it, unaware of what is happening, yet vaguely discontented. He institutes morning showers in a vain attempt to become clean and clear-headed. Yet his calabashes of wine and the heat remove all inhibitions, and he feels no shame at going naked during the day, just as he unconsciously services the *naba*'s harem each night. The two dancers, Noaga and Nagoa, remain as co-pilgrims with him in the village, while the beggar passes him on to a great, fat, easy-going eunuch, Samba Baloum. Samba is in the employ of the *naba*, and it is his job to supervise the harem. He is thus also in charge of Clarence, though Clarence doesn't know it. He is an appropriate guide to this life of the "flesh," the stage of the carnal man.

Clarence is reduced to the physical man, and to the lowest of physical creatures — the embodiment of the sexual function. Samba calls him a "fighting cock," and Clarence senses the beast in himself that comes out during the nights. His feeling of guilt — the first step towards repentance — obtrudes with the disturbing thought that he is nothing but a "stallion": "Est-ce qu'un étalon pourrait s'approacher du roi?" (1954, 150) ["Could a stallion approach the king?" (1971, 154)]. And Clarence feared the king would turn from him in disgust. Shame and pleasure vie with each other as Clarence goes from day to night: only a vague sense of progressing on his path — an intuition of direction — kept him from despair: was it not better to behave thus, as the villagers in the South, "que d'être Clarence? Et c'est pourquoi il suivait cette pente ..." ["than being Clarence? And that was why he was pursuing a downward path ..."]. Yet the doubt remained that this was not a path: "Je n'ai pas de pente" (1954, 152) ["I have no particular path," he said (1971, 156)].

Each stage in Sufism must be transcended by overcoming the obstacles appropriate to it. Sensuality is opposed by the sense of guilt, and just as Samba assists Clarence on his life of uncomplicated pleasure, so too the *naba*'s "Master of Ceremonies" acts to awaken Clarence's conscience. The indulgent guidance of the fat, fleshy eunuch is replaced by the stern, unpitying gaze and judgment of the MC. At first Clarence resists it — but gradually it awakens a feeling of reci-procity that Clarence cannot ignore. In a dream, the MC comes to Clarence and reveals to him the truth of what he is doing: the cruel, mocking laughter, and sharp teeth, are all signs of Clarence's guilty conscience, and when Clarence takes up a stick to punish the MC, he merely adopts the MC's role; in punishing him, he identifies with him. In chasing the MC, Clarence again loses himself in a maze of corridors where at last he sees his progeny and becomes aware of what he has been doing. The beginnings of his new passage to the state of "blame," typically the second stage of Sufi awareness, are found here as he learns embarrassment and shame, and refuses to bathe in the nude publicly as he had done before.

All the burden and weight of oppressive legalism are bound up in the figure of the MC. He both punishes and is punished, and when a victim of justice, he suffers from the cruelty of its dispensation: "Peut-être est-ce cruauté, mais c'est sûrement justice . . . . Les hommes justes appellent ça justice" (1954, 169) ["Maybe it is cruelty, but it is justice . . . . just men call this justice" (1971, 172)], says Baloum. The rubbish in the corridors where justice is administered serves rather too obviously to remind us that "la sordide justice des hommes ne peut se rendre que parmi les immondices" (1954, 162) ["the sordid justice of mankind can only be meted out in foulness and filth" (1971, 165)]. The MC embodies all the worst traits of the second stage: the pride, arrogance, "love of fame and authority," and especially "opposition to people" (Trimingham 1971, 156). The first stage is schematized as "the Evidential World," or the world of the senses (Trimingham 1971, 153); the second, the "World of the Isthmus" or the "Purgatorial World." The soul is described as "carnal" on the first stage, "admonishing" on the second. All these descriptions indicate the state in which the super-ego passes judgment on the libido — and this is the function in which the MC continually appears, as disapproving of Clarence's sexual role. When Clarence assumes the identity of the MC and punishes him, he also assumes the MC's values — he begins to hate his own sexual license and feels shame and guilt over his behavior. The repeated appearances, and ultimately the dreams, of the MC show that his presence, too, is important for Clarence: the guide, *murshid*, assumes more than one form. The MC awakens Clarence's sense of guilt so that even while Clarence persists in carrying out his function as a breeder, he comes to an awareness of what he is doing, and he feels ashamed over it. But as that is all the MC can bring Clarence, he teaches him about hatred, but nothing of love. As Clarence masters the MC's teaching, he encounters his next guide, the blacksmith, who points him beyond the MC.

"The *murshid* measures the *murid's* [pupil's] progress through these stages by interpreting the dreams and visions which the *murid* experiences" (Trimingham 1971, 158). The episode following that in which Clarence beats the MC in his dream, is called "The Fishwomen." In it Clarence has a vision that brings to a head, or epitomizes, the essential meaning of his life up to this point: he comes through the forest to a river. The odor of the forest again overwhelms him and he experiences its danger to his spirit as a "winding-sheet" (1971,

198). His yearning for deliverance is commensurate to his feelings of despair over his present life: "Il était résolu à ne plus se laisser conduire par ce corps qui se comportait comme une bête immonde. Mais que pouvait-il contre l'odeur, contre le Sud?" (1954, 195). ["He was determined not to let himself be led astray by this body which kept behaving like a filthy beast. But what could he do against this odor, against the South?"] He hopes for the coming of the king, yet fears he is no longer worthy: "Pouvait-on, même par seule pitié, jeter le regard sur une bête ... Peut-être n'y avait-il rien désormais qui pût le libérer?" (1954, 195−96). ["Could one cast one's eye upon a beast, even if merely out of pity? ... Perhaps there was nothing now that would set him free from himself" (1971, 198)]. Out of the bottomless pit of this despair, Clarence then experiences a vision. Fishwomen, like sirens, with obvious female breasts — breasts like those that had drawn him South from the first festival up North — now appear with "inhuman heads" (1971, 199). Unlike the traditional, literary sirens "dont on revêt un assemblage forcément rebutant" (1954, 196) [whose beauty appears as a "seductive veil over impalatable fact" (1971, 198)], the breasts of these creatures are described as "opulent and dead white, ... gruesomely revealed." Clarence experiences the full nature of the sensual — its attraction and its deadly stagnation: he is drawn and revolted, completely: "il se sentait à la fois repoussé et attiré, plus violemment rebuté qu'il ne l'avait jamais été par l'odeur de la forêt" (1954, 196−97) ["he felt himself at once revolted and attracted, more violently attracted and more violently revolted than he had ever been by the odour of the forest" (1971, 199)]. The vision leads him to the point where feels that he will drown, drawn down the river and smothered by the breasts. The descent is here completed. In this vision Clarence sums up the experience of the Carnal stage, and realizes its nature as simultaneously attractive and repellent: he struggles against being drawn down forever, setting the stage for his transition to a higher level.

    Part III of the novel, "The King," follows this vision. Having turned away completely from his carnal being, Clarence now runs the risk of stagnating on the level of the MC. In this part he must learn to pass to the third stage, at which he would have turned towards God and completed his journey. Here the influence of the blacksmith is critical, as he is the last of the guides. Interestingly, each guide has a successively smaller role to play in his encounters with Clarence: the blacksmith meets Clarence only twice at his forge, and once at the final scene. At their first, and longest visit,

Clarence stops on his way to the river, and they discuss the issue of justice, Diallo implying that "justice" may be little more than an excuse for cruelty. The bearded judges whom he calls into question sound suspiciously like the ulama, and at first he says, "le spectacle leur plaisait dans la mesure où il est juste" [they took "pleasure" in the MC's punishment "only in so far as it satisfied their sense of justice"]. But as he continues along this train of thought, he throws the rationale for their whole sense of justice into question: "Les hommes justes seraient beaucoup moins justes, je suppose, si leur justice flattait moins leur cruauté" ["I suppose just men would be much less just if their justice pandered less to their cruelty" (1971, 190)].

Clarence is not yet capable of responding to this point of view, and so the blacksmith turns the conversation to the ax he is making for the king. The ax (significantly crescent shaped) represents Diallo's devotion: it is a gift which symbolizes the dedication and effort Diallo spent in turning his attention towards the king. Diallo calls Clarence's attention to the act of devoting oneself—to *dhikr*, meaning literally recollection, as it is called in Sufism, a practice usually taking the form of incantation or repeated prayer. Diallo's reference to *dhikr* bears the closest resemblance to the Sufi repetitions of sacred formulae: "Nous l'appelons—à chaque seconde nous l'appelons" (1954, 188) ["We call to him—every moment we are calling him" (1971, 191)]; and at the same time, in humility, he accepts the impossibility of fulfilling *that* obligation, every bit as much as that of the ethical: "Mais malgré nous, nous ne l'appelons pas toujours; nous oublions de l'appeler, nous sommes distraits, l'espace d'un quart de seconde—, et soudain il apparaît, il choisit ce quart de seconde d'apparaître" (1954, 188–89). ["However hard we try, we do not call to him all the time—we keep forgetting to call to him; we are distracted for a fraction of a second—and suddenly he appears, he chooses that very fraction of a second in which to make his appearance" (1971, 191)]. Finally, Diallo teaches Clarence that it is not the ax itself—nor the sounds of the words themselves—that gives the *dhikr* its value, but the spirit with which it is made: "Le roi malgré tout considérera-t-il ma bonne volonté" (1954, 189) ["the king will give me credit for my good will"], he proclaims, a claim Clarence himself cannot begin to make until he has made the necessary effort of the will to pass beyond the first, carnal stage.

The blacksmith's fire burns red hot, driving out the impurities of the metal. Clarence feels its force as the sense of shame for his present life grows stronger—and it is then that he goes to the river and experiences the agony of the vision of the fishwomen.

The next time Clarence passes the blacksmith, it is on the way to Dioki. Again Clarence's thoughts have returned to the question of the coming of the king whose presence he envisions at the end of an endless arcade—obviously at the end of the Path or Way. He decides to visit the sorceress, Dioki, despite the warnings he receives of the danger involved, and carries her gifts of wine and eggs for her snakes. Dioki is another dervish-like figure. Her powers of prophecy are awakened in states of ecstasy brought on by her intercourse with the snakes. Just as Clarence's descent leads him along his path to the king, so, too, is Dioki's debased ecstasy with the snakes merely a means to achieve higher mystical visions and knowledge. As she goes into her trance, Clarence, who has obeyed her injunctions not to stir from the embrace of the serpent, masters his impulse to gaze at "le spectacle de la vieille et de ses serpents" (1954, 221) ["the old woman and her snakes and their orgiastic writhings" (1971, 221)]. They are inverted images of his life, and he must turn his attention away from them if he is not to be trapped on the stage of carnality. This he succeeds in doing: "Oh! il n'y réussit pas au premier essai. Mais quand il fut parvenu à chasser de sa vue et comme à biffer de la terre la vieille folle et ses serpents, il s'émerveilla fort de la vaste étendue de cette cour" (1954, 221). ["Oh! he did not succeed in turning away his eyes straight away. But when he had managed to eradicate from his sight and as it were wipe the old woman and her serpents from the face of the earth, he marvelled at the trememdous extent of the courtyard" (1971, 221).] There then follows Clarence's vision of the coming of the king. It is a vision recapitulating Clarence's journey south, with the crowds of dancers escorting the king, with the forest parting magically before him, splitting in two like the Red Sea. Clarence seeks the king's eye, but once again fails to catch it and senses his own inadequacy. Living on the second stage, where judgment replaces carnal existence, Clarence must now experience judgment to the fullest, as he had known the life of the natural man to the fullest before. The vision gives Clarence that experience, as represented by the person of the king. "Son regard, eût-on dit, était tout tourné vers l'intérieur et comme posé sur sa propre personne .... Et où un tel regard eût-on reposé, sinon en lui-même? ... Néaumoins tant d'indifférence glaçait .... On savait bien qu'on n'avait droit qu'à l'indifférence et qu'en fait on *méritait* de la répugnance; mais tout cela ne rendait cette indifférence ... moins glaciale" (1954, 223). [The king's eye "might have been turned inward .... And where could such an eye have found a place of rest, if not in himself? .... All the same, so much indifference cast a chill .... One knew quite well that one had no *right* to anything by indifference and that one deserved in fact to be treated with repugnance: but all this did not make that indifference less chill ..." (1971, 223, my emphasis).]

Clarence's humility and self-rejection mark the turning to the last stage, the one marked by *ma'rifa* or gnosis. In this light, the old woman's words upon the conclusion of the vision appear to refer to that opening upon knowledge to which she initiated Clarence: "'Tu sais,' dit-elle. 'A présent, tu sais.' 'Oui, je sais,' dit Clarence" (1954, 224). ["'You know,' she said. 'You know now.' 'Yes, I know ...' said Clarence" (1971, 224).]

In the final episode, Clarence tries in vain to pass from the stage of blame or admonishment to that of enlightenment. He has Akissi scrub his back, and of course falls prey to that despair of pride and self-reliance as he realizes that he is still trying to overcome himself by his own exertions, the impossible struggle of what Kierkegaard refers to as the ethical pathos. Once again the MC appears, in posing the final obstacle to Clarence: "Vous n'avez aucun titre à faire valoir" (1954, 238) ["You have no claim to any kind of merit" (1971, 237)], he proclaims, and Clarence ultimately has no reply but to shout back at the MC. Clarence cannot keep his own conscience quiet, however: "I'm ... impure," he tells Akissi, and as he remembers the first barriers he passed, the reefs that lay between him and Africa, he now despairs at overcoming the final ones that lie between his desire to present himself before the king and the worthiness demanded by such a presentation. He remembered the persistence with which the crew that bore him to Africa rode over the barrier of the reef — and at the end of his journey experiences the darkest moment of doubt about the wisdom of the whole venture. With no assurance, no merit, no rights upon which to rest, he wonders who would dare to present himself before the image of purity and perfection.

It is at that moment that the two dancing boys, Noaga and Nagoa, waken him from his revery by their cries as they dance before the king. Earlier in the journey, the beggar had told Clarence that just as the boys had their dancing to offer in the service of the king, he had his loyalty itself to offer — the loyalty of the dusty foot wanderer.

Clarence's despair is the last mark of a two-fold repentance: over his unworthiness or impurity for his carnal inclinations — what Dhu

'n-Nun called the repentance of "the common herd . . . from sins" —
and even more significantly, "the repentance of the elect from in-
attention," the "momentary forgetfulness of God" (Trimingham 1971,
145), like that to which Diallo had referred. "'J'ai toujours voulu
venir,' répéta-il. Mais l'avait-il vraiment et toujours voulu? 'On finit
par ne plus attendre,' avait-il dit. Il l'avait dit, et il avait finit par ne
plus attendre le roi. Il y avait eu des moments où la venue du roi lui
avait paru incroyable et impossible; des moments où réellement il
avait mis tout en doute et désespéré de tout" (1954, 245–46). ["'I
have always wanted to come,' said Clarence. But had he really
wanted, always wanted to? . . . There had been moments when the
arrival of the king had seemed to him incredible, impossible; moments
when he had really begun to doubt everything and when everything
had filled him with despair" (1971, 224–25).] The final doubt and
despair incorporated all the obstacles he had faced up till then. "Est-
ce ainsi qu'on meurt" (250). ["'Is this the way one dies,' he whispered to
himself" (1971, 249).] The last moment of despair seems bleakest of
all.

At that second, Noaga and Nagoa began to dance, demonstrating
their devotion to the king, and setting him an example. Baloum and
Diallo also appeared, attempting to disabuse him of the MC's view
that "à chacun le destin de ses mérites" (1954, 247) ["everyone has
the fate he deserves; everyone according to his merit" (1971, 246)].
Repentance, as the means to pass from the stage of carnality to the
ethical, is experienced only temporarily — here it becomes the greatest
obstacle Clarence to try his "luck," luck that Diallo calls "pity" and
the beggar "favour" (1971, 248). It is then, as all the teachings of his
guides are summed up, as Clarence feels least worthy — at the farthest
remove from the arrogant white he had been at the beginning of his
journey — that a silence, like death, comes over him, and he falls into
a trance.

The king then appears in all his radiance, and through his window
Clarence witnesses the procession of servants bearing him gifts.
Noago and Nagoa invite Clarence to present himself, but Clarence
feels his nakedness, his unworthiness, his inability to offer anything
of worth to this figure of fragile purity, of "blazing" purity. His
repentance passes from regret and shame, the "repentance of the
herd," to contrition of the heart.

The path Clarence pursues all along is that of love. He first
experiences love when he witnesses the presence of the king in the
esplanade. Then he turns to physical love, the cloying downward

path of the night and the South. With the tears Clarence now sheds at the end, he comes to the realization of the insignificance of human love before the urgent demands of divine purity and perfection. His tears mark the end of the descent, the end of "admonition" and "blame" — his total recognition of his lack of merit or worth. As "merit" recapitulated all the obstacles he had faced, his contrition now leads him to surmount the last of those obstacles. The king's gaze falls on Clarence, and as Clarence offers the king merely his "goodwill," a gift with "no virtue in it," the obstacles fall away, "le paroi devant lui s'éffondra" (1954, 253) [the "wall melts away" (1971, 251)], and Clarence walks into the arms of the king.

The quest for God comes to its end as the king's look of love envelopes Clarence. The fire with which Diallo burnt out the impurities of his offering now burns into Clarence's heart with the gaze of the king, and standing "dans le grand rayonnement du roi, et tout meutri encore par le trait de feu, mais tout vivant et seulement vivant de ce feu, Clarence tomba à genoux, car il lui semblait qu'il était enfin au bout de sa course et au terme de toute course" (1954, 253) ["in the great radiance of the king, . . . ravaged by the tongue of fire, Clarence fell on his knees, for its seemed to him that he was finally at the end of his seeking, and at the end of all seekings" (1971, 252)]. This statement of God's love working through man, and thus fulfilling man's quest, is one of the most beautiful expressions of Sufi mysticism. It culminates with the radiant image of love, beating in the king's heart, burning into Clarence's limbs, enveloping and embracing him, and calling out to him. After all the despair and longing and searching, it is the king who shows that his will was what gave Clarence's actions their direction, when he states, "Ne savais-tu pas que je t'attendais?" (1954, 254) ["Did you not know that I was waiting for you?" (1971, 252)]. In his last act, Clarence kisses the king's heart as he is granted the union he had been seeking: "Alors le roi referma lentement les bras, et son grand manteau enveloppa Clarence pour toujours" (1954, 254). ["the king slowly closed his arms around him, and his great mantle swept about him, and enveloped him for ever" (1971, 253).]

According to Trimingham, Sufism developed mystical techniques, "to enable the seeker to arrive at *ma'rifa*, (1971, 145); *ma'rifa* is here understood as "direct perception of God" (1971, 147).

When one considers the stages through which Clarence passes, the guidance of first the beggar, and then Samba Baloum, the MC, Diallo, and the other dervish figures in the novel; when one considers the techniques such as the dancing or whirling employed especially by Noaga and Nagoa, and the visions that Clarence experiences; the attitude towards merit and the prominence of love; the small details in the acts of *dhikr*, such as the salaaming and the crescent-shaped ax; the importance attached to traveling a path and to overcoming obstacles; the fact that Sufism is primarily the "Way of Purification," marked by stages on that Path "with each stage summarized as purification/vision" (Trimingham 1971, 151); and finally the last great image of union with divine; one cannot help but conclude that the early, formative Muslim influences upon Laye—undoubtedly colored by the dominant Sufi techniques indigenous to the region— must have been the sources of inspiration for the allegory in *Le Regard du roi*.

Part II: *The Wedding of Zein*: Two Centers of Consciousness

Every verse of the Koran has "an outside and an inside".

(LINGS 1977, 29).

The full-grown Sufi is thus conscious of being, like other men, a prisoner of a world of forms, but unlike them he is also conscious of being free, with a freedom which immeasurably outweighs his imprisonment. He may therefore be said to have two centres of consciousness, one human and one Divine, and he may speak now from one and now from another, which accounts for certain apparent contradictions.

(LINGS 1977, 14).

As our quotations from Lings's *What Is Sufism?* indicate, Sufis are conscious of the possibility of two different perspectives governing one's vision of the world. The same events and phenomena may be seen as foolish or exalted, empty or full of significance, desirable or damnable, worldly or trivial. The Sufi literary tale plays with this dual vision by constructing simple parables to convey its gnosis, leaving the impression that the narrator is too diffident to state the message directly. Salih would seem to be working in this tradition when, for example, he refuses to state directly how Zein came to be engaged to Ni'ma. "But how had the miracle happened? Accounts differed." The versions of Haleema, Tureifa, and Abdul Samad all compete with the semi-authorized account, which is coyly put thus: "It is, however, more likely that things happened otherwise, and that . . . . It is likely that . . .," ultimately passing from the narrator's suppositions to the definite assertion, "(A)nd thus it was that . . ." (Salih 1978, 108).

The differing versions of the "miracle" reflect, not unnaturally, the personalities of those who hold the various opinions. Generally the perspectives we expect to encounter in the text are in line with the two opposing positions outlined by Lings. In *Wedding* there are two characters who embody this opposition, namely, the Imam and the saintly Haneen. The Imam is represented in a negative fashion: gloomy, serious, unfrivolous, continually evoking the fear of death, he tells the assemblage of believers about their moral obligations, but inspires only uneasiness or vague sentiments of guilt or self-righteousness in them. In Lings's terms, he stands for exoteric, legalistic, formalistic Islam, and is limited in his understanding of things to their outer level of meaning. The inner, Sufi meaning of the Holy Text is beyond him. For the Imam, Haneen's perspective, his truth, does not exist: "Haneen . . . represented the mystical side of the spiritual world — a side he did not recognize" (94), and as a consequence he was blind to the fact that "[Haneen] was the direct cause of Seif-ad-Din's repentance" rather than the Imam's own hell-fire-and-brimstone preaching. Appropriately the Imam has had ten years of university training and is the only one in the village to concern himself with the politics of the outside world. He is a prisoner of the world of forms, trapped by the most insidious of lures, moral righteousness grounded in literal interpretations of texts — the limitation of the exoteric.

Haneen is the ideal image of the Sufi saint. His word is wholly oral: as with the common people, God's blessing is always on his lips, like an exclamation, a form of speech, which his life, devotion, and holiness imbue with real power. Unlike the Imam, he is not attached to transient things: for six months of the year he wanders with only his prayer rug and pitcher (44); he eats at the home of the simple, has no visible wealth or position of importance, no discernable family ties. The villagers recognize his authority, and seek out his presence. He is venerated, in life and in death. The saintliness of his being attests to the divine presence, as demonstrated especially by the miracle he works in his influence over Zein. The wedding, which he foretells, and his power to restrain Zein's unstoppable force, are the visible signs of the Invisible power. He opposes the exoteric formalism of the Imam with an esoteric practive. He is the Sufi guide along whose path the adept must travel.

Thus the Word has its two opposing characteristics: written versus oral; literal, moral, judgmental, serious, and exoteric readings of the Holy Text versus popular, blessed, efficacious, miraculous, hidden, and esoteric approaches to the Holy Text. The diametrical opposition of what really constitutes two opposing texts is matched perfectly in the two figures of the Imam and the Saint; the Word is made Flesh in its embodiment of opposing textual readings, an opposition that informs the entire novel.

Both the Imam and Haneen have their own followers. The whole village is divided into different camps, especially with respect to the Imam. This division is best understood in terms of two representative figures, Seif, who turns to the Imam's camp, and Zein, the one blessed by Haneen.

Seif is the reformed sinner. When he lived in a profligate manner, he seemed to be the opposite of the Sufi ascetic — a saint's alter ego. He wore a beard and looked and lived like a mirror image of the Sufi wanderer: "He carried a thick stick of the sort used in the east of the Sudan and had no luggage whatsoever. His hair was ruffled as a *sayal* acacia tree, his beard thick and dirty" (71). Haneen, on the other hand, would "stay in the village six months praying and fasting, and then take up his pitcher and prayer rug and wander about up in the desert, disappearing for six months and then returning .... (H)e carried no provisions on his long journey" (44–45). Seif reflected the unworldliness of the dissipated, not of those above worldly concerns. The Sufi seeks *fana*, extinction in the divine, often represented as the inward intoxication of the spirit — "some Shayks describe the Supreme Station as the state of being inwardly drunk and outwardly sober" (Lings 1977, 87). Seif's intoxication, in contrast, was the reverse and had nothing of the spiritual about it. He frequented the village's red-light district, a group of straw houses described as the rendezvous of ex-slave girls, having about it something "alien." There could be heard "drunken laughter," while "beams of lamplight flickered from their doorways and windows" (Salih 1978, 69). For the Sufi who becomes the "slave" of God, drunken with the divine spirit, for whom the path to God is described as a Way of Light, and for whom the center of his being is the heart, since it is love that provides him with the means of approaching God, these images of drunken revellers, laughing in the half-light, on the periphery of conventional society, are grotesque caricatures of the ascetics — exoteric readings of Sufi images. Seif's turning from the life of dissipation to one of moral uprightness represents a failure to recognize the distinction between the light of the Sufi Way and the outward form of things. The flip side of Seif's transformation is well captured in Ahmed Isma'il's sardonic evaluation: "Badawi's son has switched his allegiance from the slave-girls to the Imam" (95). He completes the portrait of the Imam in the sense that both represent false images of the holy, false in the sense that a shell, an exterior appearance masks an inner lack of real holiness. This is most striking in the case of the image of the tomb used to describe the Imam. Superficially the tomb evokes death, and the Imam's gloomy preaching. More significantly, the tomb is the center of the Sufi's veneration as the symbol of the saint and his overcoming of the externals of existence — it is at Haneen's tomb that Zein is to be found at the end, and it is common still today to find Sufi devotees in the Sudan whirling in their dances of devotion around the saint's tomb. The false religiosity of the Imam, then, requires that a true image of sanctity, the tomb, be turned — trans-valuated — into its mere surface, the symbol of a death that carries the fear of extinction.

Playing against this figure we find the familiar character of the fool represented in Zein. In the conventions of Sufism, the adept needs the master — here Haneen — to show him the Way. Still, Zein's traits are all signs of his own state of blessedness: his laughter; his role as "emissary of Love" (142); his ugliness or foolish appearance; his inexplicable strength; his affection for the crippled, the unfortunate; and generally his detachment from worldly things. When some attachment appears, as in his gigantesque appetite, in his leaping and dancing and enthusiastic cries of love, they appear as signs or metaphors for other, higher appetites. He is the epitome of an inner truth wearing an outward disguise: his "emaciated body concealed an extraordinary, super-human strength" (62–63), and even his detractors call him a dervish (81), joining a derisive term for the Sufi holy man to his mother's boast that "her son was one of God's saints" (44). Zein's outward "foolishness" becomes his strength when considered in light of the belief, voiced by the villagers, that God "places His strength in the weakest of creatures," a reflection prompted by the contradiction between Zein's concave breast and ridiculous manner, and his "great heart" (46). He becomes in their eyes one of those saintly fools capable of assuming any proportion of greatness: "perhaps he was the legendary Leader, the Prophet of God, perhaps an angel sent down by God in lowly human form" (46). Zein's exuberance is best brought out in his special role as harbinger of love: "I am slain by love in the courtyard of Mahjoub," he cries, and love snatches up the daughter of the house, who then is courted by the best of suitors. His foolishness conquers even the high and mighty Omda and all thereafter — except for those serious brothers like Seif who refuse his playfulness, the play of the fool's dance.

The line between Seif and Zein, however, is not as absolute as it might first appear. If Seif represents a kind of obverse side of Zein, still the two bear an amazing resemblance to each other. For example, they are linked by the preoccupation with love shared by both. Seif is rejected by his father for having fallen in love with an ex-slave and for having announced this news while "reeking with alcohol" (69), just as his father had performed the evening prayer. The ex-slave Moussa, whom Seif cold-heartedly dismisses when he comes into his inheritance, becomes one of Zein's special friends among various victims of misfortune. The cluster of attributes characteristic of the Sufi — intoxication, slavery, poverty, unconventionality or marginality, lack of worldliness or possessions — join the disinherited to the dissipated as to the saint. The prodigal son who returns has had the experience of disillusionment from which he can benefit, but also, if he is guided on the "True Path," a taste of the mystic's distain for things of this world. The prodigal's alternative is to be born again into the fold of society's moral mainstream, to become one of the outwardly upright citizens. Seif does not graduate into a state of enlightenment, but adopts a conventional approach to salvation — that defined by obedience to the exoteric exigencies of the text. Salih gives us some indication of the ambivalence surrounding this choice by likening the Imam to a tomb in the cemetery (90), the tomb being seen here as a symbol for the fearful finality of death, as well as being the eternal house of the saint.

For Lings the exoteric is not, as with the Imam, a wrong choice, but one that is limited for those whose vision of creation is nothing more than a world of forms. The Outward, as Lings (1977, 93) explains, is "in Reality One with the Inward" — *i.e.*, an attribute of God who, after all, speaks of creation, in the Hadith, thus: "I was the Hidden Treasure and wished to be known and so I created the world" (23). For Lings adherence to the exoteric path leads to salvation — the goal of the righteous; the esoteric path leads to *fana* or union with God (98) — the goal of the "foremost" or God's "slaves" (31). The outer is not rejected, then, but is to be put in harmony with the inner (the symbol of which is Solomon's Seal [54–57]), while neither is to be taken alone as all in all. The isthmus connecting the two is the heart: "The Heart is the isthmus which is so often mentioned in the Qur'an as separating the *two seas* which represent Heaven and earth" (50); and further, "the Heart transmits the light of the Spirit to the darkness of the soul" (51). Zein's role as emissary of love fits this description perfectly.

If love and the heart are the clearest Sufi qualities linked to Zein, the light which completes this imagery is the most complex aspect of this constellation of attributes, and in its usage we may see something of the essence of Salih's vision. Light and dark, like the exoteric and esoteric, the moral and the mystical, the literal and the hidden, do not completely exclude each other. Light does not exhibit merely a one-sided nature, but shares with the darkness, so that the moments of greatest spirituality are to be found on the boundary between the two states. That which characterizes the magical and powerful doum tree in the first story of the volume, *The Wedding of Zein*, is precisely that nebulous quality — that of the "isthmus": "(E)verything beyond it is as cryptic as talismans, like the boundary between day and night, like the fading light which is not the dawn but the light directly preceding the break of day" (Salih 1978, 6). The prayer appropriate to that moment has special qualities: "[I]t is said that the sunset prayer is 'strange': if you don't catch it in time it eludes you" (10). Later, more explicitly, the narrator states, "[T]he time was a little before the evening prayer, a time especially appropriate for prayers" (75). This is the moment in between the human and the divine, the moment in which Haneen works his miracle — the cusp or liminal region outside time when the normal can be suspended, permitting the supernatural dialogue to take place, as on "that auspicious night between summer and autumn, just a little before the evening prayer," when Haneen's "God bless You" acted with such force that it was "as though supernatural powers in the heavens had answered in one vioce 'Amen'" (76–77). The efficacity of Haneen's intervention, his blessing, is then made clear: "After that, supernatural events came in quick succession, miracle following miracle in a fascinating manner. During its existence the village had never experienced such an auspicious and fruitful year as 'Haneen's year'" (77).

In addition to describing the visible miracle as occurring at this moment, Salih constructs perhaps the most touching and effective scene in *Wedding*, one in which he expresses his own particularly quiet, unaggressive concept of spirituality, using the same interplay of light and dark. It is a light like that used in describing the houses of the prostitutes where "beams of lamp-light flickered from their doorways and windows" (69); a romantic, soft light like that of the moon on the Nile, when "the water turns into an enormous illuminated mirror over whose surface move the shadows of the palms" (50). On such a night, at such a moment, Salih describes the gathering of Zein's friends. Mahjoub sat "not on the bench but on the sand, their favorite spot where the light from the lamp touched them with the tip of its tongue. Sometimes, when they were plunged into laughter, the light and shadow danced above their heads as though they were immersed in a sea in which they floated and dipped" (96). The soft boundary is evoked when Taher Rawwasi seats himself "quietly in the patch of sand where the light did not reach" (94). The call for the evening prayer reminds us of the auspiciousness of this moment, one in which their communion is created not with formal prayer but in a communal meal. This time of night, "the zenith of their day" (105), is joined to the experience of the faithful at the prayer when their gaze reaches for "some faraway point," a center beyond ordinary time and space. "At such times the vehemence in Mahjoub's eye lessens as they idly roam along the faint, fading line where the light from the lamp ends and the darkness begins." Echoes of the eternal reach across the space to this little group: Mahjoub's silence "takes on great depth at such moments, and if one of his friends asks him something he neither hears nor makes answer." The others share the feeling: "Way Rayyis suddenly breaks out into a single phrase, like a stone falling into a pond: 'God is living.' Ahmed Isma'il inclines his head a little in the direction of the river as though listening to some voice that comes to him from there. At this hour, too, Abdul Hafeez cracks his fingers in silence and Taher Rawwasi gives a sigh from deep within him and says, 'Time comes and Time goes'" (105–06).

The parallel between this scene and the evening prayer is perhaps best caught by the centripetal force they capture, an ebbing of the wave, as Lings would have it, or a centering on a spiritual focal point: "They would then come closer together, as though toward that point, that something in the center, to which they all strive" (98). Their "extinction" or *fana* is evoked in the flickering light/dark in which they are caught, suggesting an immersion: "[it is] as though they are drowning in a sea." For Lings, it is fitting that this goal of *fana* be achieved in the mutual striving towards a center because "Mysticism begins with the consciousness of [being a] point on a radius ... the radius being a Ray of Divine Mercy which emanates from the Supreme Center and leads back to it" (1977, 21).

Dhikr, Sufi practices of dancing and chanting, are intended to lead the adept along the radius in the ebb back to the divine center.

There, instead of seriousness of purpose and moral certitude, are to be found lightness and energy — essential attributes of the fool. In the novel's final image, Zein leaps into the center of the circle of singing celebrants, "transfusing" it with "new energy." The light floods him now as he has taken Haneen's place as the center of blessed life: "Zein stood, tall and thin, in his place at the heart of the circle, like the mast of a ship" (120). Like those who spread the gospel, he announced, "Make known the good news," and in the act brought the energy into focus, into the center. The dual consciousness is completely realized at last in this image of the harmonious relationship between the human and the divine. The Sufi path leads to the center of the circle in which the contradictions "come together" (113), and where religious chanters and beautiful women dancers join in circles within circles, "making a migration from religious rapture to clamour" (117). The "outward movement of creation is reversed" as the wedding celebration connects the inner and outer worlds, and in total harmony "everything flows back through his Heart to its Eternal and Infinite Source" (Lings, 82). The novel is completed as Zein the fool assumes the mantle of his guide, Haneen the saint.

Part III: The Word and the Way

> *This is the Book, wherein is no doubt.*   (Koran II, 2)

> *Those to whom We have given the Book*
> *and who recite it with true recitation,*
> *they believe in it; and who disbelieves in it,*
> *they shall be the losers.*   (Koran II, 115)

In the Futa Toro of northern Senegal, home to Kane's Diallobé people in *L'Aventure ambiguë*, Coulon (1981, 18—53) has shown a pattern of steady resistance on the part of the marabouts in the struggle against the French, far exceeding that which occurred in the Sudan. Eventually, however, French power directly touched the lives of the Senegalese, and the impact of French culture through schooling, economic pressures, and social advantages, as well as ideological indoctrination and political intervention, was more pervasive than that of the British in the Sudan.

The first notable West African literary reaction to the European cultural hegemony was the Negritude movement, in which there were no particular associations with Islam or Muslim traditions.

Before Kane Muslim authors like Birago Diop did construct tales in which Islamic traditions were joined to traditional African folktales, but *L'Aventure ambiguë* is the first major work of African fiction to construct an explicit defense of African Islamic life and faith against the European ideological and cultural menace. If the novel is anti-colonial, it is also the most important novel of its generation to issue its challenge on the grounds of conventional Muslim views — views earlier propounded by the leaders of the major brotherhoods such as Amadou Bamba and Al Hajj Umar.

L'Aventure ambiguë does not enter directly into the particularities of the history. Rather, the story of the Diallobé is presented as if it were paradigmatic for the whole continent ("Le pays des Diaollobé n'était pas le seul qu'une grande clameur eût réveillé un matin. Tout le continent noir avait eu son matin de clameur" [Kane 1961, 59]). [The Diallobé country wasn't alone in being awakened one morning by a great clamor.] The novel leads us to infer a French presence in this period, apparently between the World Wars, which would imply that they had arrived more recently than was actually the case. The Maître is outside history, giving the slightly misleading impression that Islam was always there, that he is carrying on a tradition with an indefinite historical past. Nonetheless, and most important, actual Senegalese history is accurately reflected in the struggle for power cast into the geometrically precise form of a triangle: one corner of the struggle is occupied by the French, standing for the "modern," technological, ostensibly secular, material values of the West. On the other corner is La Grande Royale, embodying traditional power and authority, occupying the position of what Coulon dubs the prince (Coulon 1981). Traditionally the ruling authority struggled against either the masses or a noble elite so as to maintain its position. The Sufi brotherhoods challenged the basis of the princes' authority and won favor with the masses. According to this thesis (propounded by Christian Coulon in *Les Musulmans et le pouvoir en l'Afrique noir* [1983] and in *Le Marabout et le prince* [1981]), the *marabouts*, as Coulon calls the leaders of the various Sufi brotherhoods, were not merely nationalists, expressing an opposition to the foreign Christian presence: "Mais plus largement ils manifestent un refus du pouvoir oppressif d'où qu'il vienne. Ils portent, en eux, implicitement, la méfiance envers le prince .... C'est pour avoir representé auprès des masses l'idéal de cette sagesse populaire que les marabouts ont été suivis avec autant d'enthousiasme" (Coulon 1981, 16 ff.). [But more generally they manifested a rejection of oppressive power, whatever its source.

They manifested, in themselves, implicitly, a defiance towards the prince .... It was because of having represented to the masses the ideal of this popular wisdom[3] that the marabouts achieved such a popular following.]

Thus, completing the triangle, we find the Maître who stands for the other-worldly position of what Coulon calls *le marabout*, the spiritual leader who denies the primacy of the material values of the worldly ruler. He is in direct conflict with La Grande Royale at the outset when she challenges his ascetic, esoteric teachings with respect to Samba Diallo. And he provides Samba Diallo with the spiritual foundation upon which to construct the challenge to the West.

Finally, the figures of Samba Diallo and his father are located at the point of ambivalence, the center of the triangle. As ostensible members of a ruling family, they would be traditionally opposed to the purely spiritual values of the marabout and would be concerned with laying "wood on wood" (Kane 1961, 21), or, as Samba Diallo's father puts it, with defending the spirit on the basis of the strength of the hand: "[N]ous sommes parmi les derniers hommes au monde à posséder Dieu tel qu'Il est véritablement dans Son Unicité .... Comment Le sauver? Lorsque la main est faible, l'esprit court de grands risques, car c'est elle qui le défend ..." (20). [We are among the last men in the world to possess God in his oneness .... How can He be saved? When the hand is weak, the spirit runs great risks, because the former must defend the latter ....] But Samba Diallo is also the adept, the perfect disciple, whose perplexity about reconciling his position and his faith is resolved by his father's argument that even work should be performed in the service of God (112).

To understand fully the ambiguity of Samba's position, it is necessary to consider his relationships to the principal figures in the triangle, and especially to his father. To begin with, the Maître is clearly the Sufi guide, not only to Samba but to all the Diallobé. As Samba is the only one given the sobriquet, "the Diallobé," it is clear that the Maître's guidance over him is in its essence guidance over the country. When the various representatives of all the Diallobé come to the Maître to ask his advice on whether to send their children to the new school, he refuses to answer. His domain is purely spiritual, and he refuses responsibility for the other domain. He tells Samba Diallo's father, "(N)e me demandez pas ce qu'il faut faire demain matin, car je ne le sais pas" (22). [Don't ask me what must be done tomorrow morning, because I don't know.] However, when it comes to designating those to be formed as the future spiritual guides, he doesn't hesitate in choosing Samba. "Votre fils, je le crois, est de la graine dont le pays des Diallobé faisait ses maîtres" (22) [Your son, I believe, is of that stock from which the Diallobé have drawn their masters]; and he adds, not without ambiguity, "Et les maîtres des Diallobé étaient aussi les maîtres que le tiers du continent se choississait pour guides sur la voie de Dieu *en même temps que dans les affaires humaines*" (22, my emphasis). ["And the masters of the Diallobé were also the masters whom one-third of the continent chose as guides on the path to God *as well as in human affairs.*"]

The extent to which this guidance in human affairs reaches, is uncertain. At the outset, both the Maître and Samba Diallo's father seem to share the view that European education is a necessary evil, given the need to achieve some control over the world in which they live. Misery, the Maître repeats, is the enemy of God (21, 44, 94), and in school the children would learn to construct solid houses in which God would be "saved" — in which their faith could be retained. Samba Diallo's father echoes this concern, also at the outset: "(N)ous sommes parmi les derniers hommes au monde à posséder Dieu . . . ." This position, which calls for something approaching theocracy, is totally reversed by both men in the second half of the novel: the Maître repents of his pride and hunger for power in asserting that God could be an obstacle to human happiness, in utilizing God as if He belonged to the Maître himself: "T'offrant et Te refusant, de même que si Tu leur eûsses appartenu, dans le dessein de maintenir d'autres hommes sous leur obéissance" (138).[4] ["Offering You and refusing You just as if You belonged to them, with the intention of keeping other men under their rule."]

In the second part of the novel, when Samba Diallo hears of the Maître's retirement, he sees it as a withdrawal from the arena of action: "J'ai le droit de faire comme ce vieil homme, de me retirer de l'arène . . ." (138). [I have the right to do as this old man, to retire from the arena . . . .] However, even from the outset the Maître clearly saw his vocation as being in opposition to that of the prince. In assessing the position of his prize pupil, Samba Diallo, the cream of the Diallobé nobility, he asserted: "(L')adoration de Dieu n'était compatible avec aucune exaltation de l'homme. Or, au fond de toute noblesse, il est un fond de paganisme. La noblesse est l'exaltation de l'homme, la foi avant tout humilité' . . ." (33). [The worship of God is incompatible with any exaltation of man. Now, at the base of all nobility, is a base of paganism. Nobility is the exaltation of man, faith before any humility.] This *méfiance* towards power is expressed in somewhat different terms by Samba Diallo's father who, in his letter recalling Samba Diallo home from France, recognizes his error in thinking that anything learned in the Western mold would have any impact upon the spiritual quest: "Entre Dieu et l'homme, il n'existe pas la moindre consanguinité, ni je ne sais quelle relation historique .... Voilà pourquoi il me paraît illégitime de fonder l'apologetique par l'Histoire et insensé de vitupérer Dieu en raison de notre misère" (175). ["Between God and man there exists not the least consanguinity, nor any sort of historical relationship .... This is why it appears illegitimate to me to base an "Apology" upon History, and senseless to chastise God for our misery."]

The tradition followed here by the Maître and Samba Diallo's father is in line with that ambiguous tack taken by the marabouts or spiritual rulers in the nineteenth and twentieth centuries in Senegal. According to two of the best-known marabouts, al Hajj Umar and Amadou Bamba, seeking wealth and power in this world runs counter to God's dictates. Al Hajj Umar, whose realm was the most extensive of any nineteenth-century ruler in the region, states, "Le prophète m'a dit que je serai l'un de ses hommes de confiance aussi longtemps que je ne m'associerai pas aux sultans et que je ne m'attacherai pas au monde" (Coulon 1981, 35–36) ["The prophet told me that I will be one of his companions as long as I do not associate with sultans and not attach myself to the world"]. Citing Dumont, Coulon shares the paradoxical view that this great ruler was really an "anti-sultan," or more of an "ascète soufi que d'un chef temporel" (36) [Sufi ascetic than a temporal chief]. Amadou Bamba, along with a host of Senegalese religious leaders, for the most part Tijanis, echoes this sentiment: "Quant à la poursuite de la grandeur ou de la puissance,/Pour accéder au commandement ou à la préeminence/Ou pour se distinguer parmi ses semblables,/C'est une chose qui éloigne le croyant de Dieu" (31; see pp. 30–31). ["As for the pursuit of greatness or of power,/To achieve a commanding or preeminent position/Or to set oneself apart from one's equals,/Is something which distances the believer from God."].

Here it is apparent that the ambiguity of Samba Diallo's position is not due simply to demands placed upon Diallobé society by the French presence: it is inherent in the very attitude of the Sufi adherent towards temporal power itself. This is why the first conflicts experienced by Samba Diallo involve the struggle between his religious vocation and his position as member of a ruling family. His sensitivity on this point is echoed in the Maître's harshness in repressing any sign of specialness that Samba Diallo might perceive, in receiving favored treatment or special clothing, for example. Samba Diallo's fight with Demba also brings out this same issue. More importantly, the conflict between power and religion is very quickly established in the opposition between La Grande Royale and the Maître, an opposition signalled symbolically in terms of day versus night, female versus male, robustness and great size versus frailty and physical debility, life versus death, fructification versus asceticism — in short, between worldly values and spiritual ones. The metaphor used by La Grande Royale to justify her position is an agricultural one, entailing life-giving, procreative actions such as clearing, sowing, and harvesting. The figures associated with the Maître are flesh-denying: the shadow, and, ultimately, death and what lies beyond the here and now. Royalty is seen as ruling the earthly; the Maître's realm is not of this earth. While it may appear unusual to cloak temporal authority in the person of a woman in Senegalese society, Kane uses La Grande Royale all the more effectively to heighten the values of the life force in its opposition to the Sufi guide. This explains her key role in removing Samba Diallo from the *foyer-ardent* of the Maître, and in having him placed in the new European school.

The debate between Samba Diallo's father and the Frenchman Lacroix merely reiterates that already established earlier between La Grande Royale and the Maître, and as the French become the new rulers, they eventually replace the traditional "prince" in the opposition between marabout and prince. Their position, although fully elaborated in the metaphors of the *fou* and in the developments of the second part of the novel, still strike me as being a subset of the larger debate engendered at the outset within the principal forces of society. Still, the colonial presence is introjected into the situation, with the colonialists' own particular set of problems, and with their own world view. In terms of our geometrical figure, they complete the last corner of our triangle that embraces Samba Diallo at the center.

The ambiguity of Samba Diallo's position is inherent in his loyalty to both principal figures — the Maître and La Grande Royale — a situation repeated in Part II in his devotion to the two opposing systems of education he pursues. But it may also be viewed as being more fundamentally inherent in the family position he inherits. Neither Samba Diallo nor his father have clearly designated professions — and in this they differ from all the other characters in the novel. We know that Samba Diallo is studying philosophy, that he had been removed from the tutelage of the Maître just at the moment that he would have begun to learn on more than a rote basis, and that this prevented him from becoming the heir-presumptive of the Maître. We know, also, that Samba Diallo's father, like Samba Diallo, had had Western schooling, knew of such philosophers as Pascal, read and spoke French, and exercised some profession in the town of L. requiring an office and desk. He also took a long voyage through the capital cities of the Diallobé, and on his return was greeted like a dignitary by the local visitors who wished to salute "ce fils du pays que ses fonctions administratives maintenaient de longue periods durant, loin de son terroir" (Kane 1961, 18) ["this son of the country whose administrative functions kept him, for long periods, far from his native homeland"]. While not resembling any particular function-ary, his peripetatic vocation recalls that of Al Hajj Umar, another non-princely ruler, described thus by Coulon: "La 'croisade' d'El Hadj Omar est une sorte de longue marche sans fin qui tient de l'errance du *chevalier* de l'Islam plus que de la construction d'empire" (Coulon 1981, 37, my emphasis). ["The 'crusade' of Al Hajj Umar is a sort of long march without end which denotes the wonderings of the 'knight' of Islam more than the construction of an empire."] Note that the only designation applied to Samba Diallo's father is also "chevalier."

Samba Diallo's father lacks the traditional authority of the *chef*, a designation reserved for Samba Diallo's cousin. It is the family elders who decide, ultimately, on Samba Diallo's removal from the *Foyer-Ardent* and enrollment in the French school, although Samba Diallo's father is the one who calls Samba Diallo home from Europe. In short, Samba Diallo appears to be following his father's path, and this is all the more significant in that he, the father, is *not* clearly identified with any particular power or rule, while he is clearly shown to adhere to the same religious values as the Maître. The vagueness of his position suggests that he symbolizes the universal dilemma of the Western-educated African, and more generally, of those caught between worldly Power and other-worldly Spirit. This opposition troubles Samba Diallo, and is at the base of his question to his father about the problem of remaining faithful to God while still working, of maintaining the contact with the Divine while not occupied with prayer. The father's answer does not reflect a com-promise, but a hierarchy of values in which the spiritual give substance to the non-spiritual: "Si un homme croit en Dieu, le temps qu'il prend à sa prière ... le travail se justifie de Dieu dans la stricte mesure où la vie qu'il conserve se justifie de Dieu" (Kane 1961, 112) ["If man believes in God, the time he takes for his prayer ... the work, is justified before God to the precise extent that the life he preserves is justified before God"]. His answer resembles Lings's identical statement on Sufi practice, or *dhikr*, as "being capable of embracing and penetrating the whole of life" (Lings 1977, 78).

Like Salih, Kane represents the moment of closest contact with the Divine by the evening prayer, the liminal moment when awareness of death is at its greatest, when one's smallness before the immensity of what the Sufis call Reality or the Truth—attributes of God—is most sensibly felt. And, as with Salih, the prayer best evokes this by virtue of the power invested in the liturgical text, in words spoken in prayer. Earthly power, the printed word, the Europeans' alphabet, mastery of which seemed to be linked to the domination of the Africans, cedes before the Word— "la Parole" —the creative, generative matrix whose force is manifested in the *baraka* of the Maître, a power perhaps best represented in the very act of transmitting it to the adept.

The Word is the sword of the Maître with which he conquers not only La Grande Royale, but death itself: "(I)l a la Parole qui n'est faite de rien, mais qui dure ... qui dure" (Kane 1961, 75). ["He has the Word which is made of nothing, but which lasts and lasts."] In one of the Maître's more striking images of "la Parole" as generative, he calls it "l'architecture du monde" [the architecture of the world] and even "le monde même" (15) [the world itself]. Linking Creation to the other-worldly he adds, later on, "le Paradis était bati avec les Paroles qu'il récitait, des mêmes lumières brilliantes, ... de la même puissance" (53) [Paradise was built with the Words he recited, with the same brilliant lights, ... the same power]. Lastly, the image of word-world creating is given striking form as an act of weaving, an image duplicated by the Dogon (and ancient Greeks): "La Parole *tisse* ce qui est" (131, my emphasis) [The Word *weaves* that which exists].

The conflict between "le Prince et le Marabout" is one of two orders of power. The European conquest begins, as with the authority of the traditional prince, with force—the cannon. But the fuller conquest was to be with words, in the struggle for the minds, the souls, of the black men. Thus "on commença, dans le continent noir, à comprendre, que leur puissance véritable résidait, non point dans les canons du premier matin, mais dans ce qui suivait ces canons ... l'école nouvelle .... Le canon contraint les corps, l'école fascine les âmes" (60). [In the black continent, they began to understand that the true power [of the whites] resided not in the cannons that first appeared, but in that which followed the cannons ... the new school .... The cannon controlled the body, the school fascinated the souls.] Appropriately, it is the manipulation of the written word, its structure, which seduces Samba Diallo: "Lorsque j'appris à les agencer [the letters] pour former des mots, à agencer les mots pour donner naissance à la parole, mon bonheur ne connût plus de limites" (172) ["When I learned to manipulate letters to form words, to manipulate words to give birth to the Word, my happiness knew no bounds"]. The joy of mastering knowledge is aptly characterized by the Pular play on words, in which schooling becomes the act of laying or tying wood on wood, of constructing houses with solidity. The images of death and shadows, associated with "la Parole," reach out not to earthly structures but to the end of the earth, the sunset of the earthly perspective as the prelude to salvation. Colonial power, for Amadou Bamba, is thus degenerate in that it represents a heightened delusion of the false or one-sided perspective of materialism. "Sachez, chers frères, que vous vous trouvez à la fin du monde" (Coulon 1983, 33) ["Know, dear brothers, that you are at the end of the world"], begins one of Amabou Bamba's apocalyptic poems, As for the "reserve" with respect to the prince and his power, "les marabouts la mettent d'autant plus en avant qu'ils ont une vision apocalyptique des 'turpitudes du temps présent'" (33) ["the marabouts gave it due prominence as they had an apocalyptic vision of the 'turpitude of the present time'"] — a vision recapitulated in the hallucination of Samba Diallo's father in which waves of human beings turn into pale reflections of the Europeans (Kane 1961, 82). Against this irrepressible force, only the voice of the child pronouncing the complete text of the Koran stands as a barrier. As Samba Diallo recites the words during "la nuit du Coran," he experiences the moment of *fana*, which is the goal of the Sufi mystic: "Progressivement se dissolvait, dans le bourdonnement de cette voix, quelque être qui tout à l'heure encore était Samba Diallo" (Kane 1961, 84) ["Whoever Samba Diallo had just been dissolved progressively in the buzzing of this voice"].

Conclusion

Starting with two apparently radically different conflicts — mysticism versus legalism in *Wedding*, and princely versus spiritual power in *L'Aventure ambiquë* — both texts conclude with the same Sufi vision that informs *Le Regard du roi*. Yet we might see these two different conflicts in the works of Salih and Kane as having a common character.

Both help explain the shape of the fundamental relationships among
the major sets of characters, relationships best described as triangular:

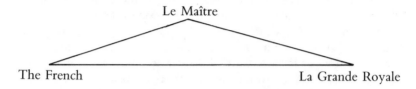

Le Maître

The French　　　　　　　　　　　　　　　　　La Grande Royale

Caught in the interior space of the triangle is Samba Diallo—as was
his father in the previous generation—trapped by his adherence to
the three figures at each corner, and by the positions they represent.
This is the true representation of the ambiguity of his position, and
not that merely given by the conflict between Western and African
cultures. In Kane's portrayal, the figures given at the positive corner
representing worldly power, especially La Grande Royale, are shown
in a positive light. The historical position of the collaborating *chefs*
might not appear to contemporary historians as being quite so attractive as that attributed by Kane to the heads of the Diallobé family. If
so, Kane utilizes the religious corner (given to the Maître) effectively
to introduce a depth of character, an element of "truth" upon which
to ground the resultant push-pull ambiguity. Samba Diallo's ambivalence is tied to the complex of the Word and its Power associated
with all three corners: the sacred Word given to the figure of spiritual
Power; the Prince's word associated with the ruler's power; and the
printed text of the colonial rulers associated with imperial, Western
power.

A similar pattern is to be seen with respect to Zein. The Maître
and La Grande Royale are represented fairly clearly by Haneen and
the circle of notables in Mahjoub's group who gather in the evening
in front of Sa'eed's shop. In the absence of a strong British ideological
and colonial presence, we have the *Imam* as a stand-in for the French:

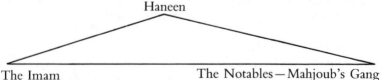

Haneen

The Imam　　　　　　　　　The Notables—Mahjoub's Gang

Not only is the *Imam*, appropriately, different from other villagers
(as the Egyptian bureaucrats were, in fact, under the British). He fits
the role of a negative surrogate for the earthly power of "le prince,"

with his concern for control over the flock based upon his mastery of the written word, upon his ability to terrify and browbeat the people. Zein floats between the saint and the prince — between Haneen, whose disciple he is, and Mahjoub's group in which he acts as a kind of peripheral member. The absence of a father, in his case, frees him to occupy this no-man's land, although we saw that in the case of Samba Diallo the position could also be an inherited one.

The general usefulness of this triangulation of power can be seen in its applicability to *Le Regard du roi* in which Clarence also stands at the center of swirling forces generated by the spiritual leadership (the king, the guides), the legalistic figures (the MC), and the conventional Westernized, secular authorities, internalized by Clarence prior to his arrival in Africa.

In the final analysis, the triangle represents the tension generated by the opposing claims of spiritual power, and its text, of political power, in its positive and negative aspects, and its texts:

Sprititual Power — The Sacred Word

Negative Worldly Power —   Positive Worldly Power —
The Printed Word   The Prince's Word

The ambiguity highlighted in *L'Aventure ambiguë* is also implicit in *The Wedding of Zein* and *Le Regard du roi*. All three works end with an equivalent mystic vision, portrayed as *fana*, in which the ambiguity or contradictions are resolved. Zein is "extinguished" in the final image of the dance, just as Clarence is "extinguished" in the embrace of the king. In both works dance becomes the figure of *dhikr*, a joyful ecstatic state whose trance-like overcoming is represented in Zein's position as the quiet center of the turbulent circle. For Lings, the meaning of this is seen as prefiguring the ultimate state of transcendence: "[T]he body stands for the Axis of the Universe which is none other than the Tree of Life. The dance is thus a rite of centralization, a foretaste of the lost Center ..." (Lings 1977, 84). That this is equivalent to the states of *fana* captured by Samba Diallo during his recitation of the Koran, during his prayers, as well as in his final disembodied return to the center, is reflected in Lings's fortuitous comment that dance is "the equivalent of the Name which also ... replaces the centre[;] and in fact the invocation of the Name, aloud or in silence, usually accompanies the dance which in any case is intended above all to plunge the dancer into a state of concentration upon Allah" (Lings 1977, 84–85). That Zein embodies the transcendence of contradictions is represented by the convergence of ex-slave-girl prostitutes and religious chanters whose singing and dancing mingle in one great synthesis and celebration.

Samba Diallo's death is also a moment in which contradictions are overcome. The voice that speaks to him out of the void evokes this state: "[Il n'y a] pas d'antagonismes" (Kane 1961, 189) ["There are no antagonisms"]. His death does not conclude the novel — its appearance is belied by the stichomythia of disembodied voices, once again ecstatic, exinguished by the expansion of human time into the infinite: "Vie de l'instant, vie sans âge de l'instant qui règne, dans l'arène lumineuse de ta durée, infiniment l'homme se déploie" (Kane 1961, 191) [Life of the instant, life without age, which reigns, in the luminous arena of your duration; infinitely, man unfolds].

Like the mystic, the novelist's path is unique, even when based on a model provided by a Master; and like the mystic, the Sufi author concludes on the same note, with an image of *fana* as the limit of the word and its power of expression. As *fana* is ineffable, it best conveys the limit of the power of human expression of the word. It also signals the limit of the power of human art, of the novelist's ability to express transcendental states through the only available means, the word.

Notes

*Substantial portions of this article have already appeared as "A Sufi Interpretation of *Le Regard du roi*" in *Research in African Literatures* and "The Power and the Word: *L'Aventure ambiguë* and *The Wedding of Zein*" in *African Studies Review*.

1. The precise character and extent of Sufism in Africa are not clearly discussed in the available literature. Trimingham's *The Sufi Orders in Islam* and *Islam in West Africa* are standard introductions to the subject, and yet their discussion is largely external, and esoteric practices are discounted. Marty is more detailed in *L'Islam en Guineé*, though its scope is more limited, as is the case with Person's elaborate study on Samori in which the Tijaniyya order is placed within its historical context. David Robinson's *The Holy War of Umar Tal: The Western Sudan in the mid-Nineteenth Century* provides a useful historical context, and Lewis's volume of essays, *Islam in Tropical Africa*, contains a variety of detailed studies, but none of them focuses upon esoteric practices.
2. Most citations in English of *Le Regard du roi* are taken from the James Kirkup translation. All translations of Coulon and *L'Aventure ambiguë* are my own.
3. "This popular wisdom" refers to the opposition to princely oppression.
4. I take "leur" to include the *maître* himself.

References

COULON, CHRISTIAN. 1981. *Le Marabout et le Prince*. Paris: Pedone.

———. 1983. *Les Musulmans et le Pouvoir en Afrique noir*. Paris: Editions Karthala.

HARROW, KENNETH. 1983. "A Sufi Interpretation of *Le Regard du roi*." *Research in African Literatures*, 14, 2 (Summer) 135-164.

———. 1987. "The Power and the Word: *L'Aventure ambiguë* and *The Wedding of Zein*." *African Studies Review*, 30, 1.

KANE, CHEIKH HAMIDOU. 1961. *L'Aventure ambiguë*. Paris: Julliard.

LAYE, CAMARA. 1954. *Le Regard du roi*. Paris: Plon, 1954.

———. 1966. *Dramouss*. Paris: Plon.

———. 1971. *Le Regard du roi*. English version translated by James Kirkup. NY: Collier.

LEWIS, I. M. 1980. *Islam in Tropical Africa*. Bloomington: Indiana University Press.

LINGS, MARTIN. 1977. *What is Sufism?* Berkeley: University of California Press.

MARTY, PAUL. 1921. *L'Islam en Guinée*. Paris: Ernst Leroux.

PERSON, YVES. 1968. *Samori*. Dakar: IFAN.

ROBINSON, DAVID. 1985. *The Holy War of Umar Tal: The Western Sudan in the mid-Nineteenth Century*. Oxford: Clarendon Press.

SALIH, TAYEB. 1969. *Season of Migration to the North*. London: Heinemann.

———. 1978. *The Wedding of Zein*. London: Heinemann.

TRIMINGHAM, J. SPENCER. 1959. *Islam in West Africa*. Oxford: Clarendon Press.

———. 1971. *The Sufi Orders in Islam*. London: Oxford University Press.

Chapter 18

▼▼▼▼▼▼▼▼▼

Through a Prism Darkly: "Orientalism" in European-Language African Writing

GEORGE LANG

*And the day will come
when the Law of the Prophet shall rule
throughout the lands, when Ethiopia
shall stretch forth her hands unto Allah, and shall
thus rise to her highest point of civilization.*

RICHARD BURTON, *cited in Hiskett 1984, 210*

One need not concur with Richard Burton's deliberately provocative vision of the inevitable victory of the nineteenth-century Fulani jihad to recognize that his admiration for Islam runs counter to the current of European-language thinking in his times as in our own. Nor need one have digested all of *Orientalism* to recognize that Burton is one of Edward Said's arch-villains, the consummate Orientalist who mastered the Orient, in all senses of the word, and penetrated "to the heart of Islam" (Said, 1979, 195). I can think of no comparable scholar of African Islam, but the absolutism and lack of nuance in Burton's prophecy does exemplify, albeit in reverse, one feature of European-langauge writing of Islam, the reduction of it to a monolith, one more often malevolent than benevolent. Of course, many Muslims also assume the unity of believers and themselves thus tend to reduce Islam's variegation. But the web of unexamined opinion about Islam that flourishes in the West holds even when transposed into Africa; and many Africanists, who were first and foremost Europeanists, have copied their script over from European learning, from what has historically been the dogmatic vision of Islam as a uniform and timeless superstition. My aim in the ensuing remarks is to discuss the effects this often-unconscious reduction of the prismatic complexity of Islam has upon African and Africanist writing and thought.

These effects are manifold, even to some extent among writers of Islamic tradition, because any language conveys with it a burden of predigested terminology and attitudes against which it is difficult, but not impossible, to write. As Mbye B. Cham has observed, writers of Islamic background run from traditional or modern promoters of Islam (Hampâté Bâ or Cheikh Hamidou Kane), to those using Islamic elements without actively fostering Islam (the *al-mukhlit*, "mixers" like Camara Laye [Fisher 1980]), to a large body of irreverents, and on to the apostates (like Sembène Ousmane and Yambo Ouologuem, though Edris Makward disputes this interpretation of Sembène elsewhere in this volume). Alongside this continuum runs another composed of writers from non-Islamic traditions. There are allies (like Edward W. Blyden, who advocated the spread of Islam, much to the consternation of the Christian missionaries of Liberia [Hiskett 1984, 210]), synthesizers (like Léopold Sédar Senghor, who saw Islam as having an important but not primordial role in African culture), misinformers (even well-intentioned ones, like some mentioned below) and, at the far extreme and corresponding to the apostates, debunkers like Ayi Kwei Armah (to whom Islam was anathema, the alien imposition of another, earlier colonizing force). To this last category also belong Christian missionaries and colonial administrators and commentators, who saw Islam as a focus of resistance to European hegemony. It is fruitful to look at the full range of these writers in light of the peculiar systematic distortion of Islam we might think of as an Africanist strain of Orientalism.[1]

Adopting, as many have, Michel Foucault's notion of discourse as a self-contained and inalterable sphere comporting an impermeable *epistémè*, Said implies that no knowledge of other beings is possible. To such epistemological monadism, I oppose a pragmatic notion of ideological hegemony as open to contradiction, and hence to correction.[2] Communication is indeed possible, but there is a deeply ingrained pattern of denial, if not of Islam itself then of its complexity, which impedes understanding not just of Islam but of Africa, and diminishes the full spectrum of its variety to a single murky hue.

There are considerable though not always consistent differences between African and non-African treatments of Islam in Africa, in part because Muslim and non-Muslim Africans have long co-existed, at least in the Sudan and Sahel. It follows that African irony about a particular facet of Islam (say, the mockery of the false marabout) is too easily missed by Western critics, or is cast out of context. That such lapses are institutional and collective rather than individual is suggested by the apparently neutral remark by my colleague Eric Sellin, who is both professionally and personally well-informed about Islam, that Aminata Sow Fall's *La Grève des bàttu* "tells of a beggar's strike after an official has tried to restrict downtown begging. This strike wreaks havoc with the almsgiving that is required by local custom" (Klein 1986, 148). Since alms-giving is one precept of Islam,[3] this is tantamount to alluding to a principle of Christian practice (say, confession in Graham Greene's *The Heart of the Matter*) as a quaint local tradition, and this in a novel dealing with the higher ambiguities of faith. There is a gamut of reaction to the marabout in Senegalese novels, some of which posit the holy man as a positive figure (e.g., Kane' *L'Aventure ambiguë* and Mamadou Dia Mbeye's *Au delà de la vertu*), some of which is gently chiding (Birago Diop in his *Contes d'Amadou Koumba*), some of which is quite negative (Sembène Ousmane or Cheikh Aliou Ndao in *Buur Tilleen: Roi de la Médina* and *Le Marabout de la sécheresse*), and some of which, like Sow Fall's novel, involve a core tenet of Islam in a complex web of ironies. Any reader who is not already *au courant* will find it difficult to situate any of these attitudes correctly, especially the last one, if misconceptions about Islam are promulgated by the critics, or for that matter if the complexity of Islamic tradition is not given its due.

The intellectual resources of that tradition are all but invisible to Europhones, and few translations from Arabic, Wolof, Hausa, and other languages necessary to understand them are available. This leads to a range of erroneous or partial readings of African literature, some of which reflect blatant Western stereotypes about Islam, others of which are more subtle, though still reductive. Take, as an example of the former, Ouologuem's denunciation of the abuse of Koranic rhetoric in the hands of petty tyrants in the opening pages of *Le Devoir de violence*, which appeared to many Western readers to be a strikingly original, but well-justified formulation of the intrinsically despotic nature of Islam (Miller 1985). Yet such criticism is a commonplace within Islamic tradition itself and was often leveled by the Sufi Qadiriyya, Tijaniyya and Mourides, or later by the

Ahmadiyya (though granted these last are notoriously unorthodox).

As an example of the subtler form of misreading, take Wole Soyinka's remark in *Myth, Literature and the African World* that Samba Diallo has assaulted the materialist atheism of the West "with the West's own dialectical weapons" (1976, 82). Soyinka himself is very willing to acknowledge the weight of the Islamic world-view in some African writing, but his readers may be too easily led to believe that Kane/Diallo's antithesis to materialism derives from the West, whereas the line of thought Kane followed both has roots in Sufi thought and goes back as far as the ninth century A.D. to the Mutakallim or Islamic scholastic movement.[4] So Mercier and Battestini claim, which demonstrates that some Western Africanists are aware of the larger Islamic world: "L'ambiguïté pour les Mutakallimoun se matérialisait dans la discussion. Ce mouvement de pensée aurait pu être repris par les musulmans actuels, adaptant le Coran aux nécessités modernes; dans la lignée islamique, Samba Diallo aurait pu voir là une issue" (Mercier and Battestini 1964, 15). ["For the Mutakallim, ambiguity was in the nature of discussion. This line of thought could have been taken up by today's Muslims, adapting the Koran to modern exigencies. Samba Diallo could have found therein an Islamic solution to his problem".] Seen in these terms, Cheikh Hamidou Kane's work reverberates with meaning far greater than the culture-conflict or "psycho-culturalist" molds into which it has been too easily crammed by, for example, Dominique Desanti or Guy Ossito Midiohouan. One understands that Midiohouan's socialist perspective would lead him to dismiss religion as escapism, but read within an Islamic framework or with some knowledge of what that framework might be, *L'Aventure ambiguë* is a most "committed" novel. Indeed, it is hard to think of any other work of African literature of traditional, Christian, or Marxist orientation that taps so deeply into its avowed tradition for a radical alternative.

Not even eminent Africanists escape from the "created consistencies" of which Said speaks (1979, 3). The noted Islamist J. Spencer Trimingham is not above observations like the following: "Muslims place extreme emphasis on the externals of religion and make no important ethical demands. They have a unified and attainable religious-social code of behavior. They do not live, as Christians do, in a state of tension, feeling that their lives fall short of their religious standard. Therefore no strain is put on them. Their religious life is wholly a matter of behavior and conformity" (1965, 107). Yet are not the very criticism of the charlatan marabout and the gallery of prayer, alms, fasting and *hadj* deviants drawn up by Debra Boyd-Buggs *prima facie* evidence that African Muslims are sensitive to the tension between essence and appearance, ethics and externals?[5]

There *have* been an increasing number of re-readings of West African fiction in the light of Islam: insistence upon the Sufi sub-text in *Le Regard du roi*(Obumselu 1980) and *L'Aventure ambiguë* (Harrow 1983)[6]; explanation of the inclusion of "Arab" Islam as part of the "white death" in Ayi Kwei Armah's *Two Thousand Seasons* (Lang 1987); Thomas Hale's reading of *Le Devoir de violence* against both contemporary Songhay griot versions of the legend of Askia Mohammed and the Islamic chronicles *Tarikh es-Sudan* and *Tarikh es-Fettach* (Hale, 1990); plus the aforementioned typology of Islam in Senegalese literature by Mbye Cham, the study by Debra Boyd-Buggs, Simon Battestini's "Muslim Influences on West African Literature and Culture," and, of course, the contributions to this present volume. Still, these revisionist readings are largely thematic or involve layers of translation, and the translation of Islamic material into English or French faces a daunting double barrier.

It is perhaps easier to understand the first of those hurdles, the political motives for which reference to African resistance to the West in any form is either masked or expunged. As Thomas Hodgkin observed in 1966: "the average Ghanaian university student will usually know something of the works of H. G. Wells or Arnold Bennett, but is unlikely to know anything of the works of their approximate contemporary, al-Hajj 'Umar ibn Abi Bakr al-Salghawi. Yet al-Hajj 'Umar's writing would seem to be at least as significant for an understanding of the recent social history of Ghana as are the writing of Wells and Bennett for the social history of Britain" (1966, 443). It is patent that something more than lack of "communication between two distinctive literary traditions" is at stake here. Al-Hajj 'Umar was hardly neutral about Western thought and politics, and it is, conversely, hardly surprising that the English or French have been so inhospitable to Islamic thought. Muslims were literally mortal enemies to the first European travelers into the Sudan, Mungo Park, René Caillé, and Heinrich Barth; and the first concrete reactions to African Islam were introduced into the English, French, and German languages by their publications, which set the foundations for the colonial novel in Europe. In the early part of this century both the English in Northern Nigeria and the French in Mali used Arabic and/or a vernacular for administrative purposes, but these practices were terminated when it became evident they inadvertently promoted Islam. The barrier between European languages and Islamic traditions in Africa was thus a deliberate one, and this obstacle affects all writers, Islamic or not—the former insofar as they must strive against the prejudice inherent in the language they are using, the latter because of the blackout that prevails as a matter of policy at all but the most learned levels of the Western intellectual world.

Yet whatever ideological challenge Al-Hajj 'Umar and other West African Muslim writers posed to the West, there are additional "literary" reasons for their relegation to marginality. Arabic and *a'jami* (African languages in Arabic script) have, in the words of Albert Gérard, "[leurs] propres critères d'excellence, qui n'ont rien de commun avec ceux de l'Occident moderne. Essentiellement, ils se ramènent à deux grandes exigences: la fidélité aux thèmes et aux structures établies, et la virtuosité dans le maniement du langage et du vers" (Gerard 1984, 132) ["their own standards of excellence which have nothing in common with those of the modern West. Essentially, they come down to two important requirements: faithfulness to established themes and structures, and virtuosity in language and verse"]. Apart from the purely political barriers to incorporating Islamic tradition into European languages, the twentieth-century European modernist penchant for "open" literary forms is at odds with the practice of "virtuosity in language and verse"—a virtuosity exemplified by the Wolof verse studied by Amar Samb and the Hausa verse Hiskett has explored. Since this mode of poetry has no counterpart flourishing in the West, Islam, perceived through the veil of Europhone translation, seems, if not limited to prose, then prosaic. The shift of matter from Islamic to Europhone spheres entails a reorientation of genres, therefore to some extent a distortion. Hiskett argues convincingly that the development of Islam in West Africa is united by a "single, unbroken thread ... [and represents] a triumph for the power of literate ideas" (1984, 318). But the nature and forms of that literacy remain invisible to the West or the Westernized, for they have roots in Islamic theology and in the unique traditions of literacy derived therefrom.[7]

One of the most interesting conclusions drawn by Said is that "the modern Orient participates in its own Orientalizing" (1979, 325), largely by adopting Western views of itself. An analogous assimilation of course occurred in Africa during the years preceding Négritude (which explicitly argued against such), but one still-pervasive aspect of "self-Orientalizing" is the marginalization of

Islam within Africa implied by setting the Sahara as a significant *cultural* boundary, and this despite the fact that Islam extends well south of the desert and that the desert has never been an absolute barrier. There are to be sure some cases, such as the politically defined Sudan, in which culture and race fall into relatively neat, sometimes violent demarcations, but the assumption that the Sahara is more than a geographical feature is an implicitly racist one, and is a corollary of the two most common presumptions about African Islam: the first that it is an anomaly in the Islamic world, the second that its impact on Africa has been due to some fantastic misunderstanding ("malentendu fantastique" [Moreau 1982, 39]). This latter point of view includes the insinuation that Islamic polygamy and amenability to superstition predisposed Africans to it. Islamists of this persuasion manage to tar both Islam and Africans with a single brush. Islamists of a different, presumably purist bent (like Jean-Claude Froelich) alternatively assert that African Islam is by its very nature condemned to schism and heresy: "L'islam doit une partie de ses succès à sa souplesse, mais il a dû payer rançon de cette facilité: l'islam en s'adaptant s'est défiguré .... En mêlant la foi nouvelle aux pratiques païennes les populations noires, sans s'en douter, ont plongé dans le schisme, sinon dans l'hérésie" (Moreau 1982, 235). ["Islam owes part of its success to its flexibility, but it has had to pay a price for it: in the process of adapting, Islam has become distorted .... Syncretizing the new faith with pagan customs, the black population unbeknownst to itself slipped into schism and perhaps heresy"]. This is not to suggest that there is no variety of sect and schism in Africa, but the contention that African Islam might have a monopoly upon diversity and variety of approach is curious. Africa is but one of the five cultural spheres in which Islam has found a home, and the Arab heartland but another. There remain the Turkish, the Irano-Indian, and the Indonesian, and the proliferation of sect within each of them certainly undermines any characterization of African Islam as especially given over to schism and heresy.[8] There is also, I would argue, a peculiar blindness towards Islamic thought practiced by philosophers like Paulin Hountondji and V. Y. Mudimbe, who see African philosophy as a synthesis of non-Muslim African civilizations and "modernity" (Mudimbe 1985, 212). In their thought, Islam is excluded from the nascent African philosophical discourse, though the terms and the methodology of contemporary post-modernist Western discourse are implicitly embraced.

There have been a number of other thinkers who have inserted

Islam into the total synthesis of cultures Africa is said to represent, the gamut here running from Léopold Sédar Senghor (whose embarrassingly opportunistic *Les Fondements de l'Africanité, ou Négritude et Arabité* is to some extent tempered by the poetic synthesis he did achieve in his *Elégies majeures*), to Hampâté Bâ (*Aspects de la civilisation africaine*) and Sulayman S. Nyang (*Islam, Christianity, and African Identity*), both active promoters of Islam. Synthesis invariably reflects its author's own ideological needs. It is hardly surprising that Senghor's *Fondements* was conceived as an address delivered in the presence of Gamal Abdel Nasser, or that as the Catholic president of a nation over 90 percent Muslim, Senghor found good reasons of his own to attribute an important role for Islam in his Universal Synthesis of cultures. Doubtless part of the popular appeal of Ali Mazrui's synthetic view of Africa as a fusion of animist, Western, and Islamic components is that such a fusion is in fact unique in world history and thus attractive to pan-African nationalists.

Historians have shown the actual complexity of West African Islamic history and thought to be a response not to European imperialism *per se*, but to the imposition of the secular European ideal of nation-states. Islamic advance and resistance to the West has flourished not along lines and among the political entities recognized by the West, but across borders and within sects, among the Wahabdis (as antagonistic to the Sufi as the Sunni are), or the Ahmadis (who count as apostates in the eyes of most Muslims). The periods and boundaries within which we interpret the chronology and the geography of West Africa frequently ignore the alternative vision Islamic tradition offers. "Islamic culture being virtually frontierless, and Muslim scholars habitually cosmopolitan and peripatetic" (Hodgkin 1966, 447), both the literary and the political endeavors of Muslims tend to slip through the grid of Western or Western-oriented analysis.

I do not wish to be programmatic. Dorothy S. Blair makes the point that in Senegal there is a "high degree of homogeneity. The Muslim majority cohabits easily with the Catholic minority and has a strong tolerance of traditional beliefs and cults." It follows that sect and syncretism, within Senegal at least, are already foregone conclusions, such that "the few traces of religious schism reflected in Senegal's literature are associated with the Mourides" (1984, 8). What this means is that a developing national culture can and will override the usually prevailing Europhone view of Muslims. Hence, in Senegal, nationalist portrayals of resistance to the French turn around historical figures who were Muslim, in particular Al-Hajj

'Umar and Lat Dior, whose conversion sparked a successful attack upon the French protectorates in 1871. Blair cites similar attitudes in Gérard Chenet's radio play *El Hadj Omar*, Cheik Aliou Ndao's *L'Exil d'Alboury*, and D. T. Niane's *Sikasso, ou la dernière citadelle* (1984, 22–30). Her point is well-taken. These statements of Senegalese nationalism are part of a syncretic national culture that rejects the Orientalist suppositions of Francophone culture. The rule this exception proves might read as follows: unless an indigenous Europhone tradition of writing or school of scholarship centered on Islamic Africa develops, the presuppositions and prejudices of the international English and French cultures regarding Islam will prevail.

West Africa offers an exemplary metaphor for interactions on the global scale. There will be no accurate and sufficiently complex representation of the Islamic world until European languages are no longer the sole curriculum of study, or at least until translation helps understand the variegation of that world. In West Africa this means a serious reappraisal of Islam, not in the provocative manner Richard Burton displayed above, but with full appreciation of its integrity as a system "of interlocking ideas, of intense intellectuality and mystical complexity" — as Mervyn Hiskett imagined Al-Hajj 'Umar imagining the *tariqa* of the Tijaniyya (1984, 318). Only then can the spectrum of Islamic thought in Africa be conveyed into Europhone scholarship and can we no longer gaze through this particular prism darkly.

Notes

1. Said's choice and understanding of the term Orientalism is not itself above reproach, and it would be unwise to apply it uncritically to Africanists, despite the common historical and institutional roots Africanists share with European Orientalists, as is apparent in the usual grouping of "African" and "Oriental" studies in English and French universities. Indeed, one must recognize that this present study would be impossible without some of these same Africanists and Islamists. We learn through approximation and error, our own as well as others'. Said himself has too blithely dismissed some Orientalists, for example the Victorian scholar of Persian, E. G. Browne, whose knowledge of his subject matter and ringing denunciation of European colonialism in the Foreword to Volume II of his *History of Persian Literature* ought to temper such categorical treatment.

2. It is revealing that prior to his recent polemic works such as *The Question of Palestine* and *After the Last Sky: Palestinian Lives*, which reflect his role as spokesman for the Palestinian National Council, Said never tried to explain the Oriental Other to his readers. In addition, he seems not to have appreciated the difference between Foucault's epistemological concept of *epistémè* and Gramsci's political and "pragmatic" understanding of

hegemony, which implies a more variegated and dynamic picture of ideological conflict.

3. The voluntary alms in Sow Fall's novel were not *zakat*, as Mbye Cham suggests (1985, 452). *Zakat* is a formal annual tithe (10 percent of one's capital goods). The *Koran* does, however, recommend the voluntary charity Sow Fall's beggar's strike cut off. See Bâ (1972, 142) and, of course, the *Koran* (II, 172).

4. *Mutakaliim* means simply theologian, but the movement itself applied dialectic and reason to the interpretation of the *Koran*, distinguishing itself from both the conservative traditionalists, from mystics, and from the "neo-Platonic and Aristotelian philosophers of the Sunnite faith . . . ." [It was based upon the] "atomistic system which was Islam's most original contribution to philosophy" (Gibb and Kramer 1965, 212).

5. To these ideological barriers must be added material ones. We lack basic and easily available research tools. In the words of Jean-Louis Triaud: "Dans le cas de l'Afrique noire, un tel capital [des ouvrages de référence essentiels à l'étude de l'Islam en Afrique] fait défaut, ou se montre largement insuffisant: où sont les travaux de références bibliographiques et bio-graphiques, les dictionnaires spécialisés, les enquêtes systématiques?" (1986, 452). ["In the case of Black Africa, such resources — works essential to the study of Islam in Africa — are lacking or very insufficient: where are bibliographical and biographical reference books, the specialized diction-aries, the systematic surveys?"] Even the compendious *European-Language Writing in Sub-Saharan Africa*, which conformed to the best models of international comparatist practice, has almost nothing to say about Islamic influence in Africa, and this despite the pioneering work of its editor, Albert S. Gérard, in making known the wealth of Islamic and related writing on the continent — and his lengthy chapters on Islamic traditions in *African Language Literatures*. The essay contained therein by Mazrui and Bakari does express the kernel of the thought Mazrui finally brought forth in *The Africans* — the now well-known but not very specific thesis that contemporary Africa is the product of indigenous, Western, and Islamic traditions.

6. It is worth observing that both Obumselu and Harrow as well as Johnson attribute Islamic influence on Laye on the basis of very general parallels between Sufi imagery and that found in the African texts, and that Sufi practice is the best known and most positively received facet of Islam in Western languages.

7. Indeed, Jack Goody's study of the Vai script demonstrates how imbued it is with West African Islamic traditions, even in the south, far from the Sudan, and how alien to Western senses of "literacy" (1987, 191 ff). For more on language use and Islam, see Brenner and Last.

8. Nor are the common attacks on and defenses of Islamic education an isolated African or Senegalese phenomenon, but part of a venerable neo-Islamic tradition well exemplified by the Egyptian Taha Hussein's "Student Days" (from *Al-Ayyam*). Scathing denunciations of the religious charlatan have a counterpart in the Iranian Sedagh Hedayat's "Caravan of Islam" and the Islamic connection extends to Indonesia where Mochtar Lubis's 1963 *Twilight in Djakarta* treated the problem of the cosmopolitan "been-

to" who returns to promulgate a modernized Islam. It is interesting in this light to consider the paucity of comparative studies of the "been-to" theme and the corresponding emphasis by Arab writers of the *nahda* (the renaissance) on the impact of Western culture on those who studied abroad (Allen 1982, 54).

References

ALLEN, ROGER. 1982. *The Arabic Novel: An Historical and Critical Introduction.* Syracuse: Syracuse University Press.

BÂ, AMADOU HAMPÂTÉ. 1972. *Aspects de la civilisation africaine* Paris: Présence Africaine.

BATTESTINI, SIMON P. K. 1986. "Muslim Influences on West African Literature and Culture." *Journal of Muslim Minority Affairs*, 7, 2 (July) 476−502.

BLAIR, DOROTHY S. 1984. *Senegalese Literature: A Critical History.* Boston: Twayne.

BOYD-BUGGS, DEBRA. 1986. "Baraka: Maraboutism and Maraboutage in the Francophone Senegalese Novel." Ph.D. thesis, Ohio State University, *Dissertation Abstracts* 47:899A.

BRENNER, LOUIS, and MURRAY LAST. 1985. "The Role of Language in West African Islam." *Africa* 55, 4, 432−46.

CHAM, MBYE B. 1985. "Islam in Senegalese Literature and Film." *Africa* 55, 4, 447−63.

DESANTI, DOMINIQUE. 1968. "Le Conflit des cultures et *L'Aventure ambiguë.*" *African Arts/Arts d'Afrique* 1 (Winter) 60−61; 106; 109−10.

DIAGNE, AHMADOU MAPATÉ. 1920. *Les Trois volontés de Malic.* Paris: Larousse.

FALL, AMINATA SOW. 1979. *La Grève des Bàttu.* Dakar: Les Nouvelles Editions Africaines.

———. 1986. *The Beggars' Strike.* Translated by Dorothy S. Blair. Burnt Mill, Essex: Longman.

FISHER, HUMPHREY J. 1980. "Crescent and Consciousness." *Research in African Literature* 11, 1 (Spring) 27.

FROELICH, JEAN-CLAUDE. 1966. "Sectes musulmanes et civilisations négro-africaines." *Le Mois en Afrique* 1 (Mai) 98−105.

GERARD, ALBERT S. 1984. *Essais d'histoire littéraire africaine.* Sherbrooke: Naaman.

GERARD, ALBERT S. (ed.) 1986. *European-Language Writing in Sub-Saharan Africa.* Budapest: Akadémiai Kiadó.

GIBB, H. A. R., and J. H. KRAMERS. 1965. *Shorter Encyclopedia of Islam.* Ithaca: Cornell University Press.

GOODY, JACK. 1987. *The Interface between the Written and the Oral.* Cambridge: Cambridge University Press.

HALE, THOMAS A. 1990. *Scribe, Griot and Novelist: Narrative Interpreters of the Sanghay Empire* Gainesville: U of Florida P, 1990.

HARROW, KENNETH. 1983. "A Sufi Interpretation of *Le Regard du Roi,*" *Research in African Literatures* 14, 2, 135−64.

HISKETT, MERVYN. 1975. *A History of Hausa Islamic Verse.* London: School of Oriental and African Studies, University of London.

———. 1984. *The Development of Islam in West Africa.* London: Longman.

HODGKIN, THOMAS L. 1966. "The Islamic Literary Tradition in Ghana," in I. M. Lewis (ed.) *Islam in Tropical Africa*. London: Oxford University Press, 442−60.

——. 1984. *The Development of Islam in West Africa*. London: Longman.

HODGKIN, THOMAS L. 1966. "The Islamic Literary Tradition in Ghana," in I. M. Lewis (ed.) *Islam in Tropical Africa*. London: Oxford University Press, 442−60.

HOUNDTONDJI, PAULIN J. 1983. *African Philosophy: Myth and Reality*. Henri Evans with the coll. of Jonathan Rée. Bloomington: Indiana University Press.

JOHNSON, LEMUEL A. 1980. "Crescent and Consciousness: Islamic Orthodoxies and the West African Novel." *Research in African Literatures* 11, 1 (Spring) 264−9.

KANE, CHEIKH HAMIDOU. 1961. *L'Aventure ambiguë*. Paris: Julliard.

KRITZECK, JAMES, and WILLIAM H. LEWIS, (eds.) 1969. *Islam in Africa*. New York: Van Nostrand Reinhold Company.

KRITZECK, JAMES. 1970. *Modern Islamic Literature*. New York: New American Library.

KLEIN, LEONARD S. 1986. *African Literatures in the 20th Century: A Guide*. New York: Ungar Publishing Company.

LANG, GEORGE. 1987. "Text, Identity and Difference: Yambo Ouologuem's *Le Devoir de violence* and Ayi Kwei Armah's *Two Thousand Seasons*," *Comparative Literature Studies* 24, 4 (December) 274−89.

MADUKUIKE, IHECHUKWU. 1983. *The Senegalese Novel: A Sociological Study of the Impact of the Politics of Assimilation*. Washington, D. C.: Three Continents.

MERCIER, ROGER, MONIQUE BATTESTINI, ET SIMON BATTESTINI (eds.) 1964. *Cheikh Hamidou Kane: Ecrivain Sénégalais*. Paris: Fernand Nathan Editeur.

MIDIOHOUAN, GUY OSSITO. 1986. *L'Idéologie dans la littérature négro-africaine d'expression française*. Paris: L'Harmattan.

MILLER, CHRISTOPHER L. 1985. *Blank Darkness: Africanist Discourse in French*. Chicago: University of Chicago Press.

MOREAU, RENÉ LUC. 1982. *Africains, musulmans*. Paris: Présence Africaine.

MUDIMBE, V. Y. 1985. "African Gnosis: Philosophy and the Order of Knowledge." *African Studies Review* 28, 2/3 (June/September) 149−233.

NYANG, SULAYMAN S. 1894. *Islam, Christianity, and African Identity*. Brattleboro, Vermont: Amana Books.

OBUMSELU, BEN. 1980. "The French and Moslem Backgrounds of *The Radiance of the King*." *Research in African Literatures* 11, 1 (Spring) 1−25.

OUOLOGUEM, YAMBO. 1968. *Le Devoir de violence*. Paris: Seuil.

SAID, EDWARD W. 1979. *Orientalism*. New York: Vintage.

SAMB, AMAR. 1968. "L'Influence de l'Islam sur la littérature volof." *Bulletin de l'IFAN*, Série B., 30, 2 (Avril) 628−41.

SENGHOR, LÉOPOLD SÉDAR. 1967. *Les Fondements de l'africanité ou négritude et arabité*. Paris: Présence Africaine.

SOYINKA, WOLE. 1976. *Myth, Literature and the African World*. Cambridge: Cambridge University Press.

TRIAUD, JEAN-LOUIS. 1986. "Review of Christian Coulon, *Les Musulmans et le pouvoir en Afrique noire.*" *Canadian Journal of African Studies* 20, 3, 451–53.

TRIMINGHAM, J. SPENCER. 1955. *Islam in the Sudan.* New York: Barnes and Noble.

WARDENBURG, JEAN-JACQUES. 1963. *L'Islam dans le miroir de l'occident.* Paris: Mouton.

Select Bibliography

▼▼▼▼▼▼▼▼▼▼▼▼▼▼▼▼▼▼

A. Works of Literature

ABDULAZIZ, MOHAMED. 1979. *Muyaka*. Nairobi: Kenya Literature Bureau.

ALKALI, ZAYNAB. 1987. *The Virtuous Woman*. Ikeja, Nigeria: Longman Nigeria.

ANDRZEJEWSKI, B. W. and I. M. LEWIS. 1964. *Somali Poetry: An Introduction*. Oxford: Clarendon Press.

ARMAH, AYI KWEI. 1973. *Two Thousand Seasons*. Nairobi: East African Publishing House.

BÂ, AMADOU HAMPÂTÉ. 1969. *Kaiidara*. Paris: Julliard (Collection classique africans).

———. 1973. *L'Etrange destin de Wangrin*. Paris: Union generale d'editions.

———. 1974. *L'Eclat de la grande étoile, suivi du bain rituel*. L. Kestleroot. C. Seydou, A. Ibrahim Sow, eds. Paris: Armand Colin.

———. 1985. *Njeddo Dewal. Mère de la Calamité: Conte initiatique peul*. Abidjan: Nouvelles editions afraicaines.

BÂ, AMADOU HAMPÂTÉ and G. DIETERLEN. 1961. *Koumen*. Paris: Mouton.

BÂ, MARIAMA. 1980. *Une si longue lettre*. Dakar: Les Nouvelles éditions africaines.

BADIAN, SEYDOU. 1958. *Sous l'orage*. Paris: Présence africaine.

———. 1976. *Le Sang des masques*. Paris: Laffont.

———. 1977. *Noces sacrées*. Paris: Présence africaine.

CAMARA, LAYE. See Laye, Camara.

DIAGNE, AHMADOU MAPATÉ. 1920. *Les Trois volontés de Malic*. Paris: Larose.

DIALLO, BAKARY. 1926. *Force-bonté*. Paris: F. Reider.

DIOP, BIRAGO. 1947. *Les contes d'Amadou Koumba*. Paris: Présence africaine.

———. 1958. *Les nouveaux contes d'Amadou Koumba*. Paris: Présence africaine.

———. 1963. *Conte et lavanes*. Paris: Présence africaine.

FALL, AMINATA SOW. 1976. *Le Revenant*. Dakar: Nouvelles éditions africaines.

———. 1979. *La Grève des bàttus*. Dakar: Nouvelles éditions africaines.

———. 1987. *L'Ex-père de la nation*. Paris: L'Harmattan.

FARAH, NURUDDIN. 1970. *From a Crooked Rib*. London: Heinemann.

———. 1976. *A Naked Needle*. London: Heinemann.

———. 1980. *Sweet and Sour Milk*. London: Heinemann.

———. 1981. *Sardines*. London: Heinemann.

———. 1983. *Close Sesame*. London: Allison & Busby.

———. 1986. *Maps*. London: Pan Books.

FODÉBA, KEITA. 1950. *Poèmes africaines*. Paris: P. Seghers.

GOLOGO, MAMADOU. 1963. *Le Rescapé de l'ethylos*. Paris: Présence africaine.

HARRIES, LYNDON. 1962. *Swahili Poetry*. London: Oxford University Press.

KA, ABDOU ANTA. 1972. *Théâtre*. Paris: Présence africaine.

———. 1975. *Mal*. Dakar: Nouvelles éditions africaine.

KANE, CHEIKH HAMIDOU. 1961. *L'Aventure ambiguë*. Paris: Julliard.

KANE, MOHAMDOU. 1982. *Roman africain et tradition*. Dakar: Nouvelles éditions africaines.

KNAPPERT, JAN. 1964. *Four Swahili Epics*. Leiden: Brill.

———. 1970. *Myths and Legends of the Swahili*. Nairobi: Heinemann.

———. 1971. *Swahili Islamic Poetry*. Leiden: Brill.

———. 1983. *Epic Poetry in Swahili and Other African Languages*. Leiden: Brill.

———. 1985. *Islamic Legends: Histories of the Heroes, Saints and Prophets of Islam*. Leiden: Brill.

KOUROUMA, AHMADOU. 1968. *Les Soleils des independances*. Paris: Le Seuil.

———. 1988. Monnè, outrages, et défis. Paris: Le Seuil.

LAYE, CAMARA. 1953. *L'Enfant Noir*. Paris: Plon.

———. 1954. *Le Regard du Roi*. Paris: Plon.

———. 1966. *Dramouss*. Paris: Plon.

———. 1978. *Le Maître de la parole: Kouma lafolo Kouma*. Paris: Plon.

MOHAMED, MWINYIHATIBU. 1977. *Malenga wa Mrima*. Dar es Salaam: Oxford University Press.

NASIR, SAYYID ABDALLA BINALI. 1977. *Al-Inkishafi*. Tr. and annotated by James de Vere Allen. Nairobi: African Literature Bureau.

NDAO, CHEIK ALIOU. 1962. *Kairée*. Grenoble: Imprimerie Eymond.

———. 1972. *Buurr Tillen, roi de la Medina*. Paris: Présence africaine.

———. 1983a. *Excellence, vos épouses!* Dakar: Nouvelles éditions africaines.

———. 1983b. *Du Sang pour un trone, ou, Goute ndiouli un dimanche*. Paris: L'Harmattan.

OUOLOGUEM, YAMBO. 1968. *Le Devoir de violence*. Paris: Le Seuil.

OUSMANE, SEMBÈNE. See Sembène, Ousmane.

ROBERT, SHAABAN. 1949. *Maisha Yangu*. London: Nelson.

———. 1951. *Kusadikika: Nchi iliyo angani*. London: Nelson.

———. 1967a. *Masomo yenye adili*. London: Nelson.

———. 1967b. *Utenzi wa Vita vya Uhuru, 1939–1945*. Nairobi: Oxford University Press.

———. 1968a. *Kielezo che fasili*. London: Nelson.

———. 1968b. *Siku ya watenzi wote*. London: Nelson.

———. 1969. *Koja la lugha*. Nairobi: Oxford University Press.

SADJI, ABDOULAYE. 1958. *Maimouna*. Paris: Presence africaine.

———. 1965. *Nini, mulatresse du Senegal*. Paris: Presence africaine.

SALIH, TAYEB. 1968. *The Wedding of Zein, and Other Stories*. Trans. Denys Johnson-Davies. London: Heinemann.

———. 1969. *Season of Migration to the North*. Trans. Denys Johnson-Davies. London: Heinemann.

SAMB, AMAR. 1973. *Matraqué par le destin, ou la vie d'un talibé*. Dakar: Nouvelles éditions africains.

SEMBÈNE OUSMANE. 1957. *O Pays, Mon beau peuple*. Paris: Le Livre contemporain-Amiot Dumont.

———. 1960. *Les bouts de bois de Dieu*. Paris: Le Livre contemporain.

———. 1962. *Voltaïque*. Paris: Présence africaine.

———. 1963. *Borom Sarret*. (Film).

―――. 1965a. *L'Harmattan*. Paris: Présence africaine.
―――. 1965b. *Vehi Ciosane, ou Blanche-Genèse suivi du Mandat*. Paris: Présence africaine.
―――. 1968. *Mandabi*. (Film).
―――. 1970. *Tauw*. (Film).
―――. 1971. *Emitaï*. (Film).
―――. 1973. *Xala*. Paris: Présence africaine. (Film adaptation 1974).
―――. 1977. *Ceddo*. (Film).
―――. 1981. *Le Dernier de l'empire. Roman sénégalais*. Paris: L'Harmattan.
Sèye, Ibrahima. 1983. *Un Trou dans le miroir*. Dakar: Nouvelles éditions africaines.
Sheikh, Amina Abubakar, and Ahmed Sheikh Nabhany, eds. 1972. *Utendi wa Mwana Kupona na Utendi wa Ngamia na Paa*. (Sanaa ya Utongo, I). Nairobi: Heinemann.
Socé, Ousmane. 1937. *Karim*. Paris: Nouvelles éditions latines.
Sow, Alfa Ibrahim, ed. 1966. *La Femme, la vache, la foi, ecrivains et poètes du Fouta-Djalon*. Paris: Julliard.
―――. ed. 1971. *Le Filon du bonheur éternal*, by Tierno Mouhammadou-Samba Mombeya. Paris: A. Colin.
Soyinka, Wole. 1964. *The Swamp Dwellers*. Oxford: Oxford University Press.
―――. 1965. *The Interpreters*. London: A. Deutsch.
―――. 1973. *A Season of Anomy*. London: Rex Collins Ltd.
Tahir, Ibrahim. 1984. *The Last Imam*. London: Routledge and Kegan Paul.
Traora, Mahama. 1974. *Njangaan*. (Film).

B. Works of Literary and Film Criticism

Allen, J. W. T. 1971. *Tendi*. London: Heinemann.
Battestini, Simon P. K. 1986. "Muslim Influences on West African Literature and Culture." *Journal of Muslim Minority Affairs* 7, 2 (July).
Boyd-Buggs, Debra. 1986. "Baraka: Maraboutism and Marabutage in the Francophone Senegalese Novel." Ph.D. thesis, Ohio State University, *Dissertation Abstracts* 47:899A.
Gerard, Albert. 1981. *African Language Literatures: An Introduction to the Literary History of Sub-Saharan Africa*. Harlow, Essex, U.K.: Longman.
―――. ed. 1986. *European-language Writing in Sub-Sarahan Africa*. Budapest: Akademaiai Kiado.
Goody, Jack, ed. 1968. *Literacy in Traditional Societies*. Cambridge: Cambridge University Press.
Harrow, Kenneth W. 1983. "A Sufi Interpretation of *Le Regard du roi*." *Research in African Literatures*, 14, 2.
―――. "The Power and the Word: *L'Aventure ambiguë* and *The wedding of Zein*." African Studies Review.
Hiskett, Mervyn. 1975. *A History of Hausa Islamic Verse*. London: School of Oriental and African Studies. University of London.
Johnson, John W. 1974. *Heelloy, Heelleellooy: The Development of the Genre Heello in Modern Somali Poetry*. Bloomington, Indiana: Indiana University Press.

JOHNSON, LEMUEL. 1980. "Crescent and Consciousness: Islamic Orthodoxies and the West African Novel." *Research in African Literatures II*, 1 (Spring).

KNAPPERT, JAN. 1967. *Traditional Swahili Poetry: An Investigation into the Concepts of East African Islam as Reflected in the Utenzi Literature.* Leiden: Brill.

———. 1979. *Four Centuries of Swahili Verse: A Literary History and Anthology.* London: Heinemann.

KRITZECK, JAMES. 1970. *Modern Islamic Literature.* New York: New American Library.

LAURENCE, MARGARET. 1964. *A Tree for Poverty.* Nairobi: Eagle Press.

MADUKUIKE, IHECHUKWU. 1983. *The Senegalese Novel: A Sociological Study of the Impact of the Politics of Assimilation.* Washington, D.C.: Three Continents Press.

PFAFF, FRANÇOISE. 1984. *The Cinema of Sembene Ousmane.* Westport, CT: Greenwood Press.

SAMATAR, SAID S. 1982. *Oral Poetry and Somali Nationalism.* London: Cambridge University Press.

SAMB, AMAR. 1972. *Essai sur la contribution du Sénégal à la littérature d'expression arabe.* Dakar: IFAN.

SHARIFF, IBRAHIM NOOR. 1988. *Tungo Zetu.* Trenton, NJ: The Red Sea Press.

SOYINKA, WOLE. 1976. *Myth, Literature and the African World.* Cambridge: Cambridge University Press.

C. Works of History, Religion, Culture, and Society

ABUN-NASR, JAMIL. 1965. *The Tijaniyya: A Sufi Order in the Modern World.* Oxford: Oxford University Press.

BÂ, AMADOU HAMPÂTÉ. 1972. *Aspects de la civilisation africaine.* Paris: Présence africaine.

———. 1980. *Vie et enseignement de Tierno Bokar: Le Sage de Bandiagara.* Paris: Editions du Seuil.

BÂ, AMADOU HAMPÂTÉ, and J. DAGET. 1962. *L'Empire peul du Macina.* Paris: Mouton.

BATTUTA, IBN. 1929. *Travels in Asia and Africa, 1325–1354.* Tr. and select. H. A. R. Gibb. London: Routledge & Sons.

BLYDEN, EDWARD D. 1967. *Christianity, Islam and the Negro Race.* (orig. 1887). Edinburgh: Edinburgh University Press.

BRAVMANN, RENÉ A. 1983. *African Islam.* Washington, D.C.: The Smithsonian Institution Press, and London: Ethnographics Ltd.

BRENNER, LOUIS. 1984. *West African Sufi: The Religious Heritage and Spiritual Search of Cerno Bokar Saalig Taal.* Berkeley: University of California Press.

CARDAIRE, MARCEL. 1954. *L'Islam et le terroir africain.* Bamako: IFAN.

CHAILLEY, MARCEL, et. al. 1962. *Notes et études sur l'islam en Afrique noire.* (Centre de Hautes Etudes Administratives sur l'Afrique et l'Asie Modèrne.) Paris: J. Peyronnet.

CHEVALIER, JEAN. 1984. *Le Soufisme.* Paris: Presses universitaires de France.

CLARKE, PETER. 1982. *West Africa and Islam.* London: E. Arnold.

COULON, CHRISTIAN. 1981a. *Le Marabout et le Prince: Islam et pouvoir au Sénégal.* Paris: A. Pedone.

———. 1981b. *Les Musulmans et le pouvoir en Afrique noire.* Paris: Karthala.

CRUISE O'BRIEN, DONAL. 1971. *The Mourides of Senegal*. Oxford: Clarendon Press.

CRUISE O'BRIEN, DONAL, and CHRISTIAN COULON. 1989. *Charisma and Brotherhood in African Islam*. Oxford: Clarendon Press.

CUOQ, JOSEPH. 1975. *Les Musulmans en Afrique*. Paris: Maisonneuve et Larose.

DEPONT, OCTAVE. 1987. *Les Confréries réligieuses musulmanes*. Paris: J. Maisonneuve.

DIA, MAMADOU. 1975. *Islam, sociétés africaines et cultures industrielles*. Dakar: Nouvelles éditions africaines.

———. 1980. *Islam et civilisations négroafricaines*. Dakar: Les Nouvelles éditions africaines.

———. 1980. *Essais sur l'Islam, II. Socio-anthropologie de l'Islam*. Dakar: Nouvelles editions africaines.

DUMONT, FERNAND. 1975. *La Pensée réligieuse de Amadou Bamba*. Dakar: Nouvelles éditions africaines.

ES-SA'DI, ABDERRAHMAN BEN ABDALLAH BEN 'IMRAN BEN 'AMIR. 1964. *Tarikh es-Soudan*. Trans. O. Houdas. Paris: Ecole des Langues orientales vivantes, 1898–1900. 2nd. edition. Paris: Adrien Maisonneuve.

FISHER, HUMPHREY. 1970. "The Western and Central Sudan." In *The Cambridge History of Islam, II*, P. M. Holt, et al., eds. Cambridge: Cambridge University Press.

FISHER, HUMPHREY J., and NEHEMIA LEVTZION, eds. 1986. *Rural and Urban Islam in West Africa*. Boulder, Colorado: Lynne Rienner.

FROELICH, JEAN-CLAUDE. 1962. *Les Musulmans d'Afrique noire*. Paris: L'Orante.

GEERTZ, CLIFFORD. 1968. *Islam Observed*. Chicago: University of Chicago Press.

GOUILLY, ALPHONSE. 1952. *L'Islam dans L'Afrique occidentale francaise*. Paris: Larose.

HALE, THOMAS. 1990. *Scribe, Griot, and Novelist: Narrative Interpreters of the Songhay Empire. Followed by The Epic of Askia Mohammed Recounted by Nouhou Malio*. Gainesville, Fla.: University of Florida Press.

HALL, MARJORIE, and BAKHITA AMIN ISMAIL. 1981. *Sisters under the Sun: The Story of Sudanese Women*. London: Longman.

HARRISON, CHRISTOPHER. 1988. *France and Islam in West Africa, 1860–1960*. Cambridge: Cambridge University Press.

HISKETT, MERVYN. 1984. *The Development of Islam in West Africa*. London: Longman.

HOLT, P. M., ANN H. S. LAMBTON, and BERNARD LEWIS, eds. 1977. *The Cambridge History of Islam*. Vol 2a: "The Indian sub-Continent, Southeast Asia, Africa and the Muslim West."; vol. 2b: "Islamic Society and Civilization." Cambridge: Cambridge University Press.

HOPKINS, J. F. P., and NEHEMIA LEVTZION, eds. 1981. *Corpus of Early Arabic Sources for West African History*. Trans. J. F. P. Hopkins. Cambridge: Cambridge University Press.

The Islamic Regime of Fuuta Tooro: An Anthology of Oral Tradition. Trans. Moustapha Kane and David Robinson. East Lansing, Mich.: African Studies Center, Michigan State University.

KATI, MAHMOUD. 1964. *Tarikh el-Fettach*. Trans. O. Houdas and M. Delafosse. Paris: Adrien-Maisonneuve.

KRITZECK, JAMES, and WILLIAM H. LEWIS, eds. 1969. *Islam in Africa.* New York: Van Nostrand Reinhold.

LEVTZION, NEHEMIA. 1968. *Muslims and Chiefs in West Africa: A Study of Islam in the Middle Volta Basin.* Oxford: Clarendon.

———. 1973. *Ancient Ghana and Mali.* London: Methuen.

LEWIS, I. M., ed. 1966. *Islam in Tropical Africa.* London: Oxford University Press.

LINGS, MARTIN. 1977. *What is Sufism?* Berkeley: University of California Press.

MARTY, PAUL. 1915–1926. *Etudes sur l'Islam en A.O.F.* 14 vols. Paris: Leroux.

MBACKE, MAME SECK. 1983. *Le Froid et le piment.* Dakar: Nouvelles éditions africaines.

MERNESSI, FATIMA. 1987. *Beyond the Veil.* Bloomington: Indiana University Press.

MONTEIL, VINCENT. 1966. *Esquisses sénégalaises: Walo, Kayor, Dyolof, Mourides, un visionnaire.* Dakar: IFAN.

———. 1980. *L'Islam noir: Une Réligion à conquête de l'Afrique.* Paris: Editions du Seuil.

MOREAU, RENÉ LUC. 1982. *Africains musulmans.* Paris: Présence africaine.

NICOLAS, GUY. 1981. *Dynamique de l'Islam au sud du Sahara.* Paris: Publications orientalistes de France.

PERSON, YVES. 1968–75. *Samori, une révolution dyula.* 3 vols. Dakar: IFAN.

"La Question islamique en Afrique noire." 1981. *Politique africaine* 4 (November). Paris: Karthala.

ROBINSON, DAVID. 1975. *Chiefs and Clerics: Abdul Bokar Kan and Futa Toro, 1853–1891.* Oxford: Clarendon.

———. 1985. *The Holy War of Umar Tal: The Western Sudan in the Mid-Nineteenth Century.* Oxford: Clarendon.

RODINSON, MAXIME. 1972. *Marxisme et monde musulman.* Paris: Editions du Seuil.

———. 1981. *La Fascination de l'Islam.* Paris: Maspéro.

SAID, EDWARD. 1979. *Orientalism.* New York: Vintage.

SCHIMMEL, ANNEMARIE. 1975. *Mystical Dimensions of Islam.* Chapel Hill, N.C.: University of North Carolina Press.

STODDART, WILLIAM. 1982. *Sufism: The Mystical Doctrines and Methods of Islam.* Northamptonshire, England: The Antiquarian Press.

STROBEL, MARGARET. 1979. *Moslem Women in Mombasa, 1890–1975.* New Haven: Yale University Press.

SY, CHEIKH TIDIANE. 1969. *La confrérie sénégalese des Mourides.* Paris: Présence africaine.

THIAM, AWA. 1978. *La Parole aux négresses.* Paris: Denoël.

TRIMINGHAM, J. SPENCER. 1949. *Islam in the Sudan.* London: Oxford University Press.

———. 1959. *Islam in West Africa.* London: Oxford University Press.

———. 1964. *Islam in East Africa.* London: Oxford University Press.

———. 1971. *The Sufi Orders in Islam.* London: Oxford University Press.

———. 1980. *The Influence of Islam upon Africa.* London: Longman.

Index

▼▼▼▼▼▼

Aaté yalla, 179

'Abd Allah Hasan, Muhammed, 35

'Abdallahi, Khalifa, 35

Abdulrahman, Sheikh, 81

Abunuwas (Ar. Abu-Nawas), 39

Addiya, 211

Addou, Mohamed, 98

African Islam (Bravmann), 233

African Language Literatures (Gérard), x

Al-Ahdal, Sayyid 'Umar bin Amin, 51

Ahmad, Muhammad, 35

Ahmadis, 306

Ahmed, Ali Jimale, 4, 17

Ajami, 151

Ake, the Years of Childhood (Soyinka), 189

Alexander, 24

Alienation, syncretism and, 12

Alkali, Zaynab, 7

Allah. *See also* God(s)
  in Somali poetry, 85, 86
  will of, 179

Allen, J. W. T., 69–70

Almamate, 111

Almamy Abdul Kader, 111

Almsgiving
  in Fulani tales of initiation, 158–59
  in Islamic culture, 301
  in Senegalese fiction, 170–71, 211

Alodia, 25

Amadu, Seku, 113

Ancestor figure, oral literature and, 143

Animal characters, as metaphors, in Wolof satirical oral narratives, 173–74

Animal fables, Swahili, 38–39

Antar ibn Shaddad, 39

Anti-Mukhlit literature, 16

Approval, in "Utendi wa Mwana Kupona," 61–62, 66

Arabo-Moors, in work of Diop, 220–26

Armah, Ayi Kwei, 13, 15, 183, 187–88, 199, 239, 240, 242, 300

Arnaud, Robert, 121–22

Art of Reciting the Qur'an, The, 83

Asceticism, in Fulani tales of initiation, 157

Asfar, Denise, 10, 11

Asfar, Gabriel, 10, 11

Askia Mohammed, 11, 132, 133–39

Asmo, 84

Aspects de la civilisation africaine (Bâ), 141, 142

Athumani, Ali wa, 43

Aventure ambiguë, L' (Kane), 3, 4, 6, 7, 9, 12, 119, 124, 169–71, 177, 181, 187, 239, 241, 247–52
  Islamic world-view in, 302
  marabouts in, 285–93
  princely versus spiritual power in, 285–94
  Senegalese history reflected in, 286–87
  Sufi components of, 261, 285–96
  Sufi guide in, 287

Axum, 25

Ayyim, marriage and, 96

Bâ, Amadou Hampâté, 11, 114, 125, 141–50, 308

Bâ, Mariama, 13

Baba, Ahmed, 110

Badian, Seydou, 13

Al-Bahaymi, Mohammad Bin Salim, 94

Al-Bakry, Rukiya binti Fadhil, 52

Balwo poetry, 83

Bamba, Cheikh Amadou, 16, 167, 201–8, 211–14, 289, 293

Bambara oral literature, 141
  ancestor figure and, 143
  gods in, 146–47
  supreme deity in, 148

Baqt, 27

Baraka, 18, 161, 208, 211

Barzakh (Ka), 167

Battestini, Simon, 147, 303

Battuta, Ibn, 8–9, 30, 109, 188–89

Baury, Fumo Liyoongo wa (al-Baury), 37–38, 53

Bayan, 115

Al-Bekkay, Ahmed, 115

Ber, Sonni Ali, 133–34

"Biche et les deux chasseurs, La" (Diop), 4

Biersteker, Ann, 17

Birago Diop (Kane), 215

Al-Bistāmî, Abu Yazî, 154

Black Africa, Islam in, 187–91, 215, 220

Blair, Dorothy, 306

Blessing, in "Utendi wa Mwana Kupona," 60–62

Blyden, Edward W., 300

Bokar, Tierno, 114, 144, 153, 160

Borom Sarret (Sembène), 178, 179–80

Bound to Violence (Ouologuem), 107, 242

Bourgeacq, Jacques, 227

Bouts de bois de Dieu, Les (Sembéne), 178, 187, 195, 198, 251–52

Boyd-Buggs, Debra, 4, 303

Bravmann, René A., 233, 254

Brenner, Louis, 111, 160

Al-Bukhari, Abu Abdallah Muhammad Ibn Ismail, 95

Bulhan, Hussein A., 85

Bulxan, Qamaan, 17

Burton, Richard, 299, 307

Al-Busary, Muhammad b. Said, 53

Calendar, coexistence of African rituals and Islam, 229–31

Caliph, British conquest of Central Sudan and, 117

"Captive Intelligentsia of Somalia, The," 85

Casril jahiliya, 86

Ceddo (Sembène), 3, 14, 107, 125, 178, 179, 181–83, 252
  attack on Islam in, 196–99
  image of Islam portrayed in, 182

Chachada, 17

Chain of initiation, 161

Cham, Mbye B., 13–14, 300, 303

Change
  fear of, 5, 7
  importance of, 23

Chantefable, 243–45

Chen, John M., 245, 246

Chevalier, Jean, 154

Christianity
  adoption of, in East Africa, 25
  Muslim conquest and, 27

Cir-gaduud, 84

Colonialism
  East African history and, 24
  hostility to traditional religion, 149–51
  maxzen complex and, 7
  of West Africa,
    by France, 117–22
    by Great Britain, 117, 123–24

Conakry, 120

Contes et lavanes (Diop), 116, 118, 219

Continuity, importance of in Islamic cultural tradition, 23

Control, individual's need for, 5

Cora, 244

Corruption, negative depiction of Islam and, 14

Coulon, Christian, 7, 286

Cruise O'Brien, Donal, 213

Curses, casting, in Somali society, 84

Cyrenaica, 26

Daara, 207, 209, 210

Dakar, Service of Muslim Affairs, 121–22

Dale, Rev. Godfrey, 40

Dar al-Harb, 9

Dar al-Islam, 9, 108, 115, 116
  in 18th and 19th centuries,

110–17

Dark Child (Laye). See *Enfant noir, L'* (Laye)

Deeqsi, Cabdi, 83

Delafosse, 189

Dernier de l'empire, Le (Sembène), 196

Destruction of Black Civilisation, The (William), 183

Devoir de violence, Le (Ouologuem), 13, 183, 187, 188, 301

Dhikr, 6, 145, 273, 278, 284, 292, 295

Dia, Mamadou, 15, 18

Diakhou, Ma Bâ, 202

Diop, Birago, 4, 6, 11, 174, 215–26, 286

Diop, Cheikh Anta, 16

Discipline, importance of, 101

Divine revelation, in tales of initiation, 145

Divine spirit, in tales of initiation, 145

Divorce, in Swahili poety, 47–49

Diwani ya Muyaka bin Haji al-Ghassaniy, 41

Djinn, 136

Dramouss (Laye), 261

Dream of Africa, A [*Dramouss*] (Laye), 242–46, 252–57

Dundari, 146, 148

Dura mandhuma, 51

East Africa, 10, 21–102
  Christianity in, 25
  city-state organization, 29–30
  early Islamic centuries (600–1500), 26–30
  historical context for study of Islam in, 23–36
  historical literature about, 23–24
  impressions of by European visitors of 16th century, 29
  incursions into by Ottoman Turks, 30–31
  incursions into by Portuguese, 31–33
  introduction of Islam in, 24–26
  later Islamic centuries (1500–1900), 30–35

new Islamic leadership in 17th and 18th centuries, 32
  new Islamic vision in, 36
  literature in, influences on, 16
  Somali literature, 79–87
  Sudanese literature, 91–102
  Swahili literature, 37–55, 59–74
  twentieth century, 35–36

Eclat de la grande étoile suivi du bain rituel, L' (Bâ), 141, 144

Education
  French, 120–21
  Koranic schools, 120–21, 221–22
  in *madrasas*, 40, 41–42
  marabouts and, 217–19
  in *medersas*, 121
  Western, 40, 41

Emitaï (Sembène), 179, 181

Empire du Macia (Bâ), 114

Empire peul du Macina, L' (Bâ), 141

Enfant noir, L' (Laye), 12, 107, 227–34, 241–42, 243, 244

Enlightenment, quest for, in *Le Regard du roi*, 275–78

Esoterism, in Fulani tales of initiation, 159–60

Ethical behavior, *maxzen* complex and, 6

Ethiopia
  containment of Islamic community in, 36
  early Islamic centuries in, 28
  Ottoman incursions into, 31–32
  resistance to conquest by, 34–35

European-language African writing, Orientalism in, 299–307

Evil
  Islam portrayed as, 14–15
  struggle against, in Islam, 13–14
  women and, 94, 95

Fall, Aminata Sow. See Sow-Fall, Aminata

Fall, Cheikh Ibra, 202, 213

Fana, 280, 284, 295, 296

Faqih, 7, 18

Faqr, 249

Farah, Nurrudin, 12, 231

"Fari l'anesse" (Diop), 221–22

Fate, written language and, 146

Fatemi, Nasrolla S., 247
Federation of French West Africa, 118
Feminisim, 4
Film, for conveying Islam as an impediment, in Senegal, 164, 175–78
Fisher, Humphrey, 109
Fodio, Usman dan, 15, 16, 109, 113
Foucault, Michel, 4, 300
France, conquest of North and West Africa by, 117–22
French education, Koranic education and, 120–21
French West Africa, 118–22
Froelich, J. C., 228
Froid et le piment, Le (Mbacké), 211–13
Fulani oral literature, 11, 141
  ancestor figure and, 143
  communication with God in, 148
  janti, 151–52
  plurality of gods in, 146
  taalol, 151
  search for self-knowledge and self-discipline in, 154
  tales of initiation, 144, 147, 153, 154
  Tijaniyya Sufis and, 144–46
Fulani tales of initiation
  almsgiving in, 158–59
  asceticism in, 157
  gods in, 146–47
  numerology in, 160
  pilgrimage in, 158
  predestination in, 158
  self-discipline in, 158
Fulani tradition, gods, 146–47
Fulani written literature, *janti*, 151
Fulbe reform movements, 111–15
Futa Jalon, 120
  jihad and, 111
Futa Toro, 119, 120
  reform movement of, 111–13

Gabay poetry, 84
Gabyow, Sheikh Ahmed, 87
Geedka haqqa iyo hukunka, 79
Geedka xeerka, 79
Geertz, Clifford, 5–7

Gérard, Albert, x, 15, 16, 306
Ghana, 124
Ghattas-Soliman, Sonia, 5, 6
al-Ghazali, Bu Hamid, 99, 101, 102
God(s)
  Allah, 85, 86, 181
  plurality of, 146–47
  quest for, in *Le Regard du roi*, 277–78
  single supreme, 146–49
Goody, Jack, 82
Gouverneurs de la rose (Roumain), 229
Grands marabouts, 179–81
Great Britain
  colonialism by, 117, 123–24
  conquest of Central Sudan by, 117
Greece, ancient, relations with Africa by, 24–26
Grève des bàttu, La (Sow-Fall), 170–71, 301
Griots
  integration with Islam, 243–45
  as masters of the word, 4
  Songhay, 134–35, 139
Grisgris, 231
Gueno, 146, 147, 159
Guinea, 120, 232
"Gyinna-Gyinna: Making the Djinn Manifest" (Bravmann), 254

Haabiil, Ali Jaamac', 87
Hadiths, Sudanese legal system and, 91
Haj, 158
Haji Hussein, Mohamed, 81
Al-Hajj Umar, 114–15, 289, 291
Al-Hajj, 'Umar ibn Abi Bakr al-Salghawi, 9, 303, 306
Hale, Thomas, 10, 303
Hamdullahi, 113–14
Hamziya poetry, 49, 53
Haqiqa, Sufism and, 158
Harakoy Dikko, 136
Harries, Lyndon, 42, 51, 70
Harrow, Kenneth, 159, 162, 236, 303, 309
Hassan, Sheikh Mohammed Abdulle, 81, 87
Hassan Ibn Tabit, 84–85
Heelooy, 82

Heerbeegti, 79
Hegira, 9
Hellenistic commerical settlements,
    in East Africa, 25–26
"Héritage, L'" (Diop), 11
Hiskett, Mervyn, 304, 307
Historical literature
    distortion in, 107–9
    East African, 23–24
    usefulness of, 109
    West African, 107–25
Hodgkin, Thomas, 303
Holeu, 136
Holy men   .
    in 17th and 18th century East
        Africa, 32–33
    siyyid and *zawiya* complexes and,
        6
Hountondji, Paulin, 305
Hubbu movement, 110
Al-Hujwiri, 249, 252
Hunwick, John O., 133–34

Idarus bin 'Uthman, 53
Identity-building, 5
Ihya al-sunna wa ikhmad al-bid'a
    (Fodio), 16
Imam, in *The Wedding of Zein*,
    279–82, 294–95
Imamate, 111
Influence of Islam upon Africa
    (Trimingham), 228
Initiation, chain of, 161
Initiation, tales of
    communication between God and
        man in, 148
    compatability with Islam, 147
    influence of Islam on, 152–61
    janti, 151–52
    Kaïdara, 151–61
    obedience to master's word in, 57
    as oral literature, 144–45
    performance of by storyteller, 152
    search for self-knowledge and
        self-discipline in, 154
    single supreme diety and, 147–48
    socialization and, 156
    Sufis and, 156–61
Inkishafi poetry, 49, 51–52, 53
Interpreters, The (Soyinka), 7

Irony, in "Utendi wa Mwana
    Kupona", 60, 68–71, 73
Islam
    African conversion to, 7–8, 9,
        228
    African and non-African
        treatment of, 301
    attitudes about, variety of, 3, 13,
        163–64, 183–84, 304
    in Black Africa, 187–90, 215, 220
    in *Ceddo*, 186, 196–99
    change and, 5, 7, 23
    compatibility with traditional
        religion, 142, 145–50, 152
    continuity of, with African
        culture, 10
    criticism of, 14–15, 219–26,
        300–302
        in *Ceddo*, 196–99
        by Diop, 219–26
        misreading, 301–2
        by Sembène, 178–83
    distortion of principles of,
        in *Njangaan*, 176–77
        in work of Sembène, 178
    in East Africa,
        early centuries (600–1500),
            26–30
        historical context for study of,
            23–36
        later centuries (1500–1900),
            30–35
        17th and 18th centuries, 32
        20th century, 35–36
    French colonial rule and spread of,
        122
    ideal of, 145
    in literature, 3–19
        criticism of, 14–15, 219–26,
            300–302
        as negative force, 14, 107
        as positive force, 13–14, 107
        promotion of, 15, 164–71, 304
    militant, 111, 113
    modes of perception, 248
    Orientalist view of, 3, 9
    in Senegal, 163–84
        attitudes toward, in literature,
            13

criticizing through film, 164, 175–78
in oral literature, 164, 172–75
promoting through fiction, 164–71
promoting through poetry, 164–71
variety of viewpoints about, 163–64, 183–84
sexual behavior and, 93
slave trade and, 33–34
Somali society and, 80
in Sudan, 91
tales of initiation and, 152–61
in Swahili literature, 37–55
three forms of, 5–7
traditional African culture and, 227–34, 244–46
traditional African religions and, 142, 145–50, 152
traditional African rituals and, 147–49, 229–33
in West Africa,
daily life and, 216–19
18th and 19th centuries, 110–17
historical literature and, 107–25
oral literature and, 141–50
three-level formula for, 109–110
in twentieth century, 117–25
Islamic belief system, Songhay belief system and, 131–39
Islamic brotherhoods, in 17th and 18th century East Africa, 32–33
Islamic holy men, in 17th and 18th century East Africa, 32–33
Islamicists, 108–9
Islamic orthodoxies, West African novel and, 239–57
Islamic sub-cultures
importance of, 123, 124–25
mystical, 125
syncretic, 125
theocratic, 124–25
Islamic virtue, 13–14
Islam noir, 122
Istihan, 8
Istiqbah, 8
Ivory Coast, 120

Iyasu, Lij, 36

Ja'afar b. Hasan al-Barzanji, 52
Jahaliya, 9
Jahn, Janheinz, x
Janti, 151–52
Jenitongo, Adamu, 138
Jihad, 13–14, 109
emergence of *dar al-Islam* and, 111
in Fulani tales of initiation, 154, 157
imperial, 114
of purification, 157
revolutionary, 114
undermining of, 115–16
Jinn, 85, 258–59
Johnson, John, 82
Johnson, Lemuel, 10, 12, 196
Journeys, tales of initiation as, 149
"Jugement, Un" (Diop), 215, 216–17
Juhe, Cerno Mamadu, 110

Ka, Moussa, 16, 167
Al-Kabir, Sidiyya, 110, 111
Kaïdara
Islam and, 146
narrative of, 151–61
Kaïdara (Bâ), 11, 141, 144, 153–61
Kan, Cerno Brahim, 110
Kane, Cheikh Hamidou, 4, 6, 7, 8, 113, 168–71, 177, 181, 187, 239–42, 302
Sufism and, 261, 285–96
Kane, Mohamadou, 8, 11–12, 13, 215
al-Kanemi, 113
Karim (Socé), 13, 205
Kashf al-Mahjub (Al-Hujwiri), 249–50, 252
Khadrou, 154–55
Khalifa, 114
"Khary-Gaye" (Diop), 216
Kheri, in "Utendi wa Mwana Kupona", 62–63, 66
Kirkup, James, 234, 247
Knappert, Jan, 42
Knowledge, quest for, 159–61
Konianké, integration with Islam, 243–45

Koranic education, 123, 217–18
    French education and, 120–21
Koumen (Bâ), 141, 147
Kourouma, Ahmadou, 5

Laayterre Koodal (Bâ), 161
Lang, George, 8
Language, as messenger between
    God and man, 148
Last Imam, The (Tahir), 7
Lat Dior Diop, 164, 202
Laye, Camara, 6, 11, 12, 13, 14,
    107, 125, 159, 227–34, 240,
    241–43, 244, 252–57
    Sufism and, 261, 262–78, 293–96
Levtzion, Nehemia, 124
Lewis, I. M., 261
Lings, Martin, 156, 248, 278–79,
    282
Literacy, memorization and, 81
Love, quest for, in *Le Regard du roi*,
    276–77

Maa Ngala, 146, 147
Madrasas, 40, 41–42
Ma dyma burati (Ka), 167
Al-Maghili, 133–34
Al-Ma'mun, Caliph, 84
Maître, 8–9
Maktoub, 146
    in Fulani tales of initiation, 158
Makuria, 25, 27–28
Makward, Edris, 6, 14
Male–female relationship, power
    and, 4
Malenga wa Mrima, 41
Malenga wa Mvita, 41
Mali, 11, 91
    European colonialism and,
    119–20
    oral literature, 141–42
"Maman Caiman" (Diop), 225
Mamar Kassaye, 134
"Mame Touba" (Mbacké), 211
Mandabi (Sembène), 181
Mandat, Le (Sembène), 192
Mansabu, Mwinyi (Sayyid Abu-
    Bakr b. Abd al-Rahman), 52
Maps (Farah), 12
Marabout et le prince, Le (Coulon),

286
Marabouts
    authority over spoken word by, 4
    colonialism and, 7
    criticism of, in work of Diop,
    223–25
    education and, 217–19
    in *L'Aventure ambigue*, 285–93
    Mouride, 202–11, 213
    in Senegalese fiction, 201–11,
    213, 303
    spiritual leadership of, 286–87,
    289
Ma'rifa, 156, 161, 279
Marriage
    importance of, 96–97
    sexual desire and, 96–97
Marty, Paul, 108–9, 122
Masa Dembali, 146, 149
Masina, Umarian conquest of, 115
Masomo Yenye Adili, 41
*Matraqué par de destin, ou la vie d'un
    talibé* (Samb), 171, 202–4,
    207–8
Mauritania, 215, 217, 210, 224
Mawlid Barzanji, 52
Al-Mawsili, Ishaq Ibrahim, 84
Maxzen complex, 6–7
    corruption and, 14
    literature critical of Islam and, 15
Mazrui, Ali, 16, 43
Mbacké, Amadou Bamba, 201–2
Mbacké, Mame Seck, 204, 211–13
Mecca, pilgrimage to, 121, 208–9
Medersas, 121
Memorization
    literacy and, 81
    of Qur'an, in Somali society,
    79–80
Men, supremacy of, 94–95
Mernessi, Fatima, 4–5, 7, 10
Meroe, 25
Metaphor, in Utendi wa Mwana
    Kupona, 71–72
Mgumi, Bwana Zahidi, 43
Militant Islam, 111, 113
Milson, Menahem, 153
Mithaq, marriage ad, 96
Monarch, sacred, *maxzen* complex

and, 6
Monogamy, vs. polygamy, 98
Monteil, Vincent, 168
Moors, in work of Diop, 219–22
Moreau, René Luc, 168
Moslem World, The, 40
Mourides (Mouridiyya), 201–14
Mouridism
  Cheikh Amadou Bamba and,
    202–3
  criticism of, 204–14
  defined, 201–2
  marabouts, 201–11, 213
  political power and, 208
  principles of, 209
  in Senegalese fiction, 4, 201–14
  spiritual values and, 211–14
  submissiveness and, 205–11
  work ethic, 202, 205, 209, 210
Mourid poetry, 16
Mudimbe, V. Y., 307
al-Mukhlit, 5, 12, 13, 239–42, 243,
  252–57, 300
Al-Mukhtar, Sidi, 110, 115
Murid, 273
  in Fulani tales of initiation, 159,
    161
Murshids, 6, 18, 159, 161, 265, 271
"Muslim Influences on West African
  Literature and Culture"
  (Battestini), 147, 303
*Musulmans et le pouvoir en l'Afrique
  noir, Les* (Coulon), 286
Muxannat, 84
Muyaka b. Haji al-Ghassany, 43, 46
Mwana Kupona binti Msham al-
  Batawy, 45–46
Mwengo, Bakari, 43, 47–51
Mystical gnosis, 156
Mysticism
  In *L'Aventure ambiguë,* 247–55
  in *L'Enfant noir,* 247, 252–55
  Islamic sub-culture, 125
  in *Le Regard du roi,* 265, 274
  Sufism and, 277–78
  in work of C. H. Kane, 261
  in work of Laye, 246–51, 261
  in work of Salih, 261
Myth, Literature and the African World
  (Soyinka), 302

Naba, 269–70
Nabbi, 142–43
Nasir, Sayyid Abdallah bin Ali bin
  51
Nasr, Seyyed Hossein, 248
Native Authority system, 117
Ndiquel, 206
Negritude movement, 285
Niane, D. T., 239, 240
Niasse, El-Hadji Ibrahima, 168
Niasse, Rokhaya, 168
Niger, 120
Nigeria, British administration of,
  123–24
Nikah, marriage as, 96
Nile valley, early Islamic centuries
  in, 28
Njangaan (Traoré), 15, 170, 175–77
Njeddo Dewal (Bâ), 141, 144, 161
Nobatia, 25
Nommo (the Word), 153
Numerology, significance of, in
  Fulani tales of initiation, 160
Nyang, Sulayman S., 306

Obedience to master's word, in
  Fulani tales of initiation, 155
Old Man and the Medal, The
  (Oyono), 240
Omar, Sheikh, 81
O Pays, mon beau peuple (Sembène),
  193–94, 198
Oral literature. *See also* Bambara
  oral literature; Fulani oral
  literature
  for conveying irreverence toward
    Islam, 164, 172–75
  quest for revelation in, 143–44
  satirical, Wolof, 172–75
  Songhay, 133–39
  West African, 141–50
Orientalism, 3, 9, 299–307
  in West African historical fiction,
    108
Ottoman Turks, 30–31
Ouologuen, Yambo, 12, 13, 15,
  107, 110, 125, 187, 188, 199,
  240, 242, 301
Oyono, Ferdinand, 240

Paganism

destruction of, 115
in French West Africa, conquest
    of, 122
Palmer, Eustace, x
Pantheism, 253
Parole, La (the Word), 148–49
Pilgrimage, in Fulani tales of
    initiation, 158
Poetry. *See also* Utendi poetry;
    Utenzi poetry
  balwo, 83
  gabay, 83
  hamziya, 49, 53
  inkishafi, 49, 51–52, 53
  Mourid, 16
  Our'am as, 55
  in Senegal, 164–68
  promotion of Islam through, 14
  Shairi, 44–49, 54
  Somali, 4, 17, 79–87
  Swahili, 16, 17, 37–38, 41–55, 68
  Tiyani Fatiha, 49, 52
  ukawafi, 49, 50, 52, 53
  utembuizo, 44
  wajiwaji, 49, 50, 53
  Wolof, 16, 165–68
Political power, Mouridism and, 208
Polygamy, Our'an and, 98–99
Portugal
  incursions into Africa by, 31–33
  slave trade by, 33–34
Power, women and, 5
Praise poems, Wolof, 165
Predestination, in Fulani tales of
    initiation, 158
Pre-Islamic animism, 153
"Prétexte, Le" (Diop), 216
Prophets, 142–43

Qadiriyya Sufis, 109, 117, 152
Qadi, 84
Qahatan, Sayyid Muhyiddin bin
    Sheikh, 50
Qamaan Bulxan, 85
Qaynah, 83–84
Quest tales
  Fulani narratives of initiation as,
    151, 159–61
  importance of, 151
  in oral literature, 143–45

in *Le Regard du roi*, 275–78
Qur'an
  memorization of, 79–80
  as poetry, 55
  polygamy and, 98
  Sudanese legal system and, 91
  Swahili translation of, 40
  warnings against poets in, 86
  widows and, 96

Race, in work of Diop, 219–221
Radhi, in "Utendi wa Mwana
    Kupona," 60–62
Al-Rahman, Sayyid Abu-Bakr b.
    Abd (Mwinyi Mansabu), 52
Ramadan, traditional rituals and,
    229–31
Al-Rashid, Harun, 39
Rassoul, 142–43
Rastam, 39
Reality, identity-building and, 4–5
Regard du roi, Le (Laye), 6, 11, 159
  Muslim legalism and, 266–68
  mysticism in, 265, 274
  quest for enlightenment in,
    275–78
  stages of Sufism in, 270–78
  submission in, 265
  Sufi components of, 261, 262–78,
    293–296
Religion
  traditional, compatibility with
    Islam, 142, 145–50, 152
  in work of Sembène, 187–199
Répond-bouche, 148
Resistance, in writings about Islam,
    12–13
Revelation, quest for, in oral
    literature, 143–44
Rhapta, 26
Ritual, religion and, 147–49
Robert, Shaaban, 45
Robinson, David, 9
Rodney, Walter, 24
Roob-doon, 85
Rouch, Jean, 136
Roumain, Jacques, 229

Saad, Sheikh Ali bin (Taji 'l Arifina),
    47–49

Sacred kingship, *maxzen* complex
  and, 6
Sada, Bokar, 111
Sahih (Bukhari), 95
Said, Edward W., 299, 300, 302, 304
Salih, Tayeb, 6, 13, 91
  Sufism and, 261, 278–85,
    293–96
Salvation, in "Utendi wa Mwana
  Kupona," 60
Samatar, Said, 87
Samb, Amar, 164–65, 170, 202–3,
  207–8, 213
al-Sanusi, Muhammad, 34
Sanusi movement, 34–35
Satirical narratives, Wolof, 172–75
Sauti ya Dhiki, 41
Sayyids, 54
Season of the Anomy, (Soyinka), 7
Season of Migration to the North
  (Salih), 5, 6, 91–102, 261
Sebaa Mansa Kolibali, Islam and,
  146
Seductive verbal eloquence, in
  "Utendi wa Mwana Kupona,"
  72
Segu, 115
Seibou, Ali, 139
Self-control, importance of, 101
Self-discipline, in Fulani tales of
  initiation, 154, 158
Self-knowledge, in Fulani tales of
  initiation, 154
Sellin, Eric, 12, 303
Sembéne, Ousmane, 6, 13, 14, 108,
  124–25, 177–83, 187–89, 240,
  242, 251–52, 257
  films of, Islam in, 107
Senegal
  cultural conflict in, 181–82
  European colonialism and, 119
  history of, in *L'Aventure ambiguë*,
    286–87
  homogeneity in, 306–7
  importance of Islam in, 163
  fiction in, 13–14, 163–64
    marabouts in, 301
    Mouridism in, 4, 201–14
    for promoting Islam, 164–71

  syncretism and, 307
  film in, for portraying Islam as an
    impediment, 163–64, 175–78
  oral narrative in, for conveying
    irreverence toward Islam, 164,
    172–75
  poetry in, for promoting
    traditional Islam, 164–68
  Wolof poetry and treatises, 16
Senghor, Léopold Sédar, 300, 306
Serigne-marabout, 181
  attack on in *Njangaan*, 175–77
  satirical narratives about, 172–75
Service of Muslim Affairs, 121–22
"Ses trois jours" (Sembéne), 194
Sexual behavior
  Islam and, 93
  marriage and, 96–97, 102
  in Wolof satirical oral narratives,
    172–73
  of women, 92–94
Sèye, Ibrahima, 204, 205–7, 209–11
Shairi poetry, 46–49
  politicians' use of, 54
Shanga city-state, 37–38
Shar'ia, Sudanese legal system and,
  91, 92, 101
Shar'ia, Sufism and, 158
Sharicah perception, 246
Shariff, Ibrahim Noor, 16–17, 70,
  82
Sheikh qadi, 79
Sheikhs, Somali, 79–87
  authority over spoken word by, 4
  disposition of, 86
  literacy and, 82
  poetry and, 79–87
  as poets, 87
*Sheria za Kutunga Mashairi na Diwani
  ya Amri*, 41
Shermarke, Abdirashid Ali, 79
Shirk, 85–86
Shustari, Andalusian Sufi, 249
Sidiyya, 117
Sierra Leone, 124
Silatigui, 154
Si longue lettre, Une (Bâ), 13
Silsila, 161
Siyyid complex, 5–6

literature praising Islam and, 15
Slave trade, 33–34
Socé, Ousmane, 13, 205
Socialization, initiation as ritualized
  form of, 156
Society for Promoting Christian
  Knowledge, 40
Sohanci, 136
Sokoto, 113, 115, 116
Sokoto Caliphate, 123, 124
Soleils des indépendances, Les
  (Kourouma), 5, 8
Somalia, 26
  casting curses in, 84
  forums in, 79
  oral culture of, 80–81, 82
  poetry, 4, 17, 79–87
    balwo, 83
    gabay, 83
Songhay belief system, 11, 110
  Islamic belief system and, 131–39
  oral narratives and, 134–39
  persistence of, 131–32
  spirits, 136–38
Souffisme, Le (Chevalier), 154
"Souleymane" (Sembéne), 194
Sow-Fall, Aminata, 168–71, 177,
  305
Soyinka, Wole, 7, 168, 187, 189, 302
Spaulding, Jay, 10
Speech behavior, in "Utendi wa
  Mwana Kupona"
  appropriate, 60, 67–68
  verbal eloquence, 72
Spiritual values, Mouridism and,
  211–14
Spoken word
  reverence for, in Somoli and
    Swahili beliefs, 17
  seductive powers of, 17
Stoller, Paul, 131, 132, 138–39
*Studies in the History of West African
  Islam* (Willis), 109
Submission
  to divine will, 155
  in *Le Regard du roi*, 265
  Mouridism and, 205–11
Sudan, 15–16
  British conquest of, 117

decline of Islam in, 116–17
French conquest of, 117–19
literature
  Islam in, 91
  Season of Migration to the North,
    91–102
Sufi Essays (Nasr), 248
Sufi guide, in *L' Aventure ambiguë*,
  287
Sufi Orders in Islam, The (Bâ), 145
Sufi path, the *The Wedding of Zein*,
  279–85
Sufi Rule for Novices, A (Milson),
  155
Sufi saint, in *The Wedding of Zein*,
  279–81
Sufism
  in *Aventure ambiguë, L'*, 247–52
  brotherhoods, 109
  influences of, 16
  in literature, 263–96
  Muslim legalism and, 266–67
  mystical techniques in, 277–78
  role of, 145
  tales of initiation and, 144–45,
    156–61
  traditional African religion and,
    152–53
  transcending stages of, 270–78
  in *The Wedding of Zein*, 282–83
  in work of Camara Laye, 247
Suluk, 159
Sundiata: An Epic of Old Mali
  (Niane), 239, 240, 254
Supernatural, 253–54
Swahili Islamic Poetry (Knappert), 41
Swahili literature
  animal fables, 38–39
  about historical personages, 39
  Islamic themes in, 37–55
  oral tradition and, 16–17, 37
  prose, 53
  secular prose, 38–39
  Swahili language and, 54–55
  western impact on, 40–41
  written tradition, 37
Swahili poetry, 16, 17, 37–38,
  41–44, 53–55
  appropriate use of language in, 68

divorce in, 47–49
forms of, 44–53
as a functional art, 54
hamziya, 49, 53
idealogy and, 73
importance of, 41–44, 53–55
inkishafi, 49, 51–52, 53
meter in, 53
religious matters in, 44–47
on secular and religious subjects,
    41–44
seductive verbal eloquence in, 72
shairi, 46–49, 54
Swahili idealogy and, 73
Tiyani Fatiha, 49, 52
ukawafi, 49, 50, 52, 53
"Utendi wa Mwana Kupona,"
    59–74
utenzi, 44–46, 49, 54
wajiwaji, 49, 50, 53
Swahili Poetry (Harries), 41
Swamp Dwellers, The (Soyinka), 7
Sy, Abu Bakr, 165
Sy, El-Hadji Abdoul Aziz, 165
Syncretism, 11–12, 240–42
    in *Enfant noir, L',* 12
    Islamic sub-culture, 125
    Senegalese literature and, 307

Taalibé, as victim, 175–77
Taalol, 151
"Tabaski de Bouki" (Diop), 216
Tabit, Hassan Ibn, 17
Tagg, 165
Taha, Mahmud Muhammad, 36
Tahir, Ibrihim, 7
Taji'l Arifina (Sheikh Ali bin Saad),
    47–49
Talibes, 205, 207, 208, 213, 217–18
Tarikh el-Fattâch, 10–11, 132–33
Tarîkh es-Sudan, 10–11, 132
Tariqa, 4, 5, 6, 265
Tasjid, 154
Tauw (Sembène), 14, 179, 181
Tcheho, I.C., 6
Tendi. *See* Utendi poetry
Tendi (Allen), 41
Tension, in writings about Islam,
    12–13
Tenzi. *See* Utenzi poetry

Thawab, 17, 42, 55, 82
Theocratic Islamic sub-culture,
    124–25
Thiam, Awa, 169
Tidjaniyya, 201
Tijaniyya Sufism, 109, 114, 117, 156
    Fulani oral literature and, 144–46
    Fulani tales of initiation and,
        160–61
    maktoub and, 158
Timbuktu, 120
Timbuktu chronicles, 132
Tiyani Fatiha, 52
Tiyani Fatiha poetry, 49, 52
Touba
    pilgrimage to, 208
    Serigne, 201, 204, 206, 213–14
Traditional culture
    coexistence with Islam calendar,
        229–31
    compatibility with Islam, 142,
        145–50, 152
    integration of Islam into, 227–34
    Islam and, syncretism of, 240–42
    ritual in, 147–49
    role of spirits and magic in, links
        with Islam, 231–33
    in work of Sembéne, 191–92
Traditional professions, 149
"Traditional Relationship of the
    African with God, The" (Bâ),
    146
Traditional Swahili Poetry
    (Knappert), 41
Traore, Mahama Johnson, 15, 170,
    175
Trimingham, J. Spencer, 9, 145,
    156, 261, 277, 302
Trou dans le miroir, Un (Sèye), 204,
    205–7, 209–11
Two Thousand Seasons (Armah), 13,
    183, 187–88, 239

Ukawafi poetry, 49, 50, 52, 53
'Ulama, 54, 274
Umar, Amandu, 115, 116
Umarians, 114–17, 120
Umm al-Qura (Said al-Busary), 53
Utendi poetry, defined, 44
"Utendi wa Mwana Kupona," 17,

59—74
appropriate speech behaviour in,
  60, 67—68
approval in, 61—62, 66
blessing in, 60—62
irony in , 60, 68—71, 73
kheri (good fortune) in, 62—63, 66
metaphor in, 71—72
salvation in, 60
seductive verbal eloquence in, 72
structure of, 60—68
wifely virtue in, 59—62, 67—71,
  73
Utenzi poetry, 16, 44—46, 49
defined, 44
forms of, 45—46
politicians' use of, 54
uses of, 53
Utenzi wa Vita vya Uhuru, 44—45
Utumbuizo poetry, 44
Uways Mohamed, Sheikh, 81, 87

Véhi-Ciosane (Blanche-Genèse)
  (Sembène), 190
Verbal eloquence. *See also* Speech
  behavior
  in "Utendi wa Mwana Kupona,"
  72
Vie et enseignement de Tierno Bokar
  (Bâ), 141
Virtue, in Islamic literature, 13—14
Virtuous Woman, The (Alkali), 7
Voltaïque (Sembène), 178

Wahabis, 306
Al-Wahdaniyya, 246—52
Wajiwaji poetry, 49, 50, 53
Waliyu, 201
Walys, 143, 144, 146, 160
Wan, 111
WaShenzi, 26
Wawa, 38
Wedding of Zein, The (Salih), 6
  imam in, 279—82, 294—95
  mysticism versus legalism in,
  278—85, 293
  Sufi components of, 261, 278—85,
  293—96
  Sufi path in, 279—85
  Sufi saint in, 279—81

West Africa, 105—234
  conquest of by France, 117—19
  Islam in, 9
    18th and 19th centuries, 110—17
    history of, 107—25
    in twentieth century, 117—25
  literature and films, 163—64
    critical of Islam in, 15
    Birago Diop's work, 215—26
    interpretations of Islam in,
    303—7
    Islamicist tradition and, 108—9
    Islamic orthodoxies and,
    239—57
    Camara Laye's work, 227—34
    Mouridism, 201—14
    oral literature, 141—50
    orientalist approach in, 108
    Sembènes Ousmane's work,
    187—99
    Senegalese, 163—84, 201—14
    tales of initiation, 141—50
  Songhay belief system, 131—40
What is Sufism? (Lings), 248, 278
"White Genesis" (Sembène), 257
Whitely, Wilfred, 16
Widows, rights of, 96, 97
Wifely virtue, in "Utendi wa
  Mwana Kupona," 59—62,
  67—71, 73
Will of Allah, 179
William, Chancellor, 183
Willis, John Ralph, 109
Wolof Muslims, 201
  conversion of, 164
  poetry by, 16, 165—68
  satirical narratives by, 172—75
  writing by, 164
Women
  as bringers of bad luck, 94
  evil and, 91, 94, 95
  male supremacy and, 94—95
  marriage and, 96—97, 102
  polygamy and, 98—99
  power and, 5
  rights of, 96, 98, 102
  sexual behavior of, 92—94
  status of, Islam beliefs and, 91
  two-sided image of, in *Season of*

Migration to the North, 91–102
as victims, 91, 100–101
widows, 96, 97
in work of Sembène, 190–91,
    194, 195–96
Work ethic, Mouridism and, 202,
    205, 209, 210
"Woundou El Hadji" (Diop),
    174–75, 216

Xala (Sembène), 179, 181, 194–95

Yu'asho, 84

Zakat, 170–71, 211
Zawiya complex, 5–6, 15
Zimbabwe
    early Islamic centuries in, 28
    Portuguese and, 32